WHERE QUEEN ELIZABETH SLEPT
&
WHAT THE BUTLER SAW

1279

WHERE QUEEN ELIZABETH SLEPT
&
WHAT THE BUTLER SAW

HISTORICAL TERMS FROM THE SIXTEENTH CENTURY TO THE PRESENT

DAVID N. DURANT

ST. MARTIN'S GRIFFIN ❧ NEW YORK

Library of Congress Cataloging-in-Publication Data

Durant, David N.
    Where Queen Elizabeth slept & what the butler saw :
historical terms from the sixteenth century to the present / David Durant.
        p.   cm.
    ISBN 0-312-19569-9
    1. English language—Obsolete words. 2. Great
Britain—Social Life and customs—Terminology. 3.
English Language—Terms and phrases. 4. Great Britain—History—Terminology. I. Title.
PE1667.D87   1997
422—dc21   97-11287
                                                CIP

First published in Great Britain as *The Country House: A
Historical Dictionary* by John Murray (Publishers) Ltd.

First St. Martin's Griffin Edition: September 1998

10 9 8 7 6 5 4 3 2 1

For Olivia and Mai-xian,
two small grandbabies

PREFACE

What is 'bote'? What were Calvin's precepts? What is a chanceling? Are marquesses outranked by earls? How were visiting cards used in the arcane ritual of 'calling'? Here you will find answers to these and many other questions. Such features of the country house as shell rooms and houses include a note of where examples may be seen. The dictionary is intended as a guide to fashions no longer fashionable, to the use of objects no longer part of our daily lives, and to past beliefs, practices, outlooks, theologies and philosophies. It also includes definitions of many social customs handed down to us, the application of which to the grand country-house life of former centuries is now generally forgotten.

Broadly speaking, the period covered is the sixteenth century to the mid twentieth century, the number of incursions into the Middle Ages reflecting the long history of many of our institutions and customs. Cross-references are indicated by SMALL CAPITALS in the text. The dates in brackets after people's names represent birth and death, except in the case of sovereigns, when they indicate the reign.

A truly comprehensive guide of this nature might easily be extended to many volumes; inevitably, I have included entries which will seem perfectly self-evident to some readers, and left out the *one* thing you were wanting to know.

Acknowledgements

I am grateful to the Authors' Foundation which supported me with a grant to write the Dictionary. I am also grateful to friends who have provided information in their own specialized fields: Ruth Bell, Dr Rosalys Coope, Christabel Durant, Dr Mark Girouard, Rosi Jarvis, Grant MacIntyre, Dr Susan Parsons, Peter Townend, Sir Peter Whiteley; and to John Murray, who has given me every encouragement, whose idea the book was in the first place, and who has laboured over the text into the small hours – it is his book as much as mine.

I also freely acknowledge the use of quotations from Lady Diana Cooper in the entries for 'Gong, dressing', 'Heating', 'Lighting', and 'Water supply', which are taken from her book *The Rainbow Comes and Goes* (1958); the quotations from Sir Harold Nicolson in the entries for 'Charades' and 'Servants' are taken from his *Diaries and Letters 1930–39* (1960); the quotation from Lady Maude Baillie in 'Nurseries' is taken from *Hardwick Hall* (1989), the National Trust guide book by Mark Girouard; and the quotation from Cynthia Asquith in 'Court, presentation at' is from her book *Remember and Be Glad* (1952).

THE DICTIONARY

Academy (Royal) of Arts. See ROYAL ACADEMY OF ARTS.

Acanthus. Distinctive sculptured leaves which distinguish Corinthian capitals from Doric and Ionic, also used in Composite capitals. Wild acanthus growing around a tomb suggested this ornamentation to the Athenian, Callimachus, in the fifth century BC. The Greeks seem to have preferred the hard and spiny *Acanthus spinosus* or bear's-foot, and the Romans the softer *A. mollis*, or bear's-breeches. See also ANTHEMION, PATERAE and CARYATID.

Act of Parliament. A law drawn up by joint action of the three 'estates' of the realm, the Lords Spiritual, the Lords Temporal, and the Commons. In its early stages any proposed Act is properly called a Bill, becoming an Act only when it has received the Royal Assent. Acts are of two kinds, public and private; public Acts have a general application, while private Acts are generally of more localized interest, intended for use by local authorities, for example. No Bill can be introduced more than once in a parliamentary session. Bills may be introduced in the Commons or the Lords (except that 'money bills', since the Parliament Act of 1911, may only be presented in the Commons). The first 'reading' of a Bill is no more than an announcement of its contents, which are then printed. In the second reading the Bill is debated in both Houses and, if passed on a vote, goes on to Committee Stage, where it is examined by either a standing committee or a committee of the whole House. It is now that the Bill receives its closest scrutiny, discussion, consideration and amendment. The amended Bill, now in its Report Stage, receives its third reading in the Commons. If it is now passed, it goes through a similar process in the Lords. After being passed by both Houses the Bill receives the Royal Assent. English statute law comprises all Acts passed by Parliament which have neither been repealed nor reached the end of their stated lives. The oldest Act still current is the Statute of Merton of 1235; it pre-dates the summoning of the Commons to Parliament, and gave land-holding barons an interest in the common-lands and wastelands.

Actresses. In Greek and Roman times female parts were played by men – or eunuchs – a convention which continued, in England, until the middle of the seventeenth century. A special Prologue to Killigrew's December 1660 production of *Othello* introduced 'the first woman that comes to act upon the stage', but her name is not known. Mrs Coleman *sang* the part of Ianthe when the first part of Davenant's *Siege of Rhodes* was performed in 1656, during Cromwell's Protectorate; but she was generally regarded as a singer rather than an actress. When the theatres reopened following the Restoration of Charles II all the companies employed actresses, who from the first acquired a reputation for easy morals and attracted wealthy 'protectors' – Charles's own liaison with

'Pretty, Witty Nell' Gwynne is only the best-known example. The idea of the loose-living actress lasted well into the nineteenth century, when Victorian morality finally won the day, and in the last quarter of the century it became rather fashionable for men of wealth and title to marry penniless 'Gaiety' girls. In the twentieth century the appearance on stage of such aristocratic ladies as Lady Diana Manners (in Max Reinhardt's *The Miracle*, 1911–12) lent 'tone' to the profession. One of the most popular marriages of actress-into-aristocracy was probably that of Fred Astaire's sister (and partner) Adele to Lord George Cavendish, grandson of the 10th Duke of Devonshire, in 1932. See also THEATRICALS.

Adam, Robert (1728–1792). A Scottish NEO-CLASSICAL architect, interior designer, furniture designer, and originator of the 'Adam Style', and the most fashionable architect in Britain between 1760 and 1780. In 1754 Robert Adam, son of William Adam (1689–1748), also a successful Scottish architect, went on the GRAND TOUR, returning in 1758. During his tour he visited, and drew in detail, many Roman Classical buildings, and in particular the ruins of Diocletian's Palace at Spalato (Split). On his return to Britain he set up in practice in London as an architect and landscape designer. He revolutionized English domestic architecture and introduced a new and elegant repertoire of architectural ornament and interior design based on a wide variety of sources from the Classical to the Cinquecento, thus rejecting the rigid rules imposed by PALLADIANISM since 1725. This new style became immediately popular, and by 1773 was widely imitated. One of his first clients, Sir Nathaniel Curzon, 1st Baron Scarsdale, confessed himself 'knocked all of a heap with wonder and amaze' on seeing Adam's proposals for his country seat, Kedleston Hall in Derbyshire; which may, incidentally, boast the only surviving Adam landscape. Adam became the most influential architect and designer (it was in interior design that he made his greatest impact) in the latter part of the eighteenth century, but by the end of the century his style was beginning to be considered too fussy, and he was superseded by James WYATT and then by the more severe GREEK REVIVAL style.

Advowson. The right to 'present a living' (appoint a vicar) in the Church of England, belonging to those whose ancestors founded or endowed a church, or to those to whom the right has been transferred.

Ague. A malarial type of fever, with hot, cold and sweating stages.

Aids. Taxes of two kinds, feudal and gracious, levied on those who held land of the king. Gracious aids were levied for particular purposes, such as for war. MAGNA CARTA (1216) restricted the levy of feudal aids to three circumstances: ransoming the king if he was captured; on the marriage of his daughter; and when his son was knighted. Aids declined in the thirteenth century, when new forms of taxation were devised. See also TAXATION and LAND TAX.

Air Force. See ROYAL AIR FORCE.

Alb. A tunic of white cloth reaching to the feet and enveloping the wearer, worn by priests in religious ceremonies and occasionally by consecrated kings. See also CASSOCK, CHASUBLE, ORPHREY, SURPLICE.

Alderman or **Earldorman.** In Anglo-Saxon times, an official (usually an earl or a political governor) appointed by the king to be in charge of a shire. He was expected to keep law and order, to enforce the judgments of local courts and to lead the local militia. Much later, between 1835 and 1972, a senior member of a town or city corporation, ranking next below the Mayor. This office was abolished in 1972, except in the City of London.

Ale. An alcoholic drink made from fermented cereal, popular in early times owing to the uncertain supply of drinkable water, particularly in towns. It was brewed both in town and country, in private houses for family consumption, and commercially for public sale. The best was made in the south of England from barley malt; in the north and west, oat malt was used. Spices were included to sharpen the taste, or to disguise it as it turned sour – ale had a short 'shelf-life'. On the other hand, although it was supposed to be left to stand for five days for the sediment to settle, unscrupulous brewers sold their ale only hours after fermentation had ceased: this was the 'pudding-ale' mentioned in William Langland's *Piers Plowman* of *c.* 1362. In the fourteenth century Flemish brewers brought the recipe for BEER to London. Beer includes the addition of hops, a preservative, and in London in 1418 cost two-thirds as much as ale; it gradually superseded ale because of its superior keeping qualities – and its finer flavour.

The terms ale and beer were often used synonymously, and both were to be found in the SERVANTS' HALL at dinner and supper. In *c.* 1769 the servants of the Duke of Portland at Welbeck Abbey, Nottinghamshire petitioned the Duke: 'We Your Grace's servants whose names are here enclosed beg leave to petition for ale: not for ourselves particular, but for the servants of Your Grace's friends, which we have been frequently refused by Mr Martin, Your Grace's butler, without giving any reason for the same, but saying I am Master and you shall have none.'

Allegiance. A bond linking a man to his lord, or the subject to his sovereign. See also RETAINER.

Amercement. In Anglo-Saxon and Norman times, a money penalty imposed in a lord's court on an offender, which came to represent an important source of income for the lord. The name derives from *à merci*, Norman-French meaning 'at the mercy of the lord'. MAGNA CARTA specified that a freeman should be amerced according to his resources; however, amercements gradually came to be of fixed amounts for particular offences, in the nature of a fixed-penalty fine.

Andirons. Metal supports for burning logs on an open hearth. Whereas logs burn best on a bed of hot wood-ash, coal requires air beneath it. As sea-coal (coal shipped by sea) became generally available in the sixteenth century, basket-grates were designed to provide the necessary draught; as coal became more widely used, andirons were often retained as decorative features standing before the coal grate. It is a solecism, one occasionally perpetuated in old houses, to fill with logs grates always intended for coal. See also FIREDOGS.

Anglo-Catholicism. A movement within the Church of England towards a return to the Catholic tradition, which developed from TRACTARIANISM and the OXFORD MOVEMENT of the mid nineteenth century. Anglo-Catholicism, the High Church movement (much loved by John Betjeman), brought new life and colour to the Church of England with the use of vestments, bells and incense − all anathema to Low Church EVANGELICALISM. See also METHODISM, PRESBYTERIANISM and PURITANISM.

Animal Graves and Monuments. Animal memorials both large and small can be found tucked away in forgotten corners of many old gardens. The fashion began in the eighteenth century, and was sometimes taken to extremes. At Shugborough Hall, Staffordshire is a mid eighteenth-century monument to Lord Anson's cat; Woburn Abbey, Bedfordshire has a pretty classical temple dedicated to a pekinese, Che Foo, who died in 1916; and Newstead Abbey in Nottinghamshire boasts the biggest monument to any dog − Lord Byron's Newfoundland, Boatswain, was placed, with typical humorous cynicism, on what the poet thought (mistakenly) was the site of the monks' high altar. Earlier, William Kent, with similar humour, had placed a memorial to a dog on the back of the Temple of Worthies at Stowe, Buckinghamshire (1735); Goodwood House, West Sussex, has a marble monument to a lioness (died c. 1760) belonging to the 2nd Duke of Richmond; and Rousham House, Oxfordshire has a stone memorial to Faustina Gwynne, a cow aged twenty-two when she died in 1882. Oddest of all must be a thirty-foot obelisk, formerly at Mount Edgcumbe, but now overlooking Plymouth, which commemorates a pet pig, Cupid.

Annates. In its strictest sense, the payment to the papacy of the first-fruits (the first year's income) of a BENEFICE by bishops on their appointment. Always a source of disagreements and disputes. As a corollary of the break with Rome over his divorce from Catharine of Aragon, Henry VIII (1509–47) in 1532/3 diverted the payment of annates from Rome to the English Crown. A charter of Queen Anne confirmed by statute in 1703 applied the Crown's income from annates to a perpetual fund, known as Queen Anne's Bounty, for the augmentation of the livings of the poorer Anglican clergy.

Ante-room. Also ante-chamber. A room leading to a more important one; in particular, the room preceding the bedchamber in houses with suites of rooms: usually three in number (ante-room, bedchamber and closet), but occasionally more. The ante-room might be used as a waiting room before presentation at a LEVÉE, or for receiving friends in more privacy than was afforded by the public reception rooms.

Anthemion. Ornamentation of stylized honeysuckle flowers, leaves and tendrils borrowed from Classical architectural design. It was very popular during the NEO-CLASSICAL period of design (1760–*c.* 1800) introduced by Robert ADAM. See also ACANTHUS and PATERAE.

Antimacassar. A crocheted or plain cloth with a lace trim, used to protect the back of an upholstered chair or sofa from the bear's grease or macassar oil which came to be used as a hair dressing in the 1860s when short hair for men became fashionable.

Apothecaries. The word derives from the Greek for a store or repository; thus an apothecary was originally a warehouseman. During the Middle Ages the term came to be applied to those who prepared and sold drugs, and dispensed medical advice. The Company of Physicians (incorporated 1518) and the Company of Barber-Surgeons (incorporated in 1461 and again in 1540) exhibited occasionally ferocious rivalry. In 1548 the apothecaries were the subject of an Act of Parliament for their protection and toleration; in 1617 they were incorporated as the Society of Apothecaries. The Hall of the Society, in Water Lane in London, was acquired in 1632, destroyed in the Great Fire of 1666 but rebuilt 1669–71, and enlarged in 1786; it is the oldest surviving City Livery Hall.

In 1673 the Society established a botanic and physic garden on land leased at Chelsea. Sir Hans Sloane, who had become the garden's landlord, gave the land to the Society in 1722 on the condition that it should present annually to the Royal Society 50 dried plant specimens, up to the number of 2,000 – a target reached in 1774. Rising maintenance costs and other factors led the Society in 1902 to hand the Chelsea Physic Garden over to a committee of management under the Charity Commissioners.

Following its incorporation in 1617 the Society of Apothecaries gradually consolidated its position, obtaining in 1772 the right to inspect practitioners' premises and destroy unfit stocks, and in 1815 it was granted powers of examination and licensing. In 1865 Elizabeth Garrett (Anderson) became the first woman to qualify in medicine when she passed the Society's examinations.

Aqua-vitae. 'Water of life' (an alchemist's term); *eau-de-vie*; now, an alcoholic distillation, a form of brandy. Said (by Brewer) to derive from a monkish mistranslation of the Spanish *aqua di vite* (water, or juice, of the vine) as *aqua vitae* rather than *aqua vitis*, 'and' (says Brewer) 'confounding the juice of the grape with the alchemists' elixir of life'. Fermented grape juice was principally used in early distilling, aqua-vitae being achieved when the distillate was concentrated enough to flame or burn – known in the Low Countries as *brandewijn* (burnt wine), hence brandy. Popular at the time of the Black Death (1343–9) and much prescribed by physicians for PLAGUE, for the feeling of warmth and well-being it induced.

The fermented juices of fruits other than grapes were also used in the distillation of aqua-vitae, as were corn and rye.

Archers, Royal Company of. See ROYAL COMPANY OF ARCHERS.

Archery. From the time of the Battle of Crécy in 1346, the longbow was valued for its lightness and speed of firing. By an Act of Edward IV (1461–83) every Englishman was compelled to possess a bow of his own height, and every town to hold compulsory longbow practice on Sundays and feast days. 'Unlawful' sports, those which might distract from this, were banned on these days. Henry VII (1485–1509) had archery butts made for him in 1502 at Woking; Henry VIII (1509–47), a skilled archer, considered second-rate the crossbow favoured by the French, and banned its use. In the sixteenth century the longbow was preferred even against firearms, as it could be fired six times faster than the early musket, and weighed less. It was last used in battle in Elizabeth I's reign (1558–1603), but was still encouraged in London in the 1640s. Requiring skill more than overt exertion, archery enjoyed a revival as a sport suitable for nineteenth-century ladies, who competed in country-house longbow contests. See also CROSSBOW.

Arches, Court of. Of medieval origin; the court of appeal of the Archbishop of Canterbury. Originally it sat at St Mary-le-Bow (St Mary-of-the-Arches, *Beata Maria de Arcubus*), London, from which it took its name, 'by reason of the steeple thereof raised at the top, with stone pillars in fashion like a bow bent archwise'. The court still sits, presided over by a Dean of Arches (properly, official Principal of the Arches Court), and hears appeals from bishops, deans and archdeacons.

Architectural styles. The earliest architecture in Britain is prehistoric – standing stones and earthworks. The first recognizable style as we know it today is Saxon which has survived in churches such as Brixworth, Northamptonshire. NORMAN (Romanesque) followed (1066–*c.* 1150), recognizable by the Norman round-headed arch. A few houses survive from this period, such as the Jew's House, Lincoln, in addition to castles, cathedrals, churches and abbeys. The basic nature of the

Norman style was one of strength. In the twelfth century EARLY ENGLISH (*c.* 1150–1290) developed out of the Norman round-arched style and was the beginning of a truly national style. It usually had acutely pointed (Gothic) arches, more slender columns, and masons of the time delighted in carving, often to be seen on corbels, capitals, etc. Windows were larger. As the DECORATED style evolved (*c.* 1290–1350), windows increased in size and were divided into two or more lights by mullions, with geometrical tracery at the top; buildings – churches were still the most prominent architecture in the land – became more airy; ornament and sculptured detail took over from discipline. The PERPENDICULAR (*c.* 1350–*c.* 1530) style which succeeded the decorated lasted longer than any previous styles; examples are the choir of Gloucester Cathedral and King's College Chapel, Cambridge. Few medieval buildings are without some trace of this style, to be recognized by the strong vertical, parallel lines of columns, tracery and stone panelling on walls, and also by its fan vaulting, as in the Divinity Schools, Oxford. Perpendicular, more than any of its predecessors, was widely introduced into domestic building. As windows could be made much larger, more light was brought into buildings. The TUDOR, ELIZABETHAN and JACOBEAN years which followed saw a great boom and revolution in the building of houses, grammar schools and colleges. Building styles became more 'homely' (Leycester's Hospital, Warwick), but this was also the era of great houses such as Longleat, Burghley, and Hardwick Hall (1590–7). Building patronage was taken over from the Church by ambitious courtiers. Great families built large houses suitable to their position. Rich men built manor houses. The craftsmen of churches turned their skills to houses, and particularly to their dining halls with wooden screens, panelling, and sometimes galleries. The seventeenth century saw the arrival of the (Italian) RENAISSANCE style pioneered by Inigo JONES (The Queen's House, Greenwich), based on usually restrained classical proportions and elements. It reached its climax as ENGLISH BAROQUE with Christopher WREN (St Paul's Cathedral), Nicholas HAWKSMOOR (The Mausoleum, Castle Howard) and VANBRUGH (Blenheim Palace). The PALLADIAN (introduced by Colen Campbell at Wanstead House, Essex, 1715–20) and GEORGIAN styles emerged in the eighteenth century, based on symmetry and an insistence on proportion. This was the age of Lord Burlington (Chiswick House), William KENT, the ADAM brothers and John WOOD (Bath); of parklands, temples, and lakes (Capability BROWN, Humphry REPTON); of villas, lodges, bridges and grottoes. It was a style as well suited to town houses and terraces as to grand country houses. In the mid eighteenth century the GOTHIC REVIVAL, mainly inspired by Horace Walpole who created his own Gothic fantasy at Strawberry Hill, Middlesex, became fashionable and continued so into the nineteenth century. The end of the eighteenth and beginning of the nineteenth centuries also saw the emergence of the GREEK REVIVAL; churches, public buildings and also houses (Attingham Park, Shropshire) were built in imitation of Greek temples, with columns, pediments, etc. Current with the Greek Revival style was the REGENCY, decorous and refined, the English counterpart of the French Directoire and Empire styles. Greek, ROCOCO, oriental, GOTHIC and Indian elements were brought together to create this fashion (Sezincote House, Gloucestershire; Brighton Pavilion; Carlton House, London (dem.) and Ashridge Park, Hertfordshire). The nineteenth century saw a Gothic Revival (Victorian Gothic) incorporating adaptions of medieval Gothic elements, asymmetrical design, steeply pitched roofs, verticality and ornate tracery, particularly suitable for public buildings (The Royal Courts of Justice, London; Royal Holloway College, Egham, Surrey; Manchester Town Hall; Scarisbrick Hall, Lancashire). It was a period of enormous energy and wealth with a great demand for new building. The Greek Revival, however, continued steadily alongside the explosion of Victorian Gothic (The British Museum, the Ashmolean Museum, Oxford). The second half of the century saw the influence of the ARTS AND CRAFTS movement in the 1860s, and the Queen Anne Revival used traditional materials, particularly brick, in a combination of towers, turrets, elaborate chimney pots, bays, projecting porches and verandas – a grand domestic style, of which Norman SHAW was a key exponent. In the hands of Sir Edwin LUTYENS this evolved into a vernacular style in the many country houses he designed (Deanery Gardens, Sonning, Berkshire; Munstead Wood, Surrey; Castle Drogo, Devon). After the First World War new building techniques and new materials such as reinforced concrete permitted new architectural experiments from which sprang Modernism. The second half of the twentieth century has seen a reaction to modernism with Post-Modernism and a return to classical detail and proportion.

Aristocracy. Literally (as contrasted with monarchy, DEMOCRACY) the government of a state in the interests of the community by its best (aristos=Greek for 'best') citizens. In practice, government by an hereditary group of noble or wealthy citizens who are held (by themselves or others!) to rank distinctly above the rest of the community. (An aristocrat *may* be a member of the nobility, or of the privileged class.) See also NOBILITY.

Armada Chests. More propertly known as 'Nuremberg chests' because they were made there in great numbers in the sixteenth and seventeenth centuries; their only connection with the Armada is that Spanish warships carried money in similar chests. Heavily iron-bound chests such as these were used as safes, their lids secured by elaborate locks the keys of which operated multiple bolts. Often a false keyhole decoyed attention away from the hidden, true keyhole. Sometimes there was a spring-trap in the keyhole; when sprung by a probing finger its teeth could cause severe lacerations, giving rise to the expression 'caught red-handed'. Originally the chests were painted, and on some the faded designs of stylized red Tudor roses can still be seen. Many of these chests survive in older historic houses.

Arms and Armour, displays of. In medieval times arms and armour were kept in the GREAT HALL, unless there was an armoury. At Hampton Court, the King's Guard Room has an elaborate display of more than 3,000 pieces, said to have been arranged by William III's (1694–1702) gunsmith (although in fact most of the weapons are fairly recent introductions). At Boughton House, Northamptonshire arms are displayed in the armoury in an eighteenth-century arrangement with muskets on racks, and swords hung in wheel formations with the tips to the hub. At Chelsea Hospital, London there is a very interesting *trompe l'oeil* trophy of arms by Henry Cooke (1642–1700) showing the fashion for radial displays of 1690. Such painted echoes of past display have gone in and out of fashion. At Canons Ashby, Northamptonshire arms, armour, drums and flags are painted over the fireplace in the Great Hall, a work of *c*. 1700; at Mawley Hall, Shropshire (1732), they appear in plasterwork over the hall fireplace, and plasterwork trophies of arms to designs by Robert Adam decorate the halls of Osterley Park, London (1773) and Newby Hall, North Yorkshire (*c*. 1770); in the hall at Blair Castle, Borders Region the plasterwork is attributed to Thomas Clayton (1750), and there is also an excellent collection of real arms and armour.

In the nineteenth century there was a romantic revival of this custom, and astonishing displays could be ordered from London suppliers not always averse to faking up some of the pieces. In the 1820s, Sir Walter Scott decorated his entrance hall at Abbotsford in the Borders with a romantic display, and there was more in his armoury. Knebworth House in Hertfordshire has a small armoury installed by the author Bulwer Lytton (Edward Bulwer-Lytton, 1st Baron Lytton, 1803–73) in the 1850s, while in the armoury at Culzean Castle, Strathclyde Region is a very dense display of arms issued to the West Lowland Regiment raised in the early nineteenth century against the threat of invasion by Napoleon I. At Erddig, Clwyd the local early nineteenth-century yeomanry swords are perilously displayed on the ceiling of the servants' hall.

Army, The. Grew out of the feudal levy which required those who held land by KNIGHT-SERVICE to assemble when called upon by the king.

These assemblies consisted of the nobility as the cavalry, and the peasants, serfs and poor as the infantry. The major drawback was that this service was restricted to forty days in a year. Edward III's (1327–77) use of scutage (payments made in lieu of knight-service) to hire mercenaries marked the end of the feudal levy and the beginning of an organized army; the Hundred Years' War (1337–1453) was fought with soldiers raised by a combination of the feudal and mercenary systems. At this time armies were invariably disbanded at the end of a campaign, but Henry VII (1485–1509) at his accession instituted the YEOMEN OF THE GUARD as a permanent military corps to act as the sovereign's bodyguard, and these became the kernel of England's standing army. Charles I (1625–49) was constantly at loggerheads with Parliament over his right to keep a standing army in time of peace; the Petition of Right (1628) declared that he had no such right. Cromwell's New Model Army, formed in 1645, was the first fully trained and professional English standing army; it was largely disbanded at the RESTORATION of 1660, except for General Monk's foot regiment, who became the Coldstream Guards, and two regiments of lifeguards formed from Cavalier supporters of Charles II (1660–85). Charles II was the first British monarch to maintain a permanent standing army: the Royal Scots were raised in 1661 and the Buffs (3rd Buffs, Holland Regiment) were formed in 1665. James II (1685–88) was condemned for keeping a standing army in peacetime without consent of Parliament, and the Mutiny Act of 1689 vested control of the army with Parliament. During the War of the Spanish Succession (1701–14) Parliament authorized the raising of an army of 200,000 men, which was drastically reduced after peace was signed. During the eighteenth and nineteenth centuries the army fluctuated in numbers between 18,000 in times of peace and 200,000 in war.

Army List. Official list of commissioned officers. The earliest known 'General and Compleat List Military of every Commission officer of Horse and Foot' – known as Nathan Brook's Army List – was printed in 1684, and an annual list for the Irish Establishment appeared from about 1733, but it was not until 1754 that a general list was issued which covered the whole of the Army Establishment. Publication continued annually until 1878. This was technically a 'private publication', under the direction of successive Clerks at the War Office, but appeared 'By permission of the Right Honourable Secretary at War', and from 1779 was headed 'War Office'. Monthly lists appeared from 1798, with interruptions, and were generally on sale to the public (again with interruptions, for example between July 1915 and December 1918, when the List was published 'For Official Use Only') until February 1939. Quarterly and half-year lists have also been published from time to time. It is, however, still published annually.

Art, Chain of. A nineteenth-century belief in civilization as a continuing process linking all national cultures. Ancient Greece was frequently considered the summit of human achievement in art.

Art Nouveau. A style of architecture and figurative and applied art, flourishing at the end of the nineteenth and beginning of the twentieth centuries, which took its name from a Parisian shop opened in 1895 to sell objects of 'modern' design uninfluenced by earlier periods; divorced from the ARTS AND CRAFTS MOVEMENT, which tended to imitate earlier styles. The highly stylized and elongated decoration which distinguishes Art Nouveau, based on graceful plant forms and distinctive sinuous shapes, can be seen in the early works of Sir Edward Burne-Jones (1833–98) and, in the 1880s, in the designs of Arthur Mackmurdo (1851–1942), an early pioneer of the style in Britain. Known in Germany as *Jugendstil*, it was far more popular on the Continent, where its exuberance can be enjoyed in, for example, the design of the entrances to the Paris Métro stations. In Britain the climax of Art Nouveau can be seen in the Glasgow School of Art, designed by Charles Rennie Mackintosh (1868–1928). Looking at this building today it is difficult to believe that it is nearly a hundred years old (designed 1897; first part completed 1899).

Arts and Crafts Movement. Arose in the second half of the nineteenth century in reaction to the increasingly banal design and poor quality of machine-made products following the INDUSTRIAL REVOLUTION. The principles of the movement, formulated by John Ruskin (1819–1900), were put into practice by William Morris (1834–96) when in 1861 he and some friends founded the firm of Morris, Marshall & Faulkner (later Morris & Co.), 'Fine Art Workmen in Painting, Carving, Furniture and the Metals'. Their aim was to re-establish the importance and dignity of the individual artist-craftsman, with a return to medieval standards of craftsmanship and design and a recognition of the beauties of form, function and materials.

With medieval standards came a revival of the idea of medieval GUILDS: these included Mackmurdo's Century Guild, formed in 1882, the Art Workers' Guild and the Home Arts and Industries Association (particularly interested in rural crafts). These groups were often short-lived, being stronger on idealism than on business acumen. See also ART NOUVEAU and PRE-RAPHAELITE BROTHERHOOD.

Ashlar. Large, usually stone, blocks used in building, wrought to even faces and square edges; also used in thin slabs to face rubble or brick walls.

Assizes. Most commonly, the annual sessions of the Judges of the High Court of Justice held in the various counties of England and Wales, arranged in Circuits (e.g., the Northern Circuit). By 1972 all Assize courts had been abolished, their functions taken over by the High Court in London. Ironically, prior to Magna Carta (1215) it was also the case that criminal cases had to be tried in London (at Westminster); the Charter made provision for some such offences to be tried annually by judges on Circuit in every county, in order to cut down on delay and inconvenience.

In Scotland, where the legal system differs in many ways from that in the rest of Great Britain, the judges of the supreme criminal court (the High Court of Judiciary) also form three separate circuit courts.

'Assize' is also used in the sense of an ordinance, or an enactment of a court or a Council of State; in 1166 the 'assize of Clarendon', for example, established (among other things) the supremacy of trial by jury over more archaic methods, such as trial by ordeal; the 'assize of bread and ale' enabled the price of these commodities to be regulated by making provision for the fixing of the price of grain.

In Scotland, an 'assize' might also mean trial by jury – or the jury itself.

Atkins, Tommy. Slang term for a private in the British Army. The original was a private in the Royal Welch Fusiliers fighting in the American War of Independence (1775–83). The Duke of Wellington chose the name as an example for the Soldiers' Account Book in 1829.

Atlantes. The male equivalent of CARYATIDS.

Attainder. The legal consequence of a judgment of death or outlawing in cases of treason or felony, resulting in the forfeiture of the guilty party's goods and lands, and 'corruption of the blood' – which is to say that the attainted person could neither inherit nor transmit lands. Bills of Attainder, originally a parliamentary method of exercising judicial authority, were first passed in 1459; by the time of Henry VIII (1509–47) they had become a means of extra-judicial procedure, and were employed by Henry against those opposing the REFORMATION. The most famous case under Charles I was that of the Earl of Strafford (1593–1641), and the last Bill of Attainder passed in England was in 1798 against Lord Edward FitzGerald, for his part in plans for a French invasion of Ireland. Attainder was abolished in 1844 except for outlawry, and completely abolished in 1938.

Attorney. A person appointed to act in another's stead. An attorney-in-fact is simply an agent, bounded by his 'powers of attorney'; an attorney-at-law was originally a public officer, conducting legal proceedings on behalf of others (his 'clients') and attached to the supreme courts of COMMON LAW at Westminster. The latter arose in medieval times, as those most frequently appointed became skilled in legal matters and established themselves as professionals. By the late thirteenth century legal representation was divided between such attorneys, who drew up the written proceedings, and serjeants, who dealt with oral proceedings. Serjeants evolved into barristers, and the position of attorney declined. Attorneys-at-law corresponded to the solicitors of the Courts of Chancery and the proctors of the Admiralty, Ecclesiastical, Probate and Divorce Courts. Since the Judicature Act of 1873 all those admitted as attorneys, solicitors or proctors of an English court have been called 'solicitors of the Supreme Court'. The principal law officer of the Crown in England is still called the Attorney-General; in Scotland he is the Lord Advocate.

In the United States an attorney-at-law exercises the functions of both solicitor and barrister, his full title being 'attorney and counsellor-at-law'.

Auction sales. Those at which objects are sold to the highest bidder. They were common in Imperial Rome, of which Robert Graves's *Claudius the God* reveals some detail. The incident concerns a fined and disgraced Roman governor, Umbonius, who transported 300 wagonloads of valuable household goods to the public auction-place. Dealers and connoisseurs lick their lips and hope for bargains, but 'when the spear was struck upright in the ground, to show that a public auction was in progress, all that Umbonius sold was his senator's gown. Then he had the spear pulled out again to show that the auction was over' and took his goods back home.

The auctions of Stuart possessions by the Puritans during the Commonwealth raised more money than any since Roman times; art patronage subsequently moved to the Continent, and it was not until the eighteenth century, when rising fortunes and political upheavals led to property changing hands on a large scale, that there was again any great demand for the buying and selling of works of art. The fashionable GRAND TOUR played its part, and it was in such a climate that Samuel Baker (d. 1778) founded in Covent Garden in 1744 the first sale-room exclusively for manuscripts, books and prints – which later became better-known as Sotheby's, after his nephew John – and James Christie (1730–1803) opened a new auction house for the buying and selling of works of art in 1766. See also FURNITURE and TASTE FOR ANTIQUE.

Augustinians, or **Austin,** or **Black,** or **Regular Canons.** An old order, originating in Northern Italy in the mid tenth century, which received official approval at the Lateran synods of 1059, their rule was based on the 109th Letter of St Augustine. Members of the order are priests and not MONKS, although like monks they take vows and live in communities doing pastoral work, and are dedicated to the *Opus Dei* and communal life. The Augustinian habit consists of a black cassock with a white surplice and a hooded black cloak, hence the name Black Canons. Augustinian churches are distinguished by their length, and some 26 survive, including the now Anglican cathedrals of Bristol, Carlisle, Oxford, Portsmouth, and Southwark; cloisters survive at Oxford and at Laycock, Wiltshire. With the secularization of ecclesiastic property at the REFORMATION, many Augustinian foundations became the sites of great houses: Anglesey Abbey (priory), Cambridgeshire (founded 1137); Lacock Abbey (nunnery), Wiltshire (1229); Longleat, Wiltshire (thirteenth century, changed to Carthusian in 1540); Michelham Priory, East Sussex (1229); Mottisfont Abbey (priory), Hampshire (1201); Newburgh Priory, North Yorkshire (c. 1145); Newstead Abbey (priory), Nottinghamshire (1163). Extending their rule from England to Scotland in about 1120, the Austin Friars founded Holyrood, St Andrews and Scone as offshoots of English houses at Merton and Nostell. Austin Friars returned to Britain in the nineteenth century; now known as the Order of St Augustine, they have eight priories, including one with a school in their old home at Carlisle. See also BENEDICTINES, CANONS REGULAR, CARMELITES, CARTHUSIANS, CISTERCIANS, CLUNIACS, DOMINICANS, FRIARS, FRANCISCANS, GILBERTINES, MENDICANT FRIARS and PREMONSTRATENSIANS.

Austin Canons. See AUGUSTINIANS, and CANONS REGULAR.

Aviary. A large cage, often decorative, used for keeping exotic birds; found in a number of country houses. An inventory of 1682 for Ham House, Twickenham lists the 'Volury Room' (derived from the French *volière*; previously the Yellow Bedchamber), with bird cages outside the bay window; perhaps the birds flew free in the room during winter. At Holland House, London in 1760 Lady Sarah Lennox had an aviary outside her dressing room. The aviary at Dropmore House, Buckinghamshire (c. 1810) still exists but is in need of repair; a similar one at Waddesdon Manor, Buckinghamshire (1870s) still houses birds. Mary Gladstone, who visited Waddesdon with her father in 1887, wrote in her diary: 'Pottered about looking at calves, hothouses . . . some rather cockney things, rockeries . . . a large aviary with gaudy plumaged birds . . .'. At Hardwick Hall in Derbyshire the 6th Duke of Devonshire (1790–1858) hung a net across the bay of the Low Great Chamber and filled that with birds. Somerleyton Hall in Suffolk has an aviary dating from the 1840s, and the owners of Clearwell Castle, Gloucestershire, still maintain an aviary in the garden.

Axminster carpets. The manufacture of knotted carpets was established at Axminster, Devon by Thomas Whitty in 1755. The patterns employed were mainly European in origin and the factory enjoyed considerable success. The looms were acquired by WILTON in 1835. See also FLOORS AND FLOOR COVERINGS and 'TURKIE' WORK.

Badge-men. An act of 1697 obliged the poor on parish relief to wear badges (hence the name) carrying the letter 'P'; they were forbidden to beg. See also GILBERT'S ACT, POOR LAW, SETTLEMENT, SPEENHAMLAND SYSTEM and WORKHOUSE.

Badminton. A game said to have been developed at Badminton House, Gloucestershire from the nursery game of BATTLEDORE AND SHUTTLECOCK; played over a net like TENNIS, but with a shuttlecock in place of a tennis ball. It appears to have been first played in England about 1873, but prior to that it was popular in India, and current rules are still based on the Poona Rules of 1876. Like CROQUET, badminton was popular with both sexes from the end of the nineteenth century.

Bailiff. In law the term signifies an officer to whom some degree of authority, care or jurisdiction is committed. The bailiff of a medieval manorial estate was responsible for managing the DEMESNE land and for running the lord's estate; since he was responsible for the collection of rents and, in the case of non-payment, for turning defaulters out, he was usually appointed from outside the lord's tenantry. As the Queen's agent, the Keeper of Dover Castle is still known as the Queen's Bailiff. Today, the name is more usually confined to SHERIFF's officers who collect fines, summon juries, and execute writs.

Baldachino, Baldacchino, Baldachin or Baldaquin. Architecturally, a CIBORIUM. A canopy over an altar or throne, particularly one which is supported on columns, especially when free-standing and disconnected from any enclosing wall; may also be suspended from the ceiling. The baldacchino became increasingly fashionable in the Renaissance, perhaps influenced by Bernini's enormous bronze one for the altar of St Peter's in Rome. There is a baldacchino in the east end of St Paul's cathedral. See also LAMBREQUIN.

Balls and **Ballrooms.** Society became more relaxed after the formality of the ENGLISH BAROQUE period ended, *c.* 1725, and balls and ASSEMBLIES became popular. In Hogarth's (1697–1764) *Wedding Dance* (1745), the dancers are swirling with enjoyable abandon beneath an emblazonment of the Royal Coat of Arms in what is undoubtedly a town hall, often the venue in county and market towns for less select balls and assemblies. From this time, county families and the NOBILITY rebuilding their outdated houses installed ballrooms, sometimes of great grandeur but only coming to life once or twice a year.

Hopetoun House, West Lothian, designed in the 1720s by William Adam (1689–1748), boasts an early ballroom, so-called, but more usually balls were held in the SALOON, as at Saltram in Devon, or in the gallery, as at Hagley, West Midlands, and Harewood House, South Yorkshire. The most fashionable balls were those held during the SEASON in London where, by the mid eighteenth century, every large house had a ballroom with a separate room for supper.

Bank of England. Founded in 1694 with the backing of Parliament and the City to finance the ever-increasing cost of William III's (1689–1702) wars with France. The 'Governor and Company of the Bank of England', with 1248 shareholders, was to borrow money at 4½ per cent interest, to lend to the Government at 8 per cent interest, the interest secured by a new duty on tonnage. The Bank was originally created for twelve years with an allowance of £100,000 per annum for costs. A new charter was granted in 1708 by which the Bank was able to issue its own notes, but these did not become legal tender until 1833.

Banneret. See KNIGHT BANNERET.

Banquet. Originally, in Tudor and Stuart times, used to describe the third and final course of a dinner; not the full, grand meal it has come to mean. The banquet emerged in the sixteenth century as a course of cakes, spiced fruit, HIPPOCRAS and wafers, at first eaten standing about while the table was cleared of the clutter and detritus from the pre-ceding courses. Gradually the custom arose of leaving the eating room altogether at this stage; the 'void' or 'voydee' (from clearing or 'voiding' the table) might be served in a withdrawing chamber, in a room spe-cially devised for the purpose – often with a splendid view (dinner was eaten earlier in the day than it is now), perhaps on the roof or in the garden. A number of banqueting houses dating from 1568–9 survive on the roof of Longleat in Wiltshire, some square and some octagonal, and none able to accommodate more than 6 or 8 people. A two-storey banqueting house (1550) also survives on the roof at Lacock Abbey, Wiltshire. The lower room can be reached through the house, the upper only by a climb across the leads, and neither is big enough for more than 6.

Baptism. A ceremonial washing, immersing, or sprinkling with water at the baptismal font to signify admission into the Christian church, often accompanied by a naming ceremony. Until comparatively recently, because of high infant mortality, it was felt important to baptise a baby at the earliest opportunity. Until the end of the eight-eenth century, the baptism and christening of babies born to rank and fortune would be carried out in the state bedroom, mother and child in the state bed; later, the ceremony might take place in the drawing-room, with the mother and her child reclining on a sofa; and some-times it was conducted in church.

Baptists. A religious sect originating among the English separatists from CONGREGATIONALISM who took refuge in Holland in 1606; dis-tinguished by their contention that only believers should be baptised, and the distinctive method of baptism, by total immersion. John Smyth (1570–1612), a Cambridge scholar and ordained minister from Gains-borough in Lincolnshire, laid the foundations of the first English Baptist

Church when he baptised himself and some of his adherents in 1609; in 1611 his declaration of faith 'of English people remaining at Amsterdam in Holland' laid down two main doctrines: 'to receive all their members by baptism upon the confession of their faith and sins'; and that 'baptism in no wise appertaineth to infants'. The year of Smyth's death his chief follower returned to England and established a little church at Newgate which was the beginning of the 'General' Baptist denomination in England. The more Calvinistic 'Particular' Baptists arose from a group of members of the Jacob Church, Southwark, about 1633. It should perhaps be noted that baptism was still at this stage by affusion, the pouring-on of water. Total immersion was introduced from Holland in the mid 1640s, initially among the Particular Baptists. Like many NONCONFORMISTS, Baptists suffered fines and imprisonment during the reign of Charles II (1660–85), but the TOLERATION ACT of 1689 gave them liberty of conscience and freedom of worship. A split in 1770 led to the formation of a General Baptist New Connection, with 'Old Connection' members merging into UNITARIANISM, but in 1891, and principally due to the efforts of the Revd John Clifford (1836–1923), both General and Particular Baptists were brought together as the 'Baptist Union of Great Britain and Ireland'.

The Baptist method of church government is congregational, each church being self-governing and locally autonomous. The officers of the church are the pastor, the deacons, and the evangelists.

Baron. See the PEERAGE.

Baronet. A hereditary titled order conferring the prefix 'Sir' on the name of the holder, 'Lady' (originally 'Dame') on his wife. The lowest-ranking hereditary title, it descends through the male line; a baronet is a commoner, not a peer. James I created the order in 1611 and sold the baronetcies – originally limited to 200 in number – to raise funds for the defence of Ulster. The fee, amounting to £1,095, represented the cost of maintaining thirty soldiers in Ireland for three years (at the rate of eight pence each per day). In 1616, by a further money-raising device to encourage applicants, the eldest son of a baronet could claim a KNIGHTHOOD on coming of age; and baronets the right to charge their armorial bearings with the Red Hand of Ulster. In 1619 the baronetage of Ireland was instituted. In 1625, Charles I created the first Scottish baronets, 'of Scotland or of Nova Scotia', as an inducement to settle the colony; the required number (150) not coming forward to take up this privilege, in 1634 it was extended to English and Irish gentlemen.

Because of the large number of wrongfully assumed baronetcies, a Royal Warrant of 1783 directed that no one should be recognized as a baronet in official documents until he had proved his right, and that future creations must register their arms and pedigree at the College of Arms, but in the face of opposition from the baronets themselves, the first regulation was rescinded. The right of eldest sons of baronets to claim knighthood was revoked in 1825. In a further attempt to curb wrongful assumptions, a Royal Warrant of 1910 established an official list or roll of the rank; every person succeeding to a baronetcy must now provide proofs of succession. Baronets of the Nova Scotia creation are entitled to display on their coat of arms the saltire of that province. See also the PEERAGE.

Baroque. Not a style restricted to art and architecture but extending to all facets of life – clothes, music, plays – the Baroque originated in Rome in the late sixteenth century. At his RESTORATION in 1660 Charles II (1660–85) brought to England a familiarity with European styles and fashions in general, and in particular a taste for the French Baroque of Louis XIV's Versailles. To this was later added the Dutch influence of William III (1689–1702) of Orange; but the publication of *Vitruvius Britannicus* (1715–17) introduced the ideas which turned fashionable taste towards PALLADIANISM.

In architecture these continental influences led to the work of VAN-BRUGH, HAWKSMOOR and Archer, exponents of English Baroque between the 1690s and the 1720s. The style is distinguished by the theatrical effect of great single units massed against one another, by massiveness and vigorous ornamentation; domes were often a feature. Blenheim Palace, Oxfordshire (built by Vanbrugh and Hawksmoor between 1705 and 1724) is perhaps the culmination of the English Baroque. Emblem and allegory were important aspects of the Baroque – Blenheim's south front carries a bust of the vanquished Louis XIV (1643–1715).

Allegory and classical references – often combined – were particularly important in paintings of the Baroque period. Wall paintings by Sir James Thornhill (1675–1734) depict cloud-dwelling gods and goddesses in re-creations of scenes from Classical mythology. Court circles saw king and courtiers as inheritors of the ideals of ancient Rome. The Great Hall at Chatsworth, Derbyshire, painted by Louis Laguerre (1663–1721) in 1692–4, shows episodes from the life of Julius Caesar. For Caesar read William III: the paintings are a glorification of the king, disguised as Classical history; his queen, Mary, painted by Verrio (1630–1707), is deified as Cybele on the ceiling of the narrow stairs to the STATE APARTMENTS at Chatsworth.

With the death of Queen Anne and the accession of the Hanoverian line, political power shifted from the Court party to the Country party, from TORIES to WHIGS, and the ostentatious support the Baroque style had afforded king and court went out of fashion.

Barrister. A term applied to the class of lawyers who have exclusive audience in the superior courts of law. Every barrister in England must be a member of one of the four Inns of Court (viz., Lincoln's Inn, the Inner and Middle Temples, Gray's Inn); in Scotland, a member of the Faculty of Advocates; in Ireland, of the King's Inns. Barristers arose in medieval times when lawyers educated students in the Common Law; the degree of barrister corresponded to apprentice or bachelor, that of serjeant to doctor. See also ATTORNEY, DOCTORS' COMMONS and INNS OF COURT.

Barry, Sir Charles (1795–1860). A leading early Victorian architect whose working life began during the Regency period. Barry could turn his hand to any style his clients demanded. In 1836 he won the design competition for the new Houses of Parliament and employed PUGIN to provide the GOTHIC REVIVAL detail and interiors; Highclere Castle, Hampshire, remodelled in 1842–50, is in the Elizabethan style; Clivedon, Buckinghamshire (1850–1) is in the Italian Renaissance style and (unusually) of brick faced with Portland cement; while Halifax Town Hall (1859–62) is Classical, with a pagoda like spire. Barry's *palazzo*-style Travellers' Club in Pall Mall (1830–2) is also well known.

Bath. The chief city of Somerset, and possessing the only natural hot springs (120 °F) in Britain, Bath seems to have been a popular spa from pre-Roman times. The city's Roman remains are, with Hadrian's Wall, the best-preserved and most impressive in Britain. The Roman baths were founded early in the era of Roman occupation, in Flavian times (AD 69–96), and consist of a long series of rooms – five baths, two swimming pools, and associated sweat rooms (warmed by under-floor heating – hypocausts) and cooling rooms. Sufferers from rheumatic and allied diseases travelled to them from all over Britain and Gaul. But early in the fifth century AD the Romans left, and the town fell into decay. Excavation has revealed Saxon graves in the soil immediately above the baths.

Samuel Pepys visited 'the Bath' (as it was often known in the seventeenth century), and on 13 June 1668 noted: 'methinks it cannot be clean to go so many bodies together into the same water'. In the Cross Bath, frequented by the gentry, and also the coolest, and so the one most used in summer, gentlemen sat on seats around the cross built in the middle (from which the bath derived its name) and ladies at the side, under the arches. There were also the King's and Queen's Baths, but Pepys found them 'full of a mixed sort of good and bad'. Early in the eighteenth century, when Queen Anne came to 'take the waters' and Richard 'Beau' Nash (1674–1762) became Master of the Ceremonies, Bath and its therapeutic medicinal springs became the resort of fashion. Admired for his taste and his manners, Beau Nash became the recognized autocrat of the town, publishing rules of polite behaviour for ladies and gentlemen, discouraging the wearing of swords and duelling. Through his association with the philanthropist Ralph Allen, the 'Man of Bath' and owner of the Bath stone quarries on Coombe Down, and in particular with the architects John WOOD, father and son, much of the town was rebuilt with the Georgian terraces and crescents so familiar today, and the amenities were improved. The first Pump Room opened in 1706, a joint venture between Nash and his doctor, William Oliver, the inventor of the Bath Oliver biscuit. By the middle of the century Bath had come to rival London in sophistication, and distinguished visitors were welcomed by peals of bells from the abbey. In 1780 Fanny Burney was shocked by the appearance of the ladies at the baths: 'it is true, their heads are covered with bonnets; but the very idea of being seen in such a situation by whoever pleases to look is indelicate.' Bath as the resort of the fashionable is vividly described in the novels of Fielding, Smollett, Fanny Burney, Dickens, and others, but best-known are Jane Austen's 'Bath' novels, *Northanger Abbey* and *Persuasion*.

Bathing. Before the modern improvements of the nineteenth century, bathing reached its apogee of comfort under the Romans, famous for their baths both public and private. In the Middle Ages ablutions might be carried out in wooden tubs or, in summer, in a river or stream. Monasteries usually had good washing facilities, although the church fathers clearly viewed excessive bathing with some mistrust; St Benedict's Rule (sixth century AD) enjoins that 'the use of baths shall be offered to the sick as often as is necessary; to the healthy, especially the young, it shall not be so often conceded'. Returning Crusaders brought with them the custom of the 'Turkish' bath, and public baths ('stews') were established in towns. Their use was in decline by the fourteenth century for various reasons – the shortage of fuel for heating water, the prevalence of PLAGUE, and the immorality which came to be associated with them (as exemplified by the colloquial use of the Italian *bagnio* (bath) for a brothel).

Private bathrooms were the prerogative of the mighty. Edward III (1327–77) had one fitted with two large bronze taps, for hot and cold water. Lesser mortals filled their tubs from buckets, but even kings bathed in wood. In 1508 Henry VII (1485–1509) ordered a wooden bath tub, at a cost of twenty shillings. Probably cold water and indifferent soap (if any: the leaves of *Saponaria officinalis*, soapwort, were possibly used) was the lot of most, but in his *Boke of Nurture* (c. 1540) John Russell describes a more luxurious experience, in which the bathing area is hung about with sweet-smelling herbs and the bather is sponged by a servant from a basin of water (warm, one hopes) and herbs. When the Burgundian ambassador was entertained by Edward IV (1442–83) in 1472, one of the 'chambers of pleasance' prepared for his use contained two 'Baynes' or baths covered with tents of white cloth.

Progress was slow. As late as 1697, a bathroom or bathing room at Chatsworth in Derbyshire was so grand that Celia Fiennes described it in detail: '. . . one entire marble all white finely veined with blue . . . it was as deep as one's middle on the outside, and you went down steps into the bath big enough for two people; at the upper end are two cocks to let in, one hot the other cold, water to attemper it as persons please; the windows are all private glass'. Carshalton House, Surrey, built in 1719–20 for a director of the South Sea Company, boasted a large bath house lined with Dutch tiles at the base of a water-tower with a water-powered engine room.

Lack of demand probably slowed the spread of the private bathroom: personal cleanliness was not a high priority. When it was felt to be necessary, small quantities of water were easily carried by servants so that their masters or mistresses could wash in their own chambers. Cold baths became a health fad (the earliest known, at Rufford Abbey, Nottinghamshire, dates from 1729), but even so, as they were taken only weekly or even monthly, there was no need to have the bath in – or even very near – the house. They were often built in the garden or park – sometimes in the open air (the bath-house and remains of an open-air pool at Wynnstay in Clwyd, c. 1780) or in a garden building or grotto, as at Stourhead.

Prince Albert had a shower-bath installed at Osborne, a contraption like a modern car-wash, and Bear Wood in Berkshire, built in 1870, was unusual in having five bathrooms with running water. Most large houses built in the nineteenth century, up to about 1880, had only one bathroom, for family use: guests had to make do with a HIP-BATH placed in front of their bedroom fire and filled by the HOUSEMAID. The 'old rich' considered bathrooms vulgar, which is why Carlton Towers in Humberside, built in the 1870s, had none. See also PLUNGE BATHS.

Bathrooms. See BATHING.

Battledore and Shuttlecock. A children's game played for centuries using small parchment or gut-stringed, wooden-framed rackets and a shuttlecock made of cork or similar light material, trimmed with feathers – a forerunner of BADMINTON. Ancient Greek drawings represent a game which appears almost identical, and a similar game has also been popular in China, Japan, India and Thailand for at least 2000 years.

'Bedint'. A slang word used by Harold Nicolson (1886–1968) and his wife Vita Sackville-West (1892–1962) to indicate people or things which were or seemed lower-class; from the German *bedienen*, to serve; *ein Bediente* is a manservant, lackey or footman.

Bedlam. The popular name for Bethlehem Royal Hospital in London; an institution for the insane but originally a priory founded in 1247 in Bishopsgate Street where the sisters and brethren of the Order of the Star of Bethlehem might entertain the bishop and canons of St Mary of Bethlehem, the mother church, on their visits to England. It is not known when lunatics were first taken in, but it is mentioned as a hospital in 1330, and the presence of lunatics is noted in 1403. At the Dissolution of the Monasteries (1536) Henry VIII gave it and its revenue to the City of London as a hospital for lunatics – the first and for centuries the only asylum for the insane. In 1676 the hospital moved to Moorfields, in 1815 to what is now the Imperial War Museum, South London, and in 1930, when it became part of the King's College Hospital Group, to West Wickham, near Croydon, Surrey. The term 'Bedlam' was used for any madhouse or lunatic asylum, and has come to signify uncontrolled uproar.

Beds and **bedchambers.** The Assyrians, Medes and Persians are known to have had beds – of stone, wood or metal, sometimes elaborately decorated – as are the Greeks and Romans, while the barbarians of northern Europe were still sleeping on piles of leaves covered with skins, or in shallow depressions filled with leaves and moss. Later, benches or ledges provided some protection from draughts and vermin, but even as beds became more general, the lowest and poorest still slept among the rushes on the floor. For many centuries beds and their hangings were regarded as among a family's most valuable possessions, to be specifically named in wills. The quality of a bed and its hangings became a clear statement of the owner's rank and wealth.

The hangings themselves probably derived from the practice of curtaining off a portion of the room against draughts, and to provide an element of privacy. In the early Middle Ages the main bed would have been in the HALL, but by the fifteenth century had been removed to the GREAT CHAMBER, where cords from the ceiling supported the tester or canopy over the bed, and draperies, often sumptuous, were hung from it around the bed. Meals were sometimes taken in the Great Chamber, creating what was effectively a bed-sitting room. A mid fifteenth-century *Orders of service belonging to the degree of a duke, marquis and an erle* describes breakfast being served at the foot of the bed. Gradually, wood came to be used increasingly decoratively in the bed's structure, and the 'standing' bed came to consist of a bedstead – correctly bedstock – with solid panelling at the head end reaching up to the tester and two pillars on pedestals at each side at the foot, these together supporting a flat wooden tester with carved frieze. The carving of pillars and panels might be enhanced with painting and gilding. A bed might be found in any multi-purpose room, and the term 'bedchamber' did not become common until the mid sixteenth century, suggesting that only by then was there a room used mainly for sleeping. The earliest mention of a suite of state bedchamber furniture is from a Chatsworth inventory of *c.* 1566.

A rare survivor of a very grand oak bed (now in private hands) which may have belonged to Henry VII's stepfather, the Earl of Derby (d. 1504), has no part of its visible oak surface uncarved; it was originally brightly painted, and no doubt hung with rich materials.

By 1660 the state bedchamber had become a status symbol, offered to any visitor of higher rank than the host. The bedchamber became the final room in the BAROQUE arrangement of STATE APARTMENTS, with bed and matching chairs covered in extravagant fabric. The high point of the state bedchamber was *c.* 1700, after which it declined in importance.

Descriptions of state beds actually in use are very rare. At Stowe, Buckinghamshire, the state bed was used at a christening held *c.* 1718. The Duke of Lorraine is recorded using a state bed at Houghton, Norfolk in 1731. When the Earl of Guilford visited the Duke of Portland at Bulstrode Park, Buckinghamshire in the 1760s, the hint was dropped that 'the good Earl would find himself more comfortable if he were not honoured with the great apartment'. Nevertheless, Robert ADAM designed an abbreviated range of state apartments, complete with state bed, at Osterley Park, London, as late as 1776.

Servants' beds. Medieval and even Elizabethan household servants had no private dormitories or bedrooms. Medieval servants slept on the rushes on the Hall floor. Later, the more important slept on truckle beds in passages and on landings. Some Elizabethan servants' beds were made to fold away into chests. Care should be taken in definition, here: as late as Jacobean times, a powerful, high-ranking peer's 'servants' might include knights, etc., as well as footmen and maids, hence the early seventeenth-century instruction that servants' beds be shared 'gentlemen with gentlemen and yeomen with yeomen'. By the eighteenth century 'servants' implied no more than footmen, etc., who slept in dormitories, as they continued to do until the twentieth century. At Welbeck Abbey, Nottinghamshire, in the 1920s, the maids' dormitory was known by the Duchess of Portland as 'the virgins' wing'. A servants' dormitory, furnished with six double beds for twelve maids, was used at Mamhead House, Devon until 1939.

Box beds. By the sixteenth or seventeenth century most people above the very poorest levels of society regarded a separate room for sleeping as essential. But in Scotland, among the peasantry beds were boxed into the wall of the kitchen, the main living space, and made to look like wainscoting or cupboards. This was practical, as the warmth of the fire was not wasted. Where accommodation was restricted, often whole families would sleep in the same room, and did so until the twentieth century.

Four-poster beds. A modern name given to beds with a covering canopy, which had evolved by the fifteenth century. Few early beds in fact, had four posts. Four-poster beds were differentiated in eighteenth century trade cards from standing beds by having a *low* headboard, so that pillars to match those at the foot were required to support the tester at the bed-head. More often they had two posts with a massive headboard, carved or painted or faced with silks, rising to the height of the tester or canopy. By the late seventeenth century many beds had no posts at all, and the tester appeared to float above the beds. Beds of this type have the French name of *lits à la duchesse*, or more explicably 'angel beds', because the tester gives the happy impression of being supported by angels; in fact, chains from the ceiling are the means of suspension.

State beds. Before 1688 state beds were comparatively simple. A bed of 1629, restored in 1852, can be seen in the blue bed-chamber at Hardwick Hall, Derbyshire. Ham House, London, has several restored beds dating from the 1670s. Three beds at Knole also date from the same period, two of which, including the remarkable spangled bed, are thought to be from royal palaces. No state beds with original fabrics survive from earlier than the 1670s. After 1688, under the influence of MAROT, an interior designer brought to England by William III, state beds had much higher testers than grand French beds of the period.

Mattresses for such beds were built up on the layer principle. A straw palliasse was laid on a base of canvas laced onto the bedstock, followed by as many as three hair or wool mattresses. Feather mattresses were sometimes used – hence 'feather-bed'. The bedding might be piled on so high that steps were needed to get onto it.

Trundle or truckle bed. A basic bed, in use from medieval times to the eighteenth century. Usually it had rope, canvas or leather webbing to support a straw mattress, the feet fitted with small wheels. As the name suggests, it could be 'trundled' out of sight in daytime beneath the main bed. Used by servants who slept in the master's bedchamber, and sometimes by children. See also BED-STEPS, LEVÉES, MATTRESSES and SPARVER.

Bed-steps. Steps used for getting onto a standing or four-poster bed raised up by MATTRESSES. In the eighteenth century bed-steps often had cupboards in them to hold CHAMBER-POTS. Bed-steps were still being made in the early nineteenth century.

Beer. An alcoholic drink made from fermented cereal, first oats or wheat and then, after the thirteenth century, usually barley, with the addition of hops as a flavouring and preservative. The recipe was brought to England by Flemish brewers in the fourteenth century. Beer and ALE were commonly drunk because they were safer than water. In 1441 both beer and ale were subject to an ASSIZE duty, and beer was not permitted to leave the brewery for eight days after brewing.

In the SERVANTS' HALL beer was served at dinner and supper – in medieval times at breakfast as well – from the BUTTERY by the Yeoman of the Buttery or, by the seventeenth century, the BUTLER. By the nineteenth century, beer was served as part of wages.

In country houses beer was brewed between October and March, because it was not possible to cool the fermentations in summer. The hops and malt for brewing were often bought-in, unless barley was grown on the home farm. The brewery was usually sited to the north of the house so that the prevailing winds blew the smell of fermentation away. Charlecote House, Warwickshire, has a fully-equipped brewery, and when George Lucy died in 1845 there were 4,650 gallons of beer in the cellar. Traquair House, Borders, Scotland, and Stanway House, Gloucestershire, still brew their own beer, for sale to visitors. See also CAUDLES and POSSET.

Bell boards. In the desire for more privacy, servants awaiting instructions were gradually banished from the main living rooms and by the mid eighteenth century they spent the greater part of their time in the servants' wing. Bell-pulls situated in the upstairs rooms were connected by wires and pulleys to bells in the servants' quarters mounted on springs on a bell board, with the name of the relevant 'upstairs' room painted beneath each differently toned bell.

Prince Pückler-Muskau recalled a visit to Penryn Castle, Gwynedd, in the late 1820s: 'The servants live in a large room, generally on the ground floor, where all, male and female, eat together, and where the bells of the whole house are placed. They are suspended in a row on the wall, numbered so that it is immediately seen in what room any one has rung: a sort of pendulum is attached to each, which continues to vibrate for ten minutes after the sound has ceased to remind the sluggish of their duty.' In a large establishment a bell-boy would be stationed by the board to fetch whichever servant was required.

Belvederes and **Prospect Towers.** Belvederes were rooms built on the roofs of houses to take advantage of a view, and might take the form of an angle turret, a cupola, a loggia, or an open gallery. The most eccentric is the Prospect Room on top of Wollaton Hall, Nottinghamshire by Robert SMYTHSON, completed in 1588 for the erratic Sir Francis Willoughby. It has an immense panoramic view and is as big as a ballroom, but difficult to use as a space for entertaining since access is only by two very narrow and steep spiral staircases in turrets.

A prospect tower was a viewing tower standing on its own, more usually built to provide a focus to a view. Towers were a popular subject for amateur architects in the eighteenth century. Sanderson Miller (1716–80) built a sham castle and tower at Edgehill, Warwickshire, on the spot where Charles I (1625–49) supposedly raised his standard before the Battle of Edgehill in 1642; Alfred's Tower, built in 1772 three miles from Stourhead at Kingsettle Hill, Wiltshire, is where King Alfred is believed to have raised his standard against the Danes in 879. These are heroic towers. A more utilitarian tower is Lutterell's Tower, near Eaglehurst, Southampton, built in 1780 and giving a wide view of the sea. A tunnel runs from the cellar to the beach; clearly there is a connection with smuggling.

Benedictines. The 'Black Monks' were the largest monastic order in England by the time of the DISSOLUTION, with some 136 monasteries and 60 nunneries. Founded in Italy by St Benedict in the sixth century, it is the earliest monastic order, from which all others derive. The Benedictines were originally not strictly speaking an order, but a confederation of self-governing houses following the same rule; they were prominent in the development of learning and the arts. The following houses are on the sites of former Benedictine foundations: Bisham Abbey, Buckinghamshire, founded as Augustinian, changed to Benedictine briefly 1537–8; Horsham St Faith, Abbey Farm, Norfolk, founded 1105; The Priory, Lavenham, Suffolk. The Benedictines returned to Britain in the nineteenth century, and today the English congregation has eight abbeys of monks and four abbeys of nuns. See also AUGUSTINIANS, CARMELITES, CARTHUSIANS, CISTERCIANS, CLUNIACS, DOMINICANS, FRIARS, FRANCISCANS, GILBERTINES, MENDICANT FRIARS and PREMONSTRATENSIANS.

Benefice. A church living and its income, derived from land belonging to an ecclesiastical office; a right to enjoy certain ecclesiastical revenues on condition of discharging certain services – not necessarily a cure of souls. An appointment by a bishop to a benefice was for the lifetime of the holder. A donative benefice was an office to which a parson was appointed without presentation to a bishop.

Benefit of Clergy. Arose from a twelfth-century conflict between COMMON (state) and CANON (church) LAW. By the Constitution of Clarenden of 1164, clergy committing criminal offences were passed to ecclesiastical courts for judgment and punishment – and ecclesiastical courts did not hand down the death penalty. An offender could show that he was a member of the clergy by reading the first verse of the fifty-first Psalm – which came to be called the 'neck verse' (since it saved his neck). In time, the ability to read was sufficient, and so widespread did abuse of the privilege become that in 1487 it was enacted that every layman convicted by the ecclesiastical court should be branded on the thumb, thus disabling him from claiming the benefit a second time. In

1547 the right was extended to peers, even if they could *not* read; in 1622 (partially) and 1692 (fully) to women. The benefit was finally abolished in 1827 but the statute of 1547 was not repealed, and it was not until 1841 that peers were put on the same footing as commons and clergy. The benefit was never extended to Scotland.

Bergère. A French term for a winged armchair fashionable from the mid eighteenth century. With a high curved back, wide, deep seat and upholstered arms, it was far more comfortable than the British equivalent, the wing arm-chair.

Between-maids or **Tweenies.** A late nineteenth-century servant ranking between a kitchen-maid and a scullery-maid; her duties were to assist the cook and the housemaid, her work being shared 'between' them.

Bible, The English. The first full translation of the Bible into English from Latin was made by John Wycliffe (1324–84) in 1384. Before his time only parts had been translated: fragments by Aelfric of *c*. 1000 survive, and the Lollards produced two Middle English versions of the Vulgate (the fourth-century Latin version of the scriptures) in *c*. 1375–96. However, until the arrival of printing there was little point in attempting to produce an English Bible for general use. William Tyndale made his translation of the New Testament from the Greek and Hebrew originals; it was printed at Worms and published in 1525 (only one complete copy survives; it is now in the British Library). Tyndale was working on the Old Testament when he died in 1536. Miles Coverdale's (1488–1568) Bible, published in 1535, the first to include both the Old and New Testament, was based on German and Latin translations. The first official English Bible was brought out in 1537, the work of John Rogers (1500–55), a friend of Tyndale; it was not a new translation, but a compilation from Tyndale's and Coverdale's Bibles. The Great Bible of 1539 (also called the Treacle Bible, from the fact that 'balm' was therein translated as 'triacle' or treacle) was a version authorized by the bishops, a revision by Coverdale based on Latin, Hebrew and Greek texts. The 1540 edition, with a preface by Archbishop Thomas Cranmer (1489–1556), is known as Cranmer's Bible. The Geneva or Breeches Bible, published in Geneva in 1560 by refugees who had fled Marian persecution, became popular with the PURITANS because of the Calvinistic tone of its marginal commentary, and generally because of its quarto size and clear Roman type (earlier Bibles had been printed in the difficult black-letter type). The Bishops' Bible commissioned by Archbishop Matthew Parker (1504–75) was published in 1568, but never became popular for use in the home. All these various Bibles were superseded by the Authorized Version of 1611, a revision of the Bishops' Bible begun in 1604 which arose incidentally out of a conference between High and Low Church parties convened by James I (1603–25), and became the standard English Bible (also often known as the James I Bible). Abroad, Roman Catholic exiles published the New Reims Testament in 1582, and the Douai Old Testament in 1609–10. See also WELSH BIBLE, below.

Bible, The Welsh. The lack of printing presses in Wales and the establishment in 1536 of English as the official language militated against the publication of a Bible in Welsh, but in 1551 William Salesbury (c. 1520–1600) produced a Welsh translation of the New Testament. An Act of 1563 had authorized a Welsh Bible, but it was not until 1588 that both Old and New Testament were translated into Welsh by William Morgan (1540–1604), Bishop of St Asaph. This translation, revised and amended by Richard Parry (1560–1623), Bishop of St Asaph, and John Davies (1570–1644) was republished in 1620 and is the version in use to this day. See also BIBLE, above.

Bicycles. The first popular bicycle was the 'boneshaker' developed in 1864 by Pierre Lallement, a Frenchman. There had been earlier inventions – the 'dandy-horse' of 1808 and Kirkpatrick's bicycle of 1840 – but none achieved the popularity of the 'boneshaker', so called because its wooden wheels had iron rims and produced vibration throughout the heavy iron frame. The 'penny farthing' of 1872–1885, also called the 'ordinary', with a large front wheel and small rear wheel, was inherently impractical due to difficulties of balance. All these machines were driven by pedals directly connected to the front or rear wheel. Two further improvements to the bicycle were: (1) in 1885, two equal-sized wheels with power transmitted by a chain to the rear wheel, which was the origin of the 'Safety Bicycle'; (2) in 1888, the invention of pneumatic tyres, by J.B. Dunlop of Belfast (1840–1921).

From 1865 bicycling was enormously popular with the upper and middle classes. 'Bloomers' – loose trousers gathered at the ankles, introduced c. 1849 by Amelia Bloomer (1818–1894), American champion of 'rational dress' for women – became fashionable and permitted ladies to enjoy the recreation of cycling with propriety.

The end of the nineteenth and the early twentieth century saw bicycling parties become hugely popular, and gave women a new taste of freedom.

Biedermeier. The name given to a style of furniture and interior decoration popular in Austria and Germany (equivalent to the French Empire style) during the peaceful years between the defeat of Napoleon in 1815 and the unrest of 1848 and the following decades – a time looked back on by many with nostalgia. The style is clean and simple in design, and includes painting and sculpture as well as furniture. The name derives from two fictitious characters, Biedermann and

Bummelmeier, who were featured in a Munich satirical magazine, *Fliegende Blätter* (Flying Leaves), and represented the small, honest, dull, complacent and self-satisfied bourgeois man. Biedermeier furniture attracted some attention in Britain.

Billeting. The enforced accommodation of soldiers and sailors on private householders, the term deriving from the billet, or ticket, directing a householder to provide such board and lodging. Billeting was much abused and resented, and under Charles I (1625–49) the practice was condemned in the Petition of Right of 1628. Billeting upon private citizens against their will was forbidden from 1679, but was employed in spite of this by Charles II (1660–85) and James II (1686–88). Condemned again in the Bill of Rights of 1689, billeting was restricted to inn-keepers in 1690. It was only when George III (1760–1820) obtained parliamentary approval for the construction of permanent barracks in 1792 that billeting ceased.

Billiards. A table game with balls and cues (rods) played in England at least since the sixteenth century. The origins of the game are obscure, variously given as Classical Greek, second-century Irish, medieval English, Italian, and Spanish. Louis XI (1461–83) of France is reported to have had a billiard table, while a French woodcut of 1480 shows the game being played on the ground, lending some substance to the theory of its derivation from bowls. Mary, Queen of Scots (1542–87) complained bitterly during her captivity in England that her table had been taken from her. The earliest reference to a billiard table in a private house is found in 1588, in connection with Howard House, the London home of the Duke of Norfolk. Shakespeare, with Cleopatra's 'let's to billiards: come, Charmian', may or may not have been anachronistic, but clearly assumes his audience to be familiar with the game. The earliest known rules were printed in 1650. Traditionally the table was set up in the hall, as at Ham House, London in 1679; Celia Fiennes noted one in the gallery at Euston Hall, Suffolk in 1697. The oldest known surviving table, at Boughton House, Northamptonshire, was in the house before 1670 – and the first specially designed billiard room was at Southill, Bedfordshire (built between 1767 and 1803). More than two-thirds of the country houses built between 1835 and 1870 had a billiard room, usually with a SMOKING ROOM adjoining, for by Victorian times billiards had become almost entirely a male pastime. Cushioned edges to the tables were introduced in 1835, and slate beds covered with green baize in 1836. Snooker, played on a billiard table but using 15 red balls and 6 coloured, was first played in Jubbapore, India by British officers in 1875, and introduced to England in 1885.

Bill of Exchange. A written order to pay a sum on a given day to the drawer or a named payee; an early method of borrowing money on future receipts; an early form of cheque. Bills of Exchange originated as a device to avoid the transmission of bulky cash (specie) from place to place to settle trade debts. They are still used in the City of London, where the Bank of England, through discount houses, buys and sells hundreds of millions of pounds in bills accepted by major banks. The operation increases or reduces the supply of money to the money markets and banks, and is therefore a major factor in the cost of borrowing.

An example of a bill's working is to imagine the cotton trade in the nineteenth century. A grower in India has an order to supply £10,000-worth of cotton to a Manchester spinner. The spinner will not pay for the cotton until it is received, but the grower needs cash to pay his cotton pickers. The Bill of Exchange answers this problem when the grower makes out a bill addressed to the spinner: 'Four months after this date, pay to me the sum of £10,000'. This becomes a legal document when the Manchester spinner accepts the bill. The grower can then sell the bill to a money-lender or a bank, at a discount, and so find money to pay his pickers. Until 1971, both Bills of Exchange and cheques were subject to Stamp Duty.

William Morris's father was a partner in a City firm of bill brokers, and the novelist Anthony Trollope graphically described characters caught up in webs of borrowing at extortionate rates on bills.

Birth control. The prevention of conception has been practised by various means from early times. In the fifth century St Augustine (probably complaining about the use of herbal pessaries) condemned it as being 'unlawful and wicked', a ruling maintained by the Roman Catholic Church to this day. The subject only became a matter for open debate in the late eighteenth century when the economist Robert Malthus (1766–1834) discussed the effect of population increase. The Church recommended the effective (if impractical) method of sexual abstinence. Most commonly used, however, were condoms made from pig or sheep guts, mainly available on the Continent, hence the nickname 'French letter'.

The GRAND TOUR was often a young man's introduction to the dangers of venereal disease, and early (if unreliable) condoms offered some protection; James Boswell (1740–95) frequently refers to them. The condom was first used in the seventeenth century (ten condoms dating from the Civil War have recently been found at Dudley Castle, West Midlands) but did not become common until the eighteenth century. A London advertiser of condoms in 1774 referred to them as 'implements of safety which secure the health of my customers'. Curiously, it was political thinkers such as Francis Place (1771–1854) and Jeremy Bentham (1748–1832) who advocated artificial methods of birth control. Thereafter the subject was swept under the carpet for the greater part of the nineteenth century. In 1877 Annie Besant (1847–1933), the British theosophist and social reformer, and the politician Charles Bradlaugh (1833–1891) were prosecuted for reissuing Dr Charles Knowlton's *Fruits of Philosophy*, originally published in the USA in 1832, which for the first time in print described artificial methods of birth control. Marie Stopes (1880–1958) opened the first birth control clinic, in London in 1921, in the face of abuse principally from outraged Roman Catholic sections of the public; others, however, applauded her dedication, and such clinics became more widespread. Until the advent of the oral contraceptive in 1960, condoms and the diaphragm were the principal means of contraception, while the Roman Catholic Church has continued to recommend the much less reliable rhythm method, based on the date of ovulation.

Bishop. See CLERGY.

Blanket, Born on the wrong side of the. Illegitimate. Born outside the marriage bond. See also BYBLOW, CHANCELING and MERRYBEGOT.

Blues. The nickname of the Royal Horse Guards, one of three cavalry regiments guarding the sovereign.

Blue-stocking. About 1750 Mrs Elizabeth Montague, in an effort to introduce a more intellectual tone to society, began to hold receptions at which literary conversation and discussion between sociable, intelligent and learned men and women displaced gossip and cards. Benjamin Stillingfleet (1702–71), a poet too poor to own fine evening clothes, came to the receptions in his daytime blue worsted stockings, although Admiral Boscowen (1711–61) is said to have coined the collective name Blue Stockings and applied it to the ladies. Such receptions became very popular, and were held in the houses of Sir Joshua Reynolds (1723–92), Mrs Thrale (1741–1821), the Countess of Cork and Orrery, and many others. Dr Johnson (1709–84) attended regularly, if only to allow himself to be lionised; other regulars were Horace Walpole (1719–97), David Garrick (1717–79) and, of course, James Boswell (1740–95), Johnson's biographer. The term came to be used derisively to describe serious women affecting literary tastes and learning.

Bodley, George Frederick (1827–1907). British GOTHIC REVIVAL architect, best-known for his churches, who set the pace for Anglican church architecture. He was Gilbert SCOTT's first pupil, but favoured simpler decorative designs. He was an early supporter of William Morris, and in his interest in craftsmanship and detail belongs to the generation of the ARTS AND CRAFTS MOVEMENT. His St Martin's, in Scarborough, North Yorkshire, contains some of the movement's first work, but Bodley's own finest work is his miniature cathedral in Clumber Park, Nottinghamshire, built in 1886 for the Duke of Newcastle.

Boiserie. Lit., wainscot, wainscoting, woodwork. Wood panels, particularly the carved ROCOCO panelling, painted white and picked out in gold, fashionable in France from the early eighteenth century. There was also a fashion for *boiseries* in Britain from the mid eighteenth century; in 1756 Norfolk House in London had a music room panelled with *boiseries*, now in the Victoria & Albert Museum. The Seven Years' War of 1756–63 caused a reaction against French influence, and the style was subsequently eclipsed by Robert Adam's GROTESQUES. The rococo saw a revival when George IV (1820–30) created rooms in Windsor Castle and Buckingham Palace in the 'Old French Style', in the 1820s. Also in the 1820s, Lord Stuart de Rothsay, British Ambassador in Paris 1815–24, brought back genuine French *boiseries* to put into Highclere Castle, Hampshire. At the same time, 1825, the Duchess of Rutland fitted out the Elizabethan Saloon at Belvoir Castle, Leicestershire, with *boiseries* said to be from Mme de Maintenon's château but actually dating from *c.* 1735 – sixteen years after her death. After the French Revolution such pieces were easy to buy in Paris, where the houses of the aristocracy had been looted. French *boiseries* can also be seen at Harlaxton Manor, Lincolnshire, installed in the house begun in 1831 by SALVIN for Gregory Gregory. The ceiling heights of French rooms were lower than English ones, so the panelling often had to be ingeniously adapted to fit. English *boiseries* were made for the White and Gold Room at Petworth, Sussex, in 1828.

Book of Common Prayer. The official service book of the Church of England. The first (1549) and second (1552) Prayer Books, drawn up by Archbishop Cranmer, were condensations of the old Latin service books. The first was intended as a compromise between the traditionalists and the reformers and was not well received by either, provoking in Cornwall the Western Rebellion of 1549. The second Prayer Book, more Protestant in substance and containing revisions to the office of Holy Communion, was better received. Under Elizabeth I (1558–1603), the Act of Uniformity of 1559 enforced the use of the 1552 Prayer Book, with minor alterations in a Catholic direction. With further modifications, the Hampton Court Conference of 1604 endorsed its continued use. As a result of the rise of Puritanism the use of the Prayer Book was suppressed in 1645, its place taken by the uninspiring Presbyterian *Directory for the Public Worship of God in the Three Kingdoms*. After the Restoration the Savoy Conference of 1661 led to the reintroduction of a revised Prayer Book in 1662. The conception of toleration of alternative forms of worship being an alien one, the general and compulsory use of the Prayer Book of the day was legally enforced by the Acts of Uniformity of 1549, 1552, 1559 and 1662.

Boonwork. Feudal labour given free by tenants of a manor, originally voluntary but later compulsory. It was much resented because demands for help in ploughing, reaping and harvesting arose, naturally enough, at times when the tenant was fully occupied in these tasks on his own behalf. Boonwork lapsed as FEUDALISM declined.

Boroughs. The term is derived from the Anglo-Saxon 'burgs' (fortified places), self-governing towns designated by the Wessex kings as defensive settlements against Danish invaders. Later they were granted charters with legal liberties, and subsequently sent members to Parliament. By the sixteenth century boroughs implied those towns with corporate status and, later still, those governed by a municipal corporation. Boroughs outside London were abolished by the Local Government Act of 1972. See also ROTTEN BOROUGHS.

Borough-English. A custom of inheritance peculiar to certain ancient boroughs and manors (chiefly in southern England) whereby a man's COPYHOLD land was inherited by his youngest son. The custom was abolished by the 1922 and 1924 Property Acts. See also PRIMOGENITURE.

Bote. The common right of tenants of a feudal manor to take timber from the waste land for repairing hedges and houses, or for tools and firewood. Haybote (hedge bote) was the right to take wood or thorns for the repair of hedges, firebote for firewood, housebote for the repair of houses. With the decline of the feudal system, the right of bote lapsed.

Bottles. From the twelfth century WINE was imported in large wooden casks and transported to the customer's cellar in the summer when roads were passable. (The wine was not laid down but was drunk immediately.) Glass bottles of a squat bulbous shape for the temporary storage of wine date from the 1620s; the tops were stoppered with waxed linen. It was only with the introduction of the cork stopper *c.* 1660 that wine could be laid down in bottles. The cork stopper was probably first used for PORT. Corkscrews were in use by 1700. The cylindrical bottle, which could be laid on its side to prevent the cork drying out, dates from *c.* 1770 and was made of very dark green glass, often with a glass seal carrying the owner's coat of arms.

Boulle or **Buhl Furniture.** Ornamental BAROQUE furniture in the style of André-Charles Boulle (1642–1732), a French *ébéniste* whose speciality was marquetry. His pieces are inlaid with silver, brass or pewter, or mother-of-pearl, but his chief fame rests on his inlay work in tortoise-shell and brass shaped and laid in elaborate patterns, the tortoise-shell often of a reddish or bluish colour from being mounted on a coloured backing. Ivory and ebony are also found in boulle-work. Boulle had a large workshop employing twenty craftsmen in the

Louvre, and Garret Johnson (*fl.* 1680–1714) and Frederick Hintz made 'Boulle' furniture in London, as did Peter Langlois, a French *ébéniste*, at his workshop in Tottenham Court Road in the mid eighteenth century. Boulle was much copied in Britain in the seventeenth century, and good boulle-style furniture was still being made in the nineteenth century. There are many examples of this style to be seen in both private houses and public collections.

Bounder. One who does not behave in the accepted manner. The term arose *c.* 1900 with the arrival from the USA of the new-fangled rubber-core GOLF ball: most golfers in Britain continued to use the old gutta percha balls, but shifty players, the bounders, used the new ball, which went further, and bounced.

Bovate, also **Oxgang.** The amount of land a single ox could plough in a year. The area was one eighth of a PLOUGHLAND but varied between 10 to 18 acres, according to the quality of the soil; clayland bovates were smaller than those on light soils.

Bowls. The oldest of British outdoor pastimes after archery and dating back to at least the thirteenth century (the Southampton Bowling Club was founded in 1299). Owing to the game's association with taverns, and heavy gambling resulting in raucous disputes, bowling was subjected to repressive legislation. Bowls, as a game, is first referred to in an Act of 1511 confirming earlier Acts against unlawful games. A later Act permitted landowners to construct bowling greens by licence, but otherwise throughout the Tudor period bowls was subject to legislative interference. There was an indoor bowling alley at Richmond Palace in 1501. In 1536, as a result of a heavy fall from his horse which made him give up jousting, Henry VIII took up TENNIS, COCKFIGHTING and bowls; by 1547 there were three bowling alleys at Hampton Court. The game continued in popularity under Elizabeth I, and in subsequent reigns – but Mary disliked it. In *Richard II*, Shakespeare mentions women enjoying bowls, and later John Evelyn and Samuel Pepys frequently note the game being played. Johannes Kips' engravings (*c.* 1700) of bird's-eye views of houses and their surroundings frequently show groups of people playing bowls on bowling greens. By the mid eighteenth century the game had reverted once more to being a tavern game and fell out of fashion in England, although it retained its popularity in Scotland: the club at Haddington (1709) and greens at Gallowtree and Candleriggs date from the early eighteenth century. In the nineteenth century bowls returned to favour in England as a game which could be played by women. Municipal bowling-greens were now laid out.

Bow Street Runners. The first organized police force in London, established in 1748 by the writer Henry Fielding (1707–54), who was also chief magistrate at Bow Street, and his stepbrother John. In 1757 a government grant extended the service outside London and Bow Street became the centre for an organized campaign against HIGHWAY-MEN and footpads. In 1829 the Runners were merged with the newly formed Metropolitan POLICE; horse patrols were abolished in 1839.

Boxing. A sport of fighting with bare fists which became popular in Britain in the early part of the eighteenth century. James Figg (d. 1734) opened the first boxing booth in London in 1719, and its popularity continued through the Georgian period. Jack Broughton (1705–89) introduced gloves, or 'mufflers', for practice bouts and drew up a set of rules. Between 1750 and 1820 public interest was enormous and fights were attended by the 'Corinthians', rich patrons of the ring who wagered large sums of money on the results. Others, like Sir John Sebright, Bt, arranged public fights for their own and their friends' pleasure. In 1808 Sir John arranged a fight between John Gully (prize-fighter, publican, and MP for Pontefract 1832–37) and Tom Gregson before a large crowd of spectators at Beechwood Park, Hertfordshire. John Jackson (1769–1845), known as 'Gentleman Jim', was English Champion from 1795 to 1818 and taught the poet Lord Byron boxing. The sport lost its reputation for brutality with the introduction of rules governing the sport drawn up by the 8th Marquis of Queensberry (1844–1900) in 1864. Known as the 'Queensberry Rules' they are, with certain modifications, still followed today.

Bragot. A popular medieval drink consisting of ale mixed with honey and powdered pepper or cinnamon, often with cloves and ginger added.

Brake. An open four-wheeled horse-drawn carriage invented in the early nineteenth century. See also CARRIAGES.

Break-front. A term applied to a piece of furniture (such as a book-case or a cabinet) in which a central section projects further forward than the two flanking parts.

Breasts, bare. A matter of fashion. In England and the rest of Europe in the late sixteenth and early seventeenth centuries, many respectable women exposed their naked breasts in public, though in 1608 John Downham condemned 'pure virgins and chaste wives' who frequently lay 'out their breasts to be seen and touched'; in 1616 Thomas Tuke commented on 'the paps embossed laid forth for men's view'. In the 1630s Van Dyke (1599–1641) painted the Marchioness of Hamilton and others in dresses that left the nipples exposed. The fashion died out in England under the Puritan Interregnum (1649–60), in Europe by the 1660s. Later complaints, such as that of playwright Sir Richard Steele (1672–1729) about 'the naked bosoms of our British ladies', are directed against plunging necklines, not bare nipples.

Breeching. The point in his growing-up when a boy was taken out of baby frocks and put into breeches – between the ages of six and seven in the seventeenth century, and at three or four in the early eighteenth century. Henry Thrale, son of Hester Thrale (1741–1821), the author and friend of Dr Johnson, was breeched at the early age of two-and-a-quarter, in 1769. Once breeched, an eighteenth-century boy was dressed as a man, but in miniature, sometimes even with a small sword.

Brickwork. Bricks are manufactured from clay, either sun-dried or baked in kilns; the best bricks for firing are made from two different clays, one moist and workable, the other hard, dry and almost rock-like, which prevents the former from shrinking and cracking during firing. Not all clays are suitable for all types of brick-making; the very hard, rock-like clays of Lancashire, parts of Yorkshire, County Durham and Ruabon in Wales were unusable until machines were invented to break them up.

Clay was originally dug out in the autumn and left to be weathered by frost until the spring. The different clays were then mixed in cylindrical horse-powered pug-mills introduced in the mid nineteenth century which removed stones and impurities and reduced the mixture to a 'dough'. This dough was pressed into wooden moulds and left to dry out for at least two weeks before being fired in a kiln for about forty-eight hours. Due to the difficulty and expense of transporting bricks, brick-making was very much a local industry: many fields near villages today are marked by hollows resulting from clay digging, and ponds are sometimes found near brick buildings for the same reason.

Roman bricks were thin, almost tile-like, no more than 1½ in thick and in length and breadth as much as 18 in × 9 ins; they were of clay mixed with straw, which was thought to transfer heat to the inside of the brick during firing and so distribute it evenly. Medieval bricks varied in size but the average was 8 in × 4 in × 2 in. From Tudor times to today, the standard is approximately 9 in × 4½ in × 2½ in, although a tax per thousand bricks from 1784 to 1850 resulted in some very large bricks being used, until this means of tax evasion was stopped. The only practical way to avoid the tax after that was to use MATHEMATICAL TILES.

The use of the word 'brick', from the French *brique*, did not become general until the fifteenth century; earlier a brick was a *waltyle* (wall-tile) or the Latin *tegula*. The Romans brought brick-making to England, and it has been assumed that the industry ceased after the Romans left, but some brickwork at Brixworth Church in Northamptonshire has lately been dated to *c.* 800. Norman brickwork is found in Polstead Church, Suffolk, and in the ruins of Coggleshall Abbey, Essex there is brickwork of *c.* 1225. Brick buildings prior to 1550 are nearly all found east of a line from the Humber to the Solent, a region that lacked building stone, and was also open to Hanse and later Flemish influence, with easy transportation by sea from the Low Countries (where brick-making was well established). Flemish bricks were imported for the Tower of London in 1278, and Little Wenham Hall in Suffolk, a small fortified house of *c.* 1275, has bricks of a variety of colours, thought to be Flemish. Until the fifteenth century, the use of brick was largely confined to buildings of importance such as schools, churches, colleges, and a few large houses. Herstmonceux Castle (1440) in Sussex and Tattershall Castle in Lincolnshire, of the same date, are entirely of local brick, as is the superb brick gate-tower at Oxburgh Hall in Norfolk, all that remains of the original house of 1482.

Bonding (the various patterns in which bricks are positioned, over-lapping one another to achieve the greatest possible strength) was hap-hazard in the Medieval period, and it was only in Tudor times that English bond, alternate courses of headers (bricks positioned with the ends facing out) and stretchers (long sides facing out), became standard. Burton Agnes, Humberside (1601), Hatfield House, Hertfordshire (1607) and Blicking Hall, Norfolk (1617) show examples of English bond. The east wing at Blickling, built 1623–4, is built in Flemish bond, predating the Dutch House at Kew, Greater London, built from 1631 and usually quoted as the earliest example. In Flemish bond each *course* is laid with alternate headers and stretchers: it is more decorative than English bond, not so strong – and, strangely, seldom seen in Flanders.

No. 29 High Pavement, Nottingham, built 1820, is acknowledged to boast the finest brickwork in Britain. Each brick was rubbed exactly square, and the joints are extremely tight.

Herringbone brickwork was often used as 'nogging' to fill the spaces in a timber-framed building where the frame is the weight-bearing element. The damp-proof course of blue brick came into general use only in the late nineteenth century, and cavity wall construction not until the 1920s.

Bridewell, The. Cardinal Wolsey (*c.* 1485–1530) built Bridewell Palace in London, between Fleet Street and the river; its name was taken from the well of St Bride (St Bridget). On his disgrace and death it reverted to the Crown, and in 1553 was made over by Edward VI (1547–53) to the City of London as a place of training and education for homeless apprentices. Soon the cells meant for recalcitrant apprentices came to be used for political and religious prisoners, and the building was so used, side by side with the teaching of apprentices, until the prison was closed in the mid nineteenth century. The palace had been demolished by 1863.

Brigade. An army infantry unit, usually consisting of three battalions, and forming part of a division.

Britannia Metal. A silver substitute, an alloy of tin containing small amounts of antimony and copper. Often looks like pewter, but is harder, stronger and more resilient. Introduced about 1770. Often plated with silver after the introduction of electroplating, *c.* 1860.

British Academy, The. Founded in 1901 and incorporated in 1902 to promote 'historical, philosophical and philological studies'. Membership is limited to 350, elected for their work in one of the fields of study favoured by the Academy.

British Museum. The impetus for the foundation of the British Museum was the bequest by Sir Hans Sloane (1660–1753) of his books, manuscripts and curiosities, to be held by trustees for the use of the nation. A bill passed Parliament for the purchase of this collection for the nominal sum of £20,000, and of the Harleian manuscripts, collected by the 1st and 2nd Earls of Oxford, for £10,000. Sir John Cotton had in 1700 presented to the nation the collection of his great-grandfather, the antiquary Sir Robert Cotton, and in 1757 George II (1727–1760) donated the royal library. A lottery was authorized to defray the costs of acquisition, and of providing accommodation for the museum and library; Montague House in Great Russell Street, London, was bought, and opened to the public on 15 January 1759. Since then there have been many additions to the collection; in 1772 Parliament voted £8,400 for the purchase of Sir William Hamilton's collection of vases, antiquities and drawings; George III (1760–1820) made a gift of the marbles taken from Alexandria, and his library was acquired with public funds in 1823. A huge collection, including the Elgin Marbles and the Rosetta stone, has been built up from acquisitions made with public money and gifts. The present British Museum building, in Classical Revival style, was designed by Robert Smirke and completed in 1847. The Natural History collection was transferred to the newly formed Natural History Museum, South Kensington in 1881, and this became a separate entity in 1963. The British Museum Library became the British Library in 1973.

Broad Church Movement, The. In the nineteenth century in the wake of the OXFORD MOVEMENT and NEWMAN's subsequent conversion to Roman Catholicism, the Church of England found itself divided into two extremes with violently opposed beliefs: the High Church ANGLO-CATHOLICS, and the Low Church EVANGELICALS. The schism was further widened by Charles DARWIN's theories of evolution, which ran counter to Biblical teaching on the Creation of Man; those who, like the Evangelicals, believed that the Bible was the literal word of God, naturally rejected Darwin's theories. The Broad Church Movement (also known as Latitudinarians) attempted to find a middle course between the Anglo-Catholics and the Evangelicals.

Brougham. See CARRIAGES.

Brown, Lancelot (Capability) (1716–1783). Known chiefly as the landscape gardener who replaced the more formal gardens of earlier periods with serpentine lakes and parkland with scattered clumps of trees, Brown was also an architect. He built Croome Court, Worcestershire, begun in 1751 for the 6th Earl of Coventry, and enlarged Corsham Court, Wiltshire (1761) for Paul Methuen; but most of his architectural designs were for landscape embellishments – temples, ruins, bridges, etc. His style, evolved from the 'natural' gardens of William KENT (1685–1784), was exemplified by the removal of parterres; grass brought up to the saloon windows; and trees cleverly grouped to provide a constantly-changing series of vistas and views, often with sheep or cattle apparently grazing freely but in fact prevented from approaching too near the house by a HA-HA. He earned his nickname from his habit of reassuring patrons that their estates had 'capabilities'. Detractors referred to his work as 'clumping and belting', from his favoured pattern of tree planting, but he is responsible for many of our most beautiful landscapes. He created more than 200, of which examples are to be seen at Belton House, Lincolnshire; Holkham Hall, Norfolk; Blenheim Palace, Oxfordshire; and Stowe, Buckinghamshire. See also Humphry REPTON.

Brummell, George Bryan (1778–1840). Known as 'Beau' Brummell, he was born in London, inherited a fortune of £30,000, and for 20 years enjoyed the friendship and patronage of the Prince of Wales, later Prince Regent and George IV. The extreme elegance of his style made him the arbiter of London fashion between 1794 and 1816, and his influence on male appearance cannot be overemphasized. He insisted that his coats be cut to perfection and that his breeches fit like a skin, priding himself that his clothes showed not a single wrinkle. He invariably wore a plain dark blue coat, and although he would spend hours over the arrangement of his neckcloth (cravat), he knew himself to be so immaculately turned out when he finally emerged from his dressing-room that he did not give his appearance another thought thereafter. He preached a restraint, even understatement, which has governed men's clothing for 180 years, and his influence made London the centre of world male fashion. He quarrelled with the Prince Regent in 1813, and gambling debts drove him three years later to flee to Calais, where he lived for fourteen years; he was consul at Caen from 1830 to 1832. Later he sank into imbecility and died insane at the pauper lunatic asylum of Bon Saveur, Caen. See also MACARONIS.

Brushing rooms. Before dry-cleaning was invented, the only methods of cleaning soiled clothing were washing, which was unsuitable for some fabrics, and brushing. Grander Tudor houses often had small, airless brushing rooms off the principal bedchambers, where servants would brush mud off travelling clothes. By the early nineteenth century such brushing was done in the servants' hall, and surviving rules for servants often stipulate when the hall could be used for this purpose. A notice board dated 1812 from the servants' hall at Apley Castle, Shropshire (demolished in 1955) states firmly: 'No brushing or Cleaning Clothes after the Hall is Clean'd for Dinner, for each default pay 6d.' By the mid century, brushing rooms were included among the outside service rooms, well away from other activities.

Brut or **Brutus.** The legendary great-grandson of Aeneas, adopted ancestor of the Romans. According to medieval tradition he was banished and sailed to Britain to found a New Troy – London. The legend is found in the twelfth-century *Roman de Brut*, and this spurious connection with ancient Rome was used by Henry VII (1485–1509) to reinforce his claim to the throne. He not only asserted his descent from Brutus, but had busts of him in his palaces.

Buffet. A very ancient piece of furniture that began life as a French coffer or chest. The dukes of Burgundy brought the art of dining to a ceremonial peak in which the buffet was used as an indicator of rank and importance. These buffets were stepped shelves designed to carry a display of plate: the more shelves, the greater the display and the higher the rank. When transferred to England the buffet replaced the CUPBOARD, though in less exalted circles it continued to be so-called. In the HALL it was used for displays of pewter and copper.

Where Henry VIII (1509–47) had buffets of twelve shelves, Cardinal Wolsey (c 1475–1530) had to be content with a mere six. It was a further indicator of wealth and power when a host could furnish a dinner-table without recourse to any of the vessels on display. Henry VIII customarily had two buffets: one for vessels used during the meal and the other simply for display. By the late sixteenth century in England the buffet had evolved into a piece of two parts, the bottom having open shelves and the top often being a cupboard. Whatever its form, it was placed in the hall and silverware, in wealthy households even silver gilt, displayed on it. In a YEOMAN household pewter and copperware were displayed. See also SIDEBOARD.

Bull-baiting. Once a popular pastime in Britain, in which a bull with the points of its horns covered was tied to a stake and attacked by dogs. The bulldog was specially bred for this, its undershot jaw and set-back nose enabling it to grip the bull's nose while still breathing. Bull-baiting was made illegal in 1835.

Bullock, George (died *c.* 1819). The most innovative cabinet-maker of the late REGENCY period. He furnished Tew Park, for Matthew Boulton the industrialist, and Napoleon's lodgings on St Helena, and did work for the Duke of Atholl, the Portuguese Ambassador the Duke of Palmella, and others. Using brass inlay and gilt-bronze mounts, his designs are bold and imposing, often with an Egyptian flavour. He was much influenced by the designs of Thomas HOPE.

Bundling. The custom (believed to have been imported from Northern Europe and found among the labouring classes, especially in Wales, in the seventeenth and eighteenth centuries) of intimate courting, half-naked in bed in the dark. The feet were often tied together. An eighteenth-century description from Wales notes that the woman had her 'under petticoat fastened at the bottom with a sliding knot', while the man kept on 'an essential part of his dress'.

Bundling gave a couple the opportunity to explore one another's temperament and mind, which would have been impossible during the long working day. It is said that 'undue advantage' was rarely taken of the situation, and the practice remained socially acceptable until the nineteenth century.

Burgage. A freehold property in a BOROUGH, which in some carried rights such as grazing on common land, sometimes known as the burgage land.

Burgess. The original meaning was an inhabitant of, or chief craftsman in a guild belonging to, a BOROUGH. In time the term was applied to those freemen of a borough possessing a freehold within the borough. In January 1265 Simon de Montfort, the leader of the barons' revolt against Henry III (1216–1272), having taken the king prisoner at Lewes, summoned there a parliament which was distinctive in that for the first time writs were issued not only to knights of the shires, but to burgesses (representatives) of the boroughs. This precedent became a right which continued for many centuries but is now abolished. See also GUILDS.

Burking. William Burke (1792–1829) and his partner William Hare were Irish labourers living in Edinburgh who specialized in the macabre trade of providing medical schools with corpses for dissection; at a time when no proper arrangements existed to meet the demand, money could always be obtained for a corpse. Burke and Hare would make their victims, usually obscure travellers, drunk and then strangle or suffocate – Burke – them. They obtained from £8 to £14 for the bodies they supplied, and had committed at least 15 murders before police suspicions were aroused. Burke was hanged, but Hare escaped trial by giving evidence against his partner.

Body-snatchers, or resurrection-men, exhumed bodies from graves to sell to anatomists, and a few churches, particularly in Lowland Scotland, still have 'sentry boxes' which sheltered a man who stood guard when a new burial had taken place.

Burlington, Richard Boyle, 3rd Earl of (1694–1753). Patron of English PALLADIANISM; that England did not follow the French ROCOCO fashion was largely due to him. Burlington's enthusiasm for architecture began early, subscribing for two copies of Colen CAMPBELL's *Vitruvius Britannicus* (1715); a second GRAND TOUR in 1719 was undertaken with the specific intention of studying Palladio and his works, and he returned from it a convert and with William KENT in tow. His villa at Chiswick, begun in 1725, was, like Campbell's Mereworth, based on Palladio's Villa Rotonda in Vicenza, Italy; in the Assembly Rooms, York (1730) he realized Palladio's interpretation of the Egyptian Hall of Vitruvius. The design of Holkham Hall, Norfolk (begun 1734), based on the plan of Palladio's unbuilt Villa Moncenigo, was conceived by Burlington and Kent in conjunction with Thomas Coke (later 1st Earl of Leicester), for whom it was built, and carried out by the architect Matthew Brettingham. Pope said of Burlington that he was a 'positive man, and both the strength and weakness of Palladianism derive from his obsessive, puritanical urge to preach absolute classical standards'.

Burn, William H. (1789–1870). A Scottish architect who built up the biggest architectural practice in Victorian Britain. Before deserting Edinburgh for London in 1844 to concentrate on his enormous private house practice, he designed St John's Church (begun in 1816) and the Melville Monument (1821–2), both in Edinburgh. Very different is his John Watson's Hospital at Belford, near Edinburgh; with its large windows it seems almost modern. In England, Burn was known for his planning of complicated service wings with rooms for every speciality. Unfortunately the early promise exhibited by his work in Scotland did not last, and his English country houses lack spirit.

Bustle, or **False Rump.** Padding or wire frame in a lady's dress to throw it out at the back. The fashion first came in in a modest form in the 1670s and 1680s, returning again in the 1780s and 1790s and yet again in the 1830s. From the end of the 1860s to 1875 the bustle became ridiculously exaggerated and stuck out behind as a preposterous shelf – the guise in which it is best known. See also CRINOLINE and FARTHINGALE.

Butler. From the old French *bouteiller*; in a large medieval household, the official in charge of the butts of wine. In England, the butler's duties evolved from those of several medieval servants: the yeoman of the BUTTERY was in charge of BEER, milk, butter, cheese (wet goods) and candles, and over the centuries his post became one of increasing importance until the first half of the seventeenth century when it was amalgamated with that of the yeoman of the PANTRY, in charge of bread, salt (dry goods) and cutlery, and that of the yeoman of the cellar who had charge of the wine and the plate. The butler's power further increased in the later seventeenth century when he became responsible for the FOOTMEN; in a large household he would have an under-butler. By the eighteenth century he was responsible for the service of meals, the ordering, storage and serving of wine, and the polishing and keeping of silver, cutlery and glass in his own pantry. In a very grand household he would himself be under a STEWARD. In the nineteenth-century SERVANTS' HALL he was equal in rank to the HOUSEKEEPER; at meal times he and she occupied opposite ends of the table, with the male and female servants segregated on either side, and at the conclusion of the main course would retire together to his or her private sitting-room for DESSERT. Such formality was preserved 'below stairs' long after it had died out among the gentry, continuing up to the First World War. See also BOTTLES.

Buttery. A medieval household office in the care of the yeoman of the buttery, who was responsible for the supply of wet goods – milk, butter, cheese and BEER – and candles. Named after the butts of beer stored in an adjacent cellar, the buttery was off the SCREENS PASSAGE and entered by one of the three doors behind the screen. Even today, in Oxford and Cambridge Colleges, drinks are served from the buttery bar. See also PANTRY, BUTLER and SCREENS PASSAGE.

Byblow. An illegitimate child. See also BLANKET, WRONG SIDE OF; CHANCELING and MERRYBEGOT.

Cab. A contraction of 'cabriolet', a light two-wheeled, one-horse chaise with a large hood, the 'cabriolet de place', invented in France *c.* 1660 by Nicholas Sauvage, and introduced in London *c.* 1823. The first cabs, painted yellow and limited to twelve in number, a restriction soon removed, replaced the old hackney coaches (Pepys's 'hacquenée') of preceding centuries, and were in turn overtaken by a new type of cab invented by Mr Boulnois in which the occupants sat facing each other and the driver sat on top. In 1836 a larger, cheaper version of the brougham came into service: the four-wheeled Clarence, of improved design and known as the 'growler', from the noise made by the steel-rimmed wheels on the street cobbles. The Hansom, a light one-horse two-wheeled, two-person cab, patented in 1834 by the architect Joseph Hansom (1803–82), was the most fashionable horse-cab, and the most popular, only superseded by the motor taxi-cab.

Cabmen's shelters, first established in 1875, provided accommodation for drivers in the stands and did much to encourage sobriety. Acts regulating horse-drawn hackney cabs in London are the Hackney Carriage Acts of 1831–53, the Metropolitan Public Carriages Act 1869, the London Cab Act 1896 and the London Cab and Stage Carriage Act 1907. These Acts stated the just fares and rules for hiring, and protected drivers against fraudulent passengers. See also CARRIAGES.

Cabal (1667–73). Deriving ultimately from the Kabbalah, the mystical interpretation of the Old Testament. In the seventeenth century, it came to mean a private intrigue of a sinister nature by a small group of people, and was later widely applied to the small committee of five ministers chosen from his PRIVY COUNCIL by Charles II (1660–85) after the fall of Clarendon (1609–74) in 1667, from its secrecy and the coincidence that the initial letters of the five (Clifford, Arlington, Buckingham, Ashley-Cooper and Lauderdale) spell CABAL. The arrangement enabled easier management of the formulation of policy than was possible, as previously, through the whole Privy Council, but was abandoned by Charles II in 1673 when he had no further use for it. By some it is regarded as the precursor of the modern CABINET.

Cabinet (1). A committee of government ministers of the political party in power, recognized by constitutional convention but not by the law, originating with the CABAL of Charles II (1660–85). Checks on the monarch's power after the Glorious Revolution of 1688 made a small, like-minded committee necessary to manage parliamentary policy; known as the 'Junto' under the Whig administration, it came, in Queen Anne's reign (1665–1714), to be known as the 'cabinet' after the small room in which it met. The Cabinet in the modern sense did not emerge until William Pitt the Younger's (1759–1806) ministry of 1783, when a group of ministers serving under him as PRIME MINISTER and working together as a wholly secret body to which non-members were not admitted, except for departmental officials summoned for particular information, formulated a programme of government. The PRIVY COUNCIL now has no executive power and the Cabinet has taken over its original purpose. Traditionally the Lord President of the Privy Council is a member of the Cabinet.

Cabinet (2). 'Cabinet rooms' (cabinets) originated in the seventeenth century as the final small room in a range of STATE APARTMENTS, off the bedchamber. The idea, and the name, came from France. In his cabinet an owner would keep his curios and collections, perhaps trophies of the GRAND TOUR, hang his favourite pictures, and there show his belongings off to his friends.

By the mid eighteenth century bedchambers were no longer the last room in the range of reception rooms on the ground floor, but increasingly situated on the first floor, and the fashionable way of using the downstairs reception rooms had altered. Remodelling of interiors to reflect these changing fashions means that few cabinet rooms have survived. The cabinet room at Felbrigg Hall, Norfolk (1751), the slightly later one at Corsham Court, Wiltshire, and the Red Velvet Room at Saltram, Devon (1770s) are the only three to survive almost in their original state.

Cabinet of Curiosities. A piece of furniture of many drawers and secret places for housing curios or 'curiosities', which might be placed in the CABINET (2). The word *cabinet* was first used in early sixteenth-century France to denote a small box with a number of compartments and drawers in the form of a sloping desk, but by the mid seventeenth century this had evolved into a large chest on a stand with many small drawers and secret flaps; often made of ebony and inlaid with ivory and mother-of-pearl, in Flanders, France or Italy. A painting (*c.* 1640) by Frans Franken II (1581–1642) of the Duke of Northumberland shows him in Syon House, Middlesex with a small table-model cabinet. Spread on the table are the contents: seashells, coins, medals, letters, drawings and a dried seahorse – a magpie collection clearly dear to the duke. The collection of the gardener and plant hunter John Tradescant (1608–62) was rather larger in every way; it can be seen today in the Ashmolean Museum, Oxford, and includes dried lizards, an alligator and a chameleon. The diarist John Evelyn (1620–1706) had a French ebony cabinet and a small tortoiseshell and ebony cabinet in his 'Closset of Curiosities' at Wotton House, Surrey, in 1702. The former is now in the Victoria and Albert Museum.

Two of the most magnificent cabinets are at Alnwick Castle, Northumberland. They were made for Louis XIV in 1683, sold in 1748 by Louis XV and eventually bought by the Duke of Northumberland in 1824. The seventeenth-century Florentine Badminton cabinet, sold to the USA in 1991, was the principal showpiece in the drawing room at Badminton House, Gloucestershire.

By the mid eighteenth century, furniture such as the COMMODE and secretaire had taken over the role and prestige of the cabinet, and small collections were shown off in other rooms: in Mrs Child's dressing room at Osterley Park, Greater London, in 1782 was 'A very Elegant Gilt Cabinet . . . with plate glass . . . containing India [Eastern] and other curiosities'. By then the cabinet was often glazed, the better to display its contents – a far cry from the early models with secret drawers.

Cabriole leg. A furniture leg which swells outwards at the top or 'knee' and then curves down, often to an ornamental foot like an animal's, complete with claws (sometimes a hoof), at the floor; sometimes called a bandy-leg; found on furniture from the BAROQUE period, through the ROCOCO and to the beginning of the NEO-CLASSICAL period (1760).

Caffoy. A woollen velvet material with a cut pile popular for furnishing in the eighteenth century. An inventory of 1726 at Erddig, Clwyd contains a direct reference to caffoy on chairs which are now in the Gallery. In 1744, Mrs Delaney noted in her correspondence that she had crimson caffoy in her drawing room, and in 1765 the SALOON furniture at Stowe, Buckinghamshire was covered in crimson caffoy. See also WALLPAPER.

Calash. A light, low-wheeled carriage with a removable folding hood; from the fashionable French 'Calash' or *calèche*, a woman's large hood supported by hoops that projected beyond the face. See also CARRIAGES.

Calendar. A method of fixing the beginning, subdivisions and length of a year; the Julian Calender, introduced by Julius Caesar in 46 BC, instituted the division of the year into 365 days, with a leap year of 366 days every fourth year and the names, order and lengths of the months as in use today. Unfortunately, inaccurate calculations resulting from insufficient astronomical data meant that by the sixteenth century the calendar was ten days out, and religious feast days were not being celebrated at the right time. In 1582 a Bull issued by Pope Gregory XIII (1572–85) annulled the ten days, and the day following October 5 in that year was recognized as October 15. This more accurate Gregorian calendar was adopted throughout Catholic Europe fairly rapidly, but there was understandable resistance among the Protestant nations. The Protestant German states, Denmark and Sweden finally adopted it about 1700; Britain in 1750 by the Calendar (New Style) Act, which provided that the day following 2 September 1752 should be reckoned 14 September (the Act also provided for the legal year to begin on 1 January rather than 25 March, a change which had already been adopted in Scotland from 1600; a common if not legal usage of 1 January as New Year's Day seems to have filtered south of the border rather earlier, as Pepys mentions it in his *Diary*); the howl from the illiterate mob was considerable: 'Give us back our eleven days' was the cry! Russia retained the Julian Calendar until the introduction of the Gregorian by the Soviet government in the twentieth century.

Called to the Bar. A bencher (law student) in the Inns of Court, when authorized to practise as a BARRISTER, was 'called' to the barrier or bar dividing the qualified from the unqualified.

Calvinism. A Protestant movement named after its founder, John Calvin (1509–64), who was born in Picardy, France. Influenced by humanism, the New Learning and Luther's Reformation, in 1534 he decided to break with Rome and the Roman Catholic Church. He believed in austerity, and preached the doctrine of the Sovereignty of God – and therefore the complete freedom of the Church from State control. This naturally made him unpopular with authority. He spent several years in Geneva, and died there in 1564. Influencing the PURITANS of seventeenth-century England, Calvinism became predominant in Scotland. It was distinguished particularly by its doctrine of Pre-destination, or Particular Election, which held that God had unalter-ably chosen certain souls for salvation, others for damnation. To the elect, blessed with the God-given gift of perseverance, sufficient grace was certain. Encompassing everyday conformity to one's responsibil-ities and duties which, it was believed, were assigned by God, this gave rise to the 'work ethic', one of the foundations of the seventeenth and eighteenth centuries' economic structure and prosperity. See also ANGLO-CATHOLICISM, EVANGELICALISM, METHODISM and PRESBYTERIAN-ISM.

Cambridge Camden Society. See OXFORD MOVEMENT.

Camden Society. Founded in 1838 in honour of William Camden (1551–1623), antiquary and historian, for the purpose of publishing documents relating to English history and literature.

Camera Obscura. When a small hole is made in the wall of a dark-ened room an inverted image of the scene outside can be projected, by means (usually) of lenses, onto the opposite wall or onto a screen. This phenomenon, known as Camera Obscura (dark chamber), was used as an aid to artists, and several versions were in use in the seventeenth century. A simple box could be used, with a translucent glass screen opposite the source of light to receive the image, or an arrangement of lenses and mirrors inside could be employed to reflect the image onto a sheet of paper. A device of this kind was constructed in 1665 by Robert Boyle (1627–91), an Irish naturalist and chemist. It is thought that the painter Jan Vermeer (1632–1675) used one, and there is firm evidence that the painters Francesco Guardi (1712–1793) and Bernardo Bellotto (1720–1780) did. A camera obscura said to have belonged to Canaletto (1697–1768) is in the Museo Civico Correr, Venice, although there is no evidence that he ever used one. There is a fine Camera Obscura, still in use and open to the public, on the Royal Mile in Edinburgh. See also CLAUDE GLASS and PHOTOGRAPHY.

Campbell, Colen (1676–1729). A Scottish lawyer turned architect whose collection of engravings of classical British buildings, *Vitruvius Britannicus* (published in two parts in 1715 and 1717, with a supple-mentary volume in 1725), featured also his own designs in the manner of Inigo Jones and Palladio, and served to advertise partly his own ability as an architect, but above all, the Palladian style. He was responsible for some twenty-two commissions, including Wanstead House, Essex (1711–12, demolished 1792), the largest house built in eighteenth-century England; Mereworth Castle, Kent (1722–5), the first to be based on Palladio's Villa Rotonda, Vicenza, Italy; Stourhead, Wiltshire (1720–4); and Houghton Hall, Norfolk (1722–35). Although Camp-bell was the first of the neo-Palladians, he lacked a powerful patron; he was briefly associated with Lord BURLINGTON in remodelling the front of Burlington House in 1719, but Burlington quickly dropped him in favour of William KENT; Campbell succeeded VANBRUGH as Surveyor of Greenwich Hospital in 1726. To Campbell must be credited the Palladian revival, which in its essentials had been accomplished by the time of his death.

Canals. Artificial watercourses linking rivers and seas for inland navigation. Canals developed quickly after James Brindley (1716–72) constructed for the Duke of Bridgewater (1736–1803) a canal linking his collieries at Worsley in Lancashire to Manchester, in 1759–61. This was the first canal, in the modern sense; it halved the cost of coal delivered to Manchester, thus demonstrating the economic importance of canals: at a time when public roads were almost impassable in winter, canals provided a much more reliable form of transport, particularly for heavy, bulky goods and long hauls. James Brindley was also responsible for the Grand Trunk Canal (1765–77) linking the rivers Trent and Mersey. Between 1780 and 1800 the network of canals constructed proved vital to the expansion of the Industrial Revolution. After 1830 railway transport, faster and more flexible, led inexorably to the decline of the canals, in the same way that the late twentieth-century growth of road haulage has led to a decline in the railways. Many canals had fallen into disuse by the beginning of the twentieth century.

Canals were built and maintained by companies authorized by ACT OF PARLIAMENT, tolls being charged for carriage on the companies' barges; they were nationalized in 1947 under the British Transport Commission, and since 1962 have been controlled by the British Waterways Board. Less than 2,000 miles of navigable canals remain, but many are now being reopened for leisure and holiday use.

Candles. See LIGHTING.

Candlemas. A church festival held on 2 February, forty days after Christmas, commemorating the purification of the Virgin Mary and the presentation of Christ in the Temple; the festival dates from the late 4th century, but the blessing of candles did not become common until the eleventh century.

Canon Law. Laws relating to the government of the Christian Church, originating in the declarations of Christ and the Apostles. The large body of Canon Law which accumulated in the Western Church over the centuries was codified in 1917 and clarified in the *Corpus Juris Canonici* promulgated by Pope Benedict XV (1914–22), the greater part of the work having been accomplished by his predecessor St Pius X (1903–14); it has been supplemented by later Papal decrees. The Canon Law of the Church of England persisted as published in 1604, apart from two additions in 1892 and 1921, until the 1940s, when obsolete

canons were deleted and the remainder redrafted. See also ECCLESIAS-
TICAL COURTS.

Canons Regular. Today canons are members of a cathedral chapter.
However, before the DISSOLUTION they were members of the
AUGUSTINIAN, GILBERTINE and PREMONSTRATENSIAN orders, who were
all known as Canons. The term 'Regular' indicated one under religious
rule, and implied being bound under a rule regulating the whole day,
even to the food to be eaten.

Canopy, or **Cloth, of Estate.** A canopy supported above a CHAIR OF
STATE, accorded to monarchs, princes of the blood, and peers down to
the rank of earl in the fifteenth, sixteenth and early seventeenth centuries. Religious in origin, a transference of the colourful ceremonies
of Corpus Christi and Easter (in which the Host was carried beneath a
portable canopy for protection from the elements) to the sovereign
when on show before his people in the rituals of coronations and funerals, touching for the King's Evil, and washing the feet of the poor on
Maundy Thursday. The earliest record of a royal canopy is of one carried
over a French monarch in the late fourteenth century. Once adopted by
the sovereign, canopies were quickly usurped by great noblemen, and
enormous importance was attached to them in the late sixteenth and
early seventeenth centuries. During her itinerant imprisonment in the
1570s and 80s Mary, Queen of Scots always carried with her a folding
canopy to be placed above her Chair of State when she was holding
court. When it was completed in the 1590s, Hardwick Hall in Derbyshire had a large canopy above a Chair of State in the GREAT CHAMBER,
still in place in 1834 according to an illustration of that date. The hooks
to hold it have remained there to this day, hidden above the cornice,
and the canopy itself has recently been reinstated. The last canopy in a
private house (prior to the reinstatement at Hardwick) was at Hamilton
Palace (demolished in the 1920s). An original arrangement can also be
seen at Hampton Court Palace. See also BALDACHINO and BED.

Canterbury. This was the name given by Sheraton to a piece of
movable eighteenth-century furniture, a type of supper-tray with a
lower shelf having three compartments for knives, forks and spoons. In
the nineteenth century the term was used for a music stand with a cupboard for holding sheet music. Today it generally refers to a music or
magazine rack.

Capital punishment. Punishment by death. The term derives from
the Latin *caput* (head), since beheading was the common form of capital
punishment, and probably the most humane – although Mary, Queen
of Scots, beheaded at Fotheringhay Castle, Northamptonshire in 1587,
perhaps would not have agreed: it took her executioner three attempts
to sever her head. In pre-Norman Britain there were various forms of

capital punishment, including beheading, hanging, burning, and hurling onto rocks. After the Conquest mutilation leading to death was substituted and is the punishment mentioned in the ASSIZE of Clarendon of 1166. The extreme form, reserved for only the most serious crimes, was hanging, drawing and quartering. By the end of the seventeenth century hanging at Tyburn, a particularly unpleasant death by slow strangulation, had taken the place in England of decapitation. From 1783 executions took place at Newgate (in front of the prison until 1867, and within its walls up to 1901) and the use of the more humane drop (the release of a trap-door beneath the gallows which instantly broke the prisoner's neck) with hanging was then introduced. By the end of the eighteenth century there were in theory more than two hundred capital offences, including petty theft, that merited the death sentence, although in practice it was only invoked for twenty-five (see also BENEFIT OF CLERGY). Sir Robert Peel (1788–1850) instituted CRIMINAL LAW REFORMS in the 1820s; after 1838 the capital offences were reduced to fifteen in number, and in 1861 to four: murder or attempted murder, piracy with violence, destruction of arsenals and public dockyards, and high TREASON. Hanging for murder was abolished in Britain in 1965, and for arson in 1971, but is still available for piracy with violence, and treason. Public hangings, which ended only in 1868, were a popular event and entertainment. During the First and Second World Wars the punishment for treason was death by firing squad, as it was also for cowardice in the First World War. See also HANGERS-ON.

Cap-money (1). To encourage the wool trade, a statute of 1571 compelled all persons of 'common degree' to wear a cap made of English woollen cloth on holy days and Sundays. The penalty (called Cap-money) for non-observance was three shillings and fourpence. The statute was repealed in 1598.

Cap-money (2). Also, in hunting terminology, money collected for the huntsmen at the death of a fox.

Carmelites. A religious order of friars of Our Lady of Mount Carmel founded in Palestine by a crusader from Calabria, c. 1145, but claiming continuity with much earlier settlements of hermits in the same holy place. The order left Palestine for Europe after the failure of the CRUSADES, arriving in England by way of Cyprus, Sicily and France in c. 1240, and were reorganized as MENDICANT (rather than monastic) FRIARS, retaining some of their original austerity but adapting to western conditions. The white mantles they wore over their dark brown habits distinguished them as the 'White Friars', and they quickly became strongly established, with fifty-two houses in England and Wales and eleven in Scotland at the DISSOLUTION. In 1431 a mitigated rule was introduced, but in 1562 St Theresa of Avila founded a small convent where she attempted to restore the original austerity of the rule. This return to the character of the primitive Carmelite life was also taken up by monks, who came to be called the Discalced, or bare-footed, Carmelites, from the fact that they wore sandals rather than shoes and stockings. Both the strict and mitigated (Calced) orders still exist.

There are now few remains of Carmelite friaries in Britain; Denbigh in Clwyd, in the care of English Heritage, is the most intact. Other remains were incorporated into private houses, as at Aylesford Friary, Kent, now restored to its original purpose. The Carmelites returned to England in 1926 and there are now some eight houses of friars, and more of nuns. See also AUGUSTINIANS, BENEDICTINES, CARTHUSIANS, CIS-TERCIANS, CLUNIACS, DOMINICANS, FRIARS, FRANCISCANS, GILBERTINES and PREMONSTRATENSIANS.

Carr, John (1723–1807), of York. Practised as an architect in the Mid-lands and the north of England for more than half a century. During his career he worked on more than 120 public buildings and churches and nearly 90 private houses. As a strict follower of Palladio (1508–80) his style was somewhat unoriginal, but dignified, and suited the taste of the northern gentry and ARISTOCRACY. His best work is seen in The Crescent at Buxton in Derbyshire, built *c.* 1780–90 for the 6th Duke of Devonshire. His first work was as a mason at Kirby Hall, West York-shire (1747–*c.* 1755; demolished 1920), built to a design by Lord BURLINGTON; Harewood House, West Yorkshire (1759–71), the inter-ior finished by the ADAM brothers, was his most prestigious commis-sion.

Carriages. In 1793, when the historian Edward Gibbon crossed Europe by coach, taking three weeks to cover 650 miles, he noted that fifteen hundred years earlier Caesarius took only six days in a chariot to cover an identical distance! For centuries travel was uncomfortable, slow and expensive. Carriages broke down on atrocious roads, accidents were frequent – a runaway horse pulling a carriage almost inevitably caused injury to passengers. Carriage accidents killed the architect James Wyatt in 1813, and the Countess of Lathom in 1897 near her home, Lathom House, Lancashire. Most early travellers preferred to go on horseback, while ladies travelled in horse litters. The first coach in England was made in 1555 for the 3rd Earl of Rutland, and the 16th Earl of Arundel imported one from Germany in 1625 (the year he died); but it was not until the invention of C-shaped springs in the mid seventeenth century that coaches offered a comfortable alternative to horseback. In 1665 Samuel Pepys (1633–1703) was astounded by his friend Colonel Blount's experiments with coach springs: '. . . one did prove mighty easy (. . . the whole body of that coach lies upon one long spring) . . . it is very fine and likely to take'. This was fundamentally the same type of vehicle that carried Gladstone two centuries later – the technology changed little until the nineteenth century. The first stage-coach ran between London and Coventry in 1659, but it was not until 1784 that the first mail-coach ran between London and Bristol. The general state of the roads continued to make most travelling by coach uncertain and uncomfortable.

The leaf-spring, introduced in 1804, permitted lighter, faster, two-wheeled vehicles to be built, while the smoother roads which resulted from 'macademizing' – surfacing with broken stones, introduced in Bristol in 1816 by John Macadam (1756–1836) – meant those lighter vehicles were safer for travelling. Other two-wheeled carriages followed: the TILBURY, STANHOPE, GIG and DOG CART. Closed four-wheeled vehicles of the nineteenth century were the BROUGHAM (introduced by Lord Brougham in 1839), the LANDAU and the FOUR-IN-HAND; open four-wheeled vehicles were the PHAETON, WAGGON-ETTE and BRAKE.

The carriages to be seen in transport museums and the coach houses of country houses are only a random selection of survivors. Most nine-teenth-century families of distinction had a travelling carriage for winter travel, a town carriage, and light two-wheeled carriages for local country journeys. At Erddig, for example, may be seen a GOVERNESS CART and a gig (open two-wheeled vehicles for local journeys) and two phaetons (open four-wheeled vehicles), but there is nothing in the way of a closed carriage for winter travel. Raby Castle in County Durham exhibits a wider range: two late eighteenth-century travelling chariots; an early nineteenth-century state coach, which would originally have been kept in London; a governess cart; a whiskey which, its light, caned body drawn by a pony, 'whisked' over the park at high speed; a station cart; and an estate wagon.

In winter the piercing draughts, unglazed windows closed by wooden shutters (though Pepys's carriage had glass windows) and the leaking carriage roofs were only tolerable when passengers were well wrapped up in fur rugs and using muff-warmers – small hand heaters – and foot-warmers – large metal hot-water bottles (there is one in the back hall at Lanhydrock, Cornwall). Straw on the floor gave a closed carriage a particular smell; Vita Sackville-West recalled that her father's coach-of-all-work at Knole in Kent, which was used to collect visitors from the station, smelled of musty hay. Arlington Court in Devon has a very good museum of horse-drawn carriages, Braemore House in Hampshire has a small collection, and the Royal Mews shows the Queen's spotlessly maintained and still-used carriages. See also CAB,

CALASH, CHAISE, CHARABANC, CHARIOT, CURRICLE, GROWLER, POST CHAISE and VICTORIA; also TURNPIKE ROADS.

Carsey. See KERSEY.

Carthusians. A strict monastic order founded in 1086 by St Bruno at Chartreuse. Unlike other orders, each monk had his own cell, and ate only vegetables and coarse bread. The life was one of almost continual fasting and solitude, the monks meeting only for vespers, the midnight office, and mass, except on Sundays and feast days. The order was established in England in 1180 at Witham, near Selwood Forest, and the London Charterhouse (a corruption of Chartreuse) was founded at Smithfield in 1371. At the DISSOLUTION there were nine foundations in England and one in Scotland. Longleat in Wiltshire was originally AUGUSTINIAN but later became Carthusian, and is the only private house now occupying a Carthusian site. The order returned to England in the nineteenth century and is now established at St Hugh's, Horsham, Sussex. Of the few remains of the medieval Carthusian monasteries, Mount Grace in North Yorkshire is the most substantial. See also AUGUSTINIANS, BENEDICTINES, CARMELITES, CISTERCIANS, CLUNIACS, DOMINICANS, FRANCISCANS, GILBERTINES, MENDICANT FRIARS and PRE-MONSTRATENSIANS.

Carucate. As much land as an ox-team (8 oxen) could plough in a year; an average of 120 acres, depending on the soil. Of Danish origin, and used in areas where the Danelaw had run, where it had been an area of ploughland assessed for taxation; William the Conqueror adopted it as a unit of taxation in 1090. In the early thirteenth century the size of a carucate was fixed at 100 acres. See also BOVATE and PLOUGHLAND.

Caryatids. Supports and brackets in architecture (and furniture) in the form of female figures, often used instead of columns to support an entablature. Especially popular in Britain during the BAROQUE period (1660 to 1720) and in the late eighteenth-century GREEK REVIVAL. The male equivalents are known as Atlantes (literally, Atlas-figures, from the god Atlas carrying the globe).

Cassock. A long close-fitting garment worn under the ALB, surplice or gown by clergy and choristers. See also ORPHREY and CHASUBLE.

Castle. A fortified building introduced to England by the Normans. The castles built after the Conquest were of three types: the earth and timber motte-and-bailey (a mound with a wooden tower – the motte – surrounded by a palisade and ditch – the bailey); the shell-keep, a version of the motte-and-bailey in which the bailey was enclosed by a curtain wall and the palisade on the mound was replaced by a high stone wall – e.g., Lincoln, Berkeley; and the massive masonry-towered hall-keeps with living quarters, surrounded by a curtain wall.

A castle was an expression of feudal power: after the Conquest William I (1066–87) gave Saxon properties to about 150 of his loyal followers, who protected their estates by building some thousand earth and timber motte-and-bailey castles. From the beginning the Norman kings controlled castle-building by licence, but during the twenty years of anarchy of Stephen's reign (1135–54) a further thousand were built without licence (so-called 'adulterine' castles). Early castles were for purely military use, but later other factors influenced their design. Rich landowners, keen to display their wealth and power, demanded a higher standard of living than was provided in the primitive hall-keeps, and so began the conflicting demands of domesticity and defence.

The first two CRUSADES tested castle design to the limit and had an important influence on military defence. The concentric walls (1180–90) of Dover Castle are an example of this. The peak of military castle-building came in the late thirteenth century when Edward I (1272–1307) built Welsh and marcher castles, and others in the north of England, to the highest standards of military engineering. Private castles, built for protection against marauding bands, would have given no defence against a determined attacker. Gunpowder and the cannon of the early fourteenth century, together with advances in mining (sapping) techniques, sealed the fate of the castle. In fact, England was becoming a more peaceful country and castles had outlived their purpose, except in the north of England and the borders of Scotland, where many defensive PELE-TOWERS were built.

Cathedral schools. The oldest educational foundations in Britain. Canon law required a parish priest to provide instruction in singing and reading the psalter; additionally, in a tradition of learning lingering on from Anglo-Saxon times, attached to cathedrals, the larger monasteries and collegiate churches, there were (as well as singing schools) grammar schools intended for the training of the clergy. In these might be taught not only the basic Latin grammar and syntax, but also rhetoric and logical disputation – the *trivium* (grammar, rhetoric and dialectic). Gradually lay pupils came to be admitted, and at some schools the curriculum might be broadened to include elements of the *quadrivium* (music, arithmetic, geometry and astronomy). There were about 400 such grammar schools by the fourteenth century. Elsewhere, basic education was given by the parish priest. See also DAME SCHOOLS and PUBLIC SCHOOLS.

Catholic Apostolic Church, The. A religious sect which grew from discussions concerning unfulfilled prophecy, held in 1826 at Albury Park, Surrey, the home of Henry Drummond, MP (1786–1860). Among those present was the magnetic Scottish preacher Edward

Irving (1792–1834), a minister of the National Scottish Church of Regent Square, London, who turned to mysticism. In 1832 Irving, having alienated the majority of his congregation, was deposed from the ministry; he and his adherents, describing themselves as the Holy Catholic Apostolic Church, removed to a building in Newman Street, where he was chief pastor until his death. As well as a belief in the apostolic gifts of prophecy and healing, the new sect were millenarians: they believed that the Second Coming of Christ was imminent and appointed twelve apostles against the great day. Sometimes known as Irvingites, they were later drawn to the rituals of the ANGLO-CATHOLICS, and increasingly adopted full Roman Catholic doctrines. When the Coming did not materialize, support for the sect languished. The last apostle died in 1901.

Catholic Emancipation. From the time of Henry VIII (1509–47), with the exception of the brief interlude of Mary Tudor's reign (1553–8), Roman Catholics (like Protestant Dissenters) suffered legal and civil restrictions. They were not legally permitted to purchase land or inherit propery, and the Test Acts of 1673 and 1678 excluded them from civil or military office, and from both Houses of Parliament. The first movements towards freeing them from these disabilities (i.e., Catholic Emancipation) took place in Ireland, where Roman Catholics were in a majority. In 1793 the Irish Parliament in Dublin repealed some of the Penal Laws against Catholics and gave them the electoral vote, although they were still not able to sit in the Irish Parliament. It was not until after the Union of Great Britain and Ireland (1800) that in 1829 the Repeal of the Test Acts enabled Catholic MPs to sit in the House of Commons. Catholic barristers were now able to take silk, but none (at this time) were appointed to the bench.

Catholics had similarly been excluded from Oxford and Cambridge, together with Protestant Dissenters; some relaxation had enabled their attendance at lectures, etc., particularly at Cambridge, but they could not take a degree or hold any college or university appointment until the repeal of the Test Acts.

Some small Catholic churches were built in the late eighteenth century, but no major Catholic churches until after 1829; PUGIN's first church, St Mary's in Derby, was not built until 1835. See also JEWS and ROMAN CATHOLICS.

Caudle. A drink consisting of a mixture of honey and strained egg yolks in ALE. Recommended as a nourishing pick-me-up in Tudor times, and earlier.

Cedar. A wood used for chests and storage furniture, due to its aromatic, insect-repellant qualities. It was particularly popular from the mid seventeenth century.

Ceilings. Inventories from the 1550s often mention 'the room that is seeled', meaning 'sealed' by plaster overhead: the ceiling, in fact. It was obviously a novelty. Medieval ceilings were unplastered; in the early sixteenth century their timbers were painted, after the French fashion, with heraldic and geometric patterns. A late example of *c.* 1550 can be seen in the PARLOUR off the Great Hall at Haddon Hall, Derbyshire, which must by that time have seemed out-of-date, as the fashion then was for plain plastered ceilings painted with 'white' lime-wash (which would look grey to us because of the impurities it contained).

Henry VIII was very open to French influence, and the ceilings of his palaces were decorated in the latest French style, but this was not widely copied by his courtiers. The ceiling of the so-called Wolsey's Closet at Hampton Court in Surrey (1540) is richly decorated with ribbed panels picked out in gold leaf; a similar design is to be found in *Regole generale di Architettura*, published in 1537 by an Italian architect, Sebastiano Serlio (1475–1554), and it is probable that other similar ceilings in Henry's palaces have been lost. The ceiling of the King's Holyday Closet, also at Hampton Court, enriched with gilded and moulded ribs and dating from 1536, is in a style which became widely popular only at the end of the century.

The earliest surviving English examples, of *c.* 1620, of the fashion for ceilings painted with scenes are at Bolsover Castle, Derbyshire; gods and goddesses look down from contorted positions while putti cavort around them. An earlier, Scottish example (*c.* 1600) is to be seen in the LONG GALLERY of Cullen House, Banffshire. At the beginning of the seventeenth century plaster ceilings were more usually moulded with ribbed compartments or decorated with STRAPWORK. The long gallery (*c.* 1620s) at Lanhydrock House in Cornwall, the only part of the house to survive a disastrous fire in 1881, is a supreme example; its plaster mouldings are richly luxuriant with pendants, bosses, birds and beasts, together with scenes from the Old Testament.

The political atmosphere of the Commonwealth discouraged such frivolities as painted ceilings, and it was only after the RESTORATION of 1660 that the French taste for BAROQUE ceilings decorated with history paintings filtered through to England. Such painted ceilings were introduced *c.* 1672 by the Italian, Antonio Verrio (*c.* 1639–1707), and some of his early work survives at Windsor Castle. Verrio's royal commissions set the fashion and other Italian and French painters soon followed him to London; Louis Laguerre (1663–1721), a godson of Louis XIV, arrived in Britain in 1684, and both his and Verrio's work can be seen at Chatsworth in Derbyshire, where they worked between 1689 and 1694. Sir James Thornhill (1676–1734) was England's own Baroque ceiling painter, and his work also may be seen at Chatsworth, where he was employed *c.* 1702–08. Thornhill was also responsible (from a total of some 45 major schemes executed by him) for the Painted Hall at the Royal Naval College, Greenwich (formerly Greenwich Hospital – by WREN, 1708–12); the hall and saloon at Blenheim Palace, Oxfordshire (1716); and the dome, lantern and Whispering Gallery of St Paul's Cathedral, London (1714–21).

In the 1730s the Baroque taste for dramatic ceiling paintings moved towards the ROCOCO fashion for ceilings painted in compartments. The long gallery of Mereworth Castle in Kent was painted in this manner (*c.* 1739) by Francesco Sleeter (1685–1775). William KENT (1685–1748), who trained as a painter in Italy, introduced the GROTESQUE style in the 1720s; examples of his work survive at Kensington Palace, London (*c.* 1723) and at Rousham Park, Oxfordshire (after 1739). Ceilings in rococo plasterwork without paintings followed: Kirtlington in Oxfordshire has examples from 1748, and a superb late example of 1768 is at Claydon House, Buckinghamshire. By the mid century the GOTHIC REVIVAL brought in plaster vaulting; both Strawberry Hill, Twickenham (1750s), by Horace Walpole (1717–1797), and Arbury Hall, Warwickshire (*c.* 1786), are richly decorated with Gothic Revival vaults, pendants, and liernes.

Grotesques were part of the NEO-CLASSICAL style of decoration used extensively by Robert ADAM on his return from the GRAND TOUR in 1758, and an early example (1759) of his work is at Harewood House, South Yorkshire. Adam did not recommend grand ceiling paintings (which he claimed were neck-breaking to look at), preferring small bordered compartments with scenes painted perhaps by Angelica Kauffman (1741–1808) or her husband Antonio Zucchi (1726–95), with plasterwork by Joseph Rose (1745–99). The neo-classical style was continued into the nineteenth century by architects such as Henry Holland (1745–1806) and Sir John SOANE, to be overtaken by a more passionate Gothic Revival from the 1830s into the 1870s. As a refreshing alternative to the richness of Gothic detail, which like all fashions tends to debasement as its popularity increases, plain white-painted ceilings, sometimes with a central rose above a central light fitting, became fashionable, and have continued so to the present day.

Celtic Church. The church in the British Isles from the introduction of Christianity in the second or third century AD until St Augustine's mission, successful only in the south of England, from Rome in 597. Close ties were maintained with Rome until the Saxon invasions of the fifth and sixth centuries; under the Saxons these ties lapsed and doctrinal differences developed between Celtic and Roman Christians. The Celtic religions were unwilling to admit the primacy of Rome, but a resolution of the differences between the two churches – which included the date of Easter – was achieved at the Synod of Whitby (664), when it was agreed that Northumbria would follow the practices of the Roman church. The north of Britain, Ireland and Wales remained bastions of the Celtic Church until 768, when it finally submitted to Roman control.

Celtic monasticism, characterized by extreme asceticism and the eremetical (reclusive; hermit-like) tradition, was brought to Iona from Ireland by St Columba in 563; the monastic remains there show individual cells within an enclosure. Columba's followers spread Christianity through the British Isles in the sixth century (the 'age of the Saints', who included Columba and David). Foundations in Cornwall, Wales, Strathclyde, Abingdon in Oxfordshire and Crowland in Lincolnshire were followed in the seventh century by those at Lindisfarne in Northumberland (635), and Whitby (637) and Hackness (680), both in Yorkshire.

Celtic fields. The Celts, who first invaded Britain *c*. 900 BC in the late Bronze Age, finally settled in Britain between 500 and 250 BC, introducing the plough and a regular system of small rectangular fields on the chalk downs. These were later superseded by the Saxon open field system. The old Celtic fields are best seen from the air under light snow, or when the sun is casting long shadows. See CELTS and also CELTIC CHURCH.

Celts. The Celts, who overran northern Europe *c*. 900 BC, brought first the use of bronze and then, when they settled in Britain in the sixth century BC, the use of iron. The Celtic language which replaced earlier tongues was in its turn ousted by what became English, but lingers on in Wales as Welsh and in Scotland and Ireland as Gaelic. See also CELTIC CHURCH and CELTIC FIELDS.

Census Act (1800). This authorized the taking of population counts from 1801. The first three census returns lack the sort of information which would make them useful for historical research, but the 1841 Census included for the first time such details as place of residence, a guide to county of birth, employment, and exact age of children under fourteen. The returns for England for 1851 are better still, with exact age, and place of birth; but for Scotland and Ireland only country of birth is given. The Census has been taken every ten years except for 1941, and is only released for public use after one hundred years. Scotland has had its own Registrar General since 1861.

Centaur. A figure in Greek mythology with a horse's body and the torso and head of a man. Centaurs appear in works by such painters as Claude and Poussin in the seventeenth century, and also in eighteenth-century ceiling painting; they were used as a decorative element by the PALLADIANS.

Chair of State. From very early times the head of a household used a chair while everyone else sat on benches or stools, and the chair thus became a status symbol, particularly when associated with a CANOPY above it. The cross-frame chair which could be folded up and packed on to a waggon met the needs of medieval lords travelling from one castle to another and remained popular for the grandest of personages until the seventeenth century. An example in Winchester Cathedral may have been used by Mary I (1553–58) when she married Philip of Spain in 1554. Full-length portraits of Elizabeth I (1558–1603) often show her standing before a cross-framed chair beneath a canopy. The Hardwick Hall inventory of 1601 mentions a 'Chare of nedlework with golde and silk frenge', with a 'foote carpet of turkie worke', and a foot stool, in the High Great Chamber: this was the Chair of State, standing beneath a canopy. Had the Queen ever visited Hardwick it would have been used as a throne. The modern royal throne is a lineal descendant of the Chair of State.

Chaise. A light, two- or four-wheeled carriage with a folding hood, used for fast travel. See also CARRIAGES.

Chambermaid. Housemaid at a hotel.

Chamber music. Prior to the era of public concerts (late seventeenth century), musical performances fell into three classes: for the church, the theatres, and the halls or chambers (private drawing-rooms) of royalty and aristocracy. The novelist Fanny Burney's father, Dr Charles Burney (1726–1814), defined chamber music as 'compositions for a small concert room, a small band, and a small audience'; he also included vocal music, and instrumental solos, whereas today we would confine it to music performed by between two and six instruments, of which the string quartet (two violins, viola and cello) is the most important grouping. Gregorio Allegri (1582–1652) is believed to have composed the first string quartet. The English composers William Byrd (*c.* 1543–1623) and Orlando Gibbons (1583–1625) both wrote pieces known as fancies, 'apt for viols and voyces'.

   In the seventeenth and eighteenth centuries, the HARPSICHORD provided a figured bass accompaniment to strings – perhaps two violins and a cello; Antonio Vivaldi (*c.* 1675–1741) and Arcangelo Corelli (1653–1713) were notable composers in this style. Franz Joseph Haydn (1732–1809) worked out the true 'equal terms' principle of chamber music, and discarded the harpsichord – though Scarlatti (1660–1725) expressly marked his four string quartets 'without harpsichord', a very early (1715) example.

Chamber-pot. A pot used in the bedchamber for calls of nature in the night, the direct descendant of the medieval 'original' – a vase, usually of glass but occasionally of metal or glazed earthenware, in shape very much like the modern invalid's bed-bottle. The chamber-pot had evolved by the fourteenth century, in pewter, tin or copper; very grand ones were made of silver or gold. By the late sixteenth century such a pot enclosed in a locked box was called a CLOSE-STOOL.

In the eighteenth century a screen in the corner of the dining-room would conceal a pot for the use of the gentlemen, and one is still to be found in a discreet cupboard in the library at Flintham Hall, Nottinghamshire. In France the custom was followed by ladies as well – to the horror of British visitors, but then French habits have always fascinated the British – and vice versa. In 1784 the young Frenchman, François de la Rochefoucauld, on a visit to Houghton Hall in Norfolk reported that, after the ladies had retired, 'The sideboard is garnished also with chamber-pots, in line with the common practice of going over to the sideboard to pee, while others are drinking. Nothing is hidden. I find that very indecent.'

Greater decorum prevailed in the nineteenth century, when the chamber-pot was less in evidence in public rooms. See also GARDE-ROBES, SERVICE, and SEWAGE.

Chanceling. An illegitimate child. See also BLANKET, WRONG SIDE OF THE; BYBLOW and MERRYBEGOT.

Chancellor of the Exchequer. See under EXCHEQUER.

Chantry. An endowment for a priest, or priests, to sing masses for the soul of the founder, or for someone named by him; usually connected with a chantry chapel in or adjoining a parish church. Chantries commonly date from the fifteenth century, when the Council of Florence (1438–45) ordained that souls in PURGATORY could be helped by the prayers of the faithful on earth – one of the doctrines denied by Luther, but reaffirmed by the Council of Trent (1545–63). The DISSOLUTION of the chantries was begun by Henry VIII in 1545, but the official survey of chantries had not been carried out at his death, and a new Act was required in 1547 before confiscation of chantry property could be completed and chantry priests pensioned off.

However, belief persisted in the beneficial power of prayer for the souls of the departed, and by the end of the sixteenth century wealthy donors were founding almshouses for the poor with a condition that the inmates should pray daily in a chapel for the souls of the founder and his or her family. See also DISSOLUTION OF THE MONASTERIES.

Chapels, private. An essential part of a medieval castle (and later of many larger houses) was the chapel, and some of these private chapels survive today. Used for daily prayer until this century, the private chapel in no way replaced the parish church, where family banners, HATCH-MENTS, and tomb monuments were to be found. At a time when private practice of their religion was tolerated, Roman Catholic families often added chapels to their houses, having nowhere else to worship. The Chapel at Ugbrooke, Dorset stands apart from the house and was built for the Catholic Clifford family by Robert ADAM in 1760; it is also the Catholic parish church, and claims to be the earliest post-Reformation Roman Catholic church in the south of England. The magnificence of the BAROQUE chapel at Chatsworth in Derbyshire, built in the 1690s, cannot be outdone in any private house. A spectacular Georgian GOTHIC chapel of the 1750s is at the Vyne in Hampshire.

The nineteenth century saw many private chapels built in the Gothic style deemed suitable for places of worship, possibly the grandest of which is at Eaton Hall, Cheshire (although the house built for the 1st Duke of Westminster in 1870–82 was demolished in 1961, this chapel remains); there is also one at Ashridge, Hertfordshire by James Wyatt (1808–13; completed *c.* 1814–17 by Sir Jeffry Wyatville). The ARTS AND CRAFTS chapel (1901) at Madresfield Court, Worcestershire, with exquisite murals by H.A. Payne, is one of the most attractive anywhere.

Chaperon. A married or significantly older woman accompanying a younger, unmarried woman at social events, for the sake of propriety.

Chapter. A term with two meanings: first, the governing body, composed of dean, archdeacon, chancellor, precentor and treasurer, of a secular college or cathedral, the chapter house being their meeting-place; second, the assembly of a religious community at which a chapter from the order's rules is read out.

Charabanc. A long, light, open horse-drawn carriage in which the seats are forward facing; the term was later applied to early, open motor buses. See also CARRIAGES.

Charades. A game of guessing a word from an acted clue for each syllable and for the whole word. A favourite country-house game originating in the mid eighteenth century; severely frowned upon by Sir Thomas Bertram in Jane Austen's *Mansfield Park*. The real-life family of Sperling at Dynes Park, Essex had no inhibitions about charades, as Diane Sperling's watercolour dated 1818 shows. Charades were often played after dinner to entertain a house-party – not always with success, as Harold Nicolson noted in his diary on a visit to Cliveden, Buckinghamshire in 1939: 'Thirty-two people in the house. Cold and draughty. Great sofas in vast cathedrals; little groups of people wishing they were alone: lack of organisation and occupation; a desultory drivel. The party is in itself good enough . . . but it does not hang together. After dinner in order to enliven the party, Lady Astor dons a Victorian hat and a pair of false teeth. It does not enliven the party.'

Chariot. A four-wheeled, horse-drawn carriage with only forward-facing passenger seats, and the driver on a high seat at the front, above a boot.

Charity. The foremost of the three theological virtues: 'And now abideth faith, hope, charity, these three: but the greatest of these is charity.' Traditionally the Church taught that charity was love of God and love of one's neighbour, the latter having no meaning without the former, and encouraged the giving of ten per cent of annual personal income to the poor. The DOLE cupboard (sometimes known as an aumbry, or ambry, by association with the locker or recess in the wall of a church in which sacramental vessels were kept) was filled with left-over food from the tables of the wealthy, to be distributed as alms; but, generally speaking, monasteries were the principal benefactors throughout the Middle Ages. After the DISSOLUTION there was nothing to replace monastic charity until an Act of 1601 which made provision for relief of the poor out of local taxation; the support of the poor, particularly after bad harvests, such as were experienced between 1594 and 1597, fell heavily on the private individual. The Countess of Shrewsbury, then building Hardwick Hall in Derbyshire, customarily gave 3s. 4d. weekly 'to the poor at the gates'; in 1595 she increased the donation to 15s., in 1596 to 20s. Her donations moved about with her, and when she went to Chatsworth in Derbyshire the donations were to the poor at Chatsworth. Her gifts might occasionally be increased on special days, such as Easter, and for no identifiable reason she gave £16 in June 1594. Although these were substantial sums for the time they in no way amounted to a tenth of her annual income of £10,000.

In times of national distress a legal charge would be made on parishes to raise money. In 1665 a tax was imposed on all landowners for the relief of those infected by PLAGUE. At Woburn Abbey in Bedfordshire, the Earl of Bedford exceeded his share of 22s., giving £10 towards the erecting of a pesthouse, £10 to the poor of Westminster, and another £10 for the poor at St Paul's, Covent Garden. Every few months he gave money for the inmates of London and Bedford prisons, principally through St Paul's Church, Covent Garden.

Household account books of the seventeenth century record many payments to beggars at the gates, particularly to ex-soldiers. In the mid eighteenth century, Dudley North, a Suffolk landowner, gave detailed instructions to his STEWARD as to which villagers were to receive gifts at Christmas and the New Year. The Duke of Chandos's usher at Cannons House, Middlesex had orders in 1721 'That he likewise takes care all the meat that remains not fit for any other use be laid up to be delivered to the poor upon the day or days of the week mentioned in the Instructions.' Sir Charles Bunbury of Barton Hall, Suffolk, in 1773–4 gave £49 7s. 8d. to charities and £2 10s. for 'the poor on St Thomas's Day as usual'. These were all official payments passed through the books of the steward and in 'closed' villages owned by the landlord.

There is no record of payments from the private purse on the impulse of a moment, and the poor in 'open' villages with no paternalistic landlord had a harder time.

By the nineteenth century the giving of charity was more organized. The squire's wife and daughters made clothes for the tenants' babies, ran 'clothing clubs' and distributed soup and food-hampers in times of scarcity, while the squire himself might give more substantial support. Declining rents in the 1880s and '90s were reflected in charitable donations. At Wilton in 1882 the Earl of Pembroke gave £206 for fuel and £207 to clothing charities; in 1902, £93 and £104.

The personification of Charity in paintings, tapestries, sculpture, china figures, and so on is an indication of its historical importance. See also POOR LAW.

Chartism. A revolutionary democratic movement originating from disappointment in the 1832 Reform Bill, which enfranchised only the middle classes. *The People's Charter* was published in 1838 by the founder of the London Workingmen's Association, William Lovett (1800–77), a London cabinet-maker, and contained six demands: universal male suffrage, voting by secret ballot, payment of MPs, the end of the property qualification for MPs, annual parliaments, and equal electoral areas. The movement lacked cohesion, being at first influenced by Lovett, who favoured moral force – persuasion and negotiations – and later, particularly in the north, by Feargus O'Connor, who initially favoured force. A petition of 1,200,000 signatures was rejected by Parliament in 1839 and was followed by proposals for a general strike, sporadic local strikes, and outbreaks of violence. In 1842 a second petition of 3,000,000 signatures was presented, and again rejected by Parliament, resulting in such serious violence, particularly in the north, that O'Connor himself was horrified. O'Connor was organizing a mass procession to present a third petition following an open-air rally on Kennington Common on 10 April 1848; but the march on Westminster was forestalled by determined military resistance, rain and lack of enthusiasm affected attendance at the rally, and O'Connor and a handful of his supporters instead carried the petition to the House of Commons in three CABS. This marked the end of Chartism as a political movement, although it continued as an organization for another ten years. O'Connor died in an insane asylum in 1855. See also FRANCHISE, REFORM ACTS and SUFFRAGETTE MOVEMENT.

Chasuble. A sleeveless mantle covering the body and shoulders, worn over the ALB and stole by a priest at the celebration of the Mass. As a garment it is directly derived from the Roman *peonula*, a cloak worn by all classes and sexes, but the word itself is from the Latin *casula*, a little house or hut. The chasuble must be of silk, and was originally plain;

now it is frequently richly embroidered and decorated with ORPHREYS. Its colour varies according to the liturgical sequence, depending upon the season and the occasion; examples are: white, on ordinary days, during Christmas, and for the funerals of infants; red, Whit Sunday, festivals of apostles and, in England, at the 'Red Mass', the mass of the Holy Spirit attended by Roman Catholic judges and barristers at the opening of term; green, between Trinity and Advent; violet at Advent, and when giving absolution after confession; black at masses and funeral services for the dead, and on Good Friday. In the Protestant church the garment was abolished at the REFORMATION, but is used today in HIGH CHURCH services. See also CASSOCK.

Chauffeur. Liveried, car-driving employee; from the French for a forge or furnace stoker – the first motor-cars were steam driven.

Chess. An intellectual game of skill for two players, using thirty-two chessmen on a chequered board of sixty-four squares. Known also as 'the royal game'. Its origins are lost in obscurity, but it is generally accepted that it existed in India before it is known to have been played anywhere else. From Persia it passed to Arabia, thence to Spain and the rest of Europe, between the eighth and tenth centuries. It was known throughout Europe by the time of the CRUSADES.

Chesterfield. A sofa with upholstered seat, back, and ends, named after a nineteenth-century Earl of Chesterfield.

Chest of drawers. Evolved over the centuries from, as its name implies, the storage chest. A stage in its development was the provision of a lower compartment or drawers at the base of the chest; an example made about 1567, with two bottom drawers, can be seen at Hardwick Hall, Derbyshire. Such chests 'with drawers' developed into both chests of drawers as we know them (late seventeenth–early eighteenth centuries) and into TALLBOYS. See also COMMODE.

Chiltern Hundreds. A principle of English parliamentary law, dating from the days when local gentry were compelled to sit in Parliament, held that a member of the House of Commons, once duly elected, could not *resign*; however, a statute of 1707 enacted that any member accepting an office of profit under the Crown must *vacate* his seat. The stewardship of the Chiltern Hundreds, a track of Crown lands in the Chiltern Hills in Buckinghamshire, is the last surviving of an original eight such nominal offices of profit noted in the Place Act of 1742, and a Member of Parliament wishing to vacate his seat is spoken of as applying for the Chiltern Hundreds. The grant is at the discretion of the CHANCELLOR OF THE EXCHEQUER.

Chimney-glass or **overmantel mirror.** A French architect, Robert de Cotte (1656–1735), is credited with the introduction of mirrors placed over fireplaces, and the fashion came to Britain in the early eighteenth century. From the beginning it posed problems; British glass-makers could not produce large pieces of flat glass, so mirrors were therefore made up of smaller pieces, the joins covered by fillets of decorated gold-work. In France the secret of making large pieces of glass was discovered at the St Gobain glass works in Picardy at the end of the seventeenth century, and larger and larger pieces were produced as the eighteenth century progressed. However, French glass was expensive even in France, and in Britain the cost was even greater, so it was rarely used. Overmantel-mirrors of French glass may be seen at Osterley Park, Greater London, refitted by Robert ADAM in the 1760s, and at Newby Hall in North Yorkshire, again by Adam (1770s). It was only in the 1790s that the Ravenhead Glass Works in Lancashire was able to manufacture glass of comparable size to the French. See also PIER GLASS and PLATE GLASS.

Chinese export porcelain. The Dutch were dealing in Chinese blue and white porcelain as early as the beginning of the seventeenth century, and it became so popular that the Chinese began to make or copy designs specifically to suit European taste. Polychrome wares – the *famille verte* of the K'ang Hsi period (1662–1722) and the *famille rose* of the reigns of Yung Cheng (1723–1735) and Ch'ien Yung (1735–1795) – were much in vogue, decorated with allegorical or mythological scenes – the 'Judgement of Paris' was a popular subject – or as dinner or tea services decorated with coats-of-arms: armorial porcelain. 'Some 5,000 dinner and tea services of the armorial type are known to have been sent to Europe, and of these 4,000 were intended for the British market.' The Chinese lavished their skill on such services, which might take two years to complete, but did not always understand the intricacies of the blazoner's art: details of the coats-of-arms were sent out from England, but very occasionally one sees examples where the colours of the blazon have been spelt out (as on the original diagram), rather than actually used – the Chinese being meticulous copyists!

Chinoiserie. A term used to describe ROCOCO decoration using Chinese motifs, popular particularly during the middle of the eighteenth century. Found in silver, porcelain, architecture (Sir William CHAMBERS's Pagoda at Kew (1762)), and interior design (the Chinese tea pavilion at Claydon House, Buckinghamshire, about 1755–75), but perhaps especially associated with the furniture designs of Thomas CHIPPENDALE – the well-known 'Chinese Chippendale'. The appeal of Chinoiserie lay partly in the fact that its elements of the exotic and the picturesque fitted in so well with the underlying themes of the rococo.

Chippendale, Thomas (*c.* 1718–79). A London cabinet maker. Born in Yorkshire, he came to London *c.* 1745, and published a book of designs, *The Gentleman and Cabinet Maker's Directory*, in 1754. This was a valuable source of designs for his competitors, which is why there is so much furniture ascribed to his name. There is, in fact, very little which can be traced to his manufacture, and there is no way in which he could have turned out the enormous number of pieces ascribed to him. His workshop, employing twenty-two cabinet-makers, was burnt out in 1755, but quickly re-established. In 1753 he was joined in partnership with James Rennie until the latter's death in 1766. In 1771, with John Haig, Chippendale traded under the style of Chippendale Haig and Co. After Chippendale's death in 1779, his son Thomas II succeeded to the business, continuing the partnership with Haig until 1796. He opened showrooms in the Haymarket, London in 1814, moved to Jermyn Street in 1821, and died in 1823. During his working lifetime Chippendale Senior followed current fashions, moving from the ROCOCO style to the NEO-CLASSICAL, and making furniture designed by the ADAM brothers.

Although the number of pieces of furniture which can be ascribed to the Chippendales, father and son, is not great, the following houses have genuine Chippendale furniture: Claydon House, Buckinghamshire; Harewood House, West Yorkshire; Nostell Priory, West Yorkshire; and Stourhead, Wiltshire.

Chivalry. Nearly synonymous with KNIGHTHOOD. (1) A mode of feudal tenure; (2) a personal attribute; (3) a scheme of manners. Probably ultimately derived from early Teutonic customs, later absorbed into the military organization of feudalism to give a code of conduct for medieval warfare. When fighting was accepted both as a glorious necessity and as one of the very few callings open to a man of any pretensions to birth, its barbarity was a little softened by combining it – in theory, if not invariably in practice – with the highest standards of behaviour and honour, elements of Christian devotion and mysticism and, later, the fashion of courtly love which grew up in the courts of southern France. The fabulous tales of King Arthur and Merlin related by Geoffrey of Monmouth in his *Historium Regum Britanniae* (1135) were translated into French and gave rise to the *romans bretons* or *romans de la Table Ronde* of the twelfth and thirteenth centuries which came to epitomise 'chivalry' in a world of TOURNAMENTS, battles, heroic deaths, sorcerers, the saving of damsels from fierce dragons and other forms of distress, and the courtly love or *amour courtois* in which the knight, ennobled by his passion, wins the love of a beautiful and virtuous woman by his prowess, courtesy and patience. These *romans* continued in popularity in verse and prose versions throughout the medieval period and were printed in the early sixteenth century.

In English law, chivalry came to mean the tenure of land by KNIGHT SERVICE – not finally abolished until 1662. Edward III (1327–77) instituted the Court of Chivalry, in which the Lord High Constable and the EARL MARSHAL of England, as joint judges, had summary criminal jurisdiction as regards all offences of knights, and in military matters generally; when the Earl Marshal alone presided, it was a court of honour deciding upon points of procedure, coats-of-arms and so on. This court sat for the last time in 1737, and the heraldic side of its duties is now vested in the Earl Marshal, as head of the Heralds' College.

The supremacy of archery and, later, the invention of gunpowder made the heavily armoured knight an anachronism, but the attraction of the ideal persisted. Henry VIII (1509–47) had his Field of the Cloth of Gold, and in the reign of Queen Elizabeth I (1558–1603) extravagant Court tournaments served both to entertain, and to emphasize the attractions of the Virgin Queen for whose favours the courtly knights competed. Edmund Spenser (c. 1552–99) wrote the *Faerie Queene* (published in 1580), and Sir Thomas Malory's (d. 1471) *Morte d'Arthur* was continually reprinted until 1634. There was a brief revival of castle building, of which Bolsover Castle, Derbyshire, begun in 1614, is an example.

The science of HERALDRY continued to flourish, although a coat-of-arms now only gave evidence (if it was accurate) of gentle birth, and no longer served as identification in battle; the Orders of the Bath and the Garter maintained their prestige; at his coronation the King's Champion threw down the gauntlet on his behalf, and other archaic knightly characters played parts derived from medieval pageantry. Towards the end of the eighteenth century, George III commissioned Benjamin West (1738–1820) to paint a series of chivalric episodes from the reign of Edward III for the King's Audience Chamber at Windsor Castle (1787–9). The interior of Alnwick Castle, Northumberland was done over in the GOTHIC style by Robert ADAM in 1770–80, and the designers of the numerous castles being built, particularly in Scotland and the North of England, in the Georgian GOTHIC and later GOTHIC REVIVAL styles turned to the annals of chivalry for inspiration. The Eglinton Tournament of 1839 was a straightforwardly romantic revival of Chivalry.

The revival was over by the 1860s, but chivalric notions persisted in the ideal of a Victorian GENTLEMAN. For many, the First World War saw the last gasp of chivalry.

The 'flower of Chivalry' was Sir William Douglas of Liddesdale, who fell fighting Edward III's forces at the Battle of Halidon Hill in 1333, but the term has also been applied to Sir Philip Sidney (1554–1586), and the Chevalier de Bayard, 'le Chevalier sans peur et sans Reproche' (1476–1524).

Chivalry, Orders of. Those carrying knighthoods are, in descending order of precedence: most noble Order of the Garter, most ancient Order of the Thistle, most illustrious Order of St Patrick, most honourable Order of the Bath, most exalted Order of the Star of India, most distinguished Order of St Michael and St George, most eminent Order of the Indian Empire, Royal Victorian Order, Order of the British Empire. No Knights of St Patrick have been appointed since 1921; and no Knights of the Indian orders since 1947.

Cholera. A term applied to a variety of acute diarrhoeal diseases, formerly endemic (probably since remote antiquity) in India in the Ganges delta and lower Bengal. The first world-wide epidemic (pandemic) of *cholera morbus* originated in India in 1826 and arrived in Sunderland in October 1831 by way of Russia and Eastern Europe. Before it was over 30,000 mainly poor and undernourished Britons had died. The main causes of its uncontrollable spread were ineffective medical treatment, appalling living conditions, and the contamination by sewage of drinking water in towns and cities. A second pandemic between 1848–9 and 1852 killed 60,000 in Britain, and outbreaks recurred periodically until 1910. A Central Board of Health was set up in 1848 to study the cause of the disease. The London Water Act of 1852, designed to safeguard the purity of water supplies, was not fully implemented for thirty-three years.

Chrisom cloth. A robe – originally a head-cloth (or shawl?), used to prevent the chrisom (consecrated oil and balm) used in the Roman Catholic Church for anointing during baptism from being rubbed off. Later, the term was applied to the white baptismal robe (a token of innocence), which was used as the child's shroud if it died within the month, but was otherwise given to the church by the mother at her CHURCHING. Children dying within the month were known as 'chrisom-children' or 'chrisoms'.

Christenings. See BAPTISM.

Christmas customs. The actual day of the Nativity has never been settled beyond dispute; the Church Fathers of the fifth century, therefore, sensibly tied the celebration of the birth of Christ to the winter solstice, a highly significant event in pagan religions, with the aim of facilitating the conversion of pagans to Christianity. The Romans exchanged gifts during the Saturnalia and decorated their temples with greenery; the Druids gathered mistletoe with great ceremony; the Saxons decorated their homes with holly, ivy and bay. In medieval times a Lord of Misrule (in Scotland, the Abbot of Misrule; another survival from the Roman Saturnalia) was chosen to direct Christmas sports and revelries; in some places the secular celebrations might extend from All Hallows' Eve (31 October) or St Thomas's Day (21 December) until

Candelmas (2 February), but in England the festive period was usually Christmas Eve to Epiphany (6 January). Under the Lord of Misrule a favourite entertainment was to turn life upside down, with masters waiting upon servants. As late as Elizabeth I's reign (1558–1603), Christmas day itself was kept as a day of religious ceremony and prayer, and gifts were exchanged on New Year's day. The general licence of the Christmas celebrations found little favour with the PURITANS, and the observance of Christmas was forbidden by Act of Parliament in 1644. Charles II revived the feast, but the Scots PRESBYTERIANS maintained the Puritan view. By the eighteenth century, the custom of giving presents on Christmas day was established. See also CHRISTMAS TREE and PAGAN SURVIVALS.

Christmas tree. It was not, as is popularly supposed, Prince Albert who introduced the Christmas tree to Britain; Princess Charlotte of Mecklenburg-Strelitz, who married George III (1760–1820) in 1761, brought with her the German custom of decorating a candle-lit tree with small gifts of all kinds, including toys and sweetmeats. It is said that Boniface, an English missionary in Germany in the eight century, replaced the sacrifices to Odin's sacred oak with a fir tree adorned in tribute to the Christ Child, and Martin Luther (1483–1546) is widely held to have introduced the idea of a candle-lit tree. See also CHRISTMAS CUSTOMS and PAGAN SURVIVALS.

Churching of women. A thanksgiving or blessing ceremony performed by or for a mother after the birth of a child, derived from a purification ceremony in the Old Testament. In 1466 at a dinner given for Edward IV's (1461–83) Queen, Elizabeth, to celebrate her churching after the birth of her daughter, she sat by herself on a gilt chair. Everyone remained kneeling while she ate except for her mother and sisters-in-law, who were permitted to sit after the serving of the first course, 'and she ate for three hours . . . And all were silent; not a word was spoken.' Custom varied, but the usual date for churching was forty days after the confinement (reflecting the presentation of the Virgin and Child at the Temple), and it was formerly held to be unlucky for a woman to leave the house after her confinement until she went to be churched.

Ciborium. A canopy above the high altar, normally a dome carried on columns. (Also refers to the dove-shaped vessel which hung beneath it, in which the Eucharist was kept.) See also BALDACCHINO.

Cipher. A Tudor term meaning a device or monogram; today it generally means a secret code.

Cistercians. 'Grey' or 'white monks' (from the colour of the habit, over which is worn a black scapular or apron). In 1098 Robert de Molesme settled with twenty monks at Cîtaux, not far from Dijon in

France, to live a life of strict observance of St Benedict's rule, without the ameliorations of severity and the elaboration of the Divine Office which had grown up over three centuries. They returned to manual labour, and became the great agriculturalists of their day, introducing and spreading many farming improvements. Unnecessary decoration was forbidden, and Cistercian abbeys were usually built in wild and desolate places; the interiors of their churches were simply painted white, and their habits were made from undyed wool. Cistercian chapter houses were always quadrangular, with two or three aisles. At the DISSOLUTION the Cistercians were the largest order in Scotland, with eleven monasteries and nunneries, and in England and Scotland as a whole there were eighty-six monasteries and thirty-three convents. Today there are three Cistercian foundations in Britain: Mount St Bernard, Leicestershire (1835); Caldey, Dyfed (1931); and Nunraw, Lothian (1946). All are 'Trappists', of the Order of Reformed Cistercians, a rule of a severity beyond Cistercian practice and far beyond St Benedict's rule, stemming from renewed reforms in France in the middle of the seventeenth century and named from the abbey of La Trappe near Soligny. Trappists observe strict silence and seclusion from the world, hard labour, and total abstinence from wine, meat, fish, and eggs. Pre-DISSOLUTION Cistercian monasteries, now ruins, are at Fountains and Rivaulx, North Yorkshire; Furness and Whalley, Lancashire; Vale Royal, Cheshire; Tintern, Monmouthshire; Valle Crucis, Clwyd; Holmcultram, Cumberland. Houses occupying former Cistercian sites are Beaulieu Abbey, Hampshire (abbey founded 1204); Buckland Abbey, Devon (1278); Forde Abbey, Dorset (1140); Rufford Abbey, Nottinghamshire (1146); Woburn Abbey, Bedfordshire (1145). See also AUGUSTINIANS, BENEDICTINES, CARMELITES, CARTHUSIANS, CLUNIACS, DOMINICANS, FRANCISCANS, GILBERTINES, MENDICANT FRIARS and PREMONSTRATENSIANS.

Cistern. See SESTERN.

Civil List, The. The account which contains the expenses of the sovereign's household in upholding the dignity and honour of the Crown; the amount voted by Parliament for such expenses. From early times the expenses of the sovereign, the civil government and defence were paid from the income of the Crown. In the reign of William III (1695–1702) Parliament took a step towards recognizing the principle that the expense of supporting the Crown should be separated from the ordinary expenses of the state. Between 1697 and the reign of George II (1728–60), £700,000 was allotted annually to defray the expenses of the Civil Service, the payment of civil pensions, the cost of the royal household, and the sovereign's own expenses – in effect, all the expenses of government except charges relating to the National Debt and defence. The Civil List was altered as circumstances dictated, but it was not until the accession of William IV (1831–37) that it was finally freed from all charges relating to government service, as distinguished from those of the court and the royal family, and fixed at £510,000. At Queen Elizabeth II's accession in 1952 the Civil List was fixed at £475,000, with a provision of £40,000 for the Duke of Edinburgh. No provision is made for the sovereign's heir, but as Duke of Cornwall the Prince of Wales receives the income from the Duchy of Cornwall; the Princess of Wales, however, is provided for separately in the Civil List. On the death of a sovereign his or her successor places the hereditary revenues of the Crown at the disposal of Parliament, and a Select Committee of the House of Commons then considers costs and allocates an annual sum for the support of the new sovereign.

Civil War (1642–9). The Civil War was made inevitable by mounting and irreconcilable religious, economic and constitutional differences between Charles I (1625–49), his Parliament and his people during the 1630s. Matters were brought to a head on 4 January 1642 when Charles, having failed to persuade the House of Lords to impeach five Members of Parliament for treason, went down with 300 armed men to the House of Commons to arrest them himself. The five – John Pym, John Hampden, Denzil Holles, Sir Arthur Haselrig, and William Strode – forewarned, took refuge with the TRAINBANDS in the City: the King found that 'all the birds are flown'. Charles I withdrew from Whitehall, and entered it again only for his trial.

The royal standard was raised in Nottingham on 22 August 1642. Support for Charles (the Cavaliers) centred mainly in the north and west, and that for the Parliamentarian cause (the Roundheads) in the south and east, particularly in London and East Anglia. The first battle of the Civil War, at Edgehill on 23 October 1642, was inconclusive. Charles failed to take London and gathered his court at Oxford, which remained the Royalist capital for the duration of the Civil War. An agreement in September 1643 for a monthly payment of £30,000 and a promise to introduce PRESBYTERIANISM into England brought the Scottish army in on the Parliamentarian side. Each side enjoyed successes and suffered defeats, but the formation of the Parliamentarian New Model Army under Oliver Cromwell (1599–1658) and Sir Thomas Fairfax (1612–1721) proved decisive, and led to the defeat of the King's army at Naseby in June 1645 and at Langport in July. In January 1647 the King surrendered to the Scots army besieging Newark.

Charles then engaged in complicated negotiations with the victors and briefly escaped to the Isle of Wight, where he successfully enlisted the Scots as allies, the Parliamentarians having been slow to pay the

Scots and slower still to introduce Presbyterianism. Royalist risings in Wales, Kent and Essex were put down by the New Model Army in March 1648, and in July a Scottish army was defeated at Preston after a three-day battle. The 'man of blood', Charles Stuart, was taken to London, tried for the treason of waging war upon his Parliament and people, and beheaded outside the Banqueting Hall in Whitehall on 30 January 1649. Charles II, crowned King at Scone in Scotland after his father's execution, led a second Scottish invasion in 1651 but was decisively defeated at Worcester on 3 September; he fled to France, and opposition from Royalist adherents was effectively at an end. See also PURITANS.

Clans. Derived from the Gaelic *clann* (offspring, family, race) and in this sense a patriarchal organization, highly developed in the Highlands of Scotland and in Ireland. In theory all members of a clan are descendants of a common ancestor, from whom the name of the clan is usually derived; in the Highlands, descent is held to be ultimately from several of the great historic royal clans. The chief, usually the oldest member, represents the common ancestor.

An interesting example is that of the Clan Gregor, from the 'three glens' of the rivers Orchy, Strae and Lochy, descended from Kenneth MacAlpin, the King of Albany, High King of the Picts and Scots in the tenth century. At the end of the thirteenth century the line of Iain of Glenorchy ended with a childless heiress who carried the 'superiority of the glens' to the Campbells, her husband's clan. The male line of the old family, 'apparently descended from Iain of Glenorchy's nephew Gregor', 'the name-father of the clan', would not submit to the Campbells and held their ancestral territory by the sword as long as they could.

In 1519 the Campbells managed to establish a MacGregor chieftain of a junior branch as Chieftain of the Clan Gregor; the disinherited line became known as the Children of the Mist and carried on their feuding and resistance to the point where in 1603 the whole Clan Gregor were outlawed, and the name of MacGregor was proscribed on pain of death – hence the many variations which occur, such as Grierson and Gregory. In 1774 the penal laws against the Clan Gregor were repealed, and shortly thereafter the head of the rightful but long-disinherited Children of the Mist was officially recognized as chief of the whole clan.

The clans' lawlessness represented a threat to government, and many official documents refer to them in terms of opprobrium. The clans continued to play an important part in Scottish history until after the JACOBITE rebellion of 1745, when their dress was prohibited, and with the clearances a determined attempt was made to break the allegiance of clansmen to their chief. Clan traditions linger on, and the chiefs of some clans maintain the clan title, but nowadays the spirit is more social than partisan and the tartan is a symbol of this past. See also SURNAMES.

Clarendon Code. A series of narrow and tyrannical measures of Parliamentary legislation against Dissenters, aimed at the re-establishment of the Anglican church following the RESTORATION of Charles II in 1660. These were named after the King's chief minister, Edward Hyde, 1st Earl of Clarendon (1609–74), although he gave them only reluctant support. The Corporation Act of 1661 demanded a declaration from the members of the governing bodies of all corporate towns (a) that the Covenant of 1643 which promised the establishment of Presbyterianism in England was an unlawful oath (b) that it was unlawful under any circumstances to bear arms against the king. The Act of UNIFORMITY (1662) imposed on clergymen of every rank, all university fellows and officials, all tutors and schoolmasters, assent to a revised Prayer Book which was largely unpalatable to Puritans; they were also to make the declarations imposed by the Corporation Act, and any who did not were to vacate their livings – probably about 2,000 in all were ejected. The Conventicle Act of 1664, designed to prevent clergy ejected by the Act of Uniformity from forming their own congregations, was directed particularly against small groups (a conventicle was defined as a meeting of five or more people over and above the members of a household) of Quakers, Presbyterians, and Independents. The Five Mile Act of 1665 prohibited ejected NONCONFORMIST ministers from residing within five miles of any corporate town or teaching in any public or private school unless they took the oath of non-resistance imposed by the Corporation Act, and further pledged not to 'endeavour at any time any alteration of government either in Church or State'.

Claret. An English term, since the beginning of the seventeenth century, for the light red wines of Bordeaux. The three centuries of English rule over the Bordeaux region which began with the marriage in 1152 of Henry II (1154–89) to Eleanor of Aquitaine, bringing trading privileges in London to the Bordeaux merchants, firmly fixed the English fondness for claret. Also slang, from about 1606, for blood. See also PORT and SACK.

Claude glass. A device used by landscape artists, mainly in the seventeenth and eighteenth centuries. It was a darkened, convex lens, often provided with a hanging chain, which showed the view in miniature, as in a painting by Claude Lorraine (1600–82), who was said to have used such a lens and from whom the name is derived; Corot (1796–1875) certainly used one. Many of those making the GRAND TOUR took a Claude glass with them, often hanging in their carriage window. See also CAMERA OBSCURA.

Clerestory. In a church, the upper part of the nave's main walls pierced by windows to admit 'clear' light (pronounced 'clear-story').

Clerical collar. More usually called a 'dog collar', it evolved in the mid nineteenth century from the eighteenth-century male neckerchief. See also CASSOCK and ORPHREY.

Clergy, The. A collective term for those in holy orders. The lowest rank of ordained Anglican clergy is that of CURATE, an assistant to a parish priest; a curate-in-charge is one who takes charge of a parish during the suspension or incapacity of the incumbent. A vicar was originally the incumbent of a parish of which the TITHES had been impropriated or conveyed to a religious community or to a layman, while a rector was the incumbent of a parish in which the tithes had not been so impropriated. A Roman Catholic rector is the head priest of a parish; 'rector' is also used of the head or master of a college, university, school, or religious institution (especially a Jesuit seminary). In the Anglican church a dean is the incumbent of a cathedral or collegiate church; in dioceses created in the twentieth century, the incumbent of a cathedral is usually appointed as a provost rather than a dean; like 'rector', 'dean' is also used of some non-ecclesiastical academic appointments. A rural dean supervises a group of parochial clergy, as deputy of the bishop and archdeacon, with particular concern for the fabric of the churches and parsonages within the district. In Tudor times it was customary for a priest who was a university graduate to have the courtesy title of 'Sir'.

In earlier times a deacon collected and distributed alms for the poor, a responsibility now echoed in the Presbyterian church, where the deacon (a layman) has charge of finances. Today in both the Roman Catholic and Anglican churches the diaconate is a step to the priesthood, conferred by episcopal ordination. An order of deaconesses existed in the Eastern church before the fourth century, but never became popular in the Western church and fell into abeyance in the middle ages. In modern times the first deaconess of the Church of England was Miss Elizabeth Freard, who was 'set apart' by the Bishop of London in 1862; deaconesses now work under the control of the parochial clergy.

Bishops are the highest-ranking Anglican clergy after the Archbishops of Canterbury and York; they are consecrated diocesan governors with powers of ordination, confirmation and dispensation. The appointment of bishops is technically vested in the Crown, though the formality of consulting the dean and chapter is observed and the choice nowadays normally rests with the PRIME MINISTER, acting on advice from the Church establishment. The forty-three dioceses of the Church of England, each with its own bishop, are organized into two sees, under the Archbishops of Canterbury, who is 'primate of all England' (twenty-nine), and York (fourteen). Both archbishops have a seat in the House of Lords, the Archbishop of Canterbury taking precedence immediately after Princes of the Blood and over every peer, including the Lord Chancellor; the Archbishop of York takes precedence *after* the Lord Chancellor. Deriving from the medieval status of bishoprics as Crown baronies, some bishops also have seats in the House of Lords as spiritual peers. All sat until 1878, since when only the Bishops of London, Durham and Winchester are always entitled to do so; the remaining 21 places are filled according to seniority of consecration (except for the Bishop of Sodor and Man, who sits in the Manx House of Keys but not in the House of Lords). When a vacancy arises it is filled by the senior Diocesan Bishop without a seat, and the vacated see goes to the bottom of the waiting list. Bishops rank in order of precedence immediately above barons, but their wives enjoy no title or precedence. Suffragan bishops are nominated by diocesan bishops of large sees to assist them in their pontifical functions; they usually take their name from some ancient town in the see.

The Church in Wales has six bishops and six suffragan bishops; it was disestablished in 1921 and so its bishops do not take seats in the House of Lords, nor do the seven bishops of the Episcopal Church of Scotland, since the Episcopal Church is not the State Church of Scotland.

The Roman Catholic Church in England and Wales has five archbishoprics under an Apostolic Delegate, with twenty-one bishops; Scotland has five archbishops and six bishops, and Northern Ireland one archbishop and five bishops under a Papal Nuncio.

Clock-jack. Sometimes called a roasting-jack. This is an eighteenth-century clockwork device in a case of brass or japanned tin, used for turning meat in front of the hearth for roasting. See also KITCHENS, JAPANNING and SPITS.

Clocks. All clocks – by definition, machines designed to record and to indicate the passing of time – are made on the principle of linking a device that performs regular movements in equal intervals of time to a counting mechanism that will record the number of those movements. Until the Industrial Revolution most people had no need to measure time precisely; sunrise and sunset were sufficient. In monasteries the passing of time was measured by church services, for which both monks and priests required some notion of time. Sundials had been in use since Anglo-Saxon times, but were of course useless at night or in cloudy weather. The first clocks were striking clocks driven by weights; a dial was added later with a single hand and a twenty-four-hour face. The oldest mechanical clock in virtually complete and working condition in Britain – possibly in the world – is at Salisbury Cathedral, made of iron about 1386; it is not in its original position, and was restored in 1956. The clock at Wells Cathedral, of the same design and probably by the same hands, dates from 1390. Church clocks were usually in the south transept, and in the care of the sacrist. Elsewhere clocks were found only in the wealthiest of households; Edward III (1327–77) had clocks in his palaces from about 1360.

With the invention of the spring to store energy, clocks came down off the wall. Portable spring-driven clocks, first made in Germany in the sixteenth century, are sometimes to be seen. The accuracy of time-pieces was revolutionized in the seventeenth century by the application of balance springs to watches, and pendulums to clocks; at this time, London was the centre of British clock-making. Brass lantern clocks of the mid to late seventeenth century were wall-mounted and weight-driven; there are several at Temple Newsam House, Leeds. Thomas Tompion (1639–1713) is the clockmaker we associate with the spring-driven bracket or mantel clocks whose portability made them so popular well into the nineteenth century. The finest examples are showpieces of superb craftsmanship, not only the clockmaker's but the casemaker's and engraver's. The decorative aspect of bracket clocks reflected current fashion, from the majestic symmetrical curves of the BAROQUE to the free-form arabesques of the ROCOCO. Temple Newsam House also has a fine, waisted satinwood clock reminiscent of Shera-ton, *c.* 1795. It was only after *c.* 1725 that clocks stood on overmantels.

The weight-driven long-case clock ('grandfather' is quite a modern term) evolved after the introduction of the pendulum control from Holland in 1658, and such clocks by Tompion and other British makers survive from as early as 1670; an example by Fromanteel, a London clockmaker of Dutch origins, is in the British Museum. Although British clockmakers produced accurate timepieces, the best and most elaborate were made in France in the eighteenth century.

A separate development in the second half of the seventeenth century was the invention of the night-clock with a striking mechanism using bells. The bells tended to wake the household, and the real night-clock with a dial illuminated by its own oil lamp was not invented until the very end of the century. Few survive, as the lamp tended to set fire to the clock. The problem of telling the time at night was not solved until 1675, when striking watches and repeater watches with subdued tones began to be made. Other unusual clocks are to be seen in country houses – such as the water-clock, worked by a regulated flow of water and ball-bearings on a balanced slide.

Close stools. Close stools, or *chaises-percées*, were no more than a modern COMMODE – a pot set in a chair-seat. They came into fashion toward the end of the sixteenth century as an improvement on the medieval GARDEBROBE or PRIVY. They were in widespread use until the mid nineteenth century, when they were superseded by the much more efficient WC. The pots were taken by personal servants and emptied into outside privies.

The sovereign was usually waited upon by gentlemen who deemed the most intimate task an honour. The office of Groom of the Stole, for example, was held in 1689 by William Bentinck, at a salary of £5,000 a year for doing no more than emptying William III's close-stool.

In cities pots were emptied out of windows into the street to the cheerful shout of 'Gardy-loo', and bad luck on anyone walking beneath. Gardy-loo is a corruption of the French *gardez-l'eau*, shouted politely as a warning.

Euphemisms of course abound for the equipment for this essential human function: it has also been known as a garderobe or night-stool, the jaques, the gongs, the WC or water-closet, more recently the Latinised lavatory, now the deplorable 'toilet' and the even more deplorable 'loo'. The *Oxford Dictionary* gives 'origin uncertain' for loo, but could it be a contraction of 'Gardy-loo'?

People living outside cities on a lower social level had for centuries to be content with an earth closet – a simple hole in the ground – until mains sewage became more general in this century. See also CHAMBER-POT and SEWAGE.

Clothes press. The forerunner of the wardrobe: a large cupboard fitted with shelves and/or sliding trays above, and drawers below. Large garments were folded on the shelves.

Clubs (of London). Most were founded, for gambling, in the late eighteenth and early nineteenth centuries; White's (1693), Boodle's (1762; originally the 'Sçavoir Vivre'), the Guards (1813 – but banned gambling), Arthur's (1707) and Crockford's (1827) were all in the West End. Of these only Brooks's (see below), Boodle's and White's still exist in their eighteenth-century homes. The Guards merged with the Cavalry Club (1890) in 1976. Others were political clubs, such as the Carlton (Conservative, 1831), the Reform Club (1834), and the National Liberal Club (1882). The Grillion Club, dining at the Grillion Hotel in Albemarle Street, was founded by Sir Thomas Acland in 1813 with the purpose of bringing together politicians of divergent opinions to dine together in harmony, after abusing each other in Parliament. Their portraits, commissioned by Sir Thomas, hang in Killerton House, Devon. Almack's was founded in 1764 in a house in Pall Mall by Macall, a Scotsman who made up the name as a near anagram of his own; bought in 1774 by a man named Brooks and trans-ferred in 1778 to a new house by Henry Holland in St James's Street, it became known as Brooks's, and noted for its high play and aristo-cratic exclusiveness. (This Almack's should not be confused with the assembly rooms of the same name in King Street, also run by Macall, where the socially select went to dance.)

Captain Gronow wrote nostalgically in 1814, 'The members of clubs in London many years since were persons, almost without exception, belonging exclusively to the aristocratic world. Bankers and merchants had not then invaded White's, Boodle's and Brooks' . . .'. See also DIVAN CLUB, HELL-FIRE CLUBS, KIT-CAT CLUB and LITTLE BEDLAM CLUB.

Cluniacs. A reformed Benedictine order founded at Cluny, France in 910. Before the end of the twelfth century there were 32 Cluniac houses in England, with Bermondsey as the only abbey. The most com-plete remains are at Castle Acre, Norfolk and Wenlock, Shropshire. Delapré Abbey in Northamptonshire occupies the site of a Cluniac nunnery founded c. 1145, and Castle Acre Priory (1087), Norfolk is on the site of another. See also AUGUSTINIANS, BENEDICTINES, CARMELITES, CARTHUSIANS, CISTERCIANS, DOMINICANS, FRANCISCANS, FRIARS, GILBERTINES, MENDICANT FRIARS and PREMONSTRATENSIANS.

Coade stone. A composition cast stone invented in 1769, and very successfully marketed from her Lambeth factory, by Mrs Eleanor Coade; production by Coade & Sealy of London continued well into the nineteenth century. Coade is extremely durable, and many eigh-teenth- and nineteenth-century examples survive as garden ornaments, architectural decoration, on church monuments, and even as over-mantels. The formula for the stone is known and is used for repairs. True Coade stone usually has the name stamped on the base. Confus-ingly, others imitated the formula and with no stamp it is difficult to distinguish the true from the imitations. See also 'COMPOSITION'.

Cockfighting, Cocking. Cockfighting was an essentially male sport, of ancient lineage in the east and introduced into Greece in the time of Themistocles. Henry VIII (1509–47) was the first English king to build cockpits; the one at Whitehall was an elaborate octagonal building with a central lantern, and another was built at Greenwich in 1533. The opportunities it afforded for betting made the sport popular, particu-larly in the eighteenth century. Bouts were known as 'mains'. After its prohibition by Act of Parliament in 1849, the specially-built cockpits were demolished, used for other purposes, or disguised, so that the occasional illicit main could take place. As a consequence, few cockpits survive in their original state. At West Wycombe Park in Bucking-hamshire a room above an archway into the stable-yard is said to be a cockpit, but this designation may owe more to the rakish reputation of its owner Sir Francis Dashwood (1708–81), founder of the HELL-FIRE CLUB, than to fact.

Codpiece. Originated early in the fifteenth century as a modest gusset in the crotch of trunk-hose – necessary because of the fashion for short tunics – and amplified into what the *Oxford Dictionary* calls 'a bagged appendage'. It clearly appealed to the male ego, and even when tunics later lengthened it remained as an ornamental item, proudly shown off through an opening in the Tudor DOUBLET; by Henry VIII's (1509–47) reign the codpiece had become outrageously phallic, as can be seen in his full-length portrait by Holbein at the National Portrait Gallery in London. By the 1570s the codpiece was becoming smaller, and the fashion of 'Venetians', which look like bloomers, had effected its demise by 1590.

Coffee-houses. The first coffee-house, Jacob's, was set up in Oxford in 1650; two years later Jacob established himself in Holborn, and by the time of the RESTORATION (1660) there were more than 80 coffee-houses in the capital, serving coffee at a penny a dish. They provided a place for friends to meet, for the transaction of business and, most importantly, in pre-NEWSPAPER days, for the exchange of gossip and news. They also provided a venue for various clubs, whether the virtuosi who later formed the Royal Society, or men who were more interested in political debate. Political discussion of this sort clearly had its dangers, and officialdom kept a wary eye on the coffee-houses. In 1666 Clarendon favoured a proposal to close them down because of the danger (at the time of the Dutch wars) of the spreading of false news, but later took the view that this could be turned to the government's advantage; a proclamation of 1675 closing down coffee-houses was withdrawn after a few weeks. The coffee-houses prospered, and there were more than 2,000 in London in the eighteenth century. Matthew Green (1696–1737) wrote: 'Or to some coffee-house I stray,/ For news, the manna of the day,/ And from the hipp'd discourses gather/ That politics go by the weather.'

Cold baths. See PLUNGE BATHS.

Combination Acts. These, passed in 1799 and modified in 1800, were the reaction of a troubled Parliament after naval mutinies and the Irish Rebellion of 1789. The intention was to prevent the formation of TRADE UNIONS. Two or more people were forbidden to 'combine' to obtain better wages, or to press for shorter hours of work or better working conditions. These laws were repealed in 1824 and replaced in 1825 with an Amendment Act, by the terms of which combination for better wages or shorter hours was no longer an offence.

'Coming Out'. A term used of unmarried young ladies (DEBUTANTES) who were presented to the sovereign at Court at the start of their first London SEASON, and were thereby 'out' in society. See also COURT, PRESENTATION AT.

Commode. A French term, understood in eighteenth-century Britain as a highly decorative piece of drawing-room furniture with drawers, or doors concealing shelves, but since changed to that of a CHEST OF DRAWERS – which originally would only have been found in the bedroom. To further confuse us, in the nineteenth century a *chaise-percée*, or CLOSE-STOOL, came to be known by the euphemism '(night) commode', a term still used today.

Common Law. The universal law of the realm, of which the fundamental principles, based on general custom, existing from time immemorial, are embodied in precedent – the reports of judicial decisions made in previous cases. It is also described as 'unwritten law', as opposed to the 'written law' or legislation. English Common Law became the basis of law in the USA. Compare EQUITY and STATUTE LAW; also CANON LAW.

Common Pleas, Court of. The first of the three COMMON LAW courts (the others are the court of KING's – or Queen's – BENCH and Court of EXCHEQUER) to evolve as a distinct judicial body from the CURIA REGIS (King's Court), in the time of Henry II (1154–89). As part of the *Curia Regis* the court, though usually held at Westminster, still followed the king from place to place. Article 17 of MAGNA CARTA laid down that it should be held 'in some certain place', and it finally settled in Westminster Hall. From 1272 the court had its own Chief Justice, and its separation from the Curia Regis might be considered complete. Rivalry developed between the court of KING'S BENCH and that of Common Pleas, resolved in 1832 when their jurisdiction was exactly defined. By the JUDICATURE ACT of 1873 the court of Common Pleas became a division of the High Court of Justice, and in 1881 it was amalgamated with the Queen's Bench division.

Common, Rights of. The feudal rights of a tenant of a medieval manor, vested in the house or land he held. These rights were of three kinds: Common of Turbary, the right to cut turf or peat for fuel; Common of Stock, right of common of pasture, the right to graze a given number of cattle and sheep on the fallow and on recently harvested land; and Common Appurtenant, a right vested in the land held, rather than the house.

Company. In military usage, usually a sub-unit of an infantry battalion, normally comprising 100–130 men. A company is usually commanded by a major or captain, and divided into platoons.

'Composition'. A material used in the decorative arts; similar to GESSO but less likely to crack with age, it was a mixture of resin, size and whiting cast in moulds which, when set, was used for decorative detail in place of plasterwork or, on doors and fireplaces, in place of carving. First used by the ADAM brothers in the 1760s. See also COADE STONE, PAPIER-MÂCHÉ.

Congregationalists. Members of an independent NONCONFORMIST denomination which originated within the Church of England. Sometimes known as Separatists, Independantists or Brownists, in doctrine they were close to Calvinists.

Robert Browne (1550–1633) (a kinsman of Lord Burghley) founded the first separate congregation in Norwich in 1580; Browne was imprisoned and other leaders were hanged for distributing his forbid den treatises. In 1608 they emigrated to Amsterdam, but before 1620 some had returned to London, where they gave shelter to some of those noncomformists due to sail in the *Mayflower* to Virginia. Under the Commonwealth they enjoyed a period of freedom from persecution. The Act of UNIFORMITY of 1662 suspended the right of Congregationalists and other Nonconformist sects to freedom of worship; the TOLERATION ACT of 1689 ended their persecution, but like other Nonconformists they were subjected to the hazard of applying to the county JUSTICES or to the diocesan bishop or archdeacon for a licence to worship in their meeting places. Like other Nonconformists, they were also barred from holding public office until 1823. See also ANGLO-CATHOLICISM, EVANGELICALISM, CALVINISM, METHODISM, NONCONFORMISTS and PRESBYTERIANISM.

Conservatories. These developed from ORANGERIES towards the end of the seventeenth century, when it was discovered that plants other than orange trees could be protected – 'conserved' – under glass. The conservatory, with a raised and heated floor, was a more solid structure than the greenhouse or glasshouse, which had developed from the cold-frame; the greenhouse was used for forcing and protecting, while the conservatory was a structure for enjoyment, and usually attached to the house. John Evelyn (1620–1706) is credited with being the first to use 'conservatory' to describe a place where tender plants were kept in winter.

By the mid nineteenth century the conservatory had evolved into the winter garden, a much larger glass building. The Victorians, who were above all technicians, enjoyed the escapism of sitting in a subtropical environment surrounded by exotic plants while rain or snow fell outside.

Often the conservatory was called 'the Stove'. The Great Stove at Chatsworth was designed by Joseph Paxton and opened in 1839, an enormous structure built to contain a complete tropical garden, and served by a railway line to carry the coal required for heating it. This exotic extravagance ended when fuel became scarce in the First World War. The Great Stove was – rather eccentrically – blown up in 1920. Somerleyton Hall in Suffolk had a winter garden (built *c.* 1855) 125 feet long by 90 feet wide, which was also demolished when it became too costly to heat. The winter garden at Halton House, Buckinghamshire, built for Sir Lionel (later 1st Baron) Rothschild in 1855, was roofed with two large and nine small domes, and had an adjoining skating rink. Some of the smaller nineteenth-century conservatories survive; an Italianate one at Flintham Hall, Nottinghamshire (1851); a Classical conservatory with a dome at Syon Park, Greater London (1827); another Classical structure at Broughton Hall, North Yorkshire (completed in 1853). Then, of course, there is the astonishing Palm House at Kew Gardens, Greater London, built in 1848.

Conservation walls. See HOT WALLS.

Consols. Short for 'Consolidated Annuities', also known as 'the 3 per cents', which were government securities created by an Act of Parliament of 1786 which consolidated certain perpetual and lottery annuities carrying interest at 3 per cent per annum. Before the days of the stock market, Consols were one of the few available investments, apart from land; they could be bought and sold, but not redeemed.

Constable. Derived from the Latin for Master of the Horse, and originally the chief military officer of the royal household, a usage surviving today in such offices as Constable of the Tower of London. A Lord High Constable is appointed by the sovereign for Coronation Day only. The ancient parish office of Petty Constable (with responsibilities for maintaining law and order traceable to the Statute of Winchester, 1285) survived until the growth of the POLICE force in the nineteenth century; various alterations to their provision were enacted between 1839 and 1869 as the county police force was developed, although the Parish Constables Act of 1872 enabled vestries to appoint paid constables under the Chief Constable of the County.

Contraception. See BIRTH CONTROL.

Co-operative movement. Robert Owen (1771–1858) is regarded as the inspiration behind the idea of selling goods without profit to members, or with profit distributed annually among members as dividends, but the first successful co-operative was the Rochdale Pioneers' Equitable Society, founded in 1844. The Industrial and Provident Societies Act of 1852 established a legal basis for the co-operative movement, and it grew rapidly; the Co-operative Wholesale Society (the CWS) was established in 1863, the Scottish CWS in 1868. Members' banking, national trading, and manufacturing was funnelled through the CWS and SCWS. The Co-operative Party, founded in 1917, was closely allied to the Labour Party.

By the 1960s the CWS was the largest co-operative organization in the world, owned and controlled by 850 societies with sales of more than £1,000m. The CWS has, however, found it difficult to meet the fierce competition from efficient nationwide retailers such as Sainsbury,

Tesco and Marks & Spencer, and is now a shadow of what it was thirty years ago.

Copyhold. An ancient form of land tenure, legally defined as a 'holding at the will of the lord according to the custom of the manor', and so called because the tenant had no deed of transfer in his possession, merely a copy of the record of his holding taken from the manorial court-roll; distinct from FREEHOLD, and originally held in return for agricultural service, but by Tudor times in return for payment of rent in money. In law the tenure could not be transferred, only given up to the lord, but in practice, by payment of the customary fines or dues, son could succeed father. At the death of a tenant the lord was entitled to the HERIOT. The Reform Act of 1832 gave £10 copyholders (those with land worth £10 annually) the vote, and the Second Reform Act of 1867 extended the franchise to £5 copyholders. Copyholders were permitted to change their tenure to that of freeholder by an Act of 1841. The tenure was abolished in 1926. See also FRANCHISE and VILLEIN.

Corn dollies. The last sheaf of a wheat harvest was considered to embody the spirit of the harvest, and after being cut was plaited into a 'kern baby' or corn dolly (usually female), decorated with ribbons, which was carried back to the farmhouse in triumph to preside over the harvest supper. See also HARVEST CUSTOMS.

Cornet. The fifth, and lowest, commissioned rank in a cavalry troop, who carried the troop's colours. The rank, abolished in 1871, was equivalent to an ENSIGN in the infantry.

Corn Laws. Regulations governing the import and export of wheat are found as early as 1177 (prohibitions on export without licence); in most normal years some English corn was exported, but in 1463 imports from abroad were prohibited except when the home price exceeded 6s. 8d. a quarter. Through the centuries which followed, the general aim was to balance the interests of consumers, requiring a regular supply of grain at low prices, and producers, who were anxious to secure a market and a fair price in good as well as bad years.

During the twenty years of the Napoleonic wars crisis succeeded crisis and Napoleon's blockade prevented the import of foreign grain; a succession of bad harvests between 1806 and 1813, followed by a bumper harvest in 1815 and the cessation of war, led to the Corn Law of 1815, which was designed to maintain the price of grain in peacetime at 80 shillings a quarter. It proved unworkable, provoking a sense of injustice, and between 1815 and 1822 the price of corn fluctuated wildly. Prices were falling generally but bread, the staple diet of the poor, was more expensive than it need have been. The Anti-Corn Law League, formed in 1839, was promoted by wealthy manufacturers who saw that repeal would ease not only industrial depression but the burden on the poor of the high cost of living. Influenced by these arguments and, decisively, by bad harvests in 1845 and the Irish potato famine, Sir Robert Peel ended the Corn Laws in 1846. From 1849 all duties on corn ceased, except for a nominal duty of 1s. per quarter, which was abolished in 1869.

Coromandel screens. Folding screens made of Chinese lacquer panels, being 8ft or more in height and having 12 leaves. They were fashionable in the seventeenth century and the early years of the eighteenth. The name is taken from the Coromandel coast (the eastern coast of India), from where they were transhipped to Europe.

Coroner. An ancient office first referred to in the Articles of Eyre (1194; but probably instituted earlier in the century), when for each county four Keepers of the Pleas for the Crown were appointed in place of the king's serjeants of Wapentake. Three keepers were knights (later, the holding of land to the value of £70 per annum – the qualification for a knight – was deemed sufficient) and one a clerk; sitting in the shire court they heard the first stage of criminal cases, civil cases, appeals of felony and abjurations of the realm, and also held inquests on sudden deaths by violent or unnatural means or from unknown causes. Their findings were recorded and passed on to the next judicial eyre (circuit) for the cases to be tried. Coroners were elected by the KNIGHTS OF THE SHIRE, later by the freeholders of the county assembled in the county court, and the office was unpaid. Under the progressive rationalization of criminal justice the importance of the coroner declined, until today his duties consist solely of holding inquests. Coroners are required to be solicitors, barristers or qualified medical practitioners with not less than five years' experience in their profession; often they have both a legal and a medical qualification. In Scotland, the duties of the coroner are performed by the Procurator Fiscal. See also EYRE, JUSTICES IN.

Cotton. Cotton fabric was introduced to Britain in the late seventeenth century when the East India Company flooded the country with Indian textiles. A century later the Lancashire cotton industry had established itself, supplying a huge domestic market. Cotton, by itself or mixed with other fibres, replaced linen for sheets and shirts, was used to imitate silk for dresses, and replaced it as yarn for hosiery; it also replaced leather for hardwearing working breeches, and was used in place of wool for furnishing fabrics. It had the advantage of being washable, at a time when fabrics such as silks and woollens were not easily cleaned; above all, cotton goods were cheap.

Improvements in textile printing enabled manufacturers of dress fabrics to keep up with rapid changes in taste; cotton proved ideal for the flowing styles of the late eighteenth century, and cheap copies of

High Society's latest fashions found their way to the lower end of the market. Cotton came to form a conspicuous part of the wardrobes of the families, not only of the middle classes but, in London particularly, of labourers and artisans too. See also HOSE.

Couple, A. This is a term which came into use after the Second World War to refer to a married couple 'in service', living in. They might perform the tasks of cook/HOUSEKEEPER and BUTLER, or perhaps gardener/chauffeur and cook.

Court. When found as part of a house name, the word 'Court' may have historical significance, indicating that the manor court or 'COURT-BARON' was held there from late medieval times; in a house of later date, in the eighteenth century, it may indicate that the owner was a justice of the peace who held the justices' court in his own justice (or court) room. In the nineteenth century, the name was sometimes bestowed with no historical justification, to make property sound grander. Arlington Court in Devon and Grey's Court in Oxfordshire are examples where the usage has a genuine historical basis.

Court-baron. An English manorial court dating from the middle ages, originally an assembly of the freehold tenants of a manor under the lord or his steward to administer the custom of the manor; by the sixteenth century the court-baron was also dealing with the fees or dues payable by new tenants who acquired COPYHOLDS by inheritance or purchase, as well as manorial agriculture, lord's tenants' rights and duties, and disputes between tenants and changes of occupancy. The court met at intervals laid down by the custom of the manor. See also COURT-LEET and MANOR.

Court Circular. A report of royal activities, issued formerly by the Court Newsman, now by the Press Office at Buckingham Palace, published daily in NEWSPAPERS; a custom instituted by George III (1760–1820) in 1803 to prevent misstatements on such subjects.

Court-leet. Originally an English petty criminal court for the punishment of minor offences concerned with View of FRANKPLEDGE, and with matters such as policing disturbances of the peace and maintenance of the lock-up, and with the appointment of officers. See also COURT-BARON and MANOR.

Court, Presentation at. To be presented at court a young lady (DEBUTANTE) needed a sponsor, an older woman who had been presented in her turn, usually her mother or grandmother, but sometimes an aunt or a godmother or other family connection.

Presentation took place early in the SEASON at two afternoon sessions in May and June at a Royal Drawing Room: the debutante made a deep court curtsy before kissing the hand of the sovereign. For her presentation she wore a white dress with a court train (not necessarily white) trailing from the shoulders and eighteen inches along the ground, with three ostrich feathers (the Prince of Wales's feathers) in her hair and a tulle veil.

Cynthia Charteris, daughter of the Earl of Wemyss, remembers that 'The metamorphosis called Coming Out was supposed to be effected when you were presented at Court, where the wand was officially waved over your head. The picturesque rites of this social baptism were preceded by weeks of trepidation – weeks busied with long lessons in deportment . . . and panic stricken rehearsals of my curtsey . . .'. A debutante might also be presented at a royal garden-party. Women were also presented on the occasion of their marriage, and again if their husband succeeded to a higher title; on such occasions a tiara was worn as well as the feathers. Presentation gave the entrée, by invitation, to a number of royal occasions or venues, such as the royal enclosure at Ascot. Divorcees could not be presented. Court presentations ended in 1958.

Coverpanes. Strips of embroidered linen used to cover a bed. Not to be confused with counterpanes, which were quilts.

Cravat. The name given by the French in the reign of Louis XIV to the scarf worn by the Croatian soldiers of the Royal Croatian regiment, a corruption of 'Croat'; introduced to Britain from France with the return of Charles II from exile in 1660. It was usually of lace or linen or muslin with broad edges of lace, and tied round the neck, the ends falling beneath the chin; it was not long before a decorative knot became fashionable. There is a carved limewood example by Grinling GIBBONS at Chatsworth, Derbyshire.

The predecessor of the cravat was the rabat or falling collar which succeeded the RUFF; it was of decorative lace, hanging down in two points in the front, but went out of fashion when the full-bottomed WIG (which hid the collar) came in. By the end of the seventeenth century the cravat had become longer and narrower. A notable fashion arose after the battle of Steinkerk in 1692, when it was said that the French officers, taken by surprise and dressing in haste, had no time to tie their cravats but turned out with the ends twisted together ropewise and drawn through a button-hole or ring. The fashion for the Steenkirk or Steinkerk, worn by both men and women, spread widely and lasted in Britain until the 1730s. Around 1735 the lacy cravat was replaced by the stock, a straight piece of linen folded round the neck and pinned or buckled at the back, with no falling ends; by this time, shirt fronts were bordered with frilled lace, giving the effect of a cravat. From the 1760s the stock became higher and was uncomfortably stiffened. From c 1780 the cravat itself returned in a new form: a length of muslin wound two or three times round the neck and knotted to the front. From 1800 shirt collars were high and the cravat was wound round the neck outside the shirt collar, leaving the starched collar points standing up at the sides of the face. The cravat continued rising higher through to the 1840s, when it was tied with a large bow in front of a high pointed collar, rather like a scarf. During the 1850s the cravat became narrower, eventually becoming the bow-tie in the 1860s, and worn with a winged collar in the 1870s. By the 1890s the tie as we know it today was being worn.

Crest. Originally, a heraldic device worn on top of a helmet to identify the armoured wearer. The crest is also shown in some achievements of family arms. The earliest known example of an heraldic crest is one of 1198. Crests were worn at the Tudor court tournaments, again to identify the wearer. Most new grants of arms in the seventeenth century had crests, and by the eighteenth century the practice was universal for new arms. However, today, many older grants of arms still have no crests. See also HERALDRY.

Cricket. A game of Saxon origin, called *creag* and played with a bent wooden bat. The first recorded organized game was in 1711, when Kent played All England. The Hambledon Club in Hampshire (1750) was the first organized club, and the cradle of the modern game. The Hambledon was disbanded in 1791 and the Marylebone (1787) took the lead, from its grounds in Dorset Square, London; by 1814 it had moved to St John's Wood, to grounds belonging to Thomas Lord, hence Lord's. The first 'Gentlemen versus Players' match took place at Mr Lord's ground in 1806, the last in 1962. In the nineteenth and early twentieth centuries it was a popular country-house pastime to put together a scratch team to play against a village or other country house team.

Criminal Law. The law applied to the definition, trial and punishment of crimes. Its object is to preserve public order, whereas that of Civil Law is to address private wrongs. A crime is an act or omission forbidden by the law of the state under pain of punishment. Before the Norman Conquest law enforcement was rudimentary, carried out locally through the shire court. In the main, punishment was by fine, except for the capital offences of arson, murder, rape and treason. From the time of the Norman Conquest the notion of the King's (or Queen's) Peace extended progressively throughout the kingdom, and today crimes are prosecuted in the name of the Crown because they are regarded as violations of the royal peace. By the late eighteenth century it came to be seen that the punishments for many offences were unjust. For example, CAPITAL PUNISHMENT extended to some 200 offences, many of them trivial; as a result, witnesses were reluctant to give evidence, and juries to convict. The law was clearly in need of rationalization. Campaigns for reform by Sir Samuel Romilly (1757–1818), Jeremy Bentham (1748–1832), and Sir James Mackintosh (1765–1832) led to the setting up of a Commons Committee of Inquiry in 1819 which, under Sir Robert Peel (1788–1850) as Home Secretary, resulted in a series of Acts in 1832, 1826–7 and 1828–30, by which legal procedure was simplified and many obsolete offences were abolished. It was the first revision of a huge backlog of legislation reaching back to Henry III (1216–72).

Crinkum-crankum, or **crinkle-crankle, wall.** A form of wall for growing fruit against, probably first devised in the eighteenth century in Scotland. It is built in a serpentine form, usually on a north/south axis, thus providing areas of warm wall (on the south-facing façades) which would not otherwise be available on a straight wall in a similar position. In addition, the curving surfaces act as buttresses, creating a structure so strong that when built of brick it need only be one brick (4½ in) thick instead of the 9 in of a standard, double thickness wall. Crinkum-crankum walls are found in the kitchen gardens of houses in the Scottish Lowlands, and in England in the eastern counties; a good example is at Heveningham Hall, Suffolk. Thomas Jefferson (1743–1826), third President of the United States (1801–1809), saw such walls in Suffolk in 1786; while he had no great opinion of British architecture, as an enthusiast himself he praised the gardens, and used serpentine walls when he came to plan the buildings for the University of Virginia at Charlottesville (1817), to which he devoted his last years. See also KITCHEN GARDENS and HOT WALLS.

Crinoline. A stiffening material made of horsehair (French, *crin*) and linen or cotton thread. Skirts were originally made to stand out from the body by means of hoops (see FARTHINGALE), numerous petticoats, and pads of horsehair. From the use of crinoline material for petticoats, the name became transferred about the middle of the nineteenth century to the hoop-petticoat made of whalebone and steel. See also BUSTLE and PANNIER.

Crofts and crofters. Crofts have been called 'small parcels of land surrounded by legislation', and this is no exaggeration. A croft (in old English, an enclosed field) is not the building in which a Scottish crofter lives, but the land which he occupies as a tenant (customarily about 10 acres) and a share in a large area of common pasture for grazing, in the former counties of Argyll, Caithness, Inverness, Orkney, Ross and Cromarty, Shetland and Sutherland. The first Crofters' Holdings (Scotland) Act, 1886, was an attempt to redress some of the wrongs arising from the Highland Clearances in giving security of tenure to crofters and ensuring fair rents. The most recent Act (1993) consolidated all previous acts. At present it is profitable for a crofter to continue as a tenant, since he is then eligible for generous grants from the Crofters' Commission. From the landlord's point of view, crofts are often an expensive burden, as the fixed rents are so low (at Tote in Skye they were last set in 1908) that they do not cover the cost of overheads such as maintaining fencing.

Croquet. Derived from the French *croc*, a crooked stick, croquet is a very subtle and often vicious game played on a level lawn with coloured balls, hoops, wooden mallets, and two pegs. The home team always has the advantage of knowing where the bumps and valleys lie on their 'level' lawn. The game is descended from Pell Mell, or Pall Mall (from the French *paille-maille*, played in Languedoc at least as early as the thirteenth century), a game played in Pall Mall, in London, and in the Mall at Musselborough in Scotland, which became fashionable after the RESTORATION. On 16 September 1660 Samuel Pepys went to St James's Park to see 'how far they have proceeded with the pellmell', the new Mall or alley for the game; this had been completed by 2 April 1661, when Pepys saw the Duke of York 'playing at *Peslemesle* – the first time that I ever saw that sport.' The earliest English rule book for Pell Mell is dated 1717. Whatever its history, the modern game of croquet was devised in Ireland in 1852 and became popular in Britain before 1860. It was the first outdoor game in which women could compete with men on equal terms, and they took to it with enthusiasm. The All-England Croquet Club was formed in 1868 at Wimbledon, and by 1874 a women's national championship was held there; the Croquet Association (1897) is now based at Hurlingham. The rage for croquet had considerable influence on loosening the constrictions of women's dress in the 1870s.

Cross-bow. An ancient missile-shooting weapon consisting of a bow fixed at right angles in a (usually wooden) stock. The stock has a groove to guide the bolt or missile, a notch to hold the string of the bow when drawn, and a trigger to release it. The earliest cross-bows have been found in China. The arbalest was a particular type of cross-bow which usually fired quarrels or square-headed bolts, and was so stiff that a mechanical contrivance was required to bend it. Cavalry cross-bows were lighter than those used by the infantry. Cross-bows were also widely used against small game from the beginning of the sixteenth century. See also ARCHERY.

Crossword. A word puzzle based on a grid pattern for which clues are provided. The first crossword-type puzzles, of a very elementary kind, were printed in England in the late nineteenth century in various periodicals and in books of general puzzles for the nursery. It was in the USA that crosswords became an adult pastime: the *New York World* began publishing them in their Sunday supplement in 1913, and by

1923 they were published by most popular newspapers, and returned to take England by storm.

Crown, Royal. The practice of the monarch wearing a crown in public was introduced by William I (1066–87). On the three great feast days of the year, at Gloucester for Christmas, Winchester for Easter and Whitehall for Whitsun, William, if in England, wore his crown. All the great magnates of the realm were at these state events, enabling the king to keep in touch with his barons, and simplify the holding of great councils. The practice continued as late as the reign of Henry III (1216–72) by which time the divine institution of monarchy was displayed by solemn ritual. See also DIVINE RIGHT OF KINGS.

Crusades. A series of campaigns undertaken against Islam by the Christian countries of western Europe between 1096 and 1291 for the recovery, specifically, of the Holy City of Jerusalem from the Saracens (Mohammedans), to whom it had fallen in 637. Early Islam tolerated the presence of the Latin Church in Jerusalem, and pilgrimages there continued. However, the fanaticism of the Caliph Hakim caused the destruction of the Church of the Holy Sepulchre (1010); the patronage of the Holy Places – a source of strife between the Greek and Latin Churches down to the time of the Crimean War – passed to Byzantium (1021); the differences between the Churches of East and West culminated in schism in 1054; and in 1071 the Seljuk Turks not only annihilated the Byzantine army at the battle of Manzikert, but captured Jerusalem from the Fatimids of Egypt: the Holy Land had become a troubled and unquiet region. The early impulse for the Crusades was thus compounded of a desire to ease the lot of the native Christians and pilgrims (this at a time of an upsurge of religious enthusiasm, when more pilgrims than ever were thronging to the East), free the Christians of the eastern Churches and the Holy Places from Turkish oppression (the Turks were less tolerant than the Arabs, and the Pope had received appeals for help from Byzantium) and, in so doing, reunite the Latin and Greek churches.

The First Crusade (1095–99) under Robert, Duke of Normandy, recaptured Jerusalem, in 1099. The Second Crusade (1147–48) achieved nothing. The loss of Jerusalem in 1187 inspired the Third Crusade (1189–92), led among others by Richard I (1189–99) of England, who captured Acre (1191) and was within twelve miles of Jerusalem when supplies ran out and he was forced to make peace with Saladin. Returning home, he was taken prisoner and ransomed by the Emperor Henry VI (1169–97). Subsequent Crusades achieved nothing in the Holy Land. The military orders of Knights HOSPITALLARS and Knights TEMPLARS were formed to protect pilgrims in the Holy Land and fight for Jerusalem.

The Fourth Crusade was diverted to Constantinople, ending in its sacking in 1204 and in the partition of the Eastern Empire, of which Venetian trade was probably the major beneficiary. Jerusalem was briefly in Christian hands again, 1229–1239 and 1243–4; but inevitably the last remnants of 'Outremer' fell to the Muslims – Tripoli in 1289 and Acre in 1291.

Although they failed in their objective of regaining the Holy Land for Christendom, the Crusades nevertheless benefited Europe in a number of ways. Trade between Europe and Asia Minor was stimulated and the maritime states of Venice and Genoa profited from the demand for shipping to transport pilgrims and soldiers, who brought back with them eastern goods and ideas. SPICES came west, and there was a rapid increase in the very profitable spice trade; herbs growing in the eastern Mediterranean were introduced to Western Europe, as was rice; the Islamic ideal of the water-garden as Paradise was introduced; CASTLE design was perfected; but perhaps the most significant influences were those of Arabic learning – many important works in Classical Greek came to the west first, or are now only known, by way of Arabic translations.

Cubbing. September hunting of young foxes to train inexperienced hounds and riders before the FOX-HUNTING season begins.

Cucking-stool. A chair, sometimes in the form of a CLOSE-STOOL, into which a female scold or disorderly woman was fastened, then exposed to the jeers of bystanders or ducked in a pond or river. Long since corrupted to ducking-stool.

Culloden, Battle of (16 April 1746). The final battle of the second and last JACOBITE rebellion, 'The Forty-five'. The pretender to the throne, Prince Charles Edward Stuart (Bonnie Prince Charlie; the Young Pretender), was defeated by an English army commanded by the Duke of Cumberland, William Augustus, at Culloden Moor near Inverness in Scotland. After only forty minutes the Highlanders, surrounded, broke and fled, leaving 1,000 dead of their 5,000-strong army; 1,000 more died in the subsequent pursuit. Cumberland lost only 50 out of 9,000, with 200 wounded – the defeat was decisive. Culloden was the last land battle to be fought in Britain.

Cupboards. Originally, literally cup–board; that is, a board or shelf for the display of silver cups and other plate. Cupboards were at first simply tables which, over time, acquired extra shelves and stages to display larger quantities of plate, similar to the medieval Burgundian BUFFET. In evolving, the lower sections came to be enclosed by a door, and so the term cupboard gained its modern meaning. This type of medieval furniture was usually found in the HALL, where the grand company dined, but might also be found in the GREAT CHAMBER.

Curate. An ordained clergyman acting as assistant to a parish priest or other beneficed clergyman, but not yet beneficed himself – and therefore likely to be poor. A character in many eighteenth- and nineteenth-century novels.

Curia Regis. Literally, the King's Court. Under the Norman and Angevin kings in particular, monarchy was personal; the general system of government was based on the king and his household, and this included the administration of justice. The *Curia Regis* dealt with matters affecting the king's person or lands, and was the court of appeal for those who failed to obtain justice in a lower court; it also dealt with matters affecting the King's Peace. It was the *king's* court – Henry II (1154–89) was said to be particularly just in his judgments, and rolls survive of pleas heard before King John (1199–1216). The *Curia Regis* met three times a year, at Easter, Pentecost and Christmas, and was the foremost executive and legislative body in the kingdom. Under an ever-increasing burden of work, the administration of justice gradually became more decentralized in the twelfth and thirteenth centuries; courts such as the COURT OF COMMON PLEAS, KING'S BENCH and EXCHEQUER were established. The surviving records of the *Curia Regis* run from 1194 to 1272, by which time its work had passed to the newly-created courts and it ceased to exist.

Curricle. A fast, light, open, two-wheeled carriage drawn by two horses abreast, fashionable from the mid eighteenth century. See also CARRIAGES.

Curtains, window. Although curtains later became highly decorative they were originally hung to keep out draughts and insulate rooms; they were uncommon until the late seventeenth century. In late medieval times, single draw curtains might serve to keep out the multiple draughts that penetrated the diamond-shaped glass panes; at Whitehall in 1532 a long pole was made for big curtains for a large window; at Greenwich in the 1530s there were satin curtains in black, purple and white; and Thomas Cranmer's portrait by Gerlach Flicke (now in the National Portrait Gallery, London) shows window curtains. In 1601 Hardwick Hall, Derbyshire had very few curtains: the bedchamber of the Countess of Shrewsbury herself, with two windows, had only two red curtains, clearly utilitarian more than decorative. Paired curtains of light material were fitted to keep out the sunlight at Ham House, Surrey in 1640, but such symmetrical arrangements were uncommon before 1670, and many windows had no curtains at all.

By 1720 it was usual for important rooms to be fitted with curtains. Paired curtains were still popular, but the pull-up festoon curtain was considered smarter; these required pelmets, which could be highly decorative. Festoon curtains used considerably more material than draw curtains, and needed five pulleys each to operate them. These pulleys were often left in place when fashions changed, and can still be seen under the pelmet boards of some houses. Where houses of this period have decorative shutter panels, made to be seen, it is likely that festoon curtains were fitted; plain panels would be hidden by draw curtains. Festoon curtains permitted different drawing-up treatments: they could be drawn partly up, as a single curtain or divided, or they could be drawn up in the centre, with side tails of decorative swags, a style known as *à l'italienne*. The curtain had become a decorative feature.

By 1770 the popularity of festoon curtains had waned, and simple paired curtains returned to favour, often without pelmets; the rods and hooks had to be presentable, and by 1820 were often boldly treated, with elaborate brackets and fancy finials. An alternative scheme at this time was a festoon pelmet above a roller blind. After 1808 society turned to the French Empire style, in Britain known as 'Regency', and the upholsterer came into his own with pelmets made up of swags, drapes, tassels and fringes. Although these window treatments look complicated they invariably consisted of only two fabrics, a lightweight outer one to keep out the light and a heavy inner one for insulation. The most difficult window of all to design working curtains for was – and is – the three-light Venetian, a problem never satisfactorily solved, and encountered anew with the pointed windows of the GOTHIC REVIVAL.

The mid nineteenth-century taste for opulence and velvet caused rooms to become dark, draped wombs, considered 'cosy'. The simpler taste of the later ARTS AND CRAFTS influence brought in another revival of the paired draw curtain, and this remained the standard until the 1980s, which saw an outburst of festoon curtains, even in small cottage windows for which they were never intended.

Cusp. From the Latin *cuspis*, meaning point or apex; the projecting point formed by the intersection of two curves, in the foliations to be found in GOTHIC tracery, panels, arches, etc. Cusps became widespread during the latter part of the EARLY ENGLISH period; initially they sprang from the flat under-surface of an arch, with little decorative detail, but soon came to carry a continuation of the decoration of the arch, and in the later DECORATED period are to be found finished at the point with a trefoil, a leaf or a flower, sometimes even a human head. Some particularly rich examples may be seen at Lincoln Cathedral, begun in 1192.

Dalmatic. A liturgical vestment of the Western Church, proper to deacons and bishops; originally a tunic, now in most countries a scapular-like cloak with an opening for the head and square lappets falling from the shoulder over the upper part of the arm – in Italy, open up the side but retaining sleeves. It is worn at Mass, also at solemn processions and Benediction, except in the penitential season. 'May He cover thee with the dalmatic of righteousness for ever' is the bishop's prayer at the ordination of deacons. A silk dalmatic is also one of the undermost garments of the British coronation robes, and with the other robes symbolizes the quasi-religious character of the Crown.

Dame. The legal title of the wife or widow of a knight or baronet ('Lady' in customary usage); also, the feminine equivalent of a knight of an Order of Chivalry. Dames (Grand Cross, or Commander) are appointed to the Order of St Michael and St George, the Royal Victorian Order and the Order of the British Empire. In the past, 'Dame' was used in courtesy to any elderly lady – as it still is in pantomimes. See also HONOURS and KNIGHTHOOD.

Dame-school. In the nineteenth century and earlier, a private school giving primary education, run by a lady. These schools filled a need only partly answered by Forster's Education Act of 1870 (making elementary education available to all children between the ages of 5 and 11), which resulted in the setting up of Board Schools in every city. MUNDELLA'S ACT of 1880 (making elementary education compulsory for all children) ended the need for dame-schools.

Dances. Unlike most other fashions, dances tend to rise through the social scale. In its earliest form, dancing was an expression of strong emotion, channelled by priests into religious ceremonies: all primitive civilizations have danced. In Britain, the Egg dance and the Carole were Saxon dances, the Carole a Yule-tide festivity of which the present-day Christmas carol is a remnant. Many country dances survived until the nineteenth century; among the oldest is the MORRIS dance, thought to be derived from the Spanish *morisco*, similar to a fandango, and popular in Europe in early medieval times; it came to England in the reign of Edward III (1327–77) and is usually performed by six men, one of whom may wear girl's clothing. The national dances of Scotland are reels, strathspeys and flings; the Irish have the jig in many varieties and shades of emotion; the Welsh, though so musical, seem to have developed no national dance.

Many dances involved the participants forming up in two lines, one each of men and women, with the top nearest the band; the head couple, or quartet, would 'lead off', perform their dance and then leave the lines for the next couple or quartet. The standing about awaiting one's turn gave an opportunity for conversation and flirtation.

Court dancing – fashionable dancing – was based on country dances, which might be from *any* European country, polished, perfected and sophisticated, usually by the French. The *danse basse* was solemn and dignified; the more lively *gaillard* was introduced from Italy by

Catherine de'Medici. The stately *pavane* was Spanish in origin, more of a procession than a dance, and must have been a splendid sight, well-suited to the stiff brocades of the ladies and the swords and heavily-plumed hats of the gentlemen. Even in the pavane, kissing formed an important part, no doubt explaining the popularity of dancing. The *minuet* was originally a country dance from Poitou which came to Paris in 1650 and was set to music by Giovanni Lully (1632–1687), becoming grave and dignified rather than gay and lively. The *gavotte*, often danced after the minuet, was another country dance which became stiff and artificial when taken up by society. By the early nineteenth century dances always began with the *quadrille*. This is a dance of some antiquity, in fact, first brought to England by William the Conqueror, and was common in Europe in the sixteenth and seventeenth centuries; the steps are very elaborate, and when well danced it could be as graceful as the minuet – but often wasn't.

All these dances were formal executions of figures, so it is easy to appreciate what a sensation the *waltz* caused. Lord Byron (1788–1824) referred to it as the 'Seductive Waltz' and 'voluptuous Waltz'. It was thought indecent by the staid and the older generation, and young ladies had to secure the permission of one of the patronesses before dancing it at Almack's, where it achieved popularity when Tsar Alexander of Russia danced it there in 1816, after Waterloo. The waltz in the form it came to England in 1812 was Bavarian (*waltzen* – to revolve), but its origins go much further back, to an ancient Provençal dance, the *Lavolta*, in which the Valois courts of the sixteenth century delighted.

Each century seems to have a dance that typifies it, the gaillard of the sixteenth century and the minuet of the eighteenth, for example. Other fashionable dances of the eighteenth and nineteenth centuries were the *ländler*, popular in Vienna in the 1770s, which came to London in 1791; the *polka*, a Bohemian national dance adopted by society in Prague in 1835, and in Paris in 1840, whence it spread like an infection; the *Lancers* came to England from Paris in 1850. Twentieth-century dances are too many to list, but shortly before the First World War ballroom dancing became more lively, leading to a burst of popular and energetic dances in the 1920s – of which the *Charleston* is probably the most famous. The *fox-trot*, and its variations, the *turkey-trot*, the *bunny-hug* and the *slow fox-trot*, were popular in the 1930s, as was the *tango* from South America, and the *rumba* from Cuba. Various dances originated in North America, based on Negro originals, watered down for European taste.

Dandyism. The Dandy (a late eighteenth-century term for a man unduly devoted to the smartness and fit of his clothes) was epitomised by Beau BRUMMELL (1778–1840). A snug fit was the essence of Dandyism, but it also extended to the elaboration of neckwear. There is a story of a morning visitor to Brummell finding him standing in a large pile of discarded CRAVATS. When asked what they were, the valet replied, 'Sir, those are our Failures'. The stiffness of the cravat or neckcloth made it difficult for the Dandy to lower or turn his head, thus adding to his imperturbable air. High-crowned top hats, with the crown top wider than the brim, were worn at all times of the day, but Brummell disapproved of the excesses of some of those who aped him, with their corsets worn to narrow the waist, and padded shoulders. By the 1820s trousers were universal for Dandies. See also MACARONIS.

Danelaw. The term was first used in King Cnut's (1017–35) time, in reference to the northern and eastern areas of England which had been settled by the Danes in the ninth and tenth centuries and in which Danish customary law subsequently prevailed, as opposed to the Mercian or Saxon customary law of the rest of the country. The Danelaw as recognized by Cnut lasted less than fifty years, but left its mark particularly in Yorkshire, where the division of land was into OXGANGS rather than hides, and the Scandinavian *wapentake* replaced the Anglo-Saxon hundred.

Darnix, darnick. A fabric, of the late fifteenth/early sixteenth centuries, probably of wool and linen, sometimes worked with silk patterns, used as cheap tapestry, for wall-hangings, etc; the patterns, therefore, must usually have stood out. The name, from Doornick, the Flemish name for Tournai, was given to materials made there.

Darwin, Charles Robert (1809–82). From observations made off the coast of South America during the famous voyage of the *Beagle* (1831–6), Darwin formulated his theory of evolution by natural selection – the survival of the fittest. Published in *On the Origin of Species* (1859), it provoked a furious reaction from those who took the Bible and the story of the Creation as the literal word of God. The following year a historic debate took place at Oxford between Thomas Huxley (1825–95), supporting Darwin, and Bishop Wilberforce (1807–73), on whether man descended from 'Apes or Angels'. Darwin's *The Descent of Man* (1871) added further fuel to the debate.

Davenport. Small, narrow writing desk with a sloping top covering a fitted well, and cupboards or drawers opening on the right-hand side of the pedestal. First made *c.* 1790 for a Captain Davenport, by GILLOW of Lancashire. Most are nineteenth-century in date.

Death duty. Estate duty, inheritance tax. The HERIOT (a fee paid to the lord of the manor at the death of a tenant) was an early form of estate duty; in a more familiar form, death duties were first introduced in 1889 by the Chancellor of the Exchequer, George Goschen, 1st Viscount Goschen (1831–1907), as Estate Duty, a tax paid on the capital value of assets owned by a person at his or her death, which was superseded by Sir William Harcourt's Death Duty in the Finance Act of 1894. The highest rate levied then was eight per cent, on very large estates of £1m or more, which was not onerous and could be met out of income or by insurance, or avoided by passing the estate to an heir before the death of the owner.

Death duties gradually increased, and did enormous harm to many estates in the First World War, when they became payable several times in succession as one heir after another was killed in action (in the Second World War the tax was not payable upon death in action). By 1919 the duty was a punishing forty per cent on an estate of £2 million. 'The old order is doomed,' wrote the Duke of Marlborough of the time. The scope of the tax was extended by succeeding Chancellors, but it was not difficult to avoid payment by taking advantage of the many loopholes. Death duties (estate duties, inheritance tax) were largely replaced in 1975 by Capital Transfer Tax payable on gifts made in a person's lifetime, as well as at death. See also TAXATION.

Debutantes. Young ladies 'coming out', or making their social début. The term was applied to those who had been presented at Court; their first London SEASON following presentation was a round of balls and other social events. See also 'COMING OUT' and COURT, PRESENTATION AT.

Decorated Period. A quite arbitrary although graphic description applied to the second period of English GOTHIC architecture, c. 1290–1350; derived from the type of window tracery used during that period. The classifications, devised by Thomas Rickman (1776–1841) c. 1811, are still used today. See also EARLY ENGLISH STYLE, GOTHIC ARCHITECTURE and PERPENDICULAR STYLE.

Demesne. A part of the manor kept in hand by the lord for his own use, not granted out in freehold tenancy; the equivalent of what came to be called the HOME FARM.

Democracy. In Abraham Lincoln's words, 'Government of the people, by the people, for the people'; a system of government based upon self-rule; in modern times, upon freely elected representative institutions and an executive accountable to the people, and embracing also freedom of speech and of the press. Until well into the nineteenth century, a term which for many signified mob-rule. Thomas Hobbes (1588–1679) wrote: 'They that are discontented under monarchy, call it tyranny, . . . and displeased with aristocracy, call it oligarchy, . . . and finding themselves grieved under democracy, call it anarchy.'

Dessert. Originally, the last course of a medieval dinner, dating from the ceremony of the 'void', when guests stood and drank spiced sweet wine while the table with all its dinner debris and the GREAT HALL or GREAT CHAMBER in which it had been served were cleared or 'voided' and the room prepared for after-dinner activities. In the sixteenth and early seventeenth centuries this course, supplemented by fruit and spiced delicacies, was often taken in BANQUETING HOUSES. When French words became fashionable at the RESTORATION, 'void' was replaced by 'dessert', from *desservir*, to clear away, to remove the cloth.

When in 1784 the eighteen-year-old Frenchman François de la Rochefoucauld visited Houghton Hall in Norfolk, he noted of dessert: 'The middle of the table is occupied by some small quantity of fruit, and, to go with the wine, some biscuits and butter, which many English eat with their dessert. All the servants depart at this time. The ladies drink a glass or two of wine: after half-an-hour they leave together.' The ladies left to take tea or coffee, while the men devoted themselves to serious drinking.

At dinner in 1852 at Oakly Park, Shropshire Anne Maria Fay, an American, noted: 'The dessert service was of pretty china, nothing remarkable. The ices and jellies and other most beautifully arranged and delicious dishes were placed on the table. The dessert was composed of every variety of fruit, oranges, pears, grapes, etc.' That was on 1 January! See also BANQUET.

Diet. The importance of vitamins for good health was realized only in the twentieth century, with the discovery of vitamin B_1 in 1901.

Since the importance of a healthy diet was not understood, Britain's population suffered, unnecessarily, from a multitude of diseases during the preceding centuries. Throughout the Middle Ages and into the seventeenth century vegetables (onions were not considered a vegetable) were held to be unhealthy because they engendered wind and melancholy, while fresh fruit engendered fevers; soups made of shredded vegetables were acceptable, but the peasant's winter diet, of salt-bacon, bread, dried peas and beans, suggests that most would have ended the winter sadly deficient in essential vitamins. Although the diet was probably supplemented with fresh rabbit, poultry and game, there was little in it to prevent scurvy and beri-beri. Wealthier people had an equal aversion to vegetables, but did eat imported dried fruit and a great deal of fish, and fresh meat, even in winter, in the form of pigeons, lamb, beef and game – all of which, though high in gout-producing protein, would have supplied sufficient essential vitamins.

In the sixteenth century in London and in seaports such as Hull, Plymouth and Bristol it was possible to buy dates, prunes, sun-dried raisons, and Jordan almonds. Many London houses had no kitchen; cooking was done by cookshops providing pies and other hot meals ready for eating, and they would also cook a customer's own joint. This was a long-established trade: an Ordinance of the Cooks and Piebakers dated 1378 gives the prices for various dishes: The best roast pig, 8d.; Three roast thrushes, 2d.; Ten eggs, 1d.; For the paste, fire and trouble upon a goose, 2d. (customer providing his own goose); The best capon baked in a pasty, 8d.

There is indirect evidence in seventeenth-century herbals of a general vitamin A deficiency, in the number of remedies for 'sore-eyes' and for stones in the kidneys and bladder. Towards the end of the century consumption of vegetables and butter (two good sources of vitamin A) was increasing, but they were looked on as poor men's food: butter, eaten in large quantities by the peasant population, was despised by the rich, who thought it fit only for use in cooking. References abound to 'green-sickness', an anaemia of dietary origin, which was treated with herbs or iron preparations. The wholemeal bread of the poor probably provided sufficient iron in conjunction with other elements of their diet, but the white bread favoured by the better-off meant they too were likely to have been afflicted with anaemia.

The preventive for scurvy, caused by a deficiency of vitamin C and for centuries the chief cause of death among seamen, was dramatically demonstrated in 1601: four EAST INDIA COMPANY ships left Woolwich for the Far East; after five months, the crews of three of the ships had been all but destroyed by scurvy, but the commander's ship had surprisingly few cases because he had taken lemon juice with him and gave each member of his crew three spoonfuls every day. Impressed, the East India Company supplied lemon juice on all its ships, but it was not until 1795 that Royal Navy regulations regarding the supply of lemon or lime juice virtually extinguished scurvy in the service.

It is well known that Elizabeth I had poor teeth, but this was not necessarily true of the population in general; the examination of 199 skulls at St Leonard's at Hythe in Kent, covering the years between 1250 and 1650, showed that half had not lost a single tooth before death, while a collection of mandibles from a burial ground in Farringdon Street covering the same period showed that 26 per cent of the males and 14.5 per cent of the females had lost no teeth before death. It seems that in general there was less tooth decay than in modern times, but it was more prevalent among the rich – Paul Hentzner probably got it right when, in an account of his visit to England in 1598, he put it down to 'their too great use of sugar'.

Dilettanti, Society of. The Society, never more than 50 to 70 members, was founded in 1732 as a dining club, meeting monthly in a tavern, a convivial gathering of 'young noblemen of wealth and position' who had been on the GRAND TOUR. Horace Walpole (1717–97), never one of them, sneered that 'the nominal qualification for membership is having been to Italy and the real one being drunk', but the Society soon came to devote itself to the study of Classical antiquities. The members took a serious interest in the architectural and archaeological remains they had seen on their visits to Greece and Italy, and financed a succession of expeditions to undertake excavations, then analyse and write up the results, thus encouraging and promoting the study of Classical archaeology: the Department of Classical Antiquities of the British Museum owes many of its finest treasures to the public spirit of the members. The Society's influence should not be under-estimated: it consciously extended the focus of the Grand Tour to include Greece as well as Italy, and through their interest in the Antique its members steered fashionable taste towards the NEO-CLASSICAL, rather than the ROCOCO style favoured in France. West Wycombe Park in Buckinghamshire, the home of a founder member, Sir Francis Dash-wood (1708–81), was an essay in the re-creation of Classical decoration.

From its earliest meetings the Society appointed a painter whose duty it was to provide a portrait of each member on his election, at his own cost. Today many of these portraits, among the Society's most treasured possessions, hang in Brooks's CLUB. A well-known group by Sir Joshua Reynolds (1723–92), painted in 1778, portrays the members with their heads all the same size, without any concession to perspective, because each was paying the same fee! The Society still exists. See also KIT-CAT CLUB.

Dining-room. A comparatively modern term, first found in the late sixteenth century but not in general use until the mid eighteenth century; even then, many people preferred to use the old term 'eating room', from the French *salle à manger* still in use today. In the 1560s William Sharrington had a room called the dining room, clearly furnished for eating in, at Lacock Abbey in Wiltshire, and Great Chalfield Manor, also in Wiltshire, built in the 1570s, had a similar arrangement; in the 1660s Samuel Pepys (1633–1703) had a room he called his dining room, and in the same decade the Duchess of Lauderdale called the salon at Ham House 'The Marble Dining Room'. All these were exceptions. Dr Johnson (1709–1784) recognized the usage in his *Dictionary* in 1755, while in the same year Mrs Delany wrote 'of my "dining-room" vulgarly so called'; Robert ADAM in the 1760s was still referring to 'eating rooms'; but by 1800 'dining-room' was in general use. See also MEALS and EATING.

Dissolution of the Monasteries. As part of the Reformation – the rejection of papal jurisdiction – of Henry VIII (1509–47), monasteries were disbanded and their property confiscated. In 1536 smaller houses with annual incomes of less than £200 were suppressed, and their property transferred to the Crown; the greater houses were coerced into 'voluntary' surrender during the years 1537 to 1540. The final Parliamentary Act for complete suppression was in 1539.

Monastery lands and buildings were sold by the Crown through the Court of Augmentations. The flood of land made for a buyers' market and bargains were to be had, if one had the cash to pay for them. Gifts of land were made to favoured courtiers, like the 1st Earl of Bedford (1485–1555), an executor of Henry's will, who was given Woburn Abbey, and Sir Thomas Audley (1488–1544), Speaker of the Parliament which passed the Acts for Suppression, who built Audley End on the site of Walden Abbey. Displaced monks were pensioned, or found employment as secular clergy. The policy brought in a considerable additional income to the Crown; an indirect result was to give the laity a majority in the House of Lords, and those peers who had profited from the Dissolution had a vested interest in maintaining Henry's break with Rome. See also CHANTRY.

Divan Club. Before Sir Francis Dashwood (1708–81) started the well known HELL-FIRE CLUB, he had inaugurated the Divan Club, for those who had visited the Ottoman Empire. The dining-room of his home, West Wycombe Park in Buckinghamshire, has portraits of the Club's members hanging on either side of one of himself in a turban and oriental coat and holding a goblet of wine, 'El Faquire Dashwood Pasha'. One member was possibly the celebrated courtesan Fanny Murray. See also CLUBS OF LONDON; DILETTANTI, SOCIETY OF; KIT-CAT CLUB and LITTLE BEDLAM CLUB.

Divine retribution. Divine retribution expresses a basic principle of justice – God's equivalent of 'an eye for an eye and a tooth for a tooth'. Eternal damnation was the fate of sinners who were not punished in this world, and a principle of much post-REFORMATION moral thinking. In secular terms, divine retribution also has an important place in criminology and systems of ensuring social justice. See also ESCHATOLOGY.

Divine Right of Kings. The theory that a monarch derived his authority from God and was answerable only to Him, and that this authority was hereditary (see PRIMOGENITURE); first put forward by Richard II (1377–1399) but only formulated in England by James I (1603–25), in his *True Law of Free Monarchy*, when James felt threatened by the powerful disruptive forces of Protestant and Catholic zealots. In England the theory was effectively ended as a political force by the Bloodless Revolution of 1688; the beheading of Charles I in 1649 had both shaken its supporters and provided them with a royal martyr. It was not intellectually demolished until the publication in 1690 of John Locke's (1632–1704) *Two Treatises on Government*.

Divorce. Marriage, as a sacrament of the Church, was regulated by the Consistory (ecclesiastical) Courts, one for each diocese, until the Matrimonial Causes Act of 1857. A marriage could not be dissolved: annulment on the grounds of non-consummation or consanguinity rendered it null and void, while adultery or gross physical cruelty were grounds for a legal separation; if both husband and wife had committed adultery, the two matrimonial offences were held by the Consistory Courts to cancel each other out. In 1670 Lord Ross was granted a private ACT OF PARLIAMENT to divorce his wife following an Act of Separation obtained in the ecclesiastical court. It was very costly. Before that date not one in England had ever achieved a divorce in the fullest sense, not even Henry VIII (1509–47).

A Parliamentary divorce was preceded by a civil suit, brought by the injured spouse before a jury in the King's Bench, to prove 'Criminal Conversation' (adultery). Whether the case was won or not made little difference, and if the suit was brought by a husband he was obliged to support his erring wife and pay her legal fees until the case was concluded; consequently, many wives appealed. A second case followed in the Diocesan Consistory Court, when the plaintiff had to prove that adultery had taken place in order to win a separation; again, the verdict could be taken to appeal, at the Court of ARCHES in London if it was heard in southern England, or at York in the north. Finally the plaintiff promoted a Bill of Divorcement through both Houses of Parliament, and its enactment dissolved the marriage and left the former spouses free to remarry. A guilty wife lost all right of access to her children, and any claim to jointure or dower after her ex-husband's death, although the Commons usually made provision for her support. A punitive award for damages for the injured husband against the wife's lover might ensure that he was imprisoned for debt – a very satisfactory result for a vengeful husband.

In brief, as secular courts held jurisdiction over property and ecclesiastical courts over matters of marriage, adultery had to be proved in both. The outlook for a divorced wife was bleak indeed; socially outcast, with but a small allowance to survive on, deprived of her children, and her lover possibly imprisoned for debt; a divorced husband, on the other hand, suffered none of these deprivations.

Between 1670 and 1857 only four wives successfully divorced their husbands. Marriage really was 'for better or worse', and if the latter, both parties were usually stuck with it. See also WIFE SALE.

Doctors' Commons. Founded in 1511 as the Association of Doctors of Laws and of the Advocates of the Church of Christ at Canterbury: a body, for practitioners of canon and civil law, analogous to the Inns of Court (whose members practised in common law and equity). Its members held degrees of Doctor of Civil Law at Oxford or Doctor of Laws at Cambridge, were admitted as advocates by the Dean of the Arches (see Court of ARCHES), and practised in the ecclesiastical courts, the Court of Admiralty, and in arbitration involving international law.

Dissolved in 1858 as part of the reforms which instituted the High Court of Justice as the umbrella beneath which all branches of the law were gathered.

Dog-cart. An open, two-wheeled horse-drawn driving-cart with two back-to-back seats, set across the vehicle; the back of the vehicle was originally made to shut up, to form a compartment for carrying dogs.

Dog collars (1). When Henry VIII sent 400 English war dogs (trained to savage enemy bowmen) to help the Emperor Charles V in his war with France, they are reported to have worn 'good iron collars', probably with iron spikes. Bonnie Prince Charlie's Italian greyhound had a silver collar engraved with the JACOBITE royal arms, and Boatswain (d. 1808), the Newfoundland dog belonging to the poet Lord Byron, had a brass collar with serrated edges. These are celebrated animals, and most surviving dog collars belong to dogs long since forgotten. Many have variations on the rhyme attributed to Alexander Pope: 'I am His Majesty's dog at Kew;/Pray tell me, Sir, whose dog are you?'; others have simply the dog's name and that of his owner, sometimes with a coat-of-arms. Occasionally the dog is famous in its own right: in a glass case on a station platform at Slough stands the preserved body of Station Jim, wearing the leather collar with padlocked leather purse-saddle in which, until his death in 1896, he collected money for railway orphans. See also DOGS.

Dog collars (2). The familiar name given to the (usually white) collars worn by most clergy.

Dogs. History seldom mentions pet dogs, and almost never working dogs; but they were certainly there, and even attended church services. When in the 1630s Archbishop Laud upset Puritan sensibilities by ordaining that church altars be placed against the east wall, he also provided that there should be a rail to keep dogs away from the altar; several churches today still possess old dog-tongs, for breaking up dog-fights, and the closed box-pews once found in every church must have ensured that dogs kept near their owners. Some houses still have dog gates at the foot of the stairs to keep animals from the upper floors. Dogs appear to have been very popular in religious houses in late medieval times. Even the stricter orders of nuns were allowed dogs as pets provided 'they were ready barkers used to drive away thieves'. Some of the laxer orders kept hunting dogs, allegedly for the use of distinguished guests.

Henry VIII had war dogs specially bred to savage enemy bowmen – see DOG COLLARS. Dogs are mentioned 167 times in Shakespeare's plays, but there is only one part for a dog, that of Crab, 'the sourest natured dog that lives', belonging to Launce, a servant to one of the *Two Gentlemen of Verona*. Mary, Queen of Scots' 'little dog' crept under her skirts when she was beheaded in 1587. Dogs often appear in royal and noble portraits: at Woburn Abbey in Bedfordshire there is a portrait (*c.* 1600) of the 4th Earl of Bedford dressed for hawking, with a pair of spaniels chained together; James I's Queen, Anne (1574–1619), was painted with a group of Italian greyhounds; Van Dyck's portrait of *c.* 1630 shows the three eldest children of Charles I (1625–49) with two King Charles spaniels; Lely's portrait (1675–80) of Mary of Modena (1658–1718), James II's second wife, now at Althorp, North-amptonshire, shows her with a spaniel; and in 1745 William Hogarth painted himself with his pug.

The sport of coursing with dogs began in the reign of Charles I, and the first coursing club was formed by Lord Orford in 1776 at Marham Smeeth, near Swaffham. An endearing eighteenth-century practice was the breeding of Dalmatians as carriage dogs to run with the owner's carriage and add style to the 'equipage'. Retrievers were bred for shooting, and favoured shooting dogs would be allowed into the house in the eighteenth century. It was then only a short step for many other breeds to be adopted as household pets: a monthly allowance for the 'house dog's' food is an item in many household accounts, and he appears in servants' group photographs. The first dog show was held at Newcatle upon Tyne in 1859, and the Kennel Club was founded in 1873 to improve breeding.

It has never been determined whether man's oldest friend is descended from the wolf, or from some distinct prehistoric breed.

Dole. Originally a charitable gift of left-over food placed in a dole-cupboard (see CHARITY) at the castle gate. Many of these cupboards still exist and there is a big collection of them at Haddon Hall, Derbyshire. After the First World War the term came to be applied to the out-of-work payments made to ex-servicemen. To be 'on the dole' now means to be out of work and in receipt of state benfits.

Dominicans. Friars Preachers; in Britain, Black Friars, from the black mantle worn over a white habit. Dominic, a Castilian AUGUSTINIAN, was sent in 1293 to preach among the heretical Albigensian churches in Languedoc; his mission, though successful, prompted him to found in 1215 an order of extreme asceticism devoted to universal (world-wide) preaching. The Dominicans, mendicants and evangelists, were based in towns, where they established themselves in cramped quarters on inconvenient sites. They were established in England by the mid thirteenth century, and at the DISSOLUTION had about sixty houses in England and Wales and sixteen in Scotland. Remains of their foundations are few, but some are to be found at St Andrews, Fife. The Dominicans returned to Britain in the nineteenth century and now have a dozen priories. See also AUGUSTINIANS, BENEDICTINES,

CARMELITES, CARTHUSIANS, CISTERCIANS, CLUNIACS, GILBERTINES, FRAN-
CISCANS, MENDICANT FRIARS and PREMONSTRATENSIANS.

Doorstops, door porters. The introduction of the rising hinge (*c.* 1775), which caused doors to swing to automatically, led inevitably to the invention of doorstops to hold them open. The earliest are of brass, round, with a lifting handle. From *c.* 1800 stops or porters were made with flat backs in a variety of metals, and even in earthenware. Iron doorstops were made in Sheffield from the 1820s; after 1842, the Coalbrookedale Company manufactured large quantities in cast iron. Many are in the form of national heroes such as Wellington, Gladstone and Disraeli, and these are easily dated. A 'dump' is a heavy glass doorstop made from scrap molten glass which would otherwise have been discarded (or dumped); often made by bottle factories as a sideline.

Dorcas Societies. Ladies' sewing-circles, originating among NON-CONFORMIST congregations in the early nineteenth century. Dorcas was a disciple of Christ, 'full of good works and almsdeeds', whom St Peter raised from the dead when he was shown garments made by her (Acts 9: 36–41).

Dormant peerage. An unclaimed peerage – i.e., one to which there is no apparent successor at the time of a holder's death.

Doublet. A close-fitting, front-fastening garment, between waist- and knee-length, with or without sleeves, worn by men – in various styles and under different names, such as *gipon* (analogous to Fr. *jupon*, an underskirt or petticoat, derived from the Arabic) and *pourpoint* – between the fourteenth and the seventeenth centuries. Derived from the *gambelin*, the padded tunic, sometimes of leather, worn under body-armour in the early Middle Ages. At first it followed the tunic shape, being high-necked and hip-length, but by 1400 it had shortened to barely cover the hips, and was worn with a low belt; by 1420 it had a small upstanding collar with a V-opening to the front, with a padded chest, and by 1450 a tight waist and padded shoulders. Between 1490 and 1530 the neckline became lower, square-cut or a deep V; for the first time it revealed the shirt, as did the fashionable slashed sleeves; the skirts were now knee-length, and the doublet was more often worn without a jerkin (sleeveless jacket) over it, laced or buttoned down the front. From 1530 the fashion for wearing jerkins returned, open at the front to show off the highly decorative buttons or lacings of the doublet, now worn close fitted round the neck and showing a frilly shirt collar above it. The Spanish modes of the latter half of the sixteenth century saw doublet skirts shorten to a mere row of tabs; the waistline became more exaggerated, often descending to a sharp point, padded and stiffened and eventually becoming the absurd artificial paunch of the 'Peascod Belly' of *c.* 1575, formed over a wooden framework and with whalebone stiffening in the seams. A standing collar became higher until it was eclipsed by the RUFF in the 1570s. By 1600 the doublet had become close-fitting, with a long waist, and by 1630 the line was more natural and the doublet more closely resembled a loose, unpadded jacket. In 1666 Charles II introduced the coat and waistcoat, as an anti-French fashion – which had the advantage of being more economical as well. Samuel Pepys (1633–1703) observed its first days: 8 October 1666 – 'The king hath . . . declared his resolution of setting a fashion for clothes . . . It will be a vest, I know not well how. But it is to teach the nobility thrift, and will do good.' 15 October 1666 – 'This day the King begins to put on his vest . . . being a long cassocke close to the body, of black cloth and pinked with white silk under it, and a coat over it, and the legs ruffled with black riband like a pigeon's leg – and upon the whole, I wish the King may keep it, for it is a very fine and handsome garment.' See also CODPIECE.

Dovecote. A building or other structure, usually round, in which pigeons were bred and kept to be used for food. The interior of a dovecote has nesting boxes set in the walls; to reach the higher ones in a round dovecote, a central rotating ladder called a potence was fitted.

A supply of fresh meat through the winter was always a problem until the invention of refrigeration; pigeons provided a partial solution, and the clergy and lords of manors had a feudal right to keep them. As pigeons will scavenge for the nearest food supply, tenants' crops suffered in proportion to the population of the dovecote. A dovecote at Kinwarden, Warwickshire, complete with potence and dating from the mid fourteenth century, may be the oldest surviving in England.

It has been estimated that there were twenty-six thousand dovecotes in England in the seventeenth century; writing shortly after the death of Elizabeth I (1533–1663), Fynes Moryson noted that 'No kingdom in the world hath so many dove-houses.' A dovecote is often the sign of a manorial holding, although by the eighteenth century feudal rights were in abeyance and many farmhouses had their own pigeon lofts.

Dowager. Originally a widow with a DOWER; first used in England of Catherine of Aragon (1485–1536), widow of Prince Arthur (d. 1502), who was known as Princess Dowager until her marriage to Henry VIII. The term was later applied to widows of titled men of high rank, to distinguish them from the wives of their sons. See also DOWRY.

Dower. A widow's life-interest in her late husband's estate, for her support and the education of their children; fixed by law at one-third of her husband's lands, until abolished in 1925. See also DOWAGER and DOWRY.

Dowry. The property in land or money brought by a wife to her husband on marriage; the marriage-portion. The means by which many families increased their wealth and power, a rich heir bargaining for a well-dowered wife – a business arrangement in which the unreliable emotion of love was seldom a consideration. See also DOWER and DOWAGER.

Dragoon. Originally, a mounted soldier trained to fight on foot only, carrying a musket or other infantry weapon. The name is derived from the 'dragon' or short musket used by the French army in the sixteenth century. Dragoons always aspired to cavalry status, and since the time of Frederick the Great (1712–86) 'dragoon' has meant 'medium cavalry'; in the eighteenth and early nineteenth centuries the British Army's light cavalry were mostly called Light Dragoons. The name is retained in certain British regiments, its original meaning of mounted infantry long gone.

Draw-table. An extendable table with leaves to pull out at either end. The first British draw-tables date from *c.* 1550. A magnificent French example of the 1560s, which may have belonged to Mary, Queen of Scots (1542–87), has stood in the State Withdrawing Chamber at Hardwick Hall, Derbyshire since 1601. The principle of the draw-table was used by Thomas SHERATON in his 'universal table'.

Dresser. A form of sideboard; derived from the French *dressoir,* used to *dresser* or arrange the various – and most ostentatious – appurtances of the dining table; or perhaps (as 'dressing board') the side-table at which food was 'dressed' or garnished before being taken to the table. Most closely related to the BUFFET.

In the *Orders of service belonging to the degree of a duke, a marquess and an earle in there own houses . . .* of *c.* 1500, we find the server of the lord's dinner, instructed to collect the food, to 'go downe to the dresser . . .' – referring to the servery where prepared food was laid out by the kitchen staff to be collected by the servers.

By the seventeenth century, what had originally been a narrow side-table now sometimes had a tall back with a varying number of shallow shelves; by the end of the century, cupboards and/or drawers might be added below the main shelf, small cupboards either side of the upper shelves. By the end of the eighteenth century, pieces with drawers and cupboards below had come to be known as Welsh dressers; a 'Yorkshire dresser' was more elaborate, with a clock set in the upper shelves. By this date, too, such pieces had been superseded in grand houses by the SIDEBOARD, and now belonged essentially to the yeoman farmhouse and lower down the social scale; by the nineteenth century, 'the dresser' in larger establishments was a useful piece of kitchen furniture.

Dressing-bell. Rung in large households in the nineteenth and early twentieth centuries to advise guests that it was time to dress for dinner. See also GONG, DRESSING.

Dressing-table. The first dressing-tables made in England exclusively for the purpose are early eighteenth-century, and have no mirror, one long drawer across the full width, and two small drawers below on either side; these last distinguish them from PIER-TABLES, which were also used as dressing-tables. Thomas CHIPPENDALE made dressing tables with swing mirrors fixed to the top; by the end of the century these pieces had, under French influence, become very elaborate pieces of furniture.

Drugget. A floor- or table-covering made of coarse woollen material. See also FLOORS and FLOOR COVERINGS.

Duelling. A pre-arranged combat, with deadly weapons, between two persons to settle a private dispute or avenge an insult. Trial by combat, although condemned by Pope Nicholas I (858–67) and many succeeding popes, was introduced to England by William I (1066–1087); duelling was banned by Oliver Cromwell (1599–1658) in 1654 and again by Charles II (1660–85), but not formally abolished by ACT OF PARLIAMENT until 1818; the laws governing the conduct of duels were not removed from the statute books until 1819. In law, a challenge to a duel now became a breach of the peace, and a fatal result a felony. Memorable duels have been fought, such as those between William Pitt (1759–1806) and George Tierney (1761–1830) in 1796; George Canning (1770–1827) and Lord Castlereagh (1769–1822) in 1809; the Duke of Wellington (1769–1852) and the Earl of Winchilsea (1791–1858) in 1829; in 1840 Lord Cardigan wounded Captain Tuckett, was tried by the House of Lords, and acquitted. The last recorded duel in England took place in 1852 when M. Barthelemey fatally wounded M. Cournet, a fellow Frenchman, at Egham, Surrey. See also HONOUR.

Dumb-waiter. A useful piece of eighteenth-century dining equipment, consisting of a central shaft with two or three tiers of revolving trays. Small dishes such as cheese, nuts or jellies would be placed on these trays and when the dumb-waiter was placed in the centre of the table, the trays could be rotated to make the contents available to everyone within reach. First introduced around 1725, it dispensed with the need for servants for the last, DESSERT course. The term is also applied in the USA to a hoist bringing food from the kitchen to the dining-room, when these are on different floors.

The Revd Thomas Talbot wrote to his wife about breakfast at Saltram, Devon in 1811: 'No domestic attends, some three footmen a Maitre d'Hotel & valet de chambre standing or laying on in the great gallery of the staircase outside the door, till summoned by a hem or whistle, his Ldship performing by a Dumb Waiter the whole ceremony himself.'

Dundreary whiskers. Long side-whiskers, worn without a beard. Lord Dundreary was a character in *Our American Cousin* by Tom Taylor (1817–80), editor of *Punch*; first performed in 1858 and a great success in the USA: President Lincoln was watching it at Ford's Theatre, Washington, DC, when he was assassinated in 1865. By this time the fashion for Dundreary whiskers had waned in Britain.

Ear-trumpet. An aid for the partly deaf, consisting of an ivory earpiece attached to a trumpet-shaped device which amplified sound; first used in 1776.

Earl Marshal of England. One of the great officers of state; originally the King's Marshal, deputy of the Lord High Constable. Under the Norman and Plantagenet kings he was a judge in the Courts of Chivalry. The office became hereditary in 1672 and vested in the family of the Dukes of Norfolk. The Earl Marshal is the head of the HERALDS' College (College of Arms), and controls state functions, particularly coronations. A similar office existed in Scotland, vested in the family of the Earls of Keith from the fourteenth century until 1716, when both earldom and office were lost by the ATTAINDER of the tenth Earl.

Early English. The first of three purely arbitrary divisions of English GOTHIC architecture, describing the style covering the period *c.* 1150–1290, when the pointed arch superseded the Norman, or Romanesque, round arch. There is a quite distinct horizontal line to the style which sets it apart from the subsequent DECORATED and PERPENDICULAR styles. The terms of classification were devised by Thomas Rickman (1776–1841) in *c.* 1811. See also GOTHIC ARCHITECTURE.

Easter sepulchre. A tomb-chest on which an effigy of Christ lay for Easter celebrations, usually found in the wall of the chancel of a church, often highly decorated, and representing the tomb in the Garden of Gethsemene from which Christ reputedly rose.

East India Company. A trading company incorporated by royal charter on 31 December 1600 for the purpose of trading with the East Indies and taking advantage of the decline of Portuguese power in that area. However, the promoters had overlooked Dutch interests there and the Dutch, always jealous of their trade, forced the Company to withdraw from the Far East after the massacre of Amboina in 1623. The Company re-established itself in Bengal and confined itself to operations in India. The earliest major factory, or depot, was in Surat; others were established at Madras, and later at Calcutta. On her marriage to Charles II (1660–85) in 1662, Catherine of Braganza (1638–1705) brought Bombay as part of her DOWRY, and Charles II leased it to the Company. Investors and factors of the Company became extremely wealthy in the late seventeenth century, despite French opposition to English expansion on the part of the Compagnie des Indes Orientales, established at Pondicherry in 1664. Open warfare followed in the eighteenth century, successfully concluded by Clive of India (1725–74), employed by the Company, whose victories at Arcot and Plassey (1757) extinguished French rivalry in Bengal. Government of the vast areas under the Company's control clashed with their commercial interests, giving rise to serious criticism of their administration. The Regulating Act of 1773 and the India Acts of 1784, 1813 and 1833 progressively transferred power from the Company to the government. The Indian Mutiny of 1857–8 revealed the dangers of a company ruling a continent, and the East Indian Company was taken over by the INDIA OFFICE in 1858. Service with the East India Company was often a short-cut, either to wealth or to an early death from disease. At a time when the eldest son inherited all (see PRIMOGENITURE), the East India Company provided a possible means for younger sons to acquire wealth, and many families sent three or four generations to serve in India. However, recruitment depended very much on whom the applicant knew within the Company, and nepotism was widespread. See also NABOBS.

Eating one's Terms. In order to be CALLED TO THE BAR, to qualify as a BARRISTER, a law student had to dine at least three times in each of twelve TERMS at the Inns of Court.

Ecclesiastical courts. Established after the Norman Conquest to administer CANON LAW, they also dealt with the laity for such offences as adultery, heresy, and cases involving marriage, inheritance and the enforcement of tithes. Excommunication was the ultimate weapon. By the sixteenth century these courts were mainly concerned with matrimonial and probate cases, a jurisdiction that lasted until 1857; they are now confined to matters concerning the CLERGY. See Court of ARCHES.

Egg–and–dart. An OVOLO moulding decorated with alternate egg-shapes and arrowheads or dart-shapes, originally Greek but revived in Britain by the Classical Revivalists. See also PALLADIAN.

Elizabethan Settlement. The accession of Elizabeth I in 1558 ended the Roman Catholic reign of her sister, Mary Tudor, which had undone much of the work initiated by their father, Henry VIII (1509–47), after his break with the Papacy. PURITAN pressure resulted in the Act of SUPREMACY of 1559, restating the breach with Rome. The Act of UNIFORMITY reinstated the Common PRAYER BOOK of 1552 and much of Henry VIII's legislation against Papal interference. By 1560 only one Marian bishop had accepted the oath of supremacy; the others were replaced by men who had been deposed by Mary and/or who had fled the country during her reign. The majority of the rest of the clergy accepted the oath, with varying degrees of enthusiasm.

Embalming. Originally Egyptian, the art of preserving dead bodies from decay. Used to preserve a corpse during its LYING-IN-STATE, but not always effective, particularly if this were lengthy, or during summer. In 1572 Mary, Countess of Northumberland, directed in her Will that her body was not to be 'opened after I am dead. I have not loved to be very bold afore women, much more would I be loath to come into the hands of any living man . . .'. Occasionally a body defied all attempts at embalming; the 1st Duke of Lennox, who died in 1624, presented this problem to his heirs, and they had him hurriedly buried. The funeral was later performed over an effigy.

Fear of being wrongly declared dead tended to discourage embalming. In 1397 John, Duke of Lancaster requested that he 'should not be buried for forty days . . .'. In 1872 the wife of Arthur Balfour (later 1st Earl of Balfour), directed: 'I wish that my body should not be consigned to the coffin till unequivocal marks of corruption have shown themselves.'

Embalming of the wealthy continued until well into the nineteenth century, as did the macabre custom of the heart, bowels and brains being placed in an urn, carried on top of the coffin and even buried separately. See also FUNERALS.

Emigration. By the end of the sixteenth century various circumstances were combining to encourage emigration. PRIMOGENITURE and land shortage was one reason, causing younger sons to seek their fortunes abroad, while religious intolerance forced PURITANS such as the Pilgrim Fathers to look outside England for freedom of worship. Once tobacco was established as a profitable crop, the Virginia colony in America became a viable settlement. Between 1630 and 1645 20,000 men, women and children emigrated to New England, and a further 40,000 to Virginia and other American colonies. English justice and customs were quickly established in the new colonies and the stream of emigrants was interrupted only by the CIVIL WAR (1642–9). Overpopulation in the nineteenth century (which terrified Thomas Malthus (1766–1834) and his followers, who argued that the increase of population could not be matched by a similar increase in production and extreme poverty would surely follow) was the cause of further waves of emigrants, to Canada, Australia and New Zealand, controlled only by emigration societies and the occasional assistance of the government. They were in part inspired by the propaganda of Gibbon Wakefield (1796–1862), who preached that emigration was the only true relief for his countrymen's economic miseries: to him is largely due the systematized and aided emigration which founded modern Australia, New Zealand and Canada.

Enclosure. The characteristic agricultural feature of the feudal era was the OPEN FIELD system, effectively a co-operative system by which the

VILLEINS arranged among themselves at an annual COURT-LEET what crops should be sown, and where. The fields were 'open' in the sense that there were no hedges or fences; division was by balks of turf. Crops were sown in strips, about 22 yards or four ox-goads wide. A rotation of crops ensured the land was not overworked. Evidence of these strips is often visible today as undulating waves crossing pasture land, particularly in light snow or during a drought. The commons were permanent pastures available for grazing for those who had the right.

The open field system was astonishingly wasteful of land and allowed no room for experiment with unusual crops or in animal husbandry. It was also inefficient for a farmer to hold his land in scattered strips, rather than in reasonably-sized fields, and by the sixteenth century pressure for change led to an inexorable dismantling of old feudal agricultural customs, and to the consolidation of scattered strips into more manageable fields by means of enclosure.

Enclosure could be brought about with the agreement of two-thirds of those having rights, at a vestry meeting or Court-Leet; otherwise, a parish had to pass its own Inclosure Act through Parliament, when Commissioners were appointed to oversee the process. (The legal term for the procedure was 'Inclosure', but the actual process was 'Enclosure'.)

Those with common grazing rights were compensated with small allocations of land, but in practice those who were given only an odd acre in return for their rights quickly sold out to farmers with larger holdings. There were many protests against enclosure, and in 1533–4 an Act was passed forbidding the process, but was widely ignored. Agitation against enclosure was most rife where large tracts of land were enclosed for sheep; since they demanded the minimum of labour, this led to real hardship. The bulk of enclosures took place between 1750 and 1850. A General Inclosure Act passed in 1834 made a process that had begun as early as the fifteenth century easier for as yet unenclosed parishes to achieve.

Today, Laxton in Nottinghamshire is the only surviving unenclosed parish, and the open field system is continued as an historical curiosity. The strips in Laxton are wider than formerly, adapted to tractors rather than horses or oxen, and crops are modern, but the principles are maintained, and the annual Court-Leet decides upon crops, rotation, and who will have which strip in the open fields. See also RIDGE-AND-FURROW.

Ensign. The lowest commissioned infantry rank in the British Army until 1871, when it was replaced by that of second lieutenant; the title is still used in the Foot Guards. The ensign carried his regimental flag into battle, as did his counterpart in the cavalry, the CORNET.

Entablature. In Classical architecture, the upper section of an order supported by columns, consisting of three horizontal divisions: architrave, frieze and cornice.

Entail. A system of inheritance through the eldest living, legitimate male heir ('of the body'). Crown lawyers were always suspicious of perpetual entails and tried to limit them to a restricted number of lives. The wealthy were continually finding ways round the law. By the later Middle Ages a system known as Uses had emerged, by which a landowner left his property to trustees for particular uses – i.e., to keep the property intact in the male line. Between the 1540s and the 1660s lawyers improved on the old system of Uses by what was known as strict settlement, under which property was entailed for three generations, a legal course which was not finally established until it was sanctioned by a court of Common Law in 1696 (Duncombe v. Duncombe). Such a settlement was usually made when the heir came of age, or on his marriage; it had the effect of making the heir a tenant for life, unable to dispose of any of the estate held in trust until the next generation came of age, when the entail would be renewed.

As long as there was a male heir, an estate would remain intact, but where the line failed and a daughter inherited, then the estate passed to her husband if or when she had one – with a long-term effect that large estates became larger. The 3rd Earl of Burlington (1694–1753) died leaving an only daughter married to the 3rd Duke of Devonshire, a factor in Chatsworth's fine art collection. In only two generations, the Lords of Ashburnham built up a fortune; they also had few children, and so did not have to find expensive dowries when daughters married – but this scarcity of progeny eventually worked against them; the title is now extinct and Ashburnham Place, Sussex, was demolished in 1959. These were the unlucky dynasties; others, like the Dukes of Norfolk and of Northumberland, have maintained their vast estates, through strict entail. The punishing death duties of the twentieth century have left large estate-owners seeking other means of preserving their holdings intact.

Epergne. An eighteenth-century dining-table centre-piece, made of silver, silver plate, or glass, having in the centre a large dish on a stand for fruit, surrounded by smaller dishes for sweetmeats, nuts and dried fruit. The design could be fantastic, and was often so during the ROCOCO period, from 1725. The idea was imported from France *c.* 1715, but the etymology of 'epergne' is unclear: in French such a centre-piece is a *surtout de table*. However, as the use of the epergne to serve DESSERT 'saved' the use of footmen in passing dishes, it may be an anglicized form of the French *épargner*, to save.

Equity. Laws established by decisions in the CHANCERY COURT, to right wrongs arising from, or deal with matters not covered by, COMMON or STATUTE LAW. Its beginnings date from the late thirteenth century, when petitions to the king by litigants who felt unfairly judged in common law cases were referred to the LORD CHANCELLOR, before whom witnesses were summoned *sub poena* (under penalty), to be heard in the Chancellor's Chancery Court. By the nineteenth century both Common Law and Equity were backed by the doctrine of judicial precedent. The JUDICATURE ACTS of 1873–5 merged the two branches in a single High Court of Justice, in which judges apply both Equity and Common Law. Witnesses are still summoned by *sub poena*, and Equity takes precedence over Common Law when the two are in conflict.

Eschatology. In Christian theology eschatology refers to the doctrine of 'last things' – i.e., the Resurrection of the Dead, the Last Judgement, Heaven and Hell, etc. – and is an attempt to explain in critical biblical terms what is meant by 'the kingdom of God' in the teaching of Jesus and Paul. It also deals with the importance to be given to Christian hope and expectations for the after-life. Eschatology developed as a means of explaining the purpose behind the particularly tough and painful existence most people experienced. Before the REFORMATION death was considered to be no more than a gateway to – it was hoped – Everlasting Life. Life was largely a matter of storing up goodness in order to have a happy after-life in Heaven. This could be done by contributing to church building, buying pardons, giving to the poor, going to church, endowing CHANTRIES for priests to offer masses for the repose of one's soul, etc. The alternative, for those who died in a state of grace but not purged of all sin, was a period in PURGATORY, when prayers were offered by the living to correct the state of the soul and send it Heavenwards; those who were incorrigible were bound for Hell. Protestants, particularly CALVINISTS, maintained that Purgatory did not exist because everyone was predestined by God, therefore both good and evil emanated from God. The dilemma was why God should countenance evil.

PURITANS in particular had the difficulty of explaining their belief that calamities were the work of God for his own inscrutable purpose. For them, good fortune was a reward for virtue, and bad a punishment for sin. When the sister of a humble NONCONFORMIST minister went up to London in the early seventeenth century without her parents' permission, returned with smallpox and died, it was taken as God's punishment for her disobedience; some Christians hold similar beliefs today.

After the Reformation, death for most Christians, particularly after illness, was a happy deliverance from the harshness of life; for friends and relatives, it was usually a calamity arising from the curse of Adam, by whom 'sin entered the world and death by sin'. Hope of reward in Heaven played a significant part in the Protestant work ethic, with its emphasis on personal and social piety in this life. See also DIVINE RETRIBUTION.

Espalier. Lattice-work on which fruit trees (usually) and other shrubs are trained, and also a term for the tree so trained. Originating from the Italian *spalliera* (*spalla*, shoulder).

Esquire. Originally, an attendant on a knight and bearer of his shield or armour. Legally the term is applied to the sons of peers, baronets and knights and their eldest sons, and to officers of the armed forces and members of the Bar. Latterly it is a term appended to the name of the eldest son of any GENTLEMAN; it carries no privileges or rights.

Estate. The modern meaning of 'landed property' has only been common from the mid eighteenth century. Previously, 'estate' meant a man's status – his social position, his rank, his wealth, his power.

Estates of the Realm. Orders or classes forming the body politic and sharing government. In England these are three in number: (1) the Lords Spiritual; (2) the Lords Temporal; (3) the Commons. The power of the Press to influence politics has led it to be termed the 'Fourth Estate'. In Scotland, until the accession of James IV of Scotland to the throne of England in 1603, the three Estates of the Realm were: (1) the nobility; (2) the boroughs; (3) the Church.

Evangelicalism. Doctrines peculiar to those Protestants who believe literally in the evangel (from the Greek for 'good news'), or Gospel, and which place supreme emphasis on the saving power of the blood of Jesus Christ shed for the redemption of mankind. Originally the term was claimed by all Protestants, but has come to be particularly applied to 'Low Church' Anglicans. Inheriting the Puritan tradition, Evangelicals were a powerful influence in the Anglican church and society from the eighteenth century. The movement placed stress on preaching rather than on worship, colliding head-on with the OXFORD MOVEMENT in the mid nineteenth century. See also ANGLO-CATHOLICISM, METHODISM and PRESBYTERIANISM.

Exchequer. The name given in England, from at least the twelfth century, to the government office receiving and responsible for public revenues. From the Latin *scaccarium*, a chess-board; hence counting-table, accounting department. In practice joined with the Treasury (the 'lower' Exchequer, an office for the receipt and payment of money where accounting practices were based on the use of the TALLY), the 'upper' Exchequer, the *scaccarium* proper, was a court closely linked to the CURIA REGIS which sat twice a year to regulate accounts; unlike the 'lower' Exchequer with its tallies, the accounting procedures of the 'upper' Exchequer were based on the use of the abacus, or counting board. The great officers of state, including the LORD HIGH CHANCELLOR, were present around 'the chessboard'; the Treasurer dictated the great roll of accounts – the 'pipe roll' – to his scribe, and the Chancellor's scribe made a duplicate – the Chancellor's roll. In the reign of Henry III (1216–72) occurred a separation of the Chancery (under the Lord High Chancellor) from the Exchequer, when a Chancellor of the Exchequer (never 'Lord' or 'High') became responsible for the custody and employment of the Exchequer Seal, and the keeping of a counter-roll as a check on the pipe rolls kept by the Treasurer. Reforms under William IV (1830–37) finally ended the great series of pipe rolls, but the Chancellorship of the Exchequer remained a relatively unimportant office during most of the nineteenth century, only of CABINET rank when it was held by the First Lord of the Treasury. Nowadays the Chancellor of the Exchequer is Minister of Finance, and so always has a seat in the Cabinet.

Excommunication. Temporary or permanent exclusion from the Communion of the Church. In the early Catholic Church, a penalty imposed by ECCLESIASTICAL COURTS for heresy, adultery, simony, church non-attendance, and the use of contumacious words. At a higher level, popes excommunicated stubborn sovereigns: John (1199–1216), Henry VIII (1509–1547) and Elizabeth I (1558–1603) were all excommunicated, and their subjects absolved from allegiance to them.

Eye-catchers and follies. Nothing can surpass in eccentricity those eighteenth-century buildings whose only purpose was to improve the view: the follies and eye-catchers. In the 1730s, at Rousham in Oxfordshire, William Kent closed a view with three ruined arches. George Durant of Tong Castle, Shropshire, who made a fortune in doubtful circumstances supplying the army in the West Indies, built a pyramid consisting of a henhouse on the ground floor and a dovecote in the upper five storeys. His main gate was flanked by two pyramids, and a pulpit from where he preached to passers-by. (He also managed to father thirty illegitimate children on the wives of his tenants at Tong, which was a very small village.)

A mock castle-ruin was a favourite eye-catcher, and the earliest as well as the most massive are at Castle Howard, North Yorkshire, built by John VANBRUGH for the 3rd Earl of Carlisle (1674–1738): the Pyramid Gate, made in 1719, a looming fortress surmounted by a pyramid, and the Carrmire Gate, with rusticated arch, broken pediment and squat obelisks – 'gargantuan BAROQUE', in Nikolaus Pevsner's words. These are not so much eye-catchers as follies. Alfred's Hall at Circencester Park, Gloucestershire, built 1721–32 by the 1st Earl Bathurst, is now sufficiently aged to be easily mistaken for a real medieval castle, but even in its early days an eminent historian was quite taken in by it. The most celebrated provider of ruins was Sanderson Miller (1717–80). His ruined tower at Hagley, Worcestershire (built in 1747–8), had the full approval of Horace Walpole, and he built another at Wimpole, Cambridgeshire in 1772. Boughton House in North-amptonshire has scattered in its Park possibly the largest selection of follies belonging to any one estate. See also BELVEDERES and PROSPECT TOWERS.

Eyre, Justices in. Itinerant courts administering COMMON LAW. They were replaced by the static ASSIZES in 1284–5 (from Anglo-French/Latin *en eyre, in itinere*).

Fairs. See MARKETS AND FAIRS.

Fancy dress. Fancy-dress parties and balls were a favourite pastime in the late nineteenth and early twentieth centuries; probably originated with Grand Tourists who had sampled the pleasures of going to parties in disguise when visiting Venice. In her diary Fanny Burney (1752–1840) gives an early mention of fancy dress in 1770. See also CHARADES.

Farthingale. A Spanish fashion in dress introduced to France about 1530 and thence to England: a canvas underskirt inset at intervals with wicker hoops, tied on at the waist. By the 1570s the fashion arose for a 'bum roll', a padded roll rising towards the back, to be tied around the waist under the kirtle or skirt, which threw it out at the sides; in the 1590s, when this style had descended through society, the 'wheel farthingale' was evolved in France. It had a cane or whalebone frame like a wheel, often four feet across, and skirts worn with it were often only ankle-length. This unbecoming fashion made women look like nothing so much as hobby-horses. The word comes from the Spanish *vertugado, verdagado*, from *verdago*, a rod or stick (Fr. *verdugale*).

Feoffment. During the feudal period, the usual method of granting or conveying a freehold or 'fee'. The oldest form of land transfer. The existing owner took the buyer to the land to be sold, handing him a blade of glass, clod or twig as a token, stating the terms of the sale. Asserting his rights as new owner the buyer then (symbolically) turned everyone off his land. This custom was called Livery of Seisin and was only part of the procedure. The terms of the sale were written as an Indenture of Feoffment, sealed and signed by both sides to the transac-tion. The document was then endorsed to the effect that the Livery of Seisin had been carried out before witnesses, without which it was not legal.

Ferneries. William (1770–1850) and Dorothy Wordsworth saw ferns as essential to romantic ruins, while part of their appeal to the late Vic-torians was that there are many varieties to collect and specimens are easily pressed. Ferneries were constructed in distant corners of gardens, in the damp conditions ferns enjoy. This seems now a quaint passion; their popularity did not outlive the Victorians, and many of these ferneries are unrecognizable today. However, a recently rediscovered fernery, made after 1870, has been restored at Brodsworth Hall in South Yorkshire, and other ferneries to be seen include a mid nineteenth century example at Tatton Park, Cheshire; a small fernery at Peckover House, Cambridgeshire of about the same date; at Standen, West Sussex an example of 1859; and a fern house at Ashridge, Hertfordshire designed by Sir Matthew Digby Wyatt in 1864 which has recently been restored. See also GARDENS.

Feudalism. One of the most influential and enduring of medieval institutions. Feudalism (from the Latin *feodum* or *feudom*, a fee or fief) evolved in Western Europe between the fourth and tenth centuries, based on legal principles and social ideas which are by no means extinct today. The two main strands of feudalism are of Roman derivation, relating to (1) land tenure, and (2) personal relationships. In theory all land belonged to the king, who granted its use – the right to exact services and, sometimes, to levy taxes and administer justice – to tenants-in-chief, who in turn might grant land to vassals The vassal's most important commitment was that of military service; the smallest practicable grant was the 'knight's fee'.

The economic unit of feudalism was the manor, whose land was worked by serfs or VILLEINS bound to the soil (in status somewhere between freemen and slaves) and holding, in return for their labour, a portion of land in the manor. Feudalism was brought to Britain by the Normans and began to decline from the thirteenth century, mainly due to the evolution of a monetary economy and, in part, to the Peasants' Revolt of 1381. Villeinage had become extinct (in practice if not in fact) in England by the sixteenth century, and feudal dues to the Crown were abolished in 1660.

Fires. The wealthy always permitted themselves the luxury of a warming fire whenever it was needed. In cottages and farmhouses the hall fire was kept in all year, to be available for cooking, while in larger establishments strict control was exercised over when the hall fire was to be lighted: household orders of the Duke of Clarence, dated 1469, lay down that the hall fire should not be lit until 1 November and never alight after Easter, but the *Book of Curtesey*, published in the mid fifteenth century, forbids a hall fire after February.

Fireplaces that smoked were commonplace. In a letter of 1603 Arabella Stuart complained of her eyes running from the smoke of coal fires in the recently built Hardwick Hall in Derbyshire. The problem was not solved until the late eighteenth century when Count Rumford

(Benjamin Thompson, an American-born Englishman, created a Count of the Holy Roman Empire by the Elector of Bavaria for services to the civil and military administration) worked out a formula for the construction of flues and fireplaces which caused a sufficient draught to take smoke away up the chimney.

Firebacks. Cast-iron plates, often decorated, placed at the back of an open hearth to reflect the heat forward and also to protect the brickwork of the chimney. The earliest known specimens date from c. 1500.

Firedogs. Metal supports placed in the hearth to hold burning logs; often highly decorative. See also ANDIRONS.

Fire engines. Before the widespread use of electricity there was always a risk of house fires, due to the use of candles and rushlights, oil lamps and, later, gas. In the stable-yards of large houses an old horse-drawn Merryweather estate fire engine can sometimes be seen, painted bright red, complete with brass helmets and hoses. These needed a nearby source of water to be effective, and until the introduction of steam pumps (on the engines invented by Braithwaite in 1829), the pressure from the manned hand pumps was very often insufficient to reach a second storey.

Serious country house fires of the past include one at Hatfield House, Hertfordshire in 1835, when the Dowager (1st) Marchioness of Salisbury died in a fire, started by her own candle, which destroyed the west wing of the house – a fire which provoked many responsible owners to acquire Merryweather engines. Landhydrock House in Cornwall was two-thirds burnt down in 1880. Sledmere House, East Yorkshire was gutted by fire in 1911 and rebuilt.

Fire engines may be seen at Polesdon Lacey, Surrey; Tatton Park, Cheshire; Raby Castle, County Durham; and Compton House, Dorset. In the 1930s the Killerton estate in Devon boasted a bull-nosed Morris open tourer, the back of which was filled with very large FIRE EXTINGUISHERS. See also FIRE INSURANCE.

Fire extinguishers. Modern versions, painted red, are easily recognized and understood by everyone, unlike some early versions.

The Harden Star and Sinclair Fire Appliance Co. was formed in 1889 and continued in business until the 1920s. In its early days it manufactured the Harden Star Grenade, described in a contemporary advertisement as 'the best, cheapest, and most reliable, and the only Hand Fire extinguisher in general use throughout the world'; these sold for 40 shillings the dozen, and were made of blue glass – in the shape of a grenade – with a filler top, and held in brackets fixed to walls at strategic points. Early models were filled only with water, later ones with carbon tetrachloride. Designed to be hurled into the seat of a fire, it is doubtful whether they were any use at all, yet they sold in their millions and may still occasionally be seen; there are many at Erddig in Clwyd, and a few survive in the service passages at Calke Abbey in Derbyshire. See also FIRE ENGINES and FIRE INSURANCE.

Fire insurance. Several insurance companies offered fire insurance to London property owners from the early eighteenth century; the Sun Insurance Company, for example, was established by 1710. To keep their losses as low as possible, the companies maintained their own fire engines, which were used to put out fires only on the properties of their clients – distinguished by metal plaques on the front of the buildings, many of which survive today. Other large towns soon followed the lead set in London. See also FIRE ENGINES.

Fireproof construction. In the late eighteenth and early nineteenth centuries textile factories and warehouses pioneered the use of what was believed to be a method of fireproof construction, consisting of floors supported on exposed cast-iron girders bridged by shallow arches of brick. It was almost inevitable that it should have been a textile family, Philips, who first used this construction in a domestic building, at Heath House in Staffordshire (1836–40); Osborne, in the Isle of Wight, followed (1840s); and another early example is at Grittleton, Wiltshire (1848–55). However, exposed iron is not fireproof, and quickly fails in extreme heat: Normanhurst, Sussex, built in 1867 using this 'fireproof' construction, was so badly damaged by fire in the 1920s that it was demolished. Tyntesfield in Somerset, remodelled in the 1860s, had hydrants on every floor, while Wadhurst Park, Sussex (1872–5; now demolished) had internal rolling shutters of iron.

Fire-screen. Used as protection from the direct heat of a fire. The earliest fire-screen known is Elizabethan, consisting of a pole with a large round wicker screen which can be raised and lowered in height by means of a central pin on the pole. A number of this type may be seen at Hardwick Hall, Derbyshire; although they may not be Elizabethan, they are similar in form. In the mid seventeenth century such pole-screens were made in metal, with a sliding, adjustable screen displaying needlework. These screens did not come into very general use until the mid eighteenth century, when they were made of wood; the adjustable screen – round, oval, or heart-shaped – was still used to display needle-work. During the nineteenth century, when ladies were particularly concerned about their complexions, many shapes and forms of pole-screen were manufactured.

The more familiar square or rectangular fire-screen, with or without folding sides and placed before the hearth, was introduced to Britain at the time of William and Mary, in 1688.

Fireworks. Fireworks came to Europe and Britain from China in the fourteenth century as part of the discovery of gunpowder. Firework displays were given in England to mark such occasions of national rejoicing as a royal birth. Handel wrote the 'Music for the Royal Fire-works' to accompany the firework display in London's Green Park which marked the Peace of Aix-la-Chapelle. From the 1840s they became increasingly popular and were used on many private and public occasions, as well as on 5 November, Guy Fawkes' Night. Behind this increase in popularity were better and cheaper means of manufacture, and amateur pyrotechnists who were encouraged by the publication in 1844 of Bruhl's *The Art of Making Fireworks* and *Practical Firework Making for Amateurs*. Members of the MECHANICS' INSTITUTES undoubtedly had a hand in spreading the popularity of fireworks, since many branches had their own enthusiastic firework makers.

First-fruits and **Tenths.** The first year's income and a tenth of the sub-sequent annual income of any newly-appointed holder of a benefice, originally paid to the pope. By the Act of ANNATES of 1532 First-fruits and Tenths were taken by Henry VIII (1509–47), and the Court of First-fruits was set up in 1540 to regulate their payment, a duty trans-ferred to the EXCHEQUER in 1554. Tenths were a tax originally imposed by the Papacy to pay for the CRUSADES and the recovery of the Holy Land. The funds for QUEEN ANNE'S BOUNTY, founded in 1703 for the relief of the poorer Anglican clergy, were derived from the income of First-fruits and Tenths.

Fish-and-chips. Perceived as quintessentially 'English', fish-and-chips derive from two immigrant sources: nineteenth-century JEWS brought a taste for fried fish to London which spread outwards across the country until around Oldham in Lancashire it met Irish immigrants with their taste for potatoes; Oldham had shops selling baked and chipped potatoes, and the two elements became combined around 1870. The fish-and-chip peak was in the 1930s, when there were about 30,000 fish-and-chip shops in Britain.

Fishing. Rights over river and lake fishing belong to the owner over whose land the water flows or on whose land it sits (in the case of a lake); the owner is not restricted in the use of machinery, so long as that machinery does not impede navigation. The principal fresh-water fish are barbel, bream, carp, chub, roach, salmon, tench and trout.

Although rod and line have been used immemorially for fresh-water fishing, other methods have had their fashion. In medieval times, monasteries and sometimes large estates maintained STEW PONDS to breed fish for meatless days, catching them in large quantities with nets, a practice which continued until the REFORMATION, when meatless days were abandoned and the ponds fell into disuse, and often into decay in the case of those belonging to monasteries. In Anglo-Saxon and medieval times, those without stew-ponds caught fish by putting a wicker fish wier across a river to trap fish running downstream.

The first work on fishing published in England was in 1496, by Wynkyn de Worde, but the most famous is undoubtedly *The Compleat Angler* by Isaac Walton, first published in 1653. Walton recognized that the finest fresh-water fishing and sport was fly-fishing for brown trout, closely run by salmon fishing. Trouts spawn in October and November and salmon from the end of autumn until the beginning of spring. See also FISHING HOUSES.

Fishing houses. Sometimes called fishing pavilions. The earliest reference to these charming retreats dates to *c.* 1570, at Anthony House in Cornwall, where Richard Carew proposed (but never built) a combined BANQUETING and fishing-house on an island; Bourne Mill in Essex is a converted banqueting-cum-fishing-house of 1591. However, fishing-houses only really came into fashion in the mid eighteenth century: in the 1760s Robert ADAM built one on the edge of a lake at Kedleston Hall, Derbyshire for the first Lord Scardsale. This comprises a fine reception room with windows opening onto the lake, for the ladies to fish from; below, at water level, is a cold PLUNGE BATH, and a boat-house. Another example is to be seen at Exton Hall in Leicestershire, built in the early nineteenth century. See also BANQUET.

Five-mile Act. By a statute of 1664 clergy ejected from their livings because they refused to conform to the Act of Uniformity of 1662 were forbidden to live within five miles of a town. The Act was designed to flush out NONCONFORMISTS, who tended to flourish in urban areas. See also UNIFORMITY, ACTS OF.

Flag officer. Admirals, vice-admirals, rear-admirals and commodores are entitled to fly a flag denoting their rank. In the days of sail, admirals carried their flags at the main-mast, vice-admirals at the fore-mast, and rear-admirals at the mizzen. Commodores of yacht clubs also fly a flag of rank.

Fleaks or **Flakes.** See HURDLES.

Fleet Prison. An infamous London gaol, established by the twelfth century in Farringdon Street on the site of the earlier Fleet Market (near the river Fleet). It was destroyed and rebuilt several times: in the PEASANTS' REVOLT (1381), in the Great Fire of London (1666), and during the Gordon Riots (1780). In the fifteenth century it was used to hold those condemned by the STAR CHAMBER; during the reigns of Mary (1553–8) and Elizabeth I (1558–1603) it was used to imprison, alternately, Protestant and Catholic martyrs, occasionally debtors and, later, those condemned by the COURT OF CHANCERY. From 1640 it was used as a prison for debtors and bankrupts. During the seventeenth, eighteenth and early nineteenth centuries it became notorious for clandestine marriages performed within its walls without benefit of banns or licence. Such marriages were declared illegal by an ACT OF

PARLIAMENT of 1753, and in 1840 the entries contained in the Fleet
Registers (dating from 1686 to 1754) were declared inadmissible as evidence to prove a marriage. The Fleet was closed in pursuance of an Act
of Parliament of 1842, and demolished in 1844.

Floors and floor coverings. For centuries the basic floor covering
was rushes or straw on a packed earth floor; as late as the early sixteenth
century, the floor of the GREAT HALL would be covered in rushes which
were only cleaned out twice yearly. Carpets were too precious to be
found on the floor: used only to cover tables, they were called table
carpets; occasionally in late medieval times a small carpet might be
placed on the floor by a nobleman's bed. A set of three carpets at
Broughton House, Northamptonshire, made in 1584, probably at
Norwich, are believed to be the earliest surviving of English manufacture. A surprising number of Persian carpets survive from the time of
Shah Abbas 1 (1557–1628), and the National Trust correctly displays
many in its keeping on tables.

In the Midlands there was a tradition of lime-ash flooring in upper
rooms; it is extremely hard-wearing, and would have been covered with
woven rush matting. A section of sixteenth-century woven rush
matting has been discovered under floor boards at Hampton Court in
Surrey, and an anonymous German painting of c. 1585, *Queen Elizabeth receiving Dutch Emissaries,* shows a Presence Chamber floor covered
with fitted rush matting. Sometimes plaster was laid on the floorboards
and painted, in imitation tiles or geometric patterns. An example of the
former can be seen in a Flemish illuminated manuscript showing
Edward IV (1461–83) enthroned; of the latter, in Holbein's painting
(1533) of *The Ambassadors* in the National Gallery in London, and in
the anonymous painting *The family of Henry VIII (c.* 1545) in the Royal
Collection.

When the GREAT HALLS passed out of fashion in the early seventeenth
century, the entrance halls which took their place were stone-flagged,
with no floor covering. At the end of the seventeenth century the
BAROQUE fashion for parquet floors in state rooms made carpets super-
fluous, although rugs were used. Oak floors were not polished or var-
nished until the late eighteenth century, a practice said to have come in
with the GOTHIC REVIVAL. In her *Servants' Directory* of 1760, Hannah
Glass does not mention polishing floors at all. Her instructions to the
housemaid are to 'be sure always to have very clean Feet', and continue:
'take some sand, pretty damp, but not too wet, and strew it all over the
Room . . . with a dry rubbing brush dry-scrub them [the boards] well
. . .' Dry-scrubbed floors survive in Syon House in the Red Drawing
Room, and in rooms at Boughton, Northamptonshire and Drumlan-
rig, Dumfries and Galloway. In 1756 Isaac Ware noted that 'The use of

carpeting at this time has set aside the ornamenting of floors in great measure'.

Fitted carpets were quite usual by the 1750s, although it is not apparent when they first came in; there was a fitted Wilton in the Drawing Room at Felbrigg in the 1760s. In 1735 the first KIDDERMINSTER factory had begun producing pileless (flatweave) carpets, and the WILTON factory opened in 1740, manufacturing looped-pile carpets. At this time carpet was made in narrow strips, then sewn together and finished off with a border. However, many people were perfectly happy to live in rooms without carpets; the evocative portraits by Arthur Devis (1711–87) show his sitters in what seem to us to be very bleak interiors, with bare floors, and although the interiors are imaginary, they show how his sitters were pleased to see themselves. Carpets designed by Robert ADAM to reflect his ceilings were specially woven in the 1760s and 70s; one at Kedleston Hall was made in Devonshire, and others are to be found at Syon House, and Osterley, Greater London; Saltram, Devon; and Audley End, Essex. In many houses, the carpets were taken up and replaced with mats in summer.

Stencilled decorations painted directly onto floor boards were once common. Examples survive at Crowcombe Court in Somerset, painted about 1760, and in the Tyrconnel Room at Belton in Lincolnshire, done in the nineteenth century; there is a border of similar date in the drawing-room at Hanbury Hall in Herefordshire.

Painted floorcloths or oilcloths were, perhaps surprisingly, used in the eighteenth century in grand houses as well as farmhouses. 'Kamptulicon', a forerunner of linoleum patented in 1844, was made from India rubber and cork. The modern linoleum floor covering in the chapel at Audley End, Essex, covers some portions of the original oilcloth of the 1770s. Linoleum was patented in the early 1860s, and linoleum 'rugs' painted in Axminster patterns were popular in the latter part of the nineteenth century.

Oilcloth proper may have been the invention of seamen who covered old sail canvas with coats of paint. However, it was not commercially produced until the second half of the nineteenth century. In New York it was called 'a new substance' in 1882. See also AXMINSTER CARPETS, and 'TURKIE' or TURKEY WORK.

Florin. A coin common in name to many European currencies, first minted as a gold coin in Florence in 1252. The British silver florin worth two shillings (or $\frac{1}{10}$ of a pound sterling) was first struck in 1849.

Follies. See EYE-CATCHERS.

Footmen. In towns, from the late middle ages to the sixteenth century a footman walked or ran beside the carriage or horse of persons of rank, wealth or prestige. He was useful in London, especially for running messages; or he might lead a spare horse; but essentially he was a status symbol. Strong footmen with good calves were particularly prized, and from the mid seventeenth century employers raced their running-footmen against each other, naturally with heavy betting on the result.

By the mid seventeenth century, footmen had also taken on some duties in the house, mainly those of waiting at lower tables, such as the STEWARD's; it was then only a short move to waiting at table upstairs, under the supervision of the BUTLER.

In 1771 Lord Clive maintained eight footmen at his Berkeley Square household in London; in 1881 the Duke of Manchester had only one footman at Kimbolton Castle in Cambridgeshire, and Earl Manvers had two at Thoresby Hall, Nottinghamshire in 1884. By that date, however, a tax was payable on male servants, and wages for male employees were higher than those for females.

Forest-work. Tapestry hangings showing forest scenes.

Forks. It is always surprising to find that something we have long taken for granted has been around for only a comparatively short time: the fork is an example. Until the late seventeenth century in England, food was eaten with the fingers of the left hand and a knife or spoon held in the right. Forks were in use on the Continent by the beginning of the seventeenth century, but more to hold the meat still while carving a slice from a shared joint than for eating with. Their use provoked a reaction; many felt no need of 'little forks to make hay with our mouths, to throw our meat into them'. Even Queen Anne, who died in 1714, preferred to eat with her fingers. See also EATING, MEALS, PLATES and TRENCHERS.

Foundlings. Literally meaning 'found' children, usually illegitimate. Unwanted babies were frequently placed in a church doorway or porch, where they would be quickly discovered. Captain Thomas Coram established his Foundling Hospital in Guilford Street, London in 1734. By the door was suspended a basket attached to a bell; when a baby was placed in the basket, the bell rang. At first, only healthy children under two months old were accepted, but from 1756, when the Hospital first began to receive an annual grant from the government, they had to accept any child under one year old, regardless of health. The hospital was flooded with children, and five branch hospitals were opened to cope with the 3,727 admitted in 1757. Between 1756 and 1760 nearly 15,000 children were taken in, but of those only about 4,500 survived (poor parents would bring dying children, to have them buried at the hospital's expense). Comprehensive acceptance was ended, and the government grant ceased in 1771, leaving the Hospital to rely exclusively on CHARITY for its funds. After 1801 the Foundling Hospital only admitted children after interviewing the mother. In 1925 they had the good fortune to sell their site for £1.6 million, and moved to Berkhamstead in Hertfordshire. Less fortunate was the demolition of the hospital buildings in 1928; but as long as you are 'accompanied by a child', you can still visit Coram's Field playground, surrounded by Classical colonnades. See also BYBLOWS; BLANKET, WRONG SIDE OF THE; CHANCELINGS and MERRYBEGOTS.

Fountains. In medieval times the overflows from spring-heads were sometimes made into fountains, often in the shape of an animal head spouting water, and the fountain and well-head remained an important feature up to the RENAISSANCE. There was a stone fountain at Windsor Castle as early as the 1260s. The earliest surviving conduit-head in England (1602) is at Trinity College, Cambridge. Paul Hentzner noted a joke fountain at Hampton Court in 1598: it spurted water at unsuspecting guests, a very Renaissance practical joke. There were other joke fountains at Wilton House, Wiltshire (1663); and at Chatsworth in Derbyshire, a willow tree drenched visitors. The modern willow fountain now at Chatsworth is hardly likely to deceive anyone. Few original waterworks survive in working order today, although Chatsworth still has the famous cascade steps, dating from 1696 and designed by a Frenchman, Grillet, and Caius Gabriel (father of the actor and dramatist Colley) Cibber's Sea Horse fountain (1688); and there are fountains at Melbourne Hall, Derbyshire dating from *c.* 1700. Remnants of fountains survive, such as basins originally designed to reflect light from the water's surface but with their water supply long since gone, and may be seen at Bramham Park, South Yorkshire; Wrest Park, Bedfordshire; Studley Royal, North Yorkshire.

For a time, in the nineteenth century, Britain held the record for the highest gravity-fed fountain in the world: this was again at Chatsworth, where the 6th Duke of Devonshire built the Emperor Fountain especially for a proposed visit in 1843 by Czar Nicholas of Russia. Alas, he never came, but the fountain remains, shooting water 290 feet into the air. Another huge piece of garden plumbing, at Castle Howard, in North Yorkshire, is in the form of a globe surrounded by four muscular tritons, all pouring water into a circular basin; it came from the Great Exhibition of 1851. Italian fountains in porcelain and cast-iron became very fashionable from the time of the Great Exhibition and some of them, or their remains, still exist. At Château Impney in Worcestershire, now a hotel, is a vast stone and cast-iron fountain installed in the 1870s. Witley Court in Worcestershire has been a burnt-out ruin since 1937, but the amazing late nineteenth-century 'Perseus Fountain' survives – a prancing horse twenty-six feet above the water – although Perseus himself has, alas, lost an arm and a knee-wing. The fountain was powered by a beam engine which threw the water 90 feet into the air. In the early part of the twentieth century Sir Edwin LUTYENS substituted taste for BAROQUE display and gradient in waterworks, relying instead on the play of sunlight and the soft tinkle of water from small jets for effect, as at The Deanery, Sonning, Berkshire.

Four-in-hand. See CARRIAGES.

Fox-hunting. Nowadays a very contentious subject, it was not always so. Hunting developed in the twelfth and thirteenth centuries, its point the pursuit of edible game, and led to the breeding of several types of hunting dog. The heavy Talbots and Gascons were used for chasing deer, and lighter gaze-hounds or greyhounds for pursuing hares and rabbits. Other specialist breeds for chasing deer, such as the Lyme mastiffs, bred at Lyme Park, Cheshire, are extinct. Lyme mastiffs were given by James I (1603–25) to the Spanish king and one is shown in a portrait by Velásquez (1599–1660) of Philip IV (1621–65) dressed as a hunter in *c.* 1632–3.

The fox, however, is only eaten by hounds, and its hunting arose from a lack of other suitable wild game – the last wild boar in Britain, for example, was killed in 1683, while enclosure and other factors caused STAG-HUNTING to withdraw in the eighteenth century to remote and uncultivated areas.

Lord Arundel was the first breeder of hounds exclusively for fox-hunting, between 1690 and 1700, and Thomas Boothby of Tooley Park, Leicestershire bred the first pack of pure foxhounds; when Boothby died, in 1752, he had ridden to hounds for fifty-two years. By then Lord Arundel's pack had descended to Hugo Meynell who, as a legendary Master of the Quorn Hunt until his death in 1800, improved the breed with a faster strain of hound. Most hunts are creations of the eighteenth century, although a few developed out of older stag-hunts. By the early nineteenth century, hunting (together with HORSE RACING) had led to improvements in horse breeding to keep pace with the faster hounds.

When the Duke of Lorraine visited newly built Houghton Hall in Norfolk in 1728, Sir Thomas Robinson recorded that 'They hunted six days a week three times with Lord Walpole's fox-hounds and thrice with Sir R[obert Walpole]'s harriers and indeed 'tis very fine open country for sport.' And hunting six days a week was not unusual for the time, nor for the next 150 years.

The hunting season runs from the first Monday in November to the following April. See also CUBBING, GAME and HUNTING PINK.

Framework knitters. See HOSE.

Franchise, The. The right to elect members to the House of Commons, of voting at elections, and the qualification upon which that is based. Derived ultimately from the rights of the freemen of a

Norman manor or BOROUGH, which later included the right to vote. From 1430 to 1832 the English county franchise was limited to forty-shilling freeholders; the franchise varied from borough to borough. In 1832 the first Reform Act unified the borough franchises; the Act of 1867 included all borough householders; and that of 1884 all county householders. All men over 21 and women over 30 were enfranchised in 1918, and since 1928 all women over 21 have had the vote. The voting age was reduced to 18 for both men and women in 1969. See also FREEHOLD, REFORM ACTS, ROTTEN BOROUGHS and SUFFRAGETTE.

Franciscans. Friars Minor; in England, Grey Friars. Founded by St Francis of Assisi in 1208 on the three-fold vow of chastity, poverty, and obedience; the order grew rapidly, but the rule of stringent poverty caused dissent, and under Pope Leo X (1513–21) the order divided into two branches: (1) the Conventuals, who lived in large groups, released from observance of extreme poverty; (2) the Observants, who continued to observe St Francis's rule as closely as possible. A further reform of 1528 led to the establishment of the Capuchins, as a third distinct Franciscan order, but they did not settle in pre-REFORMATION Britain.

The Franciscans, arriving in England in 1224, made foundations at Canterbury, Oxford, and London; the Observants were introduced by Henry VII (1485–1509), with six houses; by the DISSOLUTION there were about fifty houses, of both divisions. Of their churches, which were simple and designed for preaching, there are remains at Coventry, Lincoln, Reading and Yarmouth. The Observants were in Scotland half a century before they came to England and had nine houses there, of which there are remains only at Elgin. Little remains of five houses of Franciscan nuns (Poor Clares) except for a few ruins at Denny, near Edinburgh.

The nineteenth century saw the re-establishment of the Franciscans and the establishment of the Capuchins in Britain, and there are now about fifty houses again, with a further fifty houses of Poor Clares. The Church of England itself has one community of men and another of women, dedicated to the Franciscan ideal. See also AUGUSTINIANS, BENEDICTINES, CARMELITES, CARTHUSIANS, CISTERCIANS, CLUNIACS, DOMINICANS, FRIARS, GILBERTINES, MENDICANT FRIARS and PRE-MONSTRATENSIANS.

Frankpledge, View of. From the earliest times in England there existed a system of maintaining the peace whereby a man's relatives were responsible for his behaviour, and from this grew the principle of forming institutions for mutual responsibility in which every man was obliged to be a member of a group of ten or twelve (also called a tithing). If one member committed an offence, the others were liable for his appearance in court, and if he failed to appear the other members of the tithing paid the penalty. A manorial View of Frankpledge was held twice a year at the COURT-LEET to ensure that all men and boys on the manor were 'in frankpledge' or members of a tithing, and whether these were of adequate size and performing their duty. Great households were exempted, as the head of the household assumed full responsibility for the behaviour of all members thereof. By the fifteenth century the system was breaking down, the name only remaining, now signifying the COURT-LEET of which it had once been a part.

Freehold. Originally this was land held without terms of service tenure, although it might involve the holder in KNIGHT-SERVICE or socage – payment of a nominal rent in lieu of knight-service. A freeholder held his land in perpetuity under COMMON LAW. Freehold tenure was widespread in the DANELAW areas.

Freemasons. Probably medieval in origin, from the itinerant masons, 'free' of any employer, who travelled from site to site, as work became available, in gangs of about six under a master, and set up their lodges, or workshops, at the building site. These lodges operated as small GUILDS, the municipal craft guild as it was then known being unsuitable for the conditions (i.e., often in remote places) under which many masons worked, and by the end of the seventeenth century, after a general assembly of masons, others were accepted as honorary members. Modern Freemasonry originated with the foundation in 1717 of the first Grand Lodge of England – the governing body under a grand master. The Grand Lodge of Scotland followed in 1736. The grand master had the prerogative of creating new lodges, and later, provincial grand masters were elected. Freemasons acknowledge God as the Great Architect of the Universe, and the meetings of its members are carried out with much symbolic ritual and secrecy. A Papal Bull of 1738 excommunicated Freemasons, and they were again condemned in 1864. Today Freemasons are noted for their charitable work – schools and hospitals in particular – and have a reputation for great care of members and their families in adversity.

Friars. A generic term for members of the mendicant religious orders, as distinguished from MONKS. Monks occupied religious houses to which they were, in theory, confined, and led inward-looking lives devoted to prayer, contemplation and learning. Friars, on the other hand, were mobile, international and evangelical, using their friaries only for rest and recuperation. Initially they identified themselves with outcasts and beggars, rejecting the material things of life and living by begging for their food and clothing. It is estimated there were more than 5,000 friars in England and Wales by the end of the thirteenth century. The four great mendicant orders – Chaucer's 'alle the orders foure' – were the DOMINICANS (Black Friars), who reached England in

1221, the FRANCISCANS (Grey Frairs; 1224), the CARMELITES (White Frairs; *c.* 1240), and the Austin Friars (AUGUSTINIANS) or Hermits. See also MENDICANT FRIARS.

Friendly Societies. Sometimes called Benefit Societies, they were first formed in the seventeenth century for mutual insurance to ensure some sort of income to members during incapacity for work due to sickness, and eventual old age, together with a lump sum at death of a member or his wife, in return for payment of a regular subscription. They increased rapidly in the eighteenth century, with a total membership of 650,000 in 7,200 societies by 1797. The first Friendly Society Acts of 1793 and 1795 gave them some legal protection, and the number of societies increased further in the nineteenth century under frequent legislation designed to regulate their organization and purpose, ending the century with a membership of 5,450,000 in 27,500 registered societies. Their number declined with the introduction of the National Insurance Act of 1911, which specifically allowed Friendly Societies to be associated with national health insurance: it was this aspect (not others) which was ended by the National Insurance Act of 1946, resulting in a further decline. Nevertheless, Friendly Societies continue to exist, enjoying tax advantages which make them attractive for purposes quite other than their original ideals. See also GUARDIANS OF THE POOR.

Funerals. Funerals are for the living and not for the dead: St Augustine made this point in AD 430, but his words went largely unheeded. Between the sixth century AD and the reign of Edward VI (1547–53), prayers for the soul of the dead person were considered efficacious in ensuring its transition to Eternity; after the middle of the sixteenth century the purpose of a funeral was to give some comfort to the living, and at the same time record a peaceful transition of property to the heir.

The form of a funeral depended on the wealth of the family: the coffin of a humble villager was carried by mourners on a bier, and some of these biers still survive in dusty vestries; the nobility were buried, at increasing expense and with great pomp, by the College of Heralds. However, from the sixteenth century this expense was avoided by having night burials in which the HERALDS had no hand.

It was customary for the corpse of the head of a powerful and wealthy family to lie in state, a survival of the early medieval custom of exposing the body to demonstrate that the dead man really *was* dead, and not (apparently, at least) by foul play, thus ensuring the peaceful handing-over of power to the heir. See also EMBALMING, MAIDENS' GARLANDS, HATCHMENTS and LYING–IN–STATE.

Furniture arrangement. Until the end of the eighteenth century, furniture in rooms where company was received was arranged round the walls, which left space for numbers of guests to move about and to be seen. If a chair was needed, then servants were at hand to bring one instantly. By the 1780s a new fashion had evolved, of placing furniture out in the room, and especially round the fireplace, with sofas placed at right-angles to the hearth instead of alongside. This fashion brought with it the need for various light pieces of furniture which could be carried and placed by members of the family, such as work-boxes, games-tables, occasional tables – and the sofa-table, which was placed before the sofa and not behind it, as we do now. The convention, in use, of the arrangement in front of the hearth was that the women sat in a semicircle on the sofas and light chairs, the hostess occupying a seat next to the fire, while the men stood in the middle, sparkling with witty conversation. It proved neither convivial nor social; in 1782 Fanny Burney tells us that some hostesses were trying to get rid of 'the circle'. 'My whole care is to prevent a circle,' exclaimed one hostess as she moved the chairs into conversational groupings. Once the old formality had been broken, the new conversational arrangement was quickly adopted. Nineteenth-century photographs of grand interiors show what appears to be a complete muddle of furniture, but careful observers will be able to see that the chairs and sofas are arranged so that two, three or four people can sit together and converse. Today, when there is little entertaining on the grand scale, the need for large rooms filled with many conversational groupings has passed, and we are back to informal seating around the hearth.

Furniture, silver. Very grand silver furniture was a BAROQUE fashion, imported from France at the RESTORATION in 1660. Very little remains: it was melted down when it became outdated. However, Knole in Kent has some astonishing pieces of silver furniture of 1680–1, and there is an earlier set of *c.*, 1670 at Windsor Castle, presented by the City of London to Charles II.

Furniture, taste for antique. With the vogue for the PICTURESQUE and the GOTHIC REVIVAL, in the late eighteenth century, came the problem of appropriate furnishings, and thus arose an interest in old furniture. That Christie's found it profitable, in 1825, to hold a sale of old panelling, antique furniture and old wood carvings, indicates a demand. This furniture did not come in 'sets', so of necessity a mixture of pieces became fashionable; the alternative was to have specially made GOTHIC suites: Sir Walter Scott's Abbotsford House in the Borders Region, created in the 1820s, is a good surviving example of the Antiquarian Taste. See also AUCTION SALES.

Fusiliers. Originally a soldier armed with a 'fusil', a light musket (so named from the fusil, the fire-steel in the tinder box needed to ignite the powder to fire it). The term has only historical significance today, as all the Fusilier Regiments now carry firearms similar to those used by the rest of the infantry.

Fustian. A cloth with a linen warp and cotton weft; some included worsted threads.

Galleries. See LONG GALLERIES, PICTURE GALLERIES and SCULPTURE GALLERIES.

Gambling. Gambling moved into organized clubs (see CLUBS OF LONDON) in the late eighteenth century when card games such as whisk or whist, faro or Pharaoh (betting on the order in which certain cards will appear), macao (similar to *vingt-et-un*), lansquenet (of German origin and played since the 1680s), and piquet (1646) were popular. Most popular of all was hazard, a two-dice game in which the chances are complicated by the rules. The 5th Duke of Bedford (1765–1802) lost £30,000 (£2 million today) at one session of cards in 1774; about the same time, Charles James Fox (1749–1806) had gambling debts of £147,000 (nearly £10 million). Writing in 1814, Captain Gronow recalled a story of a Major-General John Scott, who won £200,000 (£12 million) at White's Club, playing whist.

Game and **Game Laws.** With certain exceptions live wild animals cannot be owned. These exceptions are: tamed or captured wild animals until they escape (swans are an exception to this), and young animals too small to run or fly away from the owner's land. A landowner who retains the hunting rights over his land may hunt his own game; someone who is granted sporting or hunting rights by the landowner has a right to the game killed. Dead wild animals on a property belong to the landowner or the person holding the sporting rights. Game laws were created to make poaching illegal, and regulation was based on game licences.

The sporting estate was a creation of the Normans, who introduced deer hunting to England as a royal monopoly. William I (1066–87) '. . . loved the tall deer', says the Anglo-Saxon Chronicler, 'as if he were their father'. He emparked 17,000 acres to create the New Forest, which made a deep impression on the resentful popular mind. The section of MAGNA CARTA (1215) dealing with Forest Law gave the barons some hunting rights, and the game laws of 1377 gave lesser landowners of a certain standard rights to some of the game on their own lands; these rights were extended in 1671 to owners with a freehold rental income of £100 a year.

Penalties for poaching were increased in the seventeenth century; although to us they seem ferocious, they were no more so than other punishments of the time. The 1773 Game Act made daytime poaching punishable by flogging, night-time poaching by transportation. By the early nineteenth century landowners were using man-traps and spring guns to maim and wound poachers. Spring guns were made illegal in 1827 and subsequent Game Acts relaxed the severity of punishments for poaching; fines took the place of flogging, and a prison sentence of hard labour replaced transportation. Nevertheless, poaching sometimes led to violence, and to pitched battles between poaching gangs and game keepers. In the churchyard of St Ethelbert's at Little Dean in Gloucestershire is the grave of a policeman killed apprehending poachers.

To raise taxation revenue, an Act of 1784 introduced game licences: two guineas (£2 2s.) for landowners and half a guinea (10s. 6d.) for gamekeepers. Licences to sell game were introduced in 1831, when game was defined as including hares, pheasants, grouse, heath or moor game, and bustards. Snipe, quail, landrail, woodcock and rabbits were not classified as game, but could only be taken by certified persons. See also SHOOTING, GUN ROOMS, FOX-HUNTING and OUTDOOR SERVANTS.

Games table. A small flat-topped table, usually inlaid with a chess-board lid, which when opened reveals other boards, backgammon for example. Beneath are cupboards or drawers for the CHESS, draughts and backgammon pieces. Fashionable during the eighteenth and early nineteenth centuries.

Gardens. The first gardens in Britain were planted by the Romans, within the confines of the courtyards in the centres of their villas, and consisted of hedged areas with ornamental plants in blocks, often with a fountain and pool in the centre. In medieval times, monks planted gardens to grow medicinal herbs, and flowers for the altar. There was no room for a garden inside the medieval castle walls, and sweet-smelling herbs used when washing and to strew among the rushes on the floors, and herbs for cooking and medicine, were grown outside the walls. Illuminated manuscripts, such as *Les Très Riches Heures du Duc de Berry* (*c.* 1411–16), show gardens of this type set out in formal square beds; Tudor gardens followed the same pattern. Nature was clearly something to be kept under control, and garden design leaned towards geometric patterns. Patterned beds called KNOT GARDENS, possibly based on needlework designs, were planned to be looked down on from the upper windows of a LONG GALLERY, or from a raised MOUND, as at Little Morton Hall and Dunham Massey, both in Cheshire. Colour from flowers might be augmented or replaced by red brick dust, coal dust or coloured pebbles. In the late sixteenth century, refugees from continental wars and religious persecutions and foreign travellers brought with them both new design ideas and exotic plants. Water-works as seen in Italy were constructed, and the first herbals were printed. Hatfield House, Hertfordshire (1607–12) had the latest fashion in gardens, with FOUNTAINS, terraces, fishponds and statues: the Queen of France sent 500 fruit trees for it. The early seventeenth-century terraced gardens at Haddon Hall in Derbyshire still retain traces of the idea of a Tuscan garden in their simple formality. Hot Italian summers demanded the shade of pergolas, and in the background of Isaac Oliver's (1556–1617) exquisitely painted miniature *Portrait of a Young Man* in the Queen's collection, we can see a couple, perhaps lovers, wandering out from a pergola into a knot garden. Another fragment of an early garden, surrounding a fountain, is that at Bolsover Castle, Derbyshire, made in 1634 for the 1st Duke of Newcastle (1592–1676) for a visit by Charles I (1625–49).

When the exiled Charles II (1660–85) returned in 1660, knot gardens gave way to those based on majestic formal BAROQUE gardens, such as those at Versailles. Vistas with intersecting *allées* (avenues), long rectangles of water (often known as canals), and distant fountains, all defied nature with their unnatural forms. These were on the giant scale: Bramham Park in South Yorkshire has many miles of intersecting *allées*, laid out in 1700. Ham House in Surrey, Hampton Court, Erddig in Clwyd, and Melbourne Hall in Derbyshire all have something left of original gardens from this period.

The weighty formality of the Baroque fashion in gardens was ended, perhaps surprisingly, by writers who had visited Italy. Joseph Addison (1672–1719) recommended the Roman *campagna*, as depicted in paintings by Poussin (1593–1665) and Claude (1600–82). The first 'natural' garden was made by Alexander Pope (1688–1744) at Twickenham in 1719. Introducing the HA-HA (from France), Bridgeman (d. 1738) did away with the need for fencing or hedges: gardens could now blend into the landscape. William KENT (1684–1748) developed the idea of the 'natural' garden: his earliest surviving work may be seen at Rousham in Oxfordshire where Nature, instead of being disciplined – clipped, trained and distorted – was set free (within limits). Stourhead in Wiltshire (made 1740–60) is a good example of a 'natural' garden.

Lancelot BROWN (1715–83), known as 'Capability' from his way of assuring patrons that their landscapes had 'capabilities', swept away most of what remained of older gardens: he banished the formal garden, and brought the park to the walls of the house. One looked out onto carefully contrived views of trees framed by a distant belt of green – indeed, 'clumping and belting' was the method he used, according to his detractors. This truly English concept became widely fashionable, and for the first time our ideas on landscaping were exported to mainland Europe. Humphry REPTON followed Brown's lead, but reintroduced the flower bed, and terraces around the house. In thirty years Repton created nearly 200 garden landscapes, an output almost equal to that of Brown.

In the nineteenth century, J.C. Loudon (1783–1843) developed schemes of planting-out of formal beds around the house; with the development of heated glasshouses and the availability of cheap labour, plants were often changed three times in a summer. During the preceding century the number of garden plants grown in England had multiplied fivefold, and Loudon's style may be seen as a response to so much choice. 'Italian' gardens were designed; even the old Tudor knot gardens were revived, by William Nesfield (1794–1881; brother-in-law to the architect Salvin), who designed more than 260 gardens – Alton Towers, Staffordshire; Holkham Hall in Norfolk – and whose work also included the installation of the impressive fountains at Castle Howard, North Yorkshire, and advising Baron Rothschild on the siting of Mentmore in Buckinghamshire. The inevitable reaction against this busy formality came from William Robinson (1839–1935), when in 1883 he published *The English Flower Garden*. Robinson abominated 'pastry-work gardening' and advocated a return to the 'natural' garden, reflected today in the flowery cottage garden: the 'gardenesque' style.

Gertrude Jekyll (1843–1932) developed and refined Robinson's ideas. Trained as a painter, she 'painted with plants' when her eyesight failed, grouping flowers and foliage to create the colour effects she desired. Her influence was immense and remains strong to this day. Hestercombe in Somerset is an excellent example of her several collaborations with the architect Sir Edwin LUTYENS. Other gardens, not made by her but developed along similar lines, are at Hidcote Manor, Gloucestershire, at Nymans in Sussex, and Vita Sackville-West's famous garden at Sissinghurst Castle, Kent. See also FERNERIES, GARDEN STAFF, GAZEBOS, KITCHEN GARDENS, KNOT GARDENS, MAZES, MOUNDS, QUINCUNX GARDENS and ROCK GARDENS.

Garden staff. In the days when labour was plentiful, gardens were worked by a head gardener and a varying number of under-gardeners and garden boys. The head gardener was in charge of all departments of the garden, from the hothouses and vegetables to the flower gardens, and often responsible as well for the arrangement of flowers to decorate the house. He was equal in rank to the HOUSEKEEPER and BUTLER, and on the rare occasions when he had time to eat in the SERVANTS' HALL, he withdrew with them for dessert. See also GARDENS, KITCHEN GARDENS and OUTDOOR STAFF.

Garderobe. The medieval equivalent of the modern lavatory: no more than a seat suspended over a shaft dropping into a moat or, more usually, down its own tower.

Within days of arriving in late 1568 at her first prison, Tutbury Castle in Staffordshire, Mary, Queen of Scots (1542–87) was complaining of the stench of the garderobes near her apartment: Tutbury was a medieval castle, designed for about 200 occupants, but Mary's court and hangers-on, and the soldiers guarding the royal prisoner, brought the numbers above 400, and the garderobes were overloaded. Fortunate was the house where the garderobes discharged straight into a surrounding moat – as they did at Little Moreton Hall, Cheshire. Where there was no convenient moat, a hatch at the base enabled the excreta at the foot of the shaft to be cleared out once a year. Haddon Hall in Derbyshire has a two-seater garderobe, with two cleaning hatches. Provided that the drop is more than twenty feet, there is no smell in the garderobe itself. At Wollaton Hall (1580–88) near Nottingham the interior garderobes discharged into shafts flushed out by rainwater.

At Audley End in Essex, built in 1603 on the site of a Benedictine monastery, the interior garderobes discharged into culverts – the old monastic drains; the system was so efficient that they were used well into the nineteenth century. England's largest garderobe was Whittington's Longhouse in London, a public garderobe with sixty-four seats, built with money left by Sir Richard Whittington (d. 1423). See also CLOSE STOOLS and SEWAGE.

Garniture de cheminée. Matching sets of three, five or seven ornaments, usually vases, to be set on a mantelpiece to make a symmetrical arrangement: originally Chinese export porcelain or Delft pottery copies. As a fashion the garniture reached its height about 1700 and declined with the onset of the ROCOCO fashion for asymmetry. In the late eighteenth century the term was used to describe clock-and-candlestick sets. See also CLOCKS.

Garter, Order of the. The most ancient order of KNIGHTHOOD in Europe, inspired by the Arthurian legends of the Knights of the Round Table and conceived by Edward III (1327–77) in 1344 (according to the chronicler Froissart) but only inaugurated on St George's Day 1348 at Windsor Castle, which has remained its base. Restricted to twenty-four members, the Sovereign and the Prince of Wales, it was initially an order exclusively for English knights, but was later occasionally bestowed upon distinguished foreign knights. The blue garter and motto of the Order are said to originate from an occasion when Joan of Kent (1328–84), later wife of the Black Prince, lost her garter at a ball at Calais; it was found and returned to her by Edward III who, teased by his retainers, said: 'Honi soit qui mal y pense' (Evil be to him who evil thinks.) Membership is bestowed at the discretion of the Sovereign, and each knight has a stall, with his banner above, in St George's Chapel, Windsor. In the late eighteenth and early nineteenth centuries the order was enlarged to include the sons and descendants of George I (1714–27). Ladies have always been admitted: effigies of Margaret Harcourt at Stanton Harcourt (Henry VI) and Alice Dee of Suffolk at Ewelme (Edward IV) wear the garter on their left arms.

Gate-houses and lodges. The entrance to a CASTLE was the fore-runner of all gate-houses. By the sixteenth century the gate-house had become a porter's lodge and, like the castle gate, guarded a forecourt. The gate-house at Burton Agnes, Humberside (built 1598–1610) echoes the idea of the old castle gate-house in being the only entrance to the forecourt: in such a case, the porter's discretion as to who was admitted and who was kept out was important. As the fashion in house design moved away from an enclosed forecourt, the porter moved to the park gate, where lodges were often built one either side of the gate. Possibly the earliest such survivors are the brick pavilions dating from *c.* 1525 at Sutton Place, Surrey which mark the entrance drive. Of more certain date are the two lodges flanking the entrance to Ham House, Greater London (*c.* 1610).

Lodges are the prelude to the great house; in some cases, as at Blenheim in Oxfordshire, they are the overture to a great performance. But their purpose was useful, as well as decorative. With a park full of deer, a gated wall or fence was needed to keep the animals in; however, to have to halt before one's own gates, even when there was a footman to get down to open them, was lacking in dignity. How much more impressive it was for the coachman to sound a horn to warn of one's approach, so that the gates would be standing open for the coach to drive through without a check. Such was the practice in the eighteenth century, when the majority of gate lodges were built. By this time the office of porter had vanished and the gates were managed by a gate-keeper, often the wife of gardener or gamekeeper, whose job was simply to prevent deer escaping from the park through the gates and to open them when summoned.

Gate lodges were built in all styles: the Classical, after Inigo JONES, as at Fonthill, Wiltshire; the GREEK REVIVAL, as at Wentworth Wood-house, South Yorkshire; the GOTHIC, as at Gisburn Park, Lancashire; the cottage *ornée*, as at Ugbrooke Park, Devon – all these of various dates in the eighteenth century; in the nineteenth century Italianate lodges were built at Alton Towers, Staffordshire. Some lodges were merely grand, like those at Eaton Hall in Cheshire, where the French-style Eccleston Lodge of 1881 was sufficiently commodious to provide a home for a recent Dowager Duchess of Westminster.

Gavelkind. A form of land-tenure associated particularly with Kent but also found in other parts of the country, and derived from two Anglo-Saxon words meaning 'holding of a family', gavelkind was a sur-vival of pre-feudal, pre-Conquest custom in which the inheritance of land was in equal parts among sons and, when there were no sons, among daughters (but never among both). A closely similar custom in Wales was abolished by Henry VIII (1509–47), but continued in other places. Curiously, PRIMOGENITURE was COMMON LAW in England except in Kent, where gavelkind remained Common Law until it was abolished by the Law of Property Act of 1922.

Gazebo. An eighteenth-century word for a small viewing tower or summer-house with a view, in a garden or park. When placed on the roof of a house it is called a BELVEDERE. It is difficult to distinguish Tudor BANQUETING HOUSES from what are effectively gazebos. One at Long Melford Hall, Suffolk (c. 1560), for example, has a fine view and could have served both purposes, while the seventeenth-century gazebo at Packwood House in Warwickshire was built for the view and nothing else, banqueting houses being by then out of fashion. A vogue for gazebos returned in the nineteenth and early twentieth centuries, when formal garden layouts (often best viewed from an elevated position) became fashionable again.

General Strike. The only General Strike in Britain, from 3 to 13 May 1926, was called by the Trades Union Congress (TUC) in support of already striking coal-miners who were resisting a reduction in wages and increase in hours imposed on them by mine owners when a temporary government subsidy ended on 1 May 1926. No agreement on the continuation of the subsidy was found to be possible between the government, under Stanley Baldwin, and the Miners' Federation, and the mine owners ordered a lock-out on 30 April. Responding to the TUC's call for a General strike, employees on the railways and docks, in printing, chemicals, iron and steel, electricity, building, gas and road transport came out on strike. Government plans made some nine months earlier immediately came into effect: the army and police supported by a willing middle class took over many of the strikers' jobs. The TUC leadership was unprepared for the emergency they had provoked, and when the strike was declared illegal their resolve was further undermined; they surrendered unconditionally on 12 May. Only the miners continued to strike, but eventually economic necessity forced them back to work, for less pay and longer hours. See also TRADES UNIONS.

Gentlemen-at-Arms. The gentlemen-at-arms form the personal consort of the sovereign, and their full title is 'Queen's [or King's, when appropriate] Bodyguard of the Honourable Corps of Gentlemen at Arms'. This corps was created by Henry VIII at his accession in 1509 and originally called 'the Pensioners', a name which remained in use until the time of James II. Parliament's declaration in 1674 that this corps, the YEOMEN OF THE GUARD and the MILITIA, constituted the only lawful armed forces in the realm testifies to their importance in the development of an organized army. However, the original character of the corps declined, until it was reconstituted on a military basis in 1862 when only decorated officers of the regular armed services were eligible for appointment. There are five officers of the corps – the captain (always a peer), lieutenant, standard-bearer, clerk of the cheque (adjutant) and sub-officer – and 39 gentlemen-at-arms.

Gentleman. A term, almost archaic today and really only used when addressing meetings, which implies something of good manners, good taste, good education and good feeling to others. In the sixteenth and seventeenth centuries the term 'gentleman' had become little more than a money-raising fiction of the office of HERALDS, applied to those who had the right to bear arms (and were therefore encouraged to apply – and pay for – a grant of arms) and who did not earn their living by labour. In his *A Description of England*, first published in 1577, William Harrison found that anyone 'who can live without manual work and thereto is able . . . will bear the port, charge, and countenance of a gentleman'. He felt that it had become far too easy.

In Anthony Trollope's (1815–1882) *The Prime Minister*, published in serial form in 1875–6, Abel Wharton, QC refuses to consider Ferdinand Lopez as a suitor for his daughter Emily on the grounds that Lopez is not a gentleman – for no other reason than that his father was Portuguese. Even at that date it was difficult to be a gentleman unless one's father had been one. Later in the same novel Wharton says, '. . . a man doesn't often become a gentleman in the first generation'. Various professions were by that date allowed to be gentlemanly: barristers, but not solicitors; some successful stockbrokers; money brokers; surgeons, but seldom doctors; bankers; successful brewers; and all clergy. However, Gerard Manley Hopkins (1844–89), a contemporary of Trollope, warned that 'the quality of a gentleman is so very fine a thing that it seems to me one should not be at all hasty in concluding one possesses it.' See also CHIVALRY.

Gesso. A material made from whiting, size and linseed oil, widely used in the early eighteenth century for decorative detail. Picture and mirror frames, for example, were covered with a layer of gesso before GILDING. It was also applied as a moulded decoration, and when applied over wire could stand clear of the frames to make swags and similar decorative details. From the 1690s gesso was used to decorate furniture with low-relief ornament, and table-tops of gilded gesso decoration were very fashionable in the reign of Queen Anne. Furniture made in the 1740s in the style of William KENT had a great deal of decoration, and it is also often seen on PIER-TABLES of the period. See also 'COMPOSITION' and PAPIER MÂCHÉ.

Ghosts. The souls of the dead in Hades, but especially the spectres of dead persons appearing to the living. See also HAUNTED SITES.

Gibbons, Grinling (1648–1721). A wood-carver and sculptor born in Rotterdam who came to Britain *c.* 1667 and in 1671 was introduced by John Evelyn (1620–1706) to Charles II (1660–85), who appointed him to the Board of Works. He worked with Christopher WREN (1632–1723) at St Paul's and in rebuilding the City of London churches burnt down in the Great Fire of 1666. Although best known for his carving in limewood, fruitwood or pine, he was just as versatile working in stone; Westminster Abbey, for example, has three of his monuments. His carving is highly distinctive, of amazing quality and remarkable realism; however, much of the work attributed to him is not in fact his. Examples which *are* can be seen at Sudbury Hall in Derbyshire and Belton House in Lincolnshire, and there is a baptismal font at St James's, Piccadilly, London. The carved, open pea-pod, often said to be his 'signature', is in fact a common feature of BAROQUE carving.

Gig. A light, two-wheeled, one-horse carriage that became fashionable in the early nineteenth century. See also CARRIAGES.

Gilbertines. A small order of CANONS REGULAR founded by St Gilbert of Sempringham in Lincolnshire, and the only religious order of English origin. Established in his native village as a women's community, it quickly drew recruits; other establishments were founded, as were communities of priests and clerics to minister spiritually to the nuns. The rule, drawn up in 1148, was modelled on AUGUSTINIAN and CISTERCIAN lines. The order never spread out of England. At the DISSOLUTION there were some twenty-five houses concentrated in Lincolnshire, Yorkshire, and East Anglia. Chicksands Priory, Bedfordshire is on the site of a Gilbertine foundation. See also AUGUSTINIANS, BENEDICTINES, CARMELITES, CARTHUSIANS, CISTERCIANS, CLUNIACS, DOMINICANS, FRANCISCANS, FRIARS, MENDICANT FRIARS and PREMONSTRATENSIANS.

Gilbert's Act (1782). This permitted parishes to combine into 585 'Unions', each with its own board of parish representatives elected by the rate-payers, and to build Union workhouses. The able-bodied were provided with work outside the establishment, and their accommodation was subsidized from parish rates. In practice, Gilbert's Act abolished the workhouse test of 1723. See also BADGE-MEN, POOR LAW, SPEENHAMLAND SYSTEM and WORKHOUSE.

Gilding. The application of gold to a metal or other surface, by various methods. In gilding metal, gold leaf (gold hammered out into very thin sheets) or powdered gold is bonded to the surface of the metal by a complex process in which the gold is chemically combined with another substance (usually mercury) and heat is used to bond the gold to the surface metal; this is known as fire-gilding.

A close examination of the surface of a gilded wooden mirror or picture frame will reveal the thin joins where the sheets of gold leaf were laid next to one another. Eighteenth-century gold leaf came in several different colours, from the best full yellow, down to a leaf with a reddish tinge produced by alloys added to make it cheaper. The cheapest of all, called Dutch gold, contained more copper than gold, and has tarnished badly over the years.

Wooden surfaces (including furniture) were gilded in one of several ways: oil-gilding, varnish-gilding, Japanner's gilding, and wet- or water-gilding. The cheapest was oil-gilding, in which gold leaf was stuck to the ground with a linseed oil-based adhesive after the ground had been primed with a drying oil mixed with yellow ochre and a little vermilion – often the red now shows through, as a result of wear from dusting or polishing. The gold leaf was picked up and laid on with a squirrel's-tail brush. In varnish-gilding, varnish took the place of the linseed oil-based adhesive; Japanner's gilding used powdered gold mixed with honey applied to the ground with a size made up from linseed oil; in water-gilding a water-based adhesive was used. Water gilding (once referred to as burnished gold) was a time consuming process. First the surface of the wood was gessoed (this was repeated 7 or 8 times), then a layer of burnished size (bole) was applied. The surface was then wet with water and the leaves of gold applied. Finally the surface was allowed to dry and the gold burnished.

Today we have become accustomed to the tarnished and subdued appearance of gilded and part-gilded (called parcel-gilt) frames and furniture – not at all what was originally intended, which may be seen to startling effect in the newly re-gilded furniture at Althorp House, Northamptonshire, now returned to its original glitter. One has to remember that gold leaf glows in candlelight, reflecting the light and revealing decorative details that would otherwise be invisible. At Chatsworth in the 1840s the 6th Duke of Devonshire had the exteriors of the wooden window frames of the STATE APARTMENTS gilded; surprisingly, this treatment proved an economy for his heirs: the frames have needed little attention until recently, and they remain gilded today.

The cardinal sin is to touch up old gilding with 'gold' paint.

Gillow of Lancaster. Cabinet-makers based in Lancaster in the eighteenth and nineteenth centuries. Unlike Hepplewhite and Chippendale, whose furniture is only or mainly known through their publications, Gillow customarily stamped theirs with the mark 'Gillows Lancaster'; another difference was that Gillow furniture was the product of a dynasty of fine cabinet-makers, rather than of one man in his lifetime. The first entry in Robert Gillow's order-book is dated 1729. His two sons Richard I and Robert followed in the business, and premises were taken in Oxford Street, London in 1769. Old Robert died in 1772, at which time the firm was known as Gillow & Taylor; by 1776 it was trading as Gillow, by 1790 as Robert Gillow & Company, Upholsterers, and in 1811, on the death of Richard I, as G. & R. Gillow Co. Richard's son, Richard II (b. 1772), succeeded to the firm; his son, Richard III (1806–66), retired in 1830 and was the last of the family in the business. From 1830 the firm continued without the family connection, and by 1900 had amalgamated with the Liverpool firm of Waring, trading as Waring & Gillow; they were responsible for the furnishing of many Atlantic liners, including RMS *Queen Mary*, and continued in business until 1961 when the Lancashire works closed down.

Gillow's were known for fine furniture; they went to great pains to select good mahogany, and imported their own supplies. Richard I invented the telescopic dining-table, the DAVENPORT desk was first made by Gillow in the 1790s, and the round mahogany library table was first made by them in 1795. Richard II took out a patent in 1800 for the Patent Imperial Dining Table.

Leighton Hall in Lancashire (the home of Richard II and III), Lotherton Hall in West Yorkshire, and Tatton Park in Cheshire, all contain the Gillow furniture made for them; Gillow furniture can also be seen at the Judge's Lodgings, York; Abbot Hall, Kendal, Cumbria; the Lancaster City Museum; and the Victoria & Albert Museum, London. See also ARCHITECTS, DRESSING-TABLE and GRAND JURY.

Glass. See WINDOW GLASS.

Glebe. Land held by a beneficed clergyman. Originally, a holding in the open fields sufficient to support a parish priest; this later proved inadequate, and additional parish levies were made. See also TITHES.

Globes, terrestrial and **celestial.** Globes mounted on stands were known, if unusual, in sixteenth-century Britain. A woodcut of *c.* 1640 by Abraham Bosse (1602–76), *Les Vierges Folles*, shows a Parisian interior in which a terrestrial globe decorates a table. Since French styles were avidly copied in England it is highly likely that globes were used in a similarly decorative manner here, and by 1700 a pair of globes had become an almost compulsory part of the furnishing of a gentleman's library. George Adams was one of the most noted eighteenth-century makers. Originally globes were supplied with protective leather covers, and such a pair (*c.* 1670), with a scorched-on pattern, can be seen at Ham House, London.

Gnomes, garden. Not the modern invasion one might suppose – gnomes began their advance from Germany in 1847, when Sir Charles Isham made a small, steep rock garden at Lamport Hall in Northamptonshire and peopled it with a tribe of quite large gnomes from Nuremberg; there is now only one left, and he is safely exhibited in a glass case. The others were taken to Longnor Hall in Shropshire and no trace of them remains. Until 1995 there was a family of four, four foot high, gnomelike creatures in the conservatory of Harlaxton Manor, Lincolnshire. These figures, carved out of gritstone, one depicting a dancing couple and two wearing large-brimmed hats, were Commedia dell'Arte characters and included the dwarf Punchinello. Commedia dell' Arte figures were popular in eighteenth-century Italian gardens and it might be that the fashion for gnomes originally went to Germany from Italy before being taken up by Sir Charles Isham. See also PUNCH AND JUDY.

Golf. A Scottish game popular at least as early as the fifteenth century, but its precise origins are not known. The name may be derived from a Celtic word, *kolbe*, meaning a club. The oldest club in the other sense is the Royal Blackheath, founded in 1608, followed by St Andrews in 1754, and the Royal Musselborough in 1774 (the Honourable Company of Edinburgh Golfers has Minutes dating back to 1744, but is not counted because it does not have a course). St Andrews took the name of 'The Royal and Ancient Golf Club of St Andrews' when William IV (1830–37) became its patron in 1834. A golf links (as distinct from a golf course) is a course consisting of tough, coarse grass on sandy ground near the seashore. See also BOUNDER.

Gong, dressing. An essentially Victorian feature of a large household. One hour before dinner was to be served, the dressing-gong would be sounded as a warning to guests to go upstairs to bathe and dress. The gong was sounded again when dinner was served; it was also sounded to announce LUNCHEON, but never for breakfast: this was self-service, and might be available for more than two hours.

Lady Diana Cooper remembered the gong man at Belvoir Castle, Leicestershire, about 1900: 'The gong man was an old retainer, one of those numberless ranks of domestic servants which have completely disappeared and today seem fabulous. He was admittedly very old, he wore a white beard to his waist. Three times a day he rang the gong – for luncheon, for dressing-time, for dinner. He would walk down the interminable passages, his livery hanging loosely on his bent old bones, clutching his gong with one hand and with the other feebly brandishing the padded knobbed stick with which he struck it. Every corridor had to be warned and the towers too, so I suppose he banged on and off for ten minutes, thrice daily.'

Gothic architecture. Gothic is the architecture of the pointed arch, which developed from the Norman or Romanesque round arch. The pointed arch was introduced to Britain by the CISTERCIANS *c.* 1160–80, as at Roche Abbey in Yorkshire and was inspired by French precedent. The first fully-fledged example of Gothic architecture in Britain is the east end of Canterbury Cathedral, begun in 1175 by William of Sens, and French in essence. The first real English Gothic was built at Wells, *c.* 1180, and Lincoln, 1192, and is distinguished by a strong horizontal line. Thereafter the style, never static, evolved until the end of the sixteenth century. The evolution is categorized in three divisions – EARLY ENGLISH, DECORATED and PERPENDICULAR – convenient terms of classification devised by Thomas Rickman (1776–1841) *c.* 1811 which have been in use ever since. See also GOTHIC REVIVAL and GOTHIC SURVIVAL.

Gothic Revival. A fashion for building and decorating in the Gothic style which began in the mid eighteenth century, when it was believed that 'Gothick' was an essentially English style (which of course it is not). It was always felt that Gothic was almost the only suitable style for church architecture, while anyone who has experienced Gothic *domestic* architecture will confirm that it is very uncomfortable to live with. Amateur rather than professional architects were responsible for the domestic Gothic Revival. Sanderson Miller (1716–1780), a country gentleman, experimented with the style on his own estate at Edgehill in Warwickshire, building there a thatched cottage and a tower (1744) before going on to other work which included the transformation of the hall at Laycock Abbey, Wiltshire (1754–5). Horace Walpole (1717–1797) used original Gothic details at his own house, Strawberry Hill, Greater London between *c.* 1750 and continuing into the 1770s. Of his house Walpole said: '[It] is a little plaything-house that I got out of Mrs Chenevix's shop, and it is the prettiest bauble you ever saw.'

At the time Gothic Revival was ideal for those who could not afford to rebuild in the latest Classical style – they could decorate and transform an older building by applying Gothic detail and still be in the mainstream of fashion.

The Victorians, who seldom did anything by halves, took to Gothic with enthusiasm, chiefly under the tutelage of PUGIN, whose *True Principles of Pointed Architecture or Christian Architecture* (1841) equated Gothic architecture with spiritual values. Gothic Revival civic buildings and country houses of all sizes were built up to the 1870s, when the fashion waned, to be overtaken by the Vernacular Revival.

Gothic Survival. Not to be confused with GOTHIC REVIVAL. The Gothic style was always considered to be particularly suited to church design, and consequently was never entirely abandoned. A church built in the Gothic style at any time up to the early eighteenth century may be considered Gothic Survival, after which increasing general enthusiasm led to the Gothic Revival.

Gout. An arthritic complaint caused by a hereditary metabolic defect which results in an excess of uric acid crystals forming in the joints, causing painful swelling, particularly of the big toe. It is provoked by the consumption of too much meat protein and oily fish, and (classically) by a heavy consumption of PORT and WINE. The Bishop of Derry, 4th Earl of Bristol, who began the building of Ickworth, Suffolk *c.* 1794 (eventually completed in 1829), was plagued by 'flying gout' throughout the latter part of his life, and when he died suddenly in Italy in 1803 was diagnosed as having died of it.

Governess. It is difficult to establish when women were first employed to supervise children's education in the family. The Elizabethans certainly wrote of 'Gardners' of their children, meaning 'guardians', but exactly what that entailed is not known. However, by the end of the eighteenth century the position was well-established, often the fate of educated, usually unmarried, women who fell on hard times, famously in the novels of the Brontë sisters (Charlotte, 1816–55, and Emily, 1818–48). Governesses were the first professional women to live and work away from home.

A governess was expected to live with her charges, to sleep with them in the night nursery, to eat with them in the day nursery, to supervise their education in the school-room, and generally to oversee their upbringing. Boys were sent to boarding school at an early age, and so were not usually governess-educated beyond the basic skills of literacy. In the nineteenth-century household, the position of the governess was socially difficult; being educated, she was not a servant, and could not be expected to eat in the SERVANTS' HALL. On the other hand, she *was* a paid employee, and could therefore not expect to eat or sit with the family. Her life, consequently, could be very lonely.

Naturally many children became fond of their governess, but not usually so fond as they were of their NANNY, who often stayed with one family until she was pensioned off at the end of decades of service. The employment of a governess became increasingly rare after the Second World War, and is almost unheard-of nowadays. See also NURSERIES.

Governess cart. A small horse-drawn, two-wheeled, tub-shaped cart, entered by a rear door and with facing side seats; named from its suitability for use by the GOVERNESS when taking her charges out for fresh air. See also CARRIAGES.

Grand Jury. Grand Juries evolved before the end of the thirteenth century as a pre-trial enquiry in criminal cases to discover from witnesses whether there was a *prima facie* case against the accused. They usually numbered twelve, but might be as many as twenty-three, and as a rule were composed of local gentry. After an address from the judge the Grand Jury retired with the bills of indictment to their own room, where the witnesses for the prosecution were examined under oath. The Grand Jury hearing was abolished for ordinary cases in 1933 and its responsibility taken over by the Public Prosecutor; it was finally completely abolished by the Criminal Justice Act of 1948. (It is still widely used in the United States.)

There still exist at Lancaster Castle the criminal court with a railed-off section for a grand jury, dating from *c.* 1800, together with the comfortable Grand Jury Room with its original GILLOW OF LANCASTER furnishings.

Grand Tour, The. From the latter part of the seventeenth and increasingly during the eighteenth century, the completion of a rich young man's education was to tour the principal cities and places of interest in Europe, and particularly to visit Rome: the two UNIVERSITIES of Oxford and Cambridge might give a very good grounding in the Classics, but provided no education in the fine arts. The Grand Tour made up for this lack.

The Grand Tourist in Italy bought paintings and sculpture, collected ancient Roman artefacts, visited the main Classical sights (and sites) – and often had his portrait painted by Pompeo Batoni (1708–87) – before returning to his country estate in Britain. The interiors of our country houses, and our museums and galleries, would be very much the poorer had it not been for the Grand Tour, which was also responsible for forming a taste for Classical architecture among Englishmen of the period. Holkham Hall in Norfolk would never have been built had not Thomas Coke (1697–1759), the future Earl of Leicester, taken a six-year Grand Tour beginning in 1712; Chiswick Villa outside London, dating from 1725 and based on Andrea Palladio's (1508–80) Villa Rotonda at Vicenza, owes its existence to the second Grand Tour taken by Lord Burlington (1694–1753) in 1719; the interior of Felbrigg Hall, Norfolk owes a great deal to the Grand Tour taken by William Windham II (1717–61) in 1738 – the list is endless. Wherever there are portraits by Pompeo Batoni or Rosalba Carriera (1675–1757), it is likely that the sitter took the Grand Tour, and that the contents of his house are the richer for his experience.

The comment of Dr Johnson (1709–84) (who never made the Grand Tour) – 'Sir, a man who has not been to Italy is always conscious of an inferiority . . .' – sums up the eighteenth-century attitude to the Grand Tour in upper-class circles.

Grange. Originally, an outlying agricultural centre belonging to a monastery, too far distant to be worked by the monks; later, simply a barn or other large place of storage; and most recently a country house.

Gray's Inn. See INNS OF COURT.

Great Chain of Being. A notion which originated with the Greeks and was expressed by Aristotle (384–322 BC), who regarded all things as closely interwoven in a natural order. The rediscovery of ancient literature in the Middle Ages revived the idea, and it became a standard element of European philosophy in the fifteenth and sixteenth centuries. The basis was a belief that all individuals are bound together in a Great Chain of Being and all are interchangeable one with another. The purpose of life was the continuance of the family, the village, the town, or the state, and individual well-being was not to be maximized. Personal ambitions and preferences were to be sacrificed to the common good. The sacrifice of personal independence was an eighteenth-century Enlightenment notion; its reward was the fulfilment of occupying a proper place in society and serving the common good. Each was dependent on another, and social position at birth was immutable – a philosophy which lost favour only comparatively recently.

Great Chamber. Originally, the principal bed chamber of a large medieval house; by Tudor times it had become the principal reception room or, in larger houses, the first of a sequence of rooms for the reception of important visitors. As the ground floor of a large Tudor house was given over to service and servants, the Great Chamber was always on the first floor, and multi-purpose. In the house of a courtier it would have a CANOPY and CHAIR OF STATE, to be used by the Sovereign, other exalted visitors, or the occupant himself if he were a man of rank and power. The Great Chamber also served as an eating-room on occasions of high state (see STATE APARTMENTS). In houses outside Court circles, the canopy and chair of state would be dispensed with, unless a visiting peer (who might or might not be related to the family) were expected. In this class of house the room would be used by the occupant and his immediate family rather as we use a living room. Chastleton House in Oxfordshire was built by a wealthy wool merchant (c. 1603) who received local dignitaries in his Great Chamber, but had no aspirations to Court circles.

Great Hall. The principal room of a medieval house. The word comes from Norman French, but the hall was known in Britain before 1066, when it was called the House, a word of Anglo-Saxon origins, and later the House-Place. In its earliest stage of development a fire burnt on a central hearth where food was cooked, and the head of the household slept there, though on a finer bed than the rest of his household, many of whom slept on the rush-strewn floor of packed earth. In time, in grander establishments, cooking was removed from the Hall to a separate kitchen.

The entrance to the Great Hall was at the lower end, by either of two facing doors set in the longer walls. The draughts this caused were mitigated by the placing of a screen across the lower end room, forming the SCREENS PASSAGE. In some halls a movable screen was used, such as survives at Rufford Old Hall, Lancashire (*c.* 1480–1523). The head of the household, with his family and guests, ate at the upper end of the hall on a raised dais. A CANOPY, a symbol of authority and rank, was sometimes fixed over the high table, again as at Rufford Old Hall. Those who know the old colleges of Oxford or Cambridge will be familiar with the form of the Great Hall, the High Table and the raised dais; in fact the Great Hall, devised for accommodating and feeding large households, has survived at these colleges, almost in its original form, for nearly six hundred years.

Behind the screen were three doorways, into: (1) the BUTTERY, (2) the PANTRY, and (3) down a passageway between buttery and pantry to the kitchen. To this day, the Buttery Bar in Oxbridge colleges is where drinks are ordered and passed into the Hall. The inconvenience of the central hearth was solved by moving the fireplace to a side wall. Boothby Pagnell, Lincolnshire (*c.* 1200) has a side hearth with a projecting stone canopy overmantel. Stokesay Castle in Shropshire, with its central hearth, and almost unaltered since it was built *c.* 1270–80, gives a very good idea of the living standards of a wealthy late medieval lord of the manor.

As they came to demand greater comfort, the lord's family attached less importance to dining in the hall, which was smoky, smelly, noisy and, with no window glass, excessively draughty. The family moved first into the PARLOUR behind the dais end, and later upstairs to the GREAT CHAMBER. Naturally these changes were regretted by all reactionaries: William Langland (1330–1400), in *The Vision of Piers Plowman* (*c.* 1362), wrote: 'Wretched is the hall . . . each day in the week/There the lord and lady liketh not to sit.'

The Great Hall went out of fashion in France in the early sixteenth century but remained the norm in Court circles in England until the early seventeenth century, when James I (1603–25) reorganized his Court, putting many of the royal household on the equivalent of board wages and so dispensing with the need for Great Halls in his palaces. There were exceptions in the continuing tradition of the Great Hall: the temporary palace put up by Henry VIII (1509–27) at the Field of the Cloth of Gold in 1520 did not have one, nor did his lesser houses, such as The More at Rickmansworth in Hertfordshire (where the original Great Hall was demolished in 1535), and Nonsuch in Surrey (begun 1538). In these, the reduced numbers required to run them, deprived of the communal Great Hall for eating in, used a 'new chamber' on the first floor, or the guard room. In fact the Eltham Ordnances of 1526 named only the King's greater houses – Windsor, Beaulieu, Hampton Court, Woodstock and Richmond – as places where Hall should be kept. This new concept did not appeal to many builders of new houses, and in remote parts of the country Great Halls were still being built in the mid seventeenth century.

Greek Revival. The great interest in 'archaeological' architecture from the middle of the eighteenth century (as part of the generally increasing interest in 'antiquity') should be distinguished from the earlier PALLADIANISM, which was simply the re-creation of the style of Andrea Palladio. The occupation of Greece by the Turks made it difficult to examine Classical Greek architecture, but in 1751 two English architects, James Stuart (1713–1788) and Nicholas Revett (1720–1804), were among the first who managed to visit Greece. In 1762 Stuart published the first volume of *Antiquities of Athens*, which earned him his nickname of 'Athenian' Stuart; there is a Greek Temple (1758) by him at Hagley Hall, West Midlands. But the Greek Revival was slow to take off and it was left to others to popularize the style after Stuart's death. In architecture and furniture it was especially fashionable at the end of the eighteenth century and the early decades of the nineteenth; by the 1840s the GOTHIC REVIVAL had taken centre-stage, although the Greek Revival style continued to be used throughout the nineteenth century.

Green baize door. The expression 'behind the green baize door' refers to the kitchen and the service rooms of a large house which, from the late eighteenth century, were shut off from the main part of the house by doors covered in green baize. The baize deadened the noise from the service wing, and laden trays could push open the door in comparative silence. The baize is not, however, always green: sometimes it is red.

Greenhouses. See CONSERVATORIES.

Green Man. The symbolism of the face with branches sprouting out of its mouth, carved in stone and wood on church bosses, goes back to the pagan era. The early Christian church in Britain was pragmatic enough to incorporate pagan symbolism where this did not conflict with Christian theology or liturgy, and the personification of the pagan tree spirit as a foliate mask was one of the recurrent themes in church decoration. It is usually associated with oak, the holy tree of the Druids and many other faiths. At the same time, the reverential pagan dancing around a tree became the maypole MAY DAY dance – sometimes transferred to dancing round a church, when it was called 'clipping' – a rite which, by a confusion of etymology, was revived earlier in this century at Painswick in Gloucestershire, around ninety-nine freshly-clipped yews. See also PAGAN SURVIVAL.

Grenadier. Originally, a soldier trained to throw hand-grenades. Initially, each company had four or five grenadiers attached to it, but in time a complete company of grenadiers was attached to each battalion or regiment. Later, when grenades went out of general use, the term 'grenadier' was applied to the 'crack' company of the finest men in the battalion. It now only survives in the Grenadier Guards, the first regiment of Household Infantry.

Gretna Green, or **Border, marriages.** Gretna Green in Scotland was only one of many border towns offering 'marriage by consent', following Lord Hardwicke's MARRIAGE ACT of 1754 which made marriages in England legal only if contracted, in a building licensed for the purpose, by licence or following the reading of banns. From that date it became necessary for runaway couples wishing to marry in a hurry to cross the border to Scotland, where marriage by consent and before witnesses remained legal; a priest was not necessary. In 1825 Old Gretna Hall was converted into an hotel and marriage centre offering the full range of marriage facilities – for the 'ceremony', and consummation – and from then the village became famous for its marriages. See also FLEET PRISON; MARRIAGE, AGE AT; MARRIAGE ACT; MARRIED WOMEN'S PROPERTY ACTS and WEDDINGS.

Greys. The Royal Scots Greys (2nd Dragoons), so called because they originally wore grey coats and for many years were also mounted on grey horses.

Grisaille. A style of painted decoration in shades of grey to black, giving the illusion of relief-sculptured stone. Examples can be seen on the main staircase at Knole in Kent, executed (*c.* 1607) in, unusually, yellowish-green to grey; and on the upper main stairs at Chatsworth in Derbyshire, where Verrio painted (1689–90) scenes showing Cybele, Bacchus and Ceres.

Grotesque. A light, fanciful form of decoration depicting fantastic human and animal figures, mythical creatures, foliage, etc. The term comes from the wall-paintings found in Nero's Golden House in Rome. The rooms in which they were painted were referred to as 'grottoes' when they were discovered in the 1480s, and later examined by a group of painters in the 1490s. The walls of the 'grottoes' revealed something quite new in Classical decoration – playful, ornate and linear, with vertical designs incorporating figures, animals, masks and natural life. Knowledge of them spread when the designs were published in 1507. Raphael (1483–1520) used them in murals in Pope Leo X's private *logie* in the Vatican in 1519. Henry VIII (1509–47), always quick to take up the latest modes, decorated his palaces with grotesque designs, the dazzling effect of which can be appreciated in the painting *The family of Henry VIII* (*c.* 1540), by an anonymous artist, in the Royal Collection. Early grotesques survive in panels of painted canvas of *c.* 1540 in the hall of Loseley House, Surrey; they incorporate the arms and initials of Henry VIII and are thought to have come from Nonsuch Palace, which Henry was then building and which was incomplete at his death in 1547. A Brussels tapestry with grotesques in the design, woven for the Palace of Whitehall in the 1540s, still survives in the Royal Collection.

In Scotland the fashion for grotesques dates only from 1550, and survivals are confined to an area bounded by Perth, Stirling and Edinburgh. Those at Prestongrange in Musselburgh, Lothian are the earliest, datable to 1581; later examples are found on the barrel-vaulted ceiling of the chapel at Grantully, Perthshire (1636) and in the Skelmorlie Aisle (1638) at Largs kirk, Strathclyde.

Hanging at Haddon Hall in Derbyshire is a set of the TAPESTRY design known as *The Senses*, made at Mortlake in the 1620s and including grotesque masks; in the late seventeenth century, the Soho tapestry works produced tapestries in grotesque designs by Jan Vandervart (1647–1721). Returning Grand Tourists renewed the fashion for grotesques, which were used by William KENT on ceilings at Kensington Palace in London in the 1720s, and at Rousham House in Oxfordshire, *c*. 1740; and by Robert ADAM after his return from Italy in 1758.

Grotto. The grotto, an artificial cavern where water-gods lurked, formed of rough rocks often decorated with shell-work and usually with a fountain or some source of gushing water, appeared in Britain as early as the late sixteenth century: there is known to have been one at Wimbledon House, Surrey (begun 1588, demolished *c*. 1720). However, it was really an eighteenth-century fashion, brought back by Grand Tourists fascinated by the effect, in Italian gardens, of the sound of falling water, and of light falling on the surface of rocks, shells and statues. Surviving grottoes are many, but a few of the best are at: Albury Park, Surrey – an early one, made by the diarist John Evelyn (1620–1708) in 1660; Claremont House in Surrey, by William KENT (1684–48), made in 1738; Chatsworth, Derbyshire (1798); Stourhead, Wiltshire (*c*. 1755); Wardour Castle (rather better), also in Wiltshire. There is a many-chambered grotto at Ascot Place in Berkshire, and at Hawkestone Hall in Shropshire, where there was no natural rock, a grotto was tunnelled into the ground.

Grouse. The grouse-shooting season opens on 12 August and closes on 10 December, as ordained by ACT OF PARLIAMENT (1773). When 'the glorious twelfth' falls on a Sunday, the opening date is moved to Monday, the 13th. Grouse are found and shot throughout the northern hemisphere, but the red grouse (*Lagopus scoticus*; in fact, a species of ptarmigan) is unique to the British Isles. The black grouse (belonging to a different genus from the red grouse) may only be shot from 21 August. Grouse rarely venture beyond their breeding grounds, and 90 per cent die within a mile of where they were reared. It is only in Britain that grouse are driven to the guns by beaters, a skill developed in the early nineteenth century. Britain has some 460 grouse moors (85 per cent privately owned), comprising 4.1 million acres; the current estimated annual value of grouse shooting to Scotland is £21 million.

The late Sir George Campbell peppered the daughter of his friend, Major Walter Waring, in the eye with shot at a grouse shoot. 'The least you can do is marry her', shouted the major. So he did. See also SHOOTING.

'Growler'. A four-wheeled, horse-drawn cab introduced in London in 1836. See CABS and CARRIAGES.

Guardians of the Poor. Responsibility for care of the poor was transferred from parishes to the Guardians of the Poor in 1834. Only those in the direst need received relief under the POOR LAW, and the able-bodied were put to work in the WORKHOUSE, under harsh conditions to discourage malingerers. In 1908 noncontributory old-age pensions were introduced, and the National Insurance Act of 1911 provided unemployment and sickness benefit, measures rendering the earlier schemes redundant. See also FRIENDLY SOCIETIES.

Guilds, gilds. Medieval associations of merchants or craftsmen formed for the prosecution of a common object, often with an admixture of religious ideals. They were, in some senses, the forerunners of the modern Trades Unions. Each guild controlled its own trade and had a monopoly granted by its charter. Guilds regulated the practices of their members, prices, costs and apprenticeships; they also performed charitable functions, such as maintaining bridges, roads and schools, and assisting members in misfortune. They flourished in Britain from the ninth century until the mid sixteenth century. One of the first recorded merchant guilds (or, as commonly found in historical texts, gilds merchant) set up by charter was at Burford in Oxfordshire, in the eleventh century. However, not every town or city had guilds; neither Norwich or London, for example, had one.

Craft guilds came into existence in the twelfth and thirteenth centuries, performing the same services for their members as the merchant guilds for theirs. By the fourteenth century craft guilds had largely taken over control of local government from the merchant guilds, but their strong position was undermined when industry tended to move out of towns and cities into the countryside after the sixteenth century, and by the early factory systems based on the use of water-power wherever it was to be found. The centralized authority of the craft guilds was unable to adapt itself to control a fragmented membership. See also ARTS AND CRAFTS.

Livery Companies are a survival of medieval guilds, the 'livery' being the distinctive costume worn by each Company's members. Their order of civic precedence was drawn up in 1515. They are situated in the City of London and have such names as the Merchant Taylors, the Apothecaries, the Fishmongers, the Armourers, etc. There are eighty-four Livery Companies in all. In addition to looking after the members of their respective trades they were also involved in considerable charitable work, which before the Welfare State was of great importance. They provided almshouses, schools (several in the sixteenth century, such as St Paul's, Merchant Taylors', Oundle and Tonbridge) and pensions for the poor.

Guilloche. In architecture, a Classical ornamentation consisting of two painted or carved interlacing bands forming rhythmic circles.

Guinea. A British gold coin first struck in 1664 and so called because some of the bullion used came from the Guinea Coast of Africa. 'Spade Guineas', which had the royal arms in a spade-shaped shield on the reverse, were issued between 1787 and 1799. As a gold coin, the guinea was replaced by the SOVEREIGN in 1817. Its value varied from £1 10s. in 1675 to £1 1s. in 1817. Until recent times 'guineas' were still used in charging professional fees and at auctions.

Gun Rooms. These first appeared in the 1870s and became essential to those landowners who ran shoots with organized beats. Before the 1870s, when shooting was still an unformalized recreation, guns were haphazardly kept in the hall along with other sporting equipment, or in the upper servants' rooms. It was perhaps inevitable that the Victorian passion for specialization eventually required gun rooms, with gun racks. The gun room at Cragside in Northumberland was installed, sometime after 1884, off the BILLIARD ROOM. See also GAME and GAME LAWS, and SHOOTING.

Gypsies. Nomadic people whose origins are uncertain. The name is derived from 'Egyptians', from a misconception regarding their native land. Gypsies refer to themselves as 'Rom', which may be derived from Romanoi, a name for the part of the Byzantine Empire to which they had migrated (perhaps from India) by the twelfth or thirteenth century. All that is certain is that they crossed the Bosporus early in the fourteenth century and settled in the Balkan peninsula, whence depredations by the Turks forced them into Western Europe in their thousands between 1438 and 1512. Their language, Romany, is related to the Indo-Aryan group and some of their words are Sanskrit. Gypsies have always borrowed words from the countries they have passed through, Slavonic and Greek being the chief quarries.

Migrating across Europe, gypsies arrived around 1500 in England where, distrusted as outsiders and speaking a strange tongue, they were persecuted almost from the beginning, accused of child-stealing, cannibalism (the first charge was in 1547) – which was probably untrue

– horse-stealing and general thievery – which probably wasn't. At Durham in 1592 five men were hanged for being 'Egyptians'. As social outcasts gypsies maintained a very close race relationship, and were forced into occupations suitable to their nomadic way of life: horse-dealing, fortune-telling, knife-grinding and the like. Always industrious and versatile, the gypsies are rightly famous for their music – even, in Wales, winning a reputation as harpists.

Ha-Ha. A ditch separating a garden from surrounding parkland. A trench was dug, and a vertical retaining wall (or fence) was built on the garden side of it while the other sloped gradually up to the natural ground level. This kept livestock away from the area immediately around the house, without interrupting the view. The ha-ha was introduced to Britain from France around 1712 by the Royal Gardener, Charles Bridgeman (d. 1738). There are several explanations for the unusual name, none of them conclusive; the most convincing suggestion is that those who saw it said 'Aha!', while those who did not, fell over it, causing their friends to say 'Ha! Ha!'

Horace Walpole (1717–1797), son of PRIME MINISTER Robert Walpole, noted that 'the common people called them Ha! Ha's! to express their surprise at finding a sudden unperceived check in their walk.' The ha-ha may derive from French military architecture.

Hangers-on. A word of curiously macabre derivation. Before the introduction in the 1780s of the more humane trap-door, which usually broke the prisoner's neck, hanging meant death by slow stangulation. The prisoner might arrange for his friends – or pay someone – to pull heavily on his feet as the execution was carried out, in an attempt to break his neck and thus ensure a speedier death. These friends were known as hangers-on. See also CAPITAL PUNISHMENT.

Hansom cabs. See CABS.

Harden Star Grenade. See FIRE EXTINGUISHERS.

Harpsichord. An early, harp-shaped, double keyboard instrument on legs, popular from the sixteenth to the eighteenth centuries, when it was superseded by the PIANOFORTE. Original harpsichords are rare, but the late twentieth-century revival of interest in BAROQUE music has led to the creation of many modern instruments. The harpsichord differs from the pianoforte in that its strings are plucked by quills and not struck by hammers. Virginals used the same principle but with one keyboard, with one string to each note, and were simply rectangular, portable and played across the knees, while the harpsichord took up more space and had up to four strings to each note. Confusingly, both instruments were referred to as virginals. Even more confusingly, the spinet, a smaller version of the harpsichord with one keyboard, and one string to each note, was also often called a harpsichord.

Despite the great musical activity in Britain between the fifteenth and the seventeenth centuries, not one British-made instrument survives from the sixteenth century, and only three harpsichords and twenty-four virginals from the seventeenth century – yet Henry VIII (1509–47) possessed about thirty virginals. The earliest surviving British-made harpsichord is at Knole in Kent, made by John Hasard in 1622; the second survivor (1651) is at Traquair House, Borders, still with its original decoration; and a third is at Hardwick Hall in Derbyshire, made by Thomas White in 1653. British-made harpsichords were highly regarded, and exported all over Europe. The Victoria & Albert Museum in London has the earliest surviving spinet in Britain; Italian-made, it is decorated with the arms of Anne Boleyn, and must therefore date from the 1520–30s. See also MUSIC and PIANOFORTE.

Harvest customs. As old as the first agriculture, and celebrated world-wide: no doubt the early inhabitants of the different kingdoms of Britain had their own versions. The Romans held their feasts in honour of Ceres, and the Druids celebrated 1 November. Before the REFORMATION, LAMMAS Day (1 August) was generally considered the first day of harvest festival, and a loaf made of wheat flour was presented in church by every member of the congregation, blessed and offered at Mass. Afterwards came the celebratory feast of gathering-in, known in Scotland as the 'kern', which marked the close of the successful harvest. Many customs were associated with the cutting of the final sheaf; in north-east England it was known as 'the old woman' and dressed up as one; in Scotland it was the 'maiden', and the youngest female member of the team cut it. In many areas the final sheaf was made into a CORN DOLLY. The church Harvest Festival ceremony had died out by the early nineteenth century.

The general thanksgiving announced for the good harvest of 1842 became the basis of the ceremonies we know today. The Revd R.S. Hawker (vicar of St Morwenna, Morwenstow, Cornwall, from 1834) was an early follower of the OXFORD MOVEMENT and credited himself with reviving the annual Harvest Festival in 1843. He took the medieval Lammas Day rites and transferred the service to later in the season (Hawker was received into the Church of Rome on his death-bed). Mr Hawker's claim is disputed by the church of St Mary at East Brent in Somerset, which dates the revival to 1857 under its own Revd G. Denison (vicar of East Brent in the 1850s). He was also High Church, and a controversial figure. *Supplement I* to the *Dictionary of National Biography* states that Denison 'originally initiated the new popular festival of "harvest home",' but the claim is very much open to doubt.

Hatchment. Usually a lozenge-shaped board (or framed canvas) carrying a deceased person's coat-of-arms or 'achievement' – of which 'hatchment' is a corruption; most often found hanging in churches. Originally part of the funeral rites: having processed with the funeral cortège to the church, it was then displayed on the outside of the deceased's house for six or twelve months, before being finally hung in the church. The fashion had generally died out by the 1920s, although the last recorded use of a hatchment in Britain was on the death of Lady Catherine Ashburnham (the last of the Ashburnhams) in 1953, when her hatchment was hung over the main door of Ashburnham Place (dem. 1959), Sussex. The custom may have come from the Netherlands, *c.* 1600.

On a hatchment, the arms of a bachelor, spinster, widower or widow were painted on a black ground; for a married man who left a wife living, the right (or dexter) side would be black and the left (or sinister), white; for a woman who left a husband living, the left side would have the black ground, and the right the white.

Seven months after Sir Ralph Verney's death, in 1696 at Claydon in Buckinghamshire, his heir wrote to the steward at Claydon, 'Do not meddle with the hatchment over the Doore in the best Court.' Hatchments took the place of, and symbolized, the deceased's armour, which women in any case were denied. Apart from the many survivors found in churches, hatchments are still to be seen in some houses; two nineteenth-century hatchments hang in the restaurant (the old Audit Room) at Petworth in Sussex, and there is one on the stairs at Milton Manor, Oxfordshire; that of the 6th Duke of Devonshire (d. 1858) hangs in the kitchens at Hardwick Hall in Derbyshire; and there are seven, formerly in the church, in the hall of Stanway House, Gloucestershire.

Haunted sites. Ghosts are claimed to haunt a good many places but the following sites, now all ruins, are more 'authentic' than most. At Castle Rising in Norfolk, which dates from the fourteenth century, the laughter of Queen Isabella (1292–1358), malicious mother of Edward III, is heard echoing over the walls on stormy nights. Hylton Castle (Tyne & Wear) is haunted by the Cauld Lad, a naked stableboy, stabbed to death with a pitchfork by Lord Robert de Hylton in 1609. At Okehampton, in the wood-enshrouded ruins of Devon's largest castle, the malevolent Lady Howard is driven by a headless coachman in a coach made from the bones of her four husbands, accompanied by a black dog whose glance means death. Old Wardour Castle, Wiltshire, a fourteenth-century castle 'slighted' or ruined in the Civil War, is 'visited' at twilight by Blanche, Lady Arundel, who refused to surrender when the castle was successfully besieged by Commonwealth troops in May 1643. At Scarborough Castle in North Yorkshire, the ghost of Piers Gaveston (d. 1312), Edward II's favourite, tries to lure lone visitors over the parapet on to the rocks below. Also in North Yorkshire, Constance de Beverley, a nun bricked up in a wall for breaking her vows, is reputed to haunt the dungeon stairs of Whitby Abbey, and the founding abbess, St Hilda (614–80), has been seen in a high window, wrapped in a shroud. Since these sites are closed at 6 p.m. in summer and 4 p.m. in winter, it is difficult to experience the night time hauntings. Scarborough Castle is the exception: Piers Gaveston does his luring in daylight. See also GHOSTS.

Hawkers and **Pedlars.** Itinerant dealers engaged in carrying their goods for sale to the public. A hawker was defined in the Hawkers Act of 1888 as 'one who travels with a horse or other beast of burden selling goods'. In the Pedlars Act (1871) – which required them to obtain a certificate from the local chief officer of police – a pedlar is defined as one who sells articles to the public, travelling and trading on foot without a horse or other beast of burden.

Hawking. The sport of using hawks trained for the purpose to hunt prey. A very ancient sport, known in Roman Britain and mentioned in the reign of King Ethelbert (560–614); King Alfred (871–899) was commended for his love of the sport, and William I (1066–87) was also devoted to it. The privilege of keeping hawks was reserved for kings and the higher aristocracy until the time of King John (1199–1216), when the right was extended to all freemen; nevertheless, hawking remained a sport for wealthy landowners because only they had the right to hunt over their own lands. It also remained a favoured royal sport of the late summer and early autumn: both Henry VII (1485–1509) and Henry VIII (1509–47) were devoted to it. MEWS were built for Henry VIII's hawks at Hunsdon (1537) and at The More (1542), both in Hertfordshire. Due to the increased accuracy of fire arms and to ENCLOSURE, the popularity of the sport declined after the Commonwealth (1649–60), and by the end of the seventeenth century it was hardly practised at all. Today hawking has been revived as a specialist sport.

Hawksmoor, Nicholas (1661–1736). Born in Nottinghamshire and a farmer's son, he became a clerk to Sir Christopher WREN in 1679 and was closely associated with him until the end of Wren's life. With Wren's influence he was in 1689 appointed Clerk of the Works at William III's newly-purchased Kensington Palace, and in 1698 Clerk of the Works at Greenwich Hospital. His first commission was for Easton Neston, Northamptonshire, 1685–95. Thereafter, he was involved with VANBRUGH in the building of Castle Howard, North Yorkshire; Blenheim Palace, Oxfordshire; and nineteen other houses. Following the New Churches Act of 1711 he designed ten London churches, and he worked on four others, including Westminster Abbey, for which he designed the west towers. Like Vanbrugh, he was an architect of the English BAROQUE style.

Hearth Tax. A national tax, first levied in 1622 at the rate of 2s. a hearth, with exemptions for the poor and tradesmen. It was dropped in 1689, to be replaced by the equally unpopular WINDOW TAX.

Heating. The under-floor heating introduced by the Romans did not survive their departure, and for centuries the only heating available was from an open fire in the hearth, although from the sixteenth century heating for the wealthy was supplemented by portable charcoal braziers. Most houses must have been very draughty and cold, since even a successful fifteenth-century yeoman farmer would have had no GLASS in his windows – nothing but shutters to supplement the oiled paper or linen and keep out winter storms. (People did, however, wear more layers of clothing, to make up for this.)

Early central heating in the form of hot air issuing from grilles in the floor was experimented with in 1790 by William Strutt, a mill owner, and fitted into his own house in Derby in 1819; a similar system was in place at Coleshill, Berkshire in 1811. Prince Pückler-Muskau, touring England in the 1820s in search of a wealthy wife, found that Wilton House in Wiltshire was '. . . rendered perfectly comfortable by the "conduits de chaleur" which heat the whole house'. The hot-air system was very inefficient, and the piped–hot–water system of heating which followed was an improvement. Numerous radiators were installed at Stratfield Saye in Berkshire in 1833, for the Duke of Wellington, and two of them – both enormous – survive.

Other house-owners followed the duke's example – but not all. Lady Diana Cooper remembered Belvoir Castle in Leicestershire, before the First World War: 'Lord John [later Duke of Rutland] was a beautiful bent old man. I can see him very clearly, walking down the endless corridors of Belvoir, wrapped very warmly in a thick black cape buttoned down the front, for these passages in winter were arctic – no stoves, no hot pipes, no heating at all. He would unbutton his cape at the drawing room door and hang it on a long brass bar with many others.' See also FIRES.

Hell–Fire Clubs. The name given in the eighteenth century to clubs devoted to debauchery, in particular the one established by Sir Francis Dashwood (1708–81) at West Wycombe Park, Buckinghamshire (Dashwood later became Chancellor of the Exchequer) which met in caves near the ruins of St Mary's Abbey, Medmenham, and also (reputedly) in the church. This secret fraternity called themselves the Medmenham Monks, and members were rumoured to indulge in

devil-worship and sexual orgies. The accusations are untrue. See also
CLUBS OF LONDON and LITTLE BEDLAM CLUB.

Hepplewhite, George (died 1786). An English cabinet-maker whose
work was influenced by the ADAM brothers. His designs were NEO-
CLASSICAL and more delicate than those of his contemporary, CHIPPEN-
DALE. Hepplewhite's influential book, *The Cabinet-Maker and
Upholsterer's Guide*, his only claim to fame, was published in 1788–9.
No particular piece of furniture can be definitely ascribed to Hepple-
white's own hand.

Herald. Originally, inviolable (in theory at least, if not always in practice) messengers between rulers; thence they became officers of the
Royal Household, entrusted with the management of State ceremonies
in conjunction with the EARL MARSHAL. By the fifteenth century they
had become involved in the granting of coats-of-arms, and from this
derived their parallel function as genealogists.

The royal officers of arms were incorporated by Richard III and the
members of this corporation, known as the College of Arms, are the
Kings of Arms (Garter Principal, Clarenceux South of Trent, Norroy
North of Trent); the Heralds (Windsor, Chester, Richmond, Somerset, York and Lancaster); and the Pursuivants, who attended the Heralds
while learning their business (Rouge Croix, Bluemantle – a title dating
from the reign of Edward III – Rouge Dragon and Portcullis). The
tabards they wear on ceremonial occasions – so reminiscent of the 'pack
of cards' at the trial in *Alice in Wonderland* – are a survival from the
Middle Ages.

The Heralds receive fees for duties such as the granting of arms, and
still carry out state ceremonials such as coronations. By the seventeenth
century their fees for organizing a peer's FUNERAL were so high that
many were held at night to avoid them, as they only applied during the
hours of daylight.

In Scotland the head of the office of arms is Lyon King of Arms; his
Heralds are Albany, Ross and Rothesay, his Pursuivants Carrick, March
and Unicorn. See also HERALDRY.

Heraldry. The science of armorial bearings. The display of arms as
we know it dates probably from the Crusades of the twelfth century,
and served to identify armoured knights to their men in the crush of
battle. The idea immediately became popular and quickly spread
throughout Europe, reaching a climax in the reign of Edward III
(1327–77). Under the influence of the GOTHIC REVIVAL in the second
half of the eighteenth century achievements (displays of arms) returned
to popularity. The complexities of heraldry are best unravelled with
the help of one of the many books on the subject. See also HERALDS
and CREST.

Heriot. Originally the arms and equipment of a soldier (*here*): these were customarily a gift or loan to a tenant or VILLEIN from the lord of the manor, and reclaimed by him on the death of the former. When military service was replaced by money payments, the heriot was paid in money or in kind (the best beast or chattel); thus, an early form of death duty.

Hermitage. A decorative feature of eighteenth-century gardens, for preference inhabited by a (paid) hermit of unkempt appearance – an unappealing job; hermits were hard to find, and often took to drink. As the charm of the idea declined in the face of the practical difficulties, the hermitage was left uninhabited. One survives at Badminton House, Avon. If the guide for 1784–1800 is to be believed, the hermitage at Hawkestone Park in Shropshire was inhabited during those sixteen years by 'The venerable barefooted father whose name is Francis . . . [and aged] about 90'. See also FOLLIES.

Highland Clearances. A particularly shameful episode in Scottish history. Economic thinking current from *c.* 1750 to the early nineteenth century held that small-holdings in the Highlands were uneconomic (as indeed they were), and that they should be amalgamated into larger units and used to run sheep on – a theory which disregarded the bleak future of the dispossessed. Many Highlanders moved to Ulster – others emigrated to the USA and Canada.

High Sheriff. A word (from Shire-reeve) and office which date from before the Norman Conquest; the office was elective until the reign of Edward II (1307–27). Nowadays, the chief administrative officer of an English county. The Sheriff, who is appointed annually by the sovereign and chosen from leading landowners, acts as returning officer for parliamentary elections. In Scotland the judicial duties of the post have greater importance and the Sherrif must be an advocate.

Highwaymen. Thieves on horseback who robbed travellers; those who operated on foot were known as footpads. In the seventeenth and eighteenth centuries the development of TURNPIKES with regular coach services provided sitting targets for highwaymen, and their activities became notorious. BOW STREET RUNNERS were organized to suppress them. Bagshot Heath in Surrey, Epping Forest in Essex, and Hounslow Heath, Middlesex were favourite haunts. Among the best-known highwaymen were Claude Duval (1643–70); Swift Nick Levison, hanged at York in 1784; Jack Sheppard (1702–24); Dick Turpin (1705–39); and Jerry Abershaw (*c.* 1773–95). Longevity was not expected in this profession; most highwaymen were caught and hanged in their twenties.

Hip-bath. A nineteenth-century bathtub in which the bather sat immersed in water to the hips. In large Victorian households hip-baths were kept in cupboards outside the bedrooms. Usually enamelled white on the inside and painted cream on the outside, they were brought into the bedroom when a bath was required. The floor in front of the fireplace was covered with towels, on which the hip-bath was placed; hot water carried up by a housemaid was poured in, and the bather was left to bathe. Afterwards the housemaid baled out the water into buckets, and removed the tub. Hip-baths kept as a curiosity can be seen at Chatsworth in Derbyshire, and at Lanhydrock in Cornwall. See also BATHING.

Hippocras. An old medicinal drink or cordial made from spiced, sweetened wine, so-called because the bag through which it was strained was thought to resemble Hippocrates' sleeve in shape. The wine, coloured with turnsole (sunflower) or cochineal, and sweetened with honey, was spiced with ginger, cinnamon, and grains of paradise (a type of ginger). Originally a medieval recipe, its popularity continued into the seventeenth century, by which time milk or cream was also strained into the mixture. When the BANQUET course went out of fashion in Stuart times, so did the recipe.

Hiring Fairs. Formerly an annual event on Martinmas Day (November 11) in every important county town, hiring fairs enabled employers to find employees, and vice versa. Those looking for work were mainly farm labourers and domestic servants. The initial contract was for a year, after which it could be ended or renewed. Thomas Hardy in his novel *The Mayor of Casterbridge* (1886) gives a vivid description of a hiring fair at which Michael Henchard gets drunk and sells his wife and child. See also WIFE-SALE.

Hock. German white wine; originally from Hockheim on the river Main, now widely applied to any dry white wine from the Rhine area. The name was in use in England prior to 1625. See also CLARET, PORT, SACK and WINE.

Home Farm, The. In medieval times, the lord of a manor farmed his own DEMESNE land, usually lying near to his house, rather than letting it out to tenants. This became in time the Home Farm, kept 'in hand' and farmed by the landowner. It was not expected to show a profit, but provided fresh eggs, milk, butter, cheese, corn for flour, sometimes barley for brewing beer, potatoes and other root crops, for the household. The National Trust maintains the Home Farms at Tatton Park, Cheshire, and Wimpole Hall, Cambridgeshire.

Honour. (1) Adherence to what is right in conventional conduct; increasingly rare today, apparently. In late medieval and Tudor times it meant respect, reputation and glory. To the 6th Earl of Shrewsbury (1528–90) his honour was almost tangible, and most jealously defended: in the 1580s he wrote, '. . . mine honour more dear to me than life itself', and meant it. At this period honour was also allied to rank, and any infringement of such honour was taken as a dire insult – a conception which was expressed in DUELLING. The notion of honour allied to gentlemanly behaviour was maintained throughout the nineteenth century. In September 1890 the Prince of Wales, attending Doncaster races, stayed with Arthur Wilson, a millionaire shipowner, at Tranby Croft, in what is now Humberside. Some of his fellow guests appear to have been of the somewhat unprincipled and raffish type the Prince found so attractive. On the first evening one of the Prince's party, Sir William Gordon-Cumming, was seen cheating at baccarat; worse followed. The next evening Sir William was seen by five witnesses to be cheating at cards, and over the two evenings won £225, mostly from the Prince. Accused, Sir William denied the charge but nevertheless, under pressure, signed an agreement never to play cards again. News of the scandal leaked out and Sir William charged the five witnesses with slander. He lost his case, and his honour, and the public exposure of his behaviour rendered him a social outcast.

(2) A legal description of the lordship of two or more manors under the control of one baron and subject to a single jurisdiction.

Honours. The 'Honours system', often in the past and today used as a cheap way of rewarding loyalty and service to Crown and Country, has two main components, both of which are arranged in a graduated scale of importance: (1) The orders of CHIVALRY, together with decorations for gallantry. The principal orders of chivalry are: The Most Noble Order of the Garter, KG (Edward III, 1348); The Most Ancient and Most Noble Order of the Thistle, KT (revived by James II, 1687); The Most Honourable Order of the Bath, KCB (revived by George I, 1725); The Order of Merit, OM (Edward VII, 1902); The Most Distinguished Order of St Michael & St George, CMG (George IV, 1818); The Royal Victorian Order, CVO (Queen Victoria, 1896); The Royal Victorian Chain, CVC (Edward VII, 1902); The Most Excellent Order of the British Empire, CBE (George V, 1917); The Order of the Companions of Honour, CH (George V, 1917). Below these come a host of others, some of the better known being The Order of the British Empire, OBE; The British Empire Medal, BEM; The Military Medal (Army), MM; and The Military Cross (Army), MC.

The principal decorations for gallantry are: The Victoria Cross, VC (instituted by Queen Victoria in 1856 and awarded for a conspicuous act of bravery in the presence of the enemy; takes precedence of all other Orders); The George Cross, GC (George VI, 1940); and the Distinguished Service Order, DSO, for officers (Queen Victoria, 1886). (2) The PEERAGE and Baronetage. See also BARONETS.

Hope, Thomas (1769–1831). A connoisseur and patron of the arts and a member of the Society of DILETTANTI, known particularly for his furniture design, and for his publication in 1807 of *Household Furniture and Interior Decoration*. Hope was the wealthy son of a banking family whose London house (in Duchess Street, built by Robert ADAM in the 1760s but enlarged and remodelled by Hope) and country house (at Deepdene in Surrey, also enlarged by him) formed the setting for his large collection of antique sculpture, vases and ornaments. His own NEO-CLASSICAL designs are based on his experience, on a GRAND TOUR made in 1787–95, of original Roman Classical examples; others are Greek, Egyptian and Indian in inspiration, less free and more 'antiquarian' than his contemporaries', using brass inlay and bronze-gilt mounts, with strongly figured veneers. Hope's particular style, although too uncompromising to be widely admired, played an important part in disseminating neo-classical ideas, and thus his influence on the design of REGENCY furniture and interiors was considerable.

Horse Guards. One of the cavalry units of the British Army which supplies the Sovereign's Escort, as part of the Household Troops. Known familiarly as the 'Blues', their full title was 'The Royal Horse Guards (The Blues)'. See also LIFE GUARDS.

Horse-racing. Racing only began to be popular in the reign of Henry II (1154–1189) and generally took place at Smithfield, where horse fairs were held every Friday. By the time of the Tudors the sport had languished, jousts and TOURNAMENTS taking its place. However, racing revived under James I (1603–25), when the best courses were at Gatherley in Yorkshire, Croydon in Surrey and Enfield Chase, Essex. It was not until 1640 that racing took place at Newmarket, and not until the RESTORATION and Charles II's (1660–85) patronage that it became the headquarters of breeding and racing. Horse racing owes its position as 'the sport of kings' to the Stuarts. James I imported the first Arab horse, the Markham Arabian, so bringing lightness and speed to what had previously been a broad-chested horse bred only for work, pulling coaches, the cart or the plough. The Duke of Newcastle (1592–1676) wrote the first English treatise on *Haute École* (first published in France in 1657, in French), in which his horses prance and cavort in front of his houses at Welbeck, Bolsover, and Ogle Castle. With the Restoration in 1660 horse racing became a serious sport. Stands were built at Epsom, Bath, and York, and the public took to the spectacle with enthusiasm. It is not usually known that the Rowley Mile at Newmarket is named after one of Charles II's race horses. Queen Anne (1702–14), the last of the Stuarts, was as keen on racing as her forebears and opened the Ascot course on the edge of Windsor Park as early as 1711. Racing and FOX-HUNTING both called for fast, enduring horses and the two sports were closely allied in breeding. As fox-hunting developed in the second half of the eighteenth century, so did horse racing. The St Leger was first run at Doncaster in 1776, and the Oaks (1779) and the Derby (1780) at Epsom Downs. In the 1750s the Jockey Club was founded, and rules for controlling racing were formulated.

Today horse-racing is a multi-million pound industry. It is best summed up by the anonymous punter who, after backing many losers, admitted that he had learned only that 'one horse will always run faster than another'. See also HORSES and STEEPLECHASING.

Horses. The prime importance of the horse before the invention of the internal combustion engine is often overlooked. Up to the mid seventeenth century the horse was little considered, hard ridden, over-worked and ill-housed. Rising costs brought a more considerate approach to livestock used for transport, reflected in the better quality of stabling provided: at Peover Hall in Cheshire, the stables (1654) have decorated ceilings and finely carved ornament. With a higher appreciation of the value of the horse as a commodity and the fashion for racing came a desire for portraits of favourite or valuable animals. John Wootton (1682–1764) consolidated his reputation with a series of paintings of Newmarket race meetings and portraits of dogs and horses. Other painters followed, and paintings of horses by George Stubbs (1724–1806), Ben Marshall (1767–1835) and John Ferneley (1782–1860) are to be seen in many collections.

Nowadays, the stable blocks of large country houses remain as expensive monuments to the animals on which so much depended. Smaller houses and cottages had rings or hooks by the front door or the gate to tie a waiting horse to; today we pass them by unthinkingly, and stepped mounting blocks remain as curiosities. Yet it is only in two life-times that man's dependence on the horse has passed. See also HORSE-RACING and STEEPLECHASING.

Hose. Any form of long stocking which covers both foot and leg. Early use may indicate a form of roughly-fitting trousers reaching to the ankle. Until the seventeenth century knitted hosiery was made of wool worsted or silk, with a back seam, and mainly imported. From the late seventeenth century COTTON became the principal yarn, particularly for cheaper stockings.

A conspicuous eighteenth-century architectural feature still to be seen in the East Midlands is the three-storeyed brick cottage with a long window on the top floor. This window provided light for the hosiery-knitting frames worked by the family who lived in the cottage, an industry which marked the beginning of the INDUSTRIAL REVOLUTION. The frames were not owned by the family but rented from a hosier, who provided yarn and paid a piece-rate for the finished goods.

The knitting frame, an immensely versatile machine designed to knit a continuous flat fabric from silk or worsted yarns, was invented in 1589 by William Lee in Nottinghamshire. The invention was before its time and it languished in Britain. However, in France and Spain the machine filled a need, its use prospered, and Britain was compelled to import silk stockings, waistcoats and gloves, made on frames invented in England. During the seventeenth century, some machines were used in London to supply the quality market. By the early eighteenth century the production of cheaper wool and worsted yarns created a potential market, and the knitting industry moved from London to the East Midlands, where labour was cheaper. The first pairs of machine-made cotton stockings were made in Nottingham from imported Indian yarn in 1730. Constant amendments to the adaptable frame saw the introduction of new meshes and new garments: the 'Derby Rib' hose of 1758, for example.

Trade was subject to wild swings of prosperity and depression, but owing to the hold the hosiers had over their tied knitters little prosperity came to the workers, and in depressions their wages were cut back savagely. In 1779 serious rioting was provoked by the defeat of a Parliamentary Bill for a minimum wage, and spontaneous riots were frequent in the East Midlands throughout the 1780s and 90s.

'Luddite' or frame-breaking riots were more serious; they were organized by desperate knitters who smashed the frames of hosiers who paid badly in a time of acute depression in 1811 and 1812. Lord Byron (1788–1824) made his maiden speech in the House of Lords in February 1812 in support of the knitters. Sporadic 'Luddite' riots continued before trade picked up sufficiently for wages to be increased in 1816. See also COTTON and LUDDITES.

Hospitals. Care of the sick, particularly the sick poor, was traditionally in the hands of monasteries until the DISSOLUTION; thereafter the only provision made for them was in London, where St Bartholomew's (founded 1123) and St Thomas's (1200), the only hospitals until as late as 1700, were supported by endowments and charitable donations. Outside London it is no exaggeration to say that until the eighteenth century the sick were mostly cared for at home. The advance of medical knowledge, and the consequent need for centres of treatment, led to the establishment of more hospitals, and in the nineteenth century real progress was made in their design, administration and staffing, particularly under the impetus of Florence Nightingale's work. By the mid twentieth century most cities could boast at least one large hospital, and small cottage hospitals were to be found in most market towns. See also MEDICINE.

Hospitallers (Knights of the Order of the Hospital of St John of Jerusalem). The toleration of some of its early Moslem rulers permitted the foundation in Jerusalem about 1070, by some citizens of Amalfi, of a hospice or hospital dedicated to St John the Almsgiver and staffed mostly by Amalfians under monastic vows, under the direction of a master who in turn was under BENEDICTINE authority, with the purpose of providing care and protection to Christian pilgrims visiting the Holy Sepulchre. After the first CRUSADE had taken Jerusalem (1099) the monks of the hospital became (c. 1113) an order in their own right, owing direct obedience to the Pope, and adopted the AUGUSTINIAN rule. Raymond de Puy, who became Master of the Hospital about 1120, decided that his order must also fight to keep the pilgrim routes open, and set up an establishment of knights bound by vows of chastity, poverty and obedience. The Knights of the Hospital were recognizable by the white cross on a black background on the tunics they wore over their armour. After the fall of Acre (1291) the headquarters of the Hospitallers moved from Jerusalem to Cyprus, then to Rhodes, to Malta, and finally to Rome. The order was organized in eight provinces, or Langues, consisting of France, Aragon, Auvergne, Provence, Castile, Italy, England and Germany.

The English headquarters of the Order was at the priory of Clerkenwell, London, which can still be visited, and the earliest houses of the Order, called commanderies or preceptories, date from the middle of the twelfth century, at Clanfield in Oxfordshire, Mount St John in Yorkshire, and Ossington, Nottinghamshire. Commanderies and preceptories offering hospitality to pilgrims, the poor and passing travellers were small farms or manors run by a commander with perhaps two other members, and secular servants. By1138 there were thirty-four knights, forty-eight sergeants and thirty-four chaplains in England. After the suppression of the TEMPLARS in 1312 their property was transferred to the Hospitallers, who then had some sixty-five houses in England. The prior of the English province was a member of the Great Council until the DISSOLUTION of the order under Henry VIII in 1540. Only one English Knight Hospitaller took part in the defence of Malta against the Moors in 1565.

Hot, or **conservation, walls.** In KITCHEN GARDENS, south-facing brick walls incorporating horizontal flues heated from a central stove were used from the mid eighteenth century to keep frost from ESPALIERED trees and to encouraged the earlier ripening of fruit. The wall might be fronted with a narrow glasshouse, or with canvas blinds to pull down over the trees, for further protection of the fruit.

Household costs. These have always depended very much on the income and rank of the head of the household. At Hardwick Hall in 1600, Bess of Hardwick, Countess of Shrewsbury, was paying expenses of some £2,000 annually out of a depressed annual income of £10,000.

Nearly a hundred years later, the Earl of Bedford's costs at Woburn, Bedfordshire were £1,500 annually. Untypically, he was charging his relatives £5 each per month to live with him – he was in straitened circumstances. The prodigality expected of the very grand is typified by the 2nd Duke of Kingston at Thoresby Hall, Nottinghamshire: in twelve weeks in 1736 his household consumed £300 in meat, and the household bills for three months totalled £1,477. At Wentworth Woodhouse, South Yorkshire the Marquess of Rockingham spent £2,050 during the year 1759. The Earl of Verulam's annual expenditure on London living in the 1790s was an average £1,000, while Earl Fitzwilliam lived at double the cost; by the 1820s Verulam was spending £2,500 and Fitzwilliam £3,500 annually.

Housekeeper. Always female, and always given the courtesy title 'Mrs', although usually unmarried. In the sixteenth century a housekeeper supervised the house of a bachelor or widower. As female staff increased in the seventeenth century (because they were cheaper than male staff), her position became more important. She was in charge of the female SERVANTS of the household, supervised the linen, the housework, the preserves made in the STILL ROOM, the candles and soap; she also (for a fee) showed visitors over the house. From the eighteenth century her status equalled that of the head BUTLER or STEWARD; with him she ruled supreme in the SERVANTS' HALL at meal times, one at each end of the table with male and female servants segregated down the two sides. After the main course was eaten the housekeeper and butler left the servants' hall to take DESSERT in either his or her room. Like so much in the servant hierarchy, this custom was an historic leftover from above-stairs.

Prince Pückler-Muskau, visiting England in search of a wife, recalled Penrhyn Castle in Gwynedd in the 1820s, before it was rebuilt: 'The females of the establishment have also a large common room, in which, when they have nothing else to do, they sew, knit and spin: close to this is a closet for washing the glass and china, which comes within their province. Each of them, as well as of the man-servants, has her separate bedchamber in the highest storey. Only the housekeeper and butler have distinct apartments below. Immediately adjoining that of the housekeeper, is a room where coffee is made, and the store-room containing everything requisite for breakfast, which important meal, in England, belongs especially to her department.' See also VAILS and SERVANT PROBLEM.

Houses, ceremonial layout of. The ceremonial layout of medieval houses and castles was comparatively modest, with a GREAT HALL and, for relative privacy, a parlour with a GREAT CHAMBER above. By the sixteenth century, houses likely to be visited by the sovereign and the court had come to require, in addition to a great chamber, a withdrawing-room and state BEDCHAMBER. Further changes came about following the accession of James I in 1603; the great hall became redundant and the French system of apartments came into fashion. The sequence comprised an entrance hall with staircase, and beyond the hall a SALOON for receptions and state meals, with two withdrawing-rooms off it and a bedchamber with closet off each withdrawing room. One of the bedchambers would be a state bedchamber for the accommodation of important visitors. This arrangement had the effect of emphasizing the importance of the occupant of the state bedchamber, since only the most privileged visitor would be offered it, and few in the household would have access to it. These rooms were invariably laid out in line – the 'axis of honour' – as at Boughton House, Northamptonshire (1695) and Chatsworth, Derbyshire, of the same date and typical of the BAROQUE period.

With the gradual transfer of government from the sovereign to Parliament following the CIVIL WAR and the Great Rebellion of 1688 it was no longer necessary for the sovereign to travel around the country accompanied by his ministers and advisors; there was a consequent decline in the use and importance of the state apartments in country houses, and life became far more relaxed. Bedchambers now moved upstairs, and the sequence of rooms on the PIANO NOBILE (usually the first floor) were used for entertainment. At Kedleston Hall, Derbyshire, built in the 1750s and 60s, a grand entrance hall leads to a SALOON where guests for dinner would gather before processing back across the hall to the eating room. After dinner the guests would move either to the intimacy of the music room or small library, or to the larger and grander withdrawing-room. In the nineteenth century guests gathered in the withdrawing-room and when dinner was announced processed in pairs, male and female, through the main rooms to the dining-room, giving guests a tour of the ground floor and an opportunity to be impressed by their host's possessions. See also DINING-ROOM.

Hudson's Bay Company. Founded by a royal charter in 1670 which gave to Prince Rupert (1619–82), as first Governor, and seventeen others, exclusive rights of trade over all lands draining into the Hudson Bay and not already granted to others. Trade was mainly in furs bartered from the Indians, and the company made vast profits in the early years, but French competition cut into their trade and erupted into open violence when Britain and France were at war. British sovereignty was recognized by France in 1713, and Canada was ceded by France to Britain in 1763. The monopoly was put to the test by competition from the North-West Fur Company of Montreal trading outside the Hudson's Bay Company charter area. The rivalry provoked cut-price competition and often violence, only ended by an enforced amalgamation of the two companies in 1821. In 1869 the Hudson's Bay Company sold its lands to the Canadian government for £300,000, but still remained a trading company with headquarters in Winnipeg, Manitoba.

Hue and cry. The old COMMON LAW process of pursuing a criminal 'with horn and voice'. Failure to raise a general alarm, or to turn out with the raiser in pursuit, was a punishable offence under a statute of 1275. This primitive policing system survives today in the obligation of the public to assist the police in enquiries which may lead to the arrest of a criminal. See also CONSTABLES and POLICE FORCES.

Huguenots. The name given to French Protestants from about the middle of the sixteenth century; the name is probably a corruption of the Swiss-German *eidgenoss* (a confederate, literally an oath-associate), the name given to a member of a league of Swiss Protestants. Mainly CALVINISTS, they were harshly persecuted by François I (1515–47) and Henri II (1547–59). During the French wars of religion the Huguenots were supported with funds and men by Elizabeth I (1558–1603), and the St Bartholomew's Day Massacre of 1572, when many French Huguenots were slaughtered by order of the French Queen, caused many others to seek refuge in England. Their persecution was eased under Henri IV (1589–1610), by the Edict of Nantes in 1598, but this was revoked in 1685 by Louis XIV (1643–1715), causing a further exodus of 400,000 refugees, again mainly to England. These succeeding waves of Huguenots settled mostly in London, and in Norwich, Bristol, Southampton, and Canterbury. The term 'Huguenots' was also applied to Protestant refugees from late sixteenth-century Spanish persecution in the Netherlands.

Hundred. An ancient territorial division of a county, dating from at least the tenth century (the Wessex hundreds may be older), which continued in use as an administrative unit of local government into the nineteenth century. In the area covered by the DANELAW the division was into WAPENTAKES. Theoretically a hundred consisted of 100 hides, the hide being as much land as would support a peasant and his family. The number of hundreds within a county varied – Berkshire had twenty-two, Staffordshire only five. New hundreds were created in medieval times, when they were chiefly of judicial importance. The Moot – the Hundred Court – met every month under the king's reeve and was concerned with criminal and lesser ecclesiastical matters, private pleas and taxation, and also view of FRANKPLEDGE. In Derby, Leicester, Lincoln, and Nottingham, wapentakes (confusingly) were divided into smaller units also called hundreds. The term survives today in the CHILTERN HUNDREDS.

Hunting. See FOX-HUNTING.

Hunting box. A comparatively small house with considerable stabling, used for accommodation in the late eighteenth and the nineteenth centuries during the FOX-HUNTING season. 'Hunting lodge' is a far older term: Worksop Manor Lodge in Nottinghamshire was built for the 7th Earl of Shrewsbury in the 1590s, a substantial building standing in Sherwood Forest only four miles from his large house, Worksop Manor.

Hunting pink. The majority of English hunts wear coats which, though known as 'pink', are in fact red. See also FOX-HUNTING.

Hurdle, flake or **fleak.** In her *Journal* for 1802, Dorothy Wordsworth (1771–1855) notes that she has put hurdles up in the orchard. Hurdles were, and to some extent still are, a very useful part of country life. Made of woven willow wattle, three feet wide and sometimes as much as seven feet long, they can be used as temporary fencing (which is what Dorothy was using them for), as gates, to make lambing pens, or for filling gaps in hedges. Before the invention of tubular steel scaffolding – when scaffolding consisted of wood poles lashed together with rope – hurdles were used for flooring the scaffolding, being lighter than wood planks and as serviceable.

Icehouses. Structure for the preservation of ice for domestic use. In the summer of 1671 ice-cream was served at a Garter dinner at Windsor Castle, its first recorded appearance in Britain. It must have been the height of luxury, and was only possible because of the icehouse, used to preserve for summer use blocks of ice cut from frozen lakes in winter. An icehouse consisted of a brick- or stone-lined pit about 25 feet deep with a drain at the bottom, covered by a dome-shaped superstructure. The entrance was always on the north side, and led into as many as four chambers in which ice, properly stacked between layers of straw, might keep for as many as three years. Icehouses, sometimes called ice wells, are a feature in the parks of many country houses, often placed conveniently near to a lake. Most were constructed in the eighteenth century, but the first recorded icehouse was built at Greenwich in 1619, a second, nearby, in 1621, followed by another at Hampton Court in 1625. At Linley Hall in Staffordshire the icehouse is designed as a Roman temple; West Wycombe Park in Buckinghamshire has two, one with a Temple of Venus above it, the other featuring a Temple of the Winds. The best preserved is to be seen at Heveningham Hall in Suffolk.

In his *Encyclopedia of Gardening* (1834), J.C. Loudon (1783–1843) gives detailed directions for the construction of an icehouse. However, the invention of hand-cranked ice-making machines in the 1840s made the icehouse redundant, and most were left to decay; some 2,000 survive in some form today.

Ice-pails. With the introduction of ice-cream in the second half of the seventeenth century came the problem of keeping it frozen at the table. By the mid eighteenth century, Sèvres ice-pails were being imported from France. These had a removable bowl which held the ice-cream, kept frozen by ice in the bottom of the pail; the lid was so constructed as to hold more ice. This design was quickly copied by the Derby, Worcester and Coalport porcelain works (between 1770 and 1820).

India Office. The successor to the EAST INDIA COMPANY. Pitt's India Bill of 1784 had 'created a board of control, as a department of the [British] Government, to exercise political, military and financial superintendence over the British possessions in India. . . . from this date the direction of Indian policy passed . . . from the company to the governor-general in India and the ministry in London', but in 1858 the Indian administration was entirely transferred to the India Office, under the Crown, following the Indian Mutiny. This led to little change in the top management, the President of the Company becoming Secretary of State for India and the Council of India being appointed mainly from the old board of control. India was then governed under a viceroy over provincial governors supervising a British-staffed Indian Civil Service. Not until 1917 were Indians admitted to the civil service, under a policy intended to lead to eventual self-government. The India Office was abolished in 1947 when independence was granted to India and Pakistan.

Industrial Revolution. A term first used by Arnold Toynbee in 1882 (*The Industrial Revolution in England*, publ. 1884) to describe the sudden acceleration of technological development in Britain between 1740 and 1850. It was marked by a change from cottage-based industry to the factory system made possible first by water- and later by steam-power. The conditions for this development came from the stability following the Glorious Revolution of 1688, the emergence of a capitalist banking system, and the invention and enterprise stemming from NON-CONFORMIST ingenuity.

The major changes took place in the textile industry, in mining, in the iron and steel trades, and in the pottery industry, taking advantage of technology which in some cases had been available for years, but only became applicable when allied to steam-power. The railway is a good example: rail tracks had been used in coal mining in the sixteenth century but only became significant with the invention of George Stephenson's (1781–1848) steam locomotive in the 1820s, bringing about a major improvement in the quick transport of merchandise. The steam locomotive in its turn evolved from James Watt's (1736–1819) Newcomen steam pump of 1765, devised to pump water out of coal mines, and later used to provide factory power.

The changes brought about unforeseen social problems, to which there was no immediate solution; vast population movements from the land to manufacturing towns created slums, filled with the unemployed in times of trade slump, where the lack of drainage caused disease and high mortality – conditions which gave rise to demands for social reform in the late eighteenth and the nineteenth centuries.

Inglenook. The 'ingle nooks' were originally the corners of a large fireplace, under the main chimney-breast opening and on either side of the hearth itself. Often from the late fifteenth century there was room for a bench or seat on each side, beneath the chimney canopy. Anyone sitting here was warm, and out of the draughts and cold of the room. It was a feature revived in the late nineteenth-century ARTS AND CRAFTS Domestic Revival Style. An example can be seen at Cragside, Northumberland, in the dining-room designed by Norman Shaw in 1891.

Inner Temple. See INNS OF COURT.

Inns of Court. Associations having the exclusive right to call BARRISTERS to the Bar. Of uncertain origin, they developed before the fourteenth century as centres for the teaching of COMMON LAW.

The four Inns of Court are the Inner Temple, the Middle Temple, Lincoln's Inn, and Gray's Inn. EQUITY and CHANCERY practitioners usually join Lincoln's Inn, while for COMMON LAW the two Temple Inns are considered superior.

'Readers' were barristers who taught the students, and recommended them for call to the bar by the Benchers, who were the senior members and formed the sole governing body of each Inn. Students who were CALLED TO THE BAR by the Benchers of their Inn were thereby recognized as qualified apprentices (barristers) and might practise law. When a barrister had practised long and successfully, he might be awarded by the Crown the degree of Serjeant-at-Law, when he at last ceased to be an apprentice.

The Inns of Chancery were subordinate to the great Inns and originally provided accommodation for Chancery clerks and students, later including those who were to become ATTORNEYS and SOLICITORS, who were excluded from the Inns of Court. Furnival's and Thavie's were attached to Lincoln's Inn; Staple and Barnard's to Grey's Inn; Clifford's and Clement's to the Inner Temple; and New Inn to the Middle Temple.

By the sixteenth century the Inns were attracting men who did not intend to practise law but needed knowledge of it, such as the sons of the gentry and nobility. A time-honoured feature of the Inns of Court is EATING ONE'S TERMS – the keeping of terms, not by attendance at lectures or residence but by eating dinners in Hall.

Ironsides. At the battle of Marston Moor in 1644 Prince Rupert referred to Oliver Cromwell (1599–1658) as 'Old Ironsides', and the name was then transferred to the troopers of his cavalry regiment, recruited in his home town of Huntingdon in 1643 from 'god-fearing' YEOMAN and FREEHOLDERS; the Ironsides were noted for their zeal and discipline.

Jacobins. Originally, British supporters of the French Revolution, but later applied to anyone in the early nineteenth century with liberal tendencies; the name is taken from the Jacobin Club, which became the principal focus of the Terror in the French Revolution.

Jacobites. Supporters of the deposed Roman Catholic James II (the name is derived from the Latin *Jacobus*, James) and his heirs, active for about sixty years after the Glorious Revolution of 1688; largely but not exclusively Roman Catholic. The principal centres of Jacobitism were in Scotland and Ireland; it was underpinned by help from France, where James took refuge as a pensioner of the French king. A Highland rising in support of James was put down in 1689 at Killicrankie; James himself was defeated in Ireland at the battle of the Boyne in 1690, and Irish resistance was crushed when his supporters surrendered at Limerick in 1691. James died in 1701 and the cause was inherited by his son James, 'the Old Pretender', whose English supporters failed to proclaim him James III on Queen's Anne's death in 1714, mainly because of his Roman Catholicism and his dependence on France. 'The Fifteen', an open Jacobite rebellion of 1715–16, failed, as did an attempted invasion in 1719 by the 2nd Duke of Ormonde, supported by Spain, and a Scottish rising the same year at Glensheil. In 1722 Francis Atterbury, TORY Bishop of Rochester and leader of the HIGH CHURCH Jacobites, plotted a seizure of the BANK OF ENGLAND to coincide with another invasion attempt by Ormonde, but their plans were foiled after being revealed by the French Foreign Minister. Thereafter support for the already lost cause waned, although war between France and Britain in 1744 provided 'the Young Pretender' (Bonnie Prince Charlie) with a last chance; but 'The Forty-Five' rebellion culminated in the bloody defeat of the Jacobite cause at Culloden in 1746 – the last battle to be fought in Britain. The last direct descendant of James II, Henry Stuart, Cardinal Duke of York, the second son of the Old Pretender, died in 1807, bequeathing the crown jewels carried off by James II to the future George IV. Until the accession of Edward VII in 1901, finger bowls were never placed on royal dinner-tables, from the Jacobite custom of drinking to the king 'over the water' (in the finger bowls).

Japanning. The art of coating metal, wood, etc., with varnishes, which are then dried and hardened in stoves or hot chambers, Japanning is an English imitation of the Japanese process of lacquering, in which the resin of a tree which does not grow in Europe is used; the resin hardens on exposure to air, and hence cannot be imported. Japanning is commonly black, the varnish consisting of asphaltum mixed with gum, linseed oil and turpentine, giving a hard and shiny finish. Japanning became fashionable in England in the late seventeenth century (William III (1694–1702) had japanned furniture) but the fashion had begun earlier and sets of japanned furniture, day beds, chairs, etc., can occasionally be found dating from the 1660s. The technique of Japanning was explained in a book, *A Treatise of Japanning and Varnishing* (1688), by John Stalker and George Parker. See also CORO-MANDEL.

Jews in Britain. There was a small group of Jewish traders in England in Roman times, since when newcomers have been immigrant refugees forming a minority group, often oppressed. In 1066 a Jewish community arrived with the Norman invasion, but in *c.* 1100, and associated with Crusading fervour, all property and wealth belonging to Jews, and Jews themselves, became the property of the king. They were forbidden to engage in agriculture or in retail trade but, as usury was forbidden to Christians, they were encouraged to be money-lenders. So began the classic view of Jews in Britain, following the pattern of the rest of Europe.

The Jewish population of Norman Britain was below 10,000, yet contributed in taxes one seventh of the royal revenue. By the end of the twelfth century taxation had so impoverished the Jewish population as to have rendered them useless as a tax milchcow, and Richard I (1189–99) ordered the expulsion of those remaining. His action resulted in a series of pogroms throughout the country in 1189–90, culminating in the massacre of 150 Jews at York. It has been calculated that by 1190 14,000 Jews had left England. Some returned, but Edward I (1239–1307) ordered a further expulsion in 1290. Although technically Jews were forbidden entry to the country, a few extraordinary individuals were accepted – mainly doctors for the royal households. Gradually anti-Jewish feeling relaxed, and about 1500 many immigrants arrived from Spain and Portugal, victims of the oppressions of the Spanish Inquisition and fleeing the policy of forced Christianization in Portugal; this Mediterranean immigration of mainly Sephardic Jews continued through the century.

The problem of Jewish status in England came to Cromwell's attention, and in 1655 the courts found that entry to the country by Jews was not illegal; the following year, a test case established the right of Jews to hold property. In 1722 and 1735 further oppression by the Inquisition resulted in two more waves of immigration, and 1880 and 1905 marked the arrival of Ashkenazim, Jews forced out of Russia by pogroms there. Finally, in the 1930s, came the biggest ever influx of Jews, fleeing from Nazi persecution.

Although Jews were not barred from Parliament, the Oath of Abjuration required a statement of Christian belief and this effectively prevented practising Jews from taking a seat in the House of Commons. As bankers in Hesse during the Napoleonic Wars the Rothschilds aided the transmission of money to the Duke of Wellington, through their London branch established in 1798. Lionel de Rothschild (1808–1879) was elected MP for the City of London in 1847 and (fruitlessly) four more times, before an Act of Parliament of 1858 permitted the omission, in particular cases, of the offending phrase from the Oath: only then was Rothschild allowed to take his seat. By the Parliamentary Oaths Act of 1866 the phrase was dropped altogether. Benjamin Disraeli (1804–1881), although the son of a Spanish Jew, had been baptized a Christian in 1817, and consequently there was no problem when he was elected to Parliament in 1837. Jews were admitted to the House of Lords in 1885.

Jigsaw puzzle. A puzzle made of a picture mounted on card or a thin sheet of wood and cut (with a jig-saw) into irregularly-shaped pieces. Introduced in the mid eighteenth century as a means of teaching children geography.

Jingo. A supporter of a bellicose, blustering, patriotic policy; adopted as a nickname for those who supported Disraeli's war-like policy toward Russia in 1878. A popular song by G. W. Hunt went:

> We don't want to fight, but, by Jingo if we do,
> We've got the ships, we've got the men, and we've got the money too.

'By Jingo' appears in Cervantes' *Don Quixote*, published in two parts in 1605 and 1615, and later in Goldsmith's *Vicar of Wakefield* (1766). The word was originally a part of seventeenth-century conjurors' gibberish.

Joint stool. A sixteenth-century rectangular wooden stool on four turned legs with stretchers at the bottom. The seat is often perforated, for easy lifting. Sometimes wrongly called coffin stools, because they were thought to have been used to support coffins. See STOOL.

Jones, Inigo (1573–1652). English architect, draughtsman, painter and designer of Court masques and plays, a genius far in advance of his time. He was first recorded as 'picture-maker' in 1603, but is principally famous for introducing the Classical style from Italy to England, at a time when medieval GOTHIC still held sway and there was little knowledge of the Renaissance in architecture. There are more than 450 of his drawings for Court masques at Chatsworth in Derbyshire, and he revolutionized English stage design after his second visit to Italy in

1613–14, introducing the proscenium arch and stage machinery. He feuded with and eventually triumphed over Ben Jonson, his collaborator in Court masques. The second of Jones's visits to Italy was influential in other ways. Travelling with the Earl of Arundel, he was able to study Palladio's buildings (see PALLADIANISM) and to gain first-hand knowledge of Roman monuments.

Jones was made Surveyor of the King's Works in 1615, and until the outbreak of the Civil War in 1642 he was continually employed on royal buildings. The Queen's House, Greenwich, begun in 1616, interrupted by Queen Anne's death in 1619 and not finished until 1635, was the first true Classical building in Britain. This was followed by the Prince's Lodgings at Newmarket (1619–22, now demolished), and his masterpiece, the Banqueting House in Whitehall (also 1619–22). The Queen's Chapel in St James's palace (1623–7) was an innovation – a Classical church. None of Inigo Jones's work for Charles I (1625–49) survives; his Corinthian portico for Old St Paul's (in the 1630s) was lost in the Great Fire of 1666, and his designs for a vast Royal Palace in Whitehall (1638) were never realized. Although Jones was for many years credited with the garden front of Wilton House, Wiltshire, it was in fact designed by his assistant, Isaac de Caus, in *c.* 1632. Badly damaged by fire *c.* 1647, it was restored by Jones's nephew and pupil, John Webb (1611–72). A pavilion at Stoke Park, Northamptonshire of *c.* 1630 (the central block of which was burnt down in 1886) is also attributed to Jones, as is a Classical façade to Houghton House, Bedfordshire (built soon after 1615, now a ruin). In his own lifetime, Inigo Jones's influence was largely confined to the immediate Court circle.

Judicature Acts. The purpose of the Supreme Court of Judicature Act of 1873, supplemented by amendments in 1876 and 1880, was to bring order to the confusion and conflict between the EQUITY and COMMON LAW courts, whose jurisdiction tended to overlap, leading to costly and cumbersome legal processes such as those ridiculed by Charles Dickens. By the Act the administration of the two branches of law was combined; the existing superior courts were consolidated into one Supreme Court consisting of two primary divisions: the High Court of Justice, with the subdivisions (1) QUEEN'S BENCH (which included COMMON PLEAS and EXCHEQUER); (2) CHANCERY; (3) DIVORCE, Probate and Admiralty; and the Court of Appeal, which heard appeals against decisions in the other courts. The House of Lords became the final Court of Appeal.

Jury. The inquest or enquiry by a panel of local men sworn to determine the facts of a disputed matter was an ancient custom, confirmed and extended by the Assize of Clarendon of 1166. Juries in each HUNDRED, comprising twelve (sometimes more) men, were directed to bring suspects to the Justices in EYRE at the HUNDRED court. Trial by ordeal (appealing to God's judgment by, for instance, the accused carrying hot iron in his bare hands, but having no scars after three days) was abolished in 1215 and the jury system extended to criminal charges; jury trials became compulsory for criminal cases in 1275. In civil cases, trial by jury dates from about 1179, following the introduction by Henry II (1154–89) of trial by Grand Assize in place of trial by battle in cases of disputes about land. See also ORDEAL, TRIAL BY.

Justice of the Peace (JP). A magistrate, not usually a lawyer, appointed to keep the peace within the jurisdiction for which he is appointed; usually unpaid in country districts, but in metropolitan areas where the weight of business is heavy, stipendiary (paid) magistrates may be appointed.

The system began in 1361 with the appointment of members of the local aristocracy or gentry as justices for the king's peace in BOROUGHS and counties with additional judicial powers to those held by the conservators of the peace of the thirteenth century. JPs' duties increased in Tudor times and included fixing fair wages. This was work congenial to the talents of the local gentry, who were also suited to it by their comparative literacy, and their local knowledge. The RESTORATION of 1660 reduced their powers, and saw an increased tendency for JPs to act in the interests of property, particularly their own. However, through QUARTER SESSIONS and PETTY SESSIONS they remained the principal instrument of county government and law enforcement until the Local Government Acts of 1888 and 1894 removed their administrative powers. Today a JP is appointed by the LORD HIGH CHANCELLOR to try certain cases (e.g., motoring cases and assault) in a magistrates' court, and to send more serious cases to a higher court.

Kent, William (1685–1748). A painter, furniture designer, landscape gardener and, later, architect. Born in East Yorkshire at Bridlington and thought to have been apprenticed to a coach-painter in Hull, he was sent to Italy by three patrons to buy paintings and works of art for their country houses, and also to study painting himself. While in Rome in 1714 he met the 3rd Earl of Burlington (1695–1753), formed what was to prove a lifelong friendship, and returned to England with him in 1719. Under Burlington's patronage Kent received numerous commissions, chiefly involving landscape design and interior decoration, as well as architecture. However, it was only about 1730, following his edition of *The Designs of Inigo Jones* (1727), that he found his true métier as a PALLADIAN architect. Among his best known interiors are the state apartments at Houghton Hall, Norfolk (1726), and his decorated rooms in Burlington House, London, which may still be seen. At Rousham House, Oxfordshire he added wings to the north front in 1738, designed the famous landscape garden, and was responsible for some interior decoration; his most representative work, Holkham Hall in Norfolk, was begun in 1734. Like ADAM, he also designed furniture for many of his buildings.

Kersey. A coarse, narrow, worsted cloth, woven from long wool, usually ribbed. Named after Kersey in Suffolk, where it was made.

Kidderminster carpets. Flatweave carpets and rugs were made at Kidderminster from the beginning of the seventeenth century, but no examples survive. From about 1735 *moquette* (wool pile, coarsely imitating silk velvet) carpets, in the style of Brussels carpets, were introduced and manufactured on a very large scale.

Kings (now **Queen's**) **Bench, Court of.** One of the three courts that evolved from the CURIA REGIS (King's Court), hearing cases which concerned the king or those privileged to be tried before him. Established by the time of Edward I (1272–1307); the king's presence was not essential, and had become a fiction by the end of the fourteenth century. It gradually evolved into one of the three courts which administered the COMMON LAW, COMMON PLEAS and EXCHEQUER being the others. The three were merged in the JUDICATURE ACT of 1873, and became the King's (or Queen's) Bench Division of the Supreme Court of Justice.

King's Bench Prison. Established in Southwark in London by the fourteenth century to hold prisoners committed by the Court of KING'S BENCH; from 1758 it was used also for debtors. Such prisoners might, by payment of fees, 'purchase the liberties' – that is, permission to live in lodgings outside the prison walls – or 'purchase day-rules' – the right to go outside the prison under certain regulations. 'The Rules' were particular areas where prisoners might live; see Charles Dickens's *Nicholas Nickleby*. Burned during the Gordon Riots (1780), and renamed Queen's Bench Prison in 1842, it was closed when imprisonment for debt was abolished in 1869, and demolished ten years later.

King's Evil. Scrofula, or tuberculosis of the lymphatic glands. A medieval belief was that a touch by the king's hand cured the disease. The custom, believed to be an hereditary power, was introduced from France by Edward the Confessor (1042–66). The king washed the affected parts of supplicants and gave the sufferer a touch-piece, usually a gold angel coin. Henry VII (1457–1509) omitted the ceremony of ablution, merely touching the afflicted person. The custom lapsed but was revived by James I (1603–25) and became popular after the RESTORATION. William III (1694–1702) declined to perform the ceremony; the last English monarch to 'touch' for the King's Evil was Queen Anne (1702–14), who touched Dr Johnson in his youth. The exiled Stuarts in Italy frequently performed the ceremony, however.

King's (or **Queen's**) **Proctor.** Prior to 1859, the representative of the Crown in the Court of Admiralty, where the practitioners were known by titles different from those used in the ordinary courts. In the Court of Admiralty, advocates took the place of BARRISTERS, and proctors of SOLICITORS, the King's (or Queen's) Advocate-General that of the Attorney-General, and the King's (or Queen's) Proctor that of the Treasury solicitor.

Under the Judicature Act of 1873 DIVORCE (originally a matter for the ecclesiastical courts) and PROBATE were linked for administrative purposes with the Court of Admiralty, and in cases of divorce it was the duty of the King's (or Queen's) Proctor to intervene at any stage in the proceedings when it could be shown to be against the tenets of morality to dissolve the marriage; or to prevent a *decree nisi* being made absolute when it was shown that there had been collusion between husband and wife, or that all material facts had not been disclosed.

Kit Kat, Kit-Cat Club. The Kit-Cat Club was a literary association founded in the early part of the eighteenth century, the secretary of which was Jacob Tonson (1656–1736), a publisher, and the members chiefly leaders of the WHIG party. The meetings were held at the house of a pastry-cook named Christopher Cat (or Kat) in Shire Lane, near Temple Bar, from whose mutton pies, called Kit-cats, the club took its name (see Addison's *Spectator*, no. 9). The club later met at Tonson's house at Barn Elms, near Putney.

Sir Godfrey Kneller (1649?–1723) was commissioned by Tonson between 1707 and 1717 to paint portraits of the members – the 'Forty-three Celebrities of the Kit-Cat Club', now in the National Portrait Gallery, London. Because Tonson's dining-room ceiling was too low to accommodate the usual half-length portrait, these, with one exception, measure 36 inches by 28, and the name Kit-cat is often still used to denote a portrait of this size, particularly when the sitter is showing only one arm. See also CLUBS OF LONDON: DILETTANTI, SOCIETY OF; DIVAN CLUB; HELL-FIRE CLUBS and LITTLE BEDLAM CLUB.

Kitchens. Today, kitchens in historic houses are often presented as orderly, shining palaces filled with gleaming copper – a thoroughly misleading impression. In Henry VIII's (1509–47) time the boys working in Hampton Court's kitchen ran about naked because of the intense heat; in the late eighteenth century François de la Rouchefoucauld noted of English kitchens: '. . . the women who worked there were as black as coal and the dirt indescribable.'

Kitchens evolved from the early medieval practice of cooking over the central hearth in the GREAT HALL. Medieval monks were the first to move the hearth to a side wall and the kitchen to a separate building, a change commonplace even in more modest dwellings by the thirteenth century. In a large house, access was by means of the central door behind the screens passage. The Abbot's kitchen at Glastonbury, Somerset, of *c.* 1370, is one of the best preserved free-standing medieval kitchens, square externally but octagonal within. Another polygonal kitchen at Berkeley Castle, Gloucestershire, dates from the fourteenth century and is integral with the main building. The fine free-standing medieval kitchen at Stanton Harcourt, Oxfordshire dates from the late fourteenth century. These of course were all part of grand establishments.

In time the kitchen was integrated into the main building. An example is Haddon Hall in Derbyshire, where the kitchen was perhaps originally separate, but was in its present position, behind the BUTTERY and PANTRY, by the mid fourteenth century. Lower down the social scale, farmhouse cooking was still done over a hall hearth, even in the seventeenth century.

Medieval kitchens were supervised by the Clerk of the Kitchen who was responsible not only for the preparation of food but for provisioning the household. A medieval custom in grand households was that the kitchen staff were forbidden to turn their backs on meat roasting on the spit: because it was to be consumed by the lord of the establishment, it acquired part of his quasi-mystical authority.

The open fire for cooking obviously presented problems of heat control, although kitchens in large houses often had more than one hearth, one for a hot fire and another kept at a lower temperature; both would have had SPITS turning in front of them. A big step forward came with the reinvention or rediscovery of the Roman charcoal range; the earliest surviving example is at Llanvihangel Court in Gwent, dated 1679, but there is evidence that Henry VIII's kitchens had them. They consisted of a range of griddles over charcoal fires burning at different heats; flues were not needed, as charcoal burns without smoke. There is a large eighteenth-century charcoal range in the kitchens at Hardwick Hall, Derbyshire. As late as 1769 Mrs Elizabeth Raffald (1733–81), in *The Experienced English House-Keeper*, condemned charcoal ranges because she found them expensive, 'as well as pernicious to the cooks'. No doubt she had also over her hearths the words so often painted in kitchens: 'Waste not, want not'.

The despised charcoal range was eclipsed by the more scientific approach of Count Rumford, who at the end of the eighteenth century invented the first true cook-stove giving a controlled heat – the forerunner of cast-iron ranges with ovens. By the mid nineteenth century the old open hearths were being filled with smart cast-iron ranges which had to be black-leaded every day to keep them from rusting. Although more efficient for cooking, these monsters, using one and a half tons of coal a month, gave a great deal more work to the kitchen-maid (who would be lucky to be paid £20 a year in the mid nineteenth century). Good nineteenth-century kitchens with cast-iron ranges can be seen at Lanhydrock, Cornwall; Longleat, Wiltshire; Brodie Castle, Grampian; and Croxteth Hall, Merseyside; and a later kitchen at Castle Drogo, Devon. See also EATING and GREAT HALL.

Kitchen gardens. Like so much else, the idea of growing fresh vegetables and fruit in a separate garden came from France. When the Elizabethans were growing the few vegetables they needed amongst their flowers, the French were growing them in a separate *potager*. By the early seventeenth century some English gardens had separate sections for herbs and vegetables. In 1653 John Evelyn, who had lived in France in the 1640s, was planting out the gardens at his home, Sayes Court in Surrey. His salad calendar was published in 1664, and he observed in 'Notes for the Kitchin-Garden' that 'Chervill is handsom and proper for the edging of Kitchin Garden beds'. A visit to Sayes Court by Charles II (1660–85) in 1662 brought the idea of the kitchen garden to the attention of influential courtiers, and it may be that we should credit Evelyn with its popularization. Many of Leonard Knyff's drawings of the late 1690s show walled kitchen gardens, notably at Chatsworth, Derbyshire, and Hampton Court, London.

High walls sheltered the plants, kept out windblown weed seeds, prevented animals breaking in, and provided warmth for trained fruit trees on south-facing walls (see also CRINKUM-CRANKUM WALLS), while cold frames brought on early plants, HEATED WALLS brought on fruit, and hot-beds made up of dung grew melons. By the eighteenth century, an orderly kitchen garden had become a place for family and guests to promenade.

With the decline of large households after the First World War, the purpose of the big kitchen garden came to an end; there was no need for enormous quantities of fruit and vegetables to supply the various inhabitants of a large house. None exist today which equal the massive output of a hundred years ago: the kitchen gardens at Erddig in Clwyd and Montacute in Somerset have been turned into visitors' car parks. Elsewhere such walled areas have been developed into ordinary gardens, or garden centres, which at least continues the theme. Many remain as overgrown wildernesses, although the occasional large establishment still maintains a kitchen garden, as at Chatsworth, Derbyshire.

Knife boxes or **cases.** Often seen on the SIDEBOARDS of country-house eating-rooms, these are containers, usually in pairs, either with sloping tops and serpentine fronts or made in the form of urns, and with partitions inside to take knives, forks and spoons. They are known from as early as 1649, but most commonly date from the 1760s. Early examples are found in walnut, covered in leather or shagreen, or japanned and gilded. Robert ADAM's designs in particular reflected the fashion for the classical urn shape, and his knife boxes often stood on their own pedestals at either side of, rather than on, the sideboard. Instead of both boxes having fittings for cutlery, one might contain instead a lead-lined cistern, to hold water for washing precious glassware in the dining-room: it would of course have a tap at the bottom, to empty it, and so the knife-box proper would have a false tap, to match.

Knight-banneret. In feudal times, a noble who had the right to lead his forces onto the field of battle under his own banner; subsequently, a rank and order of knighthood conferred for deeds of honour carried out on the field of battle in the king's presence, or in the presence of the Royal Standard. If the newly-created knight-banneret previously carried his arms on a pennant or streamer, the pointed end of this was cut off to make the banner.

It is thought that the last authentic creation of a knight-banneret was that of John Smith by Charles I at the Battle of Edgehill, when Smith rescued the Royal Standard from the Parliamentarians.

Knighthood. Originated with the military tenancies under the feudal system introduced after the Norman Conquest; those who held land in return for KNIGHT-SERVICE were liable to be called to arms by the king. Although the various fees involved continued to be a source of revenue to the Crown, the feudal system this represented was defunct long before the formal abolition of tenure by knight-service in 1660. Today knighthood is the lowest titled rank; the recipient prefixes his name with 'Sir' (Sir John Smith) and his wife becomes a Lady (Lady Smith). Knighthoods may be of two kinds: knights of the various orders of CHIVALRY, and Knights Bachelor.

The popular belief that a knight represented on his tomb with crossed legs died on Crusade is fiction; this was merely the fashion in effigies *c.* 1300.

Knights of the Shire. The Parliamentary representatives of a shire or county (not a BOROUGH); first summoned to Parliament in 1258. A statute of 1275 declared that elections for knights of the shire should be 'free from disturbance by the great', and writs to the SHERIFFS stated that those sent to Parliament should be chosen from the more discreet and law-worthy knights of the shire. These knights formed a useful link in judicial procedure between local and central government; they were active in local administration and usually substantial land-holders in the community.

Knight-service. The dominant and distinctive tenure of land under the feudal system. William the Conqueror awarded land to his tenants-in-chief in return for the service of a fixed number of knights; they could be knights hired for pay, or might be provided through a process of sub-enfeoffment. The primary obligation was service in the field when called upon, for forty days per year, suitably armed and accoutered. By 1100 knight-service could be commuted by the payment of scutage, the income from which was used by successive monarchs to raise and pay mercenary armies. Knight–service was abolished in 1660. See also KNIGHTHOOD and WARDSHIP.

Knocknobbler. Also called a dog-whipper, the knocknobbler was responsible for driving dogs out of church when they caused a nuisance.

Knot gardens. Knot gardens – small, and usually rectangular – came to Britain from France in the sixteenth century, having originated in Italy. They consisted of low hedging of rosemary, thrift, hyssop, thyme, cotton-lavender, marjoram or, after 1600, dwarf box, laid out in a pattern, the beds the hedging enclosed filled with colour from flowers or coloured soils, stones or gravel. The pattern of the hedging was taken initially from needlework designs and, by the mid sixteenth century, from published woodcuts: *Most Briefe and Pleasant Treatyse* by Thomas Hill, published in 1563, shows several knot patterns; du Cerceau's *Les Plus Excellent Bastiments de France*, published in 1576 and 1579, shows several French gardens laid out with knot gardens. Such publications doubtless helped to popularize the fashion. The intricate weaving patterns were best appreciated from above, from a raised walk or a MOUND, or from the windows of LONG GALLERIES. A modern recreation of a knot garden can be seen at Barnsley House, Gloucestershire. See also GARDENS.

Lambrequin. The Victorian name for a padded pelmet; a short piece of decorative drapery, the lower edge often scalloped, hung over a door or above a window from a pole. The name is derived from heraldic MANTLING. Decoratively, the feature most often survives today as a *trompe-l'oeil* painted detail.

Lammas. An early English harvest festival, originally held on 1 August (12 August when the Gregorian CALENDAR came into use). Said to originate from 'Loaf-Mass': a loaf made from the first ripe wheat was blessed and solemnly offered at Mass in lieu of first-fruits. See also HARVEST CUSTOMS.

Lancers. Soldiers of a cavalry regiment, originally armed with nine-foot lances. In the modern sense, lancer regiments date from Napoleon's raising in 1807 of a regiment of Polish Lancers. More common in Eastern Europe. The first British lancer regiments were created 1816 from Light DRAGOON regiments.

Landau. See CARRIAGES.

Land Tax. The longest surviving direct taxation. Initiated by the Parliamentary side during the Civil War (1642–3); the weekly or monthly assessments proved difficult to collect. A revised and more exact valuation of landed property was made in 1692, and a tax on the value of rentals was introduced which varied from 1s. to 4s. in the pound. This provided much of the finance for the wars in which England was involved under William III and Queen Anne, but was unpopular with the landowning gentry; Sir Robert Walpole (1676–1745) tended to keep the level as low as possible, in the WHIG interest. To pay for the war with France, William Pitt the Younger (1759–1806) fixed it at 4s. in 1798, and also put forward a scheme whereby fifteen years' worth of tax might be paid by a once-only lump sum: many landowners took advantage of this. In 1909 Lloyd George (1863–1945) introduced a new tax on any unearned increase in land values, but it was discontinued in 1920. Land Tax was finally abolished in 1963. See also TAXATION.

Latten. A yellow alloy of copper and zinc, similar to brass, used for plates and dishes; also used for monumental brasses, such as the screen of Henry VII's tomb in Westminster Abbey.

Laundry. A very old department of the great household, and completely independent of the HOUSEKEEPER. Under the supervision of the laundress the laundry-maids laboured week in, week out. Huge coppers were used for boiling linen, massive box mangles worked by vast wheels squeezed out water before the sheets were hung to dry over the heavy dying racks (from the mid-nineteenth century) which pulled out from a heated cupboard, or in the drying grounds in fine weather. Finally, weary laundry-maids used heavy cast-iron smoothing irons to iron the sheets and garments.

The drying ground, walled and convenient to the laundry, was a feature of the country house for centuries before the introduction of heated cupboards. A painting of Wollaton Hall in Nottinghamshire by Jan Siberechts (*c.* 1700) shows laundry drying on distant bushes. It also provided a chink in the rigid household rules; laundry-maids going out to hang up the washing were accessible to the male outside staff: parish registers in churches near country houses often show baptisms of laundry-maids' illegitimate babies.

In the nineteenth century Chatsworth in Derbyshire maintained a central laundry, and the Duke of Devonshire's dirty household linen was sent up weekly in wicker hampers by train from London. Erddig in Clwyd has a completely-equipped nineteenth-century laundry.

Lawn-mower. For centuries lawns were cut, surprisingly close, by scythe. In 1830 a Gloucestershire textile engineer, Edwin Budding, applied to lawns the principle of cutting the nap of cloth, and the first mechanical hand-propelled lawn-mower was invented. Early machines were designed to be pushed and pulled, larger mowers were pulled by donkeys or horses, with leather boots on their hooves to avoid marking the turf. In *c.* 1900 the first petrol-powered mower came on the market. There is a small lawn-mower museum at Trerice in Cornwall.

Leather mâché. Shreds of leather mixed with size and brick-dust which set hard when mixed with water and poured into moulds. Used for interior decoration, particularly on ceilings, in the sixteenth century. Leather mâché was used in the interiors of Henry VIII's Hampton Court in the 1530s. See also PAPIER MÂCHÉ.

Lending libraries. Circulating libraries from which, for a subscription, members might borrow books. Allan Ramsey (1686–1759), a Scottish poet, wigmaker and bookseller, is credited with founding the first lending library in Edinburgh in 1762. The system was successful, and at its most popular from the second half of the eighteenth century to the end of the nineteenth. The big new circulating libraries of the mid to late nineteenth century, MUDIE's, W.H. Smith's and Boots, implemented powerful moral censorship and refused to stock some writers' novels. However, they stimulated reading and, consequently, publishing. Until its popularity waned at the end of the nineteenth century, the three-volume novel of the late eighteenth and the nineteenth century was largely supported by lending libraries. Most lending libraries had closed by 1970, in the face of competition from book clubs, and from public libraries financed from local taxation.

The first British public libraries, established under the Museum Act, were at Canterbury in 1847, Warrington in 1848, and Salford in 1850. The Public Libraries Act of 1850 allowed local BOROUGHS in England and Wales with a population of more than 10,000 to spend a half-penny rate on libraries and museums. This was extended to Scotland in 1853, and in 1855 the rate was raised to a penny and the population limitation lowered to 5,000; the population limitation was removed in 1866, and the rate limitation in England and Wales in 1919.

Letter of credit. Before the modern banking convenience of cheques and credit cards, a traveller used a letter of credit to draw funds from a foreign bank. This was simply a letter written by one banker, instructing his appointed agent or another banker to pay a specified sum or sums to the person named in the document. The letter was not transferable.

Levant Company. Established in 1592 in a merger between the Turkey Company, founded in 1581, and the Venice Company, founded in 1583, with a monopoly to develop trade in the eastern Mediterranean. The Company maintained trading stations at Acre, Alexandretta, Aleppo, Cairo, Cyprus, Constantinople, Smyrna and Tripoli.

Trade was mainly in the exchange of woollen cloth for eastern silks, dried fruits and wine; it declined from the time of the Dutch wars of the 1660s, and the monopoly was finally ended in 1825.

Levée. From the French *lever*, to rise; a custom imported, like so much else, from the French Court, where the royal bedchamber, having become by the mid seventeenth century the most important room in the sequence of STATE APARTMENTS, was used for the reception of very important visitors. The *lever* of the king, in several stages (*petit lever, première entrée, grand lever*) was attended by male courtiers only, and involved the getting up and dressing of the sovereign. English noblemen later borrowed the custom for themselves; it became part of London life, and was gradually taken over by fashionable women. By the 1740s the custom had become outmoded: Hogarth, in his series *Marriage à la Mode* at the National Gallery, pokes fun at it, showing the dissolute countess holding an equally dissolute levée in her bedchamber. In the nineteenth century the Royal Levée had become a reception held by the sovereign (or, abroad, by her representative) in the late morning or early afternoon, in May or June, at which young men made their début in society. The custom ended in 1958.

Levellers. The name given to a party of radical democrats active during the CIVIL WAR and Commonwealth. Originating among MPs but found mainly among soldiers, and led by John Lilburne (1614?–1657), the Levellers were opposed to the idea of kingship and proposed various constitutional reforms, including a sovereign Parliament to be selected by universal male suffrage, together with religious toleration of all sects. Mutinies in several regiments in 1647 and outbreaks of violence in 1649 led to the arrest of Lilburne and other leaders by Oliver Cromwell (1599–1658), to whose increasing power they were opposed.

Libraries. Both royal and private libraries of any distinction appeared relatively late on the scene. Henry VII (1485–1509) had a librarian, and Henry VIII (1509–47) had libraries at Greenwich Palace, Hampton Court and Whitehall in the 1520s, but they were comparatively small – in 1542 the one at Whitehall had only 910 books. No more than two Elizabethans, Lord Lumley and Lord Burghley, had collections (totalling more than a thousand books) that might really be called libraries. Books were not displayed on open bookshelves as they are today, but stacked in cupboards, their titles written on the fore-edge, as the early seventeenth-century books at Charlcote Park in Warwickshire still show. It was only when the number of books in a household became an embarrassment that serious thought began to be given to their storage. In 1610 Sir Thomas Bodley (1545–1613) introduced double tiers of shelves reached by ladders in Duke Humphrey's Library, Oxford.

After the mid seventeenth century, as both literacy and an interest in learning increased, so did the number of books to be found in country houses. Open-fronted bookshelves remained unusual in private houses until the mid eighteenth century: the shelves of the tiny library made by the Lauderdales in 1675 at Ham House, Surrey are open, while the equally small library at Chichley Hall, Buckinghamshire, made fifty years later, gives the appearance of being a panelled room, until the panels are opened to reveal bookshelves. There is a similar 'secret' library of *c.* 1740 at Blithfield Hall, Staffordshire.

An early, recognizable library is at Holkham Hall, Norfolk: designed by William KENT in the 1740s, it is 54 feet long and attached to Thomas Coke's private apartments, not an element of the STATE APARTMENT circuit: at that date, a gentleman's library was intended for his own use, not to impress visitors with his culture. An eighteenth-century fashion in Scotland was to put libraries on an upper floor. Sometime after the middle of the eighteenth century the library became one of the 'state' rooms.

Some libraries were excellent. In the 1770s the landscape gardener Humphry REPTON used the library of his neighbour William Windham at Felbrigg Hall, Norfolk. At Stourhead in Wiltshire, the library built in 1792 became a focus for the study of local history: Sir Richard Colt Hoare (1758–1838), the owner of Stourhead, wrote his two-volume history of Wiltshire here, and it was here that meetings took place of local gentry (including the Bishop of Bath and Wells) who were fascinated by aspects of history.

By the early nineteenth century libraries had become places to sit and be comfortable in. The Irish novelist Maria Edgeworth (1767–1849) described the library at Bowood, Wiltshire in 1818: 'The library tho' magnificent is a most comfortable habitable looking room . . . it was very agreeable in the delightful library after breakfast this day.' By the middle of the nineteenth century the library had become a male domain which ladies would only visit when invited. And so it remained for the rest of the century.

Life Guards. One of the cavalry units of the British Army which supplies the Sovereign's Escort; full title 'The Life Guards (1st and 2nd)'. See also HORSE GUARDS.

Lighting. Today with the convenience of electric lighting it is easy to overlook the fact that for centuries the only artificial light available was that from the fire, supplemented by tallow candles and rush-lights.

Rush-lights were the cheapest and were used, even in great houses, in the KITCHENS. They consisted of rushes washed, bleached, dried and peeled; the pith was then dipped in mutton suet or grease, sometimes with the addition of a little beeswax. A two-foot rush-light, clamped in an iron holder, burnt for an hour. As it burnt down it often bent, and the scorch-marks indicating near-conflagrations can be seen on the vertical wooden surfaces of many a building, in the kitchens of Hampton Court for example.

Tallow candles, first using a rush-pith as a wick, later flax or cotton, were better because they burnt longer, but like rush-lights had the disadvantage of being smelly. Candles made from beeswax were the best and least offensive, but also the most expensive – beyond the purses of most people, particularly after the introduction of a tax on manufacturing candles in 1709 (repealed only in 1831).

In 1728 Sir Thomas Robinson described the new Houghton Hall, Norfolk, lit for the visit of the Duke of Lorraine: 'They dined in the hall, which was lighted by 130 wax candles, and the saloon with 50; the whole expense in that article being computed at fifteen pounds a night.' In 1789 Tottenham Park in Wiltshire was lit for the visit of George III (1760–1820) and Queen Charlotte (1744–1818) by 159 wax candles and twenty-four extra lamps in thirty-three rooms. No room had more than eighteen candles, the bedrooms had four candles, and the dressing-rooms three.

The size of candle used depended on how long an evening party was expected to last. The glass chandeliers with many candles, which we tend to think of as typical of eighteenth-century rooms, were in fact very rare, and mostly Venetian: it was not until the late 1780s that really beautiful chandeliers made in Britain were introduced into drawing rooms and SALOONS, and pre-Regency chandeliers are the exception, not the rule.

The taxation measures of 1709 included a tax on candles and then on oil lamps. This effectively slowed down the development and production of the latter, although it was far better means of lighting. A swiss, Aimé Argand (1755–1803), invented the Colza oil lamp in 1784, which burnt rape-seed oil and gave a brilliant light, but vegetable oils tended to clog the wick, which needed constant attention; refined paraffin, introduced in the 1850s, solved this problem. Probably the greatest step forward was the invention by Count Rumford (1753–1814) of the glass chimney, which fitted over the lighted wick and prevented the oil lamp from flickering.

Gas lighting was first used in 1779 by William Murdock (1754–1839) in his own house in Cornwall; in 1798 he installed it in an engineering works in Soho in Birmingham. The early burners were of the 'batswing' type, in which a flattened flame was produced by a slit in the end of the burner. Gas produced a harsh white light: the more flattering candle-light was therefore often preferred. In the sculpture gallery at Chatsworth there are two huge gasoliers, now converted to electricity, bought at a sale at Wanstead House in 1822. It was not until the invention of the Bunsen incandescent burner, finally improved in 1885 by the Welsbach mantle, that the disadvantages of gas lighting were overcome. It did, however, provide a surprising amount of heat, and high ceilings were a necessity.

Electricity was the next great step forward: Cragside in Northumberland was the first house in Britain to be illuminated by hydroelectric power, in 1880. Hatfield House, Hertfordshire, had electric lighting the following year. The first church to be lit by electricity was St Anne's, at Chasetown in Staffordshire, in 1883. Arundel Castle in Sussex retains its original electric light fittings of *c*. 1900. However, electricity was considered vulgar by many, and at first was never installed in the principal rooms – at Claydon in Buckinghamshire, for example, and Erddig in Clwyd; Burghley House in Lincolnshire was lit by gas until 1956.

Lady Diana Cooper remembered her home, Belvoir Castle in Leicestershire, in *c*. 1900: 'Then there were the lamp and candle men . . . for there was no other form of lighting. Gas was despised, I forget why – vulgar, I think. They polished and scraped wax off the candalabra, cut wicks, poured paraffin oil and unblackened glass chimneys all day long. After dark they were busy turning wicks up or down, snuffing candles, and de-waxing extinguishers. It was not a department we liked to visit. It smelt disgusting and the lamp men were too busy.'

Lincoln's Inn. See INNS OF COURT.

Linoleum. See FLOORS AND FLOOR COVERINGS.

Little Bedlam Club. A drinking club founded at Burghley House, Lincolnshire, by the 5th Earl of Exeter in the late seventeenth century. Oval framed portraits of the members hang in the billiard room there; they included Sir Isaac Newton (1642–1727) and the painter Antonio Verrio (1630–1707), who worked in the house. See also CLUBS OF LONDON, DIVAN CLUB and HELL-FIRE CLUBS.

Livery Companies. See GUILDS.

Lodges. See GATES AND LODGES.

Long galleries. Galleries evolved in France as open-sided, connecting corridors between separate buildings. The earliest surviving example in Britain is at Christchurch Priory, Canterbury (*c*. 1400), and runs between the Court Gate and Kitchen Court. The incorporation of the gallery within the building, which is how we think of them today, is also of French origin. An early English example is a two-storey gallery of *c*. 1500 in the Prior's Lodging at Wenlock Priory, Shropshire. It was only after 1550 that Tudor houses of consequence had a gallery sited on an upper floor, often in the roof space, giving a view from its windows onto KNOT GARDENS and PARTERRES. The fashion lasted until the mid seventeenth century; although some houses have galleries later in date, they were intended for a different purpose. Originally the gallery was a secondary room of reception, used also for exercise. At Ingatestone Hall, Essex in 1566 the gallery was described as '. . . a stately gallery or walk . . .'. In *c.* 1700, when the original use of the gallery was on the wane, it was described as '. . . a room for no other use but pastime and health, so far as gentle moving . . . within the walls of an house may concerne it.' Galleries had always been hung with portraits, and by the eighteenth century were used for the display of other paintings, and sculpture. They were not originally described as 'long', a term which came gradually to be added, often to distinguish it from another, shorter gallery; by the time of Celia Fiennes' journeys (between 1683 and 1703) it was in common use. The longest surviving gallery (172 feet) is at Montacute House in Somerset; longer galleries, since demolished, existed at Worksop Manor, Nottinghamshire and Longleat House, Wiltshire.

Lord Chamberlain. An officer of the sovereign's household, a member of the government of the day, a peer, and a privy councillor. Responsible for such state occasions as royal marriages, christenings and funerals, and closely involved in all court functions. His responsibility for licensing theatre performances (a form of censorship) ended on 26 December 1968.

Lord Great Chamberlain. To be carefully distinguished from the LORD CHAMBERLAIN. An hereditary and largely ceremonial office first granted in 1133 by Henry I (1100–35) to the de Veres, Earls of Oxford which passed in 1779 to co-heiresses of Lord Willoughby de Eresby and is now vested in the Marquesses of Cholmondeley. His emblem of office is a key. The Lord Great Chamberlain has charge of the Palace of Westminster, with an office in the House of Lords, and is mostly concerned with ceremonial duties in Parliament, particularly at coronations, and at the opening of Parliament when this is done by the sovereign in person.

Lord High Chancellor. The term is from the Latin *cancellarius*, meaning 'the man behind the lattice', used in Roman courts of justice; a type of legal scribe; in the reign of Edward the Confessor (1042–66), the king's chaplain and chief secretary. He also kept the great seal, and supervised the Chancery which recorded and produced acts and grants made under it. Always an ecclesiastic, until the fourteenth century. Under Edward III (1327–77) he was established as head of a permanent Court of CHANCERY to consider petitions to the king. The position is now a cabinet office; the holder also appoints judges and JUSTICES OF THE PEACE, presides over the Court of Appeal and the Court of Chancery, and acts as Speaker in the House of Lords.

Lord-Lieutenant. The sovereign's representative in a county, nominated by the sovereign; usually held by a local dignitary. An office first created by Henry VIII (1509–47) as part of an attempt to decentralize government. Originally the Lord-Lieutenant's duty (taken over from the SHERIFF or shire-reeve) was to command the county MILITIA in such emergencies as riot and invasion. The office became permanent in 1551 under Elizabeth I (1558–1603) when Lords-Lieutenant were expected to maintain order locally, with the help of JUSTICES OF THE PEACE. Until 1871, when it reverted to the Crown, the Lord-Lieutenant had the right to appoint his own officers.

Louis XV (Louis Quinze) Style (1715–1774). Much French furniture of this period is to be seen in the great houses of Britain. The style is ROCOCO at its most frivolous, easily distinguished by heavy ORMOLU decoration, beautiful marquetry and sensuous curves, particularly in the legs. The best is undoubtedly in the Wallace Collection in London, but there are a number of exquisite pieces at Boughton House, Northamptonshire, and the Rothschilds' collection at Waddesdon Manor, Buckinghamshire is well worth seeing. See also LOUIS XVI STYLE.

Louis XVI (Louis Seize) Style (1774–1793). Like the LOUIS XV style, often to be seen, and easily distinguished: a NEO-CLASSICAL style, with straight lines where the rococo of Louis XV has curves. Designs are neither so heavy, nor so much fun. Elegance is the key; ORMOLU was still applied but not so lavishly, nor was inlay so luxurious. Above all – *the* distinguishing feature – legs are always straight. The best pieces are again to be seen in the Wallace Collection in London, and at Waddesdon Manor in Buckinghamshire. See also LOUIS XV STYLE.

Love-seat. A small settee or chair wide enough for two to sit on side by side. When introduced in the second half of the seventeenth century it was termed a 'courting chair'; the French version is a *marquise* chair.

Luddites. Organized bands of workers who, from their first appearance in Nottingham in 1811, destroyed new factory machinery. The name reputedly derived from Ned Ludd, a Leicestershire youth who broke up some knitting machinery in 1779. The activities of the Luddites lasted until January 1813, with further outbreaks in 1816. The cause was unemployment and reduced wages in the cotton industries of Leicestershire, Derbyshire, and Nottinghamshire, where new power-driven machinery was taking work from the long-established, home-based, framework knitters. In January 1812 the riots spread to Lancashire and Cheshire where cotton power-looms were newly installed, and to the West Riding where the target was woollen shearing-machines. The government suppressed the riots with military force, and the breaking of machinery was made a capital offence. In 1813 some seventeen men were hanged in York for frame-breaking.

These riots, together with riots in the 1830s provoked by the REFORM ACTS, persuaded landowners that Britain was in danger of revolution, and some took steps to protect themselves. At Wollaton Hall in Nottinghamshire, Lord Middleton built a fortified gatehouse with cannon on the roof. Other less militant remedies were suggested by PUGIN who (inspired not doubt by his GOTHIC REVIVAL tastes) advocated a return to the use of the Great Hall, where landowners and tenants could meet at least three times a year at convivial dinners. See also COTTON and HOSE.

Lutyens, Sir Edwin (1869–1944). In 1887 Lutyens entered the office of (Ernest) George and (Harold) Peto, where he assimilated the English Domestic Revival styles of the practice. He also met Norman SHAW, who became his lifelong hero, and was influenced by Philip WEBB's work. In 1896 he designed Munstead Wood for Gertrude Jekyll, and this was followed by a number of houses in the ARTS AND CRAFTS style. However, Lutyens also shared to the full the ideas of grandeur of the Imperial Edwardian years, and was the ideal architect for the last of the spectacular English country houses: Lindisfarne Castle, Holy Island, Northumberland (1903), the romantic restoration of a Tudor castle; Castle Drogo, Devon, an amazing twentieth-century castle project (1910–30); and the neo-Georgian Great Maytham, Kent (1907–9) – all demonstrate Lutyens' versatility. He could be a brilliant master of composition and balance, but could also falter, as revealed by his Grosvenor Estate buildings in Marsham Street, Westminster. He will be remembered particularly for the magnificent grandeur of his government buildings in New Delhi, India, begun in 1913, and his Cenotaph in Whitehall (1919–20).

Lying-in-state. The custom of presenting a corpse to the public as a demonstration that the person in question is indeed dead and, in some circumstances, that the death had not been caused by foul play. Now, usually, only seen at the death of the sovereign and, very occasionally, of a great statesman or peer. The last lying-in-state in Britain of a commoner was that of Sir Winston Churchill in 1965.

The room of the lying-in-state would be draped in black. When Sir Ralph Verney died at Claydon House, Buckinghamshire in 1696 the Hall and the Brick Parlour were hung with black baize. Furniture in the room in which the lying-in-state took place was also customarily covered in black, or painted black, for the period of mourning. Attingham Park in Shropshire shows evidence of black paint on a skirting-board, probably from the lying-in-state of the 1st Lord Berwick in 1789. The King's Bed at Knole in Kent shows traces of having been painted in mourning black in the late seventeenth or early eighteenth century.

The problem of decomposure of the corpse was not always satisfactorily met by EMBALMING. At a royal lying-in-state an effigy might therefore be exhibited on the coffin; this was first done in 1327, at the funeral of Edward II, and the custom survived until 1685: Charles II was the last British sovereign whose effigy was displayed at his funeral. It may be seen (fully clothed) in the museum at Westminster Abbey. However, wax figures continued to be exhibited; the last time a wax effigy was used at a peer's lying-in-state was at the burial of the Duke of Buckingham in 1753; his wax likeness is still in Westminster Abbey. See also FUNERALS.

Marcaronis. Eighteenth-century dandies imitating continental fashions and reacting against the formal dress of their times. In the 1770s a younger set affected the extreme and ridiculous fashion of wearing a towering WIG, complete with a long horse-tail at the back and crowned with a very small tricorne hat. When everyone else was wearing coats cut straight to knee-length, the Macaronis wore French long-bodied coats with short tails. They also wore huge buttons, when the fashion was for small, and enormous shoe buckles. *The Town and Country Magazine* reported in 1772: 'They make a most ridiculous figure with hats an inch to the brim that do not cover but lie upon the head, with about two pounds of fictitious hair formed into what is called a "club" hanging down their shoulders.'

This fashion never became widespread, and the frivolity it expressed was swept away by the social climate engendered by the French Revolution. See also DANDYISM.

Mackintosh, Charles Rennie (1868–1928). A brilliant Scottish pioneer of modern design and the British Art Nouveau style. His best-known buildings are the Glasgow School of Art (1898–9), Hill House, Helensburgh (1902–3), and Mrs Cranston's Tea-rooms in Buchanan Street, Glasgow (1897). Mackintosh was ahead of his time, and the First World War effectively killed off his architectural practice. Examples of his work (which included furniture design) are few but influential, and after years of neglect his genius is at last appreciated.

Magna Carta. The 'Great Charter' of liberties granted by King John (1199–1216) at Runnymede on 15 June 1215. It takes its name not so much from its perceived significance, as from its great length. Arbitrary rule and a disastrous foreign policy which lost Normandy and its revenues forced John to raise money in England to pay for his military operations. Such taxation roused strong baronial opposition, led by Archbishop Stephen Langton (d. 1228), which resulted in outright revolt in the Midlands. Hostilities were only ended by a truce arranged by Langton, the terms of which were set out in Magna Carta. The charter defined the barons' feudal rights, confirmed the liberties of the Church, and stated what feudal revenues the king might raise. The best-known clauses guaranteed justice for everyone, and for every free man security from illegal interference with his person or property. Most remarkably, by Article 61 the barons were empowered to appoint a council of twenty-five to hear complaints if King John did not carry out his promises, with powers to confiscate his castles and lands. Backed by the papacy, John reneged on his promises, provoking the Barons' War in the autumn of 1215. Papal support for the Charter, John's death in 1216, and amendments to its terms, successfully ended the war in 1217. Further revisions were made by Henry III (1216–72) in 1225, and the Charter became of the greatest importance in defining the restrictions on royal power, and remained so through the thirteenth and fourteenth centuries; by the fifteenth century many of its provisions were obsolete, yet such was the veneration in which the Charter was held that even into the seventeenth century lawyers continued to find in it meanings which would have surprised its drafters. Four copies of the Charter exist, two at the British Library in London, and one each in Salisbury and Lincoln Cathedrals.

Maidens' garlands. A garland made of a wooden frame decorated with paper flowers, ribbons, and one or two pairs of gloves. These sad devices were carried on the coffin of a dead virgin, and after the funeral hung in the church. Understandably, many have perished, but examples may sometimes be found in country churches; most date from any time in the eighteenth century. St Mary's at Abbotts Ann in Hampshire has more than any other church in Britain, which may say something for the village; the latest is dated 1953.

Mail, Royal. See POST OFFICE.

Mannerism. A rather unsatisfactory art-historical term that came into use in this century. It defines the development of art and architecture in the period from the death of Raphael in 1520 to the end of the sixteenth century. Vasari (1511–74), a Florentine painter and biographer of fellow artists past and present, used the term *maniera* to define the artificial sense of style he recognized as current in his century.

Mannerist painting is distinguished by an insistence on the primacy of the human figure, and by elongated and over-muscular figures held in contorted poses. In architecture, the Mannerist style is expressed in exaggerated detail, and in stretching the rules of proportion to effect a sense of 'movement' and excitement in buildings. A typical Mannerist detail in England is to be seen in the use of the STRAPWORK motif: architecturally the feature becomes exaggerated, with little obvious relationship to the leather strapwork of its origins, and is transformed into a decorative detail in its own right.

The Mannerist search for excitement and movement developed smoothly into the BAROQUE.

Manners. A mode of life, very much a condition of society, and hence historically variable.

A mid fifteenth-century book on behaviour, *The Boke of Nurture* by John Russell, exposes some rough medieval manners. Written for young men who were placed as pages in great houses, its wealth of useful advice is revealing in what was forbidden. 'Pike not youre nose ne that hit be droppynge with no peerlis clere . . . and alle wey be ware of thy hyndur part from gunnes blastynge'. After such strictures, the admonition not to squirt or spout with your mouth or put your tongue in a dish seems tame stuff. *The Babees' Book* of 1475, when manners had apparently become more civilized, advised merely, 'Youre nose, youre teethe, your nails, from pyckynge kepe . . .'; and 'Youre knyf withe mete to your mouthe nat bere' – remember that there were no FORKS, and eating was done with a knife to cut the food and the left hand to lift it to the mouth: this straightforward and useful hint was repeated in many such subsequent books. *The Young Children's Book* of *c*. 1500 added, 'Ne spitte thow not over the tabylle, ne thereupon', and included the admonition (its first appearance) not to speak with the mouth full of food; but standards had clearly relapsed again by 1545, when Hugh Rhodes's *Book of Nurture and School of Good Manners* was first published: 'Belche thou neare to no man's face with a corrupt fumosytye.' Daughters seemingly had long been better-behaved: *How the Good Wiyf taugte her Daugtir* (1430) contains the straightforward advice, 'Don't go where your lover might get you into trouble', persistent enough in any age; 'If you get drunk often, you'll be disgraced' points, however, to some licence.

The School of Manners (1701) indicates that behaviour was by this time far more civilized, although use of the fork was not universal, and trenchers were still commonplace: 'Smell not to thy meat nor move it to thy nose'; 'Take not salt with a greazy knife'; 'Blow not thy meat but wait with patience till it be cool'; and (again) 'Drink not nor speak with anything in thy mouth'. In the section 'Rules for Behaviour in Company' the author, a schoolmaster, advises, 'Spit not in the Room, but in the corner, and rub it out with thy Foot', and 'Spit not upon the fire'; his advice is otherwise surprisingly modern.

In the recent past it was considered impolite to compliment the hostess on the quality of the dishes served at her table – it was, after all, the cook who had prepared the meal, not the hostess. The custom of leaving a little upon the plate, to indicate that one had had enough and second helpings were unnecessary, puzzled at least one child encouraged to 'leave something for Mr Manners'; why should Mr Manners be in want of anything, when Manners was the family name of the Dukes of Rutland?

Manning, Henry Edward, Cardinal (1808–92). Educated at Harrow and Bailliol; rector of Lavington-cum-Graffham from 1833, archdeacon of Chichester in 1840, and a TRACTARIAN. His conversion to Roman Catholicism in 1851 caused enormous controversy and consternation in the Church of England. He became Archbishop of Westminster in 1865 and took a leading part in the debates in the Vatican Council on Papal infallibility in the 1870s, becoming a cardinal in 1875. He was in his time an energetic and influential leader of the Roman Catholic Church in England. See also NEWMAN and OXFORD MOVEMENT.

Manor. Originally from the Old French *maneir* (now *manoir*) meaning 'a dwelling place'; introduced to England after the Norman Conquest as a lordship based on land tenure: a holding of land and its administrative centre. The manorial system had reached the peak of its development by the thirteenth century, and (like feudalism) was showing signs of decay by the fourteenth century. Usually, although not always, part of the estate – the DEMESNE – was reserved for the maintenance of the lord of the manor, and the remainder was held by tenants, in return for a money rent and (sometimes) a duty of some minor service if they were freemen, or in return for labour on the lord's demesne if they were VILLEINS. But manors were infinitely variable, as were the terms of landholding; some manors had no demesne, and others no free tenants. Manors also varied in size; a 'typical' manor might include one village, while another encompassed several. The lord possessed a limited jurisdiction over his free tenants, in the COURT-BARON, and wider powers over his villeins, in the Customary Court dealing with minor misdemeanours and breaches of manorial regulations. Some lords also had the privilege of holding a COURT-LEET half-yearly, a delegation to the lord of the powers of the royal courts. ENCLOSURE brought an end to the manorial system, although vestiges lingered on until comparatively recent times; the last links were broken when COPYHOLD tenure was abolished in 1926. See also HONOUR (2).

Mantling. Also called a LAMBREQUIN; originally, a short scarf worn by a knight in the CRUSADES to cover his steel helmet for protection from the Palestinian sun. The mantle became an element of HERALDRY, shown in blazonry as fixed to the helmet by the 'torse', a circlet of twisted silk, then falling aristically round the shield of arms, with one end (cut or jagged) pendant or floating.

Marines, Royal. See ROYAL MARINES.

Markets and **fairs.** It is suggested that fairs grew out of truces between warring tribes, and that markets evolved from fairs. Whatever their origins, they are linked together. A prohibition in 1285 of the early medieval custom of holding fairs in churchyards was largely ignored. In

Henry VI's reign (1422–71) it was prohibited to hold fairs on various feast days and Sundays. Any merchant who continued to sell after a fair closed was liable to a heavy fine of double the value of what he had sold.

Local landlords greedily collected charters to hold fairs and markets. In Northumberland in the fourteenth century, for example, the Percies were licensed to hold fairs in nine market towns; the Scropes had four, and the Nevilles had three. By the fifteenth century, most towns held at least a weekly market. It was the tolls on goods sold and fees for the use of stalls that made fairs so profitable, together with the fines that might accrue from the Court of Piepowder, the summary court held at fairs and markets to administer justice among the hawkers and pedlars.

Medieval fairs and markets were a vital part of the economy. Although a large household was largely self-sufficient, it could not be so in all things. Cloth, dried fruits and jewellery, for example, often readily available in London, were not so in the provinces: for their supply, and that of other unusual items, fairs and markets answered a need. Sturbridge Fair in Cambridgeshire, held in September and by tradition a Roman foundation, was the greatest of all British fairs and the prototype of Bunyan's 'Vanity Fair'. In 1720 one Sturbridge warehouse seen by the writer Daniel Defoe (1661–1731) held £20,000-worth of goods. The last Sturbridge Fair was held in the 1930s.

Bartholomew Fair, held in West Smithfield in London on St Bartholomew's Day (August 24) for two weeks (shortened to four days in 1691), was another great event, held regularly until 1854. Other notably important fairs were held at Winchester in Hampshire – the chief cloth fair in the kingdom – Boston in Lincolnshire, and St Ives in Cambridgeshire; many other, smaller fairs were held up and down the country, mainly in May and June. Widecombe Fair in Devon is perhaps the best known, from being celebrated in popular song – but the first recorded date for it is as late as 1850.

Although fairs and markets gradually lost their attraction as the efficiency of distribution and retailing increased, they still linger on locally, for household goods and for the sale of livestock. Some are now no more than amusement fairs, like the famous Nottingham Goose Fair held in the autumn, which today has nothing to do with the sale of anything other than candyfloss, and with having a good time.

Marot, Daniel (c. 1660–1752). A French architect, furniture designer and engraver who was immensely influential in the design of British furniture and interiors. A French HUGUENOT, he left France for the Dutch Court after the Edict of Nantes in 1685, and was appointed architect to William of Orange (1652–1702). On William's accession

to the English throne after the Glorious Revolution of 1688, he followed him to England, in 1694. Although the frontispiece to his collected works describes him as 'Architect of William III', there are no
English buildings which can be unhesitatingly ascribed to Marot; he
has however been linked with Boughton House in Northamptonshire
and Petworth House in Suffolk, both remarkably French in feeling and
both being remodelled during his years in England. He is best known
in England as a designer of gardens, furniture and interiors. He provided designs for the east parterre at Hampton Court, and perhaps for
some of the furnishings and interior decoration. His *Oeuvres*, published
in Amsterdam in 1715, following his return to the Low Countries
about 1698, became a handbook for interior decorators. His speciality was elaborately swagged and curtained BAROQUE state beds of great
height – a feature he must have developed after leaving France, where
state beds remained lower. Most beds of this kind after 1690 show his
influence, which can be seen in the tassels, fringes, bells, ruches and
festoons of the State Bed at Dyrham Park in Gloucestershire (*c.* 1704)
and the Melville bed, made for the Earl of Melville *c.* 1690 and now
in the Victoria & Albert Museum, London; each is a riotous display
of the upholsterer's art. Marot died at The Hague, where he had been
responsible for buildings such as the palace at Het Loo and the Huis
ten Bosh.

Marquetry. Inlaid work in a variety of materials such as wood, ivory,
brass, pewter, silver or tortoiseshell; see also BOULLE, in which a marquetry of metal (usually brass) and tortoiseshell is used in reverse patterns. Marquetry is similar to PARQUETRY, but generally freer in form,
not geometrical.

Marriage, age at. The age at which people married tended to be
lower among those who did not need to work to support a wife than
it was among labourers, or those who had to serve out an apprenticeship.

In the 1550s, upper-class women of an average age of twenty were
marrying husbands of twenty-four; these average ages increased steadily
over the next two hundred and fifty years, to twenty-five for women
and twenty-nine for men by 1800. The marriage pattern for manual
workers throughout Britain has not yet been established, but in
Colyton, Devon the following average ages have been recorded: 1560,
both men and women, twenty-seven; 1660, men twenty-eight, women
thirty; 1760, men twenty-seven, women twenty-five. By 1800 the ages
were little different from those of forty years earlier.

For the children of peers the average age at marriage is well recorded:
1550, men twenty-four, women twenty; 1600, men twenty four,
women nineteen; 1650, men twenty-four, women twenty; 1700, men

twenty-nine, women twenty-one; 1750, men twenty-seven, women twenty one; and 1800 men twenty-six, women twenty-four.

See also GRETNA GREEN, MARRIAGE ACT, MARRIED WOMEN'S PROPERTY ACTS, WEDDINGS and WIFE SALE.

Marriage Act. By the terms of Lord Hardwick's Act (1753), designed to prevent the clandestine marriage of minors, valid marriages could only be solemnized in a church after the publication of banns, or by special licence. Minors had to have the consent of guardians or parents. Exempted from the Act were the royal family, Jews, and Quakers, and it applied neither in the Channel Islands nor in Scotland, hence the popularity of GRETNA GREEN. An amendment in 1836 allowed marriages before a registrar or with religious rites other than Anglican. See also FLEET PRISON; MARRIAGE, AGE AT; MARRIED WOMEN'S PROPERTY ACTS; ROYAL MARRIAGES ACT; WEDDINGS and WIFE SALE.

Marriage settlement. A financial contract entered into on behalf of a husband and wife at marriage. Financial considerations played an important part in the marriages of the wealthy, and a marriage contract would be drawn up between the fathers (or financial representatives of the families) of the bride and groom. The bride's father had to provide a substantial cash sum, known as the 'portion', which was customarily paid by instalments over one or two years; he also provided the bride's trousseau and jewellery, and paid for the marriage feast: when Lord Wentworth's heir married Lord Burghley's daughter in 1581, the wedding guests were entertained for three days, at a cost to Lord Burghley of £624. The father of the groom made provision for an annual allowance to be paid to his daughter-in-law should she become a widow – her DOWRY or jointure; of only slightly less importance was the allowance he undertook to pay his son.

A third item which became common in marriage settlements after c. 1620 was that of 'pin-money', a personal allowance, paid to the bride out of her portion. When the daughter of the Earl of Rutland was proposed in marriage for the grandson of the Earl of Salisbury in 1661, Rutland wrote during the negotiations to Salisbury: 'My lord of Salisbury shall have with my daughter £9,000 and for jointure [I] expect £1,600 per an[num] . . . out of this £1,600, £300 I desire for my daughter's personal allowance made over to trustees for her.' The father of the groom was also expected to determine and reveal the portion of his estate to be settled on his son after his death (particularly important where the groom was a younger son).

The intricate negotiations provided a harvest for lawyers, and by the late seventeenth and early eighteenth centuries the legal documents involved in 'Settlements' were of formidable size: that made in 1759 when Viscount Wentworth married Lady Elizabeth Cavendish-

Bentinck covers about 300 square feet of parchment. Under English COMMON LAW there existed, from Anglo-Saxon times until its abolition in 1833, an automatic right of 'DOWER', by which a widow was entitled to one-third of her late husband's income for her life.

Married Women's Property Acts (1870, 1874 and 1882). Until the Act of 1882 a woman's property passed entirely to her husband on marriage. The first and second Acts allowed a married woman to retain some earnings and investments; that of 1882 allowed her to keep property owned on marriage or later acquired. The three Acts may now be seen as important landmarks in the women's movement, granting, as they did, basic property rights to married woman. Until the 1882 Act the only way of preventing a husband acquiring his wife's fortune was to create a trust, or 'separate estate' holding the wife's property, before the marriage – a method employed by wealthy fathers when headstrong daughters insisted on marrying apparently unsuitable fortune-hunters; an alternative was to withhold wealth on the daughter's marriage and create a trust in a will. See also GRETNA GREEN; MARRIAGE, AGE AT; MARRIAGE ACT; WEDDINGS and WIFE SALE.

Masques. A form of dramatic entertainment originating in Italy which became a favoured diversion at the courts of Henry VIII (1509–47) and Elizabeth I (1558–1609), reaching its peak of popularity under James I (1603–25). The masque was an elastic sort of composition, mixing in varying proportions declamation and dialogue, decoration and scenery, costume-dress and dancing. Allegorical themes were popular. The earliest painting showing a masque is a detail in the memorial portrait of Sir Henry Unton commissioned by his widow in 1595 (National Portrait Gallery). It shows a six-piece orchestra playing before masquers dressed as black and white cherubs, and exotically attired women with red faces; its meaning was apparently as obscure to Lady Unton as it is to us: a small cherub hands her a note of explanation.

Inigo JONES (c. 1573–1652) and Ben Jonson (1572–1637) collaborated (with increasing disharmony) on masques for Anne of Denmark, James I's queen, who was exceedingly fond of this form of drama. The Queen and her ladies played their parts in silence while actors spoke their lines from behind the scenery. The masque usually ended with players and audience joining in general dancing – probably a large element in its popularity. Masques reached the heights of allegorical fancy in the latter days of Charles I (1625–49); like the theatre they were banned during the Commonwealth (1649–60), but unlike the theatre were not revived with the return of Charles II in 1660. See also MUSIC and THEATRICALS.

Mathematical tiles. Also called mechanical tiles: a very practical way of modernizing a timber-framed house, making it appear brick-built. The tiles had one face moulded to resemble the face, or end, of a brick, and were nailed to battens fixed to a timber-framed wall; they were then pointed, like brickwork. They are found more commonly in the south-ern counties. The earliest known may be seen at the Malthouse, West-cott, Surrey; they date from 1724, which is exceptionally early – the brick tax of 1784, which did not apply to tiles, stimulated their popularity, and most date from the early nineteenth century. See also BRICKWORK.

Mattresses. Beds of past centuries were considerably less comfortable than today's. Until the invention of the sprung mattress in the twenti-eth century, most people slept on straw, later horsehair, mattresses, though those of the wealthy might have flock, feather, or down fillings. Like most novelties, horsehair mattresses, introduced in the late seven-teenth century, were thought to be unhealthy. Sarah, Duchess of Marl-borough, agreed: in furnishing the new Blenheim Palace, Oxfordshire, she ordered: 'I shall want a vast number of Feather Beds and quilts. I would have some of the Feather Beds swansdown, all good sweet feath-ers, even for the servants.' See also BEDS.

Mausoleum. A monument erected to receive the remains of a deceased person. Named after the great tomb built in the fourth century BC at Halicarnassus by Queen Artemisia for her husband, Mau-solus. Private tombs became fashionable in Britain in the eighteenth century when GRAND TOURISTS saw burial buildings in the style of Imperial Rome. One of the grandest, and possibly the earliest, is at Castle Howard. Built in 1731 by Nicholas HAWKSMOOR for the 3rd Earl of Carlisle, it dominates the landscape: one cannot overlook this ulti-mate resting-place of the Earls of Carlisle. The most elegant mausoleum is at Brocklesby Park in Lincolnshire, built 1787–94 to designs by James Wyatt (1746–1813) to contain marble monuments to the Pelhams from 1587 onwards. Blickling in Norfolk has a pyramid mausoleum (1793) designed by Joseph Bonomi (1739–1808). At West Wycombe, close by the church on a hill opposite to the Park, is a vast circular mausoleum (1764) for the Dashwoods by John Bastard (1722–78). The most exclu-sive must be the Royal Mausoleum at Frogmore, completed in 1871 for the remains of Prince Albert; Queen Victoria joined him in 1901. Built in the mid-century Italian Romantic style, it is open only in May on the nearest Wednesday (Queen Victoria's day of birth) to 24 May (her date of birth). The largest mausoleum, although strictly speaking it is only a memorial, is at Lancaster, built by Lord Ashton in 1906 for his wife. An early reinforced concrete building with a dome similar to that of St Peter's in Rome, it cost £87,000 to build and was recently restored for the sum of £600,000.

May Day. The first of May; formerly a public holiday celebrated throughout Britain and parts of France and Germany with festivities directly descended from the Roman Floralia festival. A May Queen was crowned, followed by dancing round a maypole, usually of birch wood, which was set up on 30 April, for May Day only – except in London, where permanent maypoles stood in the streets. The church of St Andrew Undershaft in Leadenhall Street, London was so called because of the maypole (the shaft) in nearby Cornhill. It was stored beneath the eaves of nearby houses, and destroyed in 1549 when local residents chopped it up and burnt it. The PURITANS banned maypoles in 1644, but the celebration was encouraged at the RESTORATION. By ancient tradition, choristers sing from the top of the Bell Tower of Magdalen College, Oxford at dawn every May Day. May Day was chosen as an international labour holiday by the International Socialist Congress of 1889, and is now utilized by Labour and Socialist parties for demonstrations of solidarity. See also GREEN MAN.

Mazes. Mazes (sometimes called labyrinths), are an attractive garden feature offering the fascination of walking into the unknown. They became fashionble in British gardens in the seventeenth century as an extension of the enthusiasm for TOPIARY, but were known in the sixteenth century, and earlier: Rosamund's 'bower' at Woodstock in Oxfordshire, made by Henry II (1154–89), was almost certainly an architectural labyrinth. A Parliamentary survey made of Wimbledon House, London, *c.* 1650 shows a maze, but the yew Maze at Hampton Court, London (*c.* 1699) is undoubtedly the best known. Others, all made in the nineteenth century, may be seen at Woburn Park, Bedfordshire; Somerleyton Hall, Suffolk (by William Nesfield); and Wooton Court, Warwickshire.

The concept of the labyrinth goes back many hundreds of centuries and is based on the Cretan legend of the Minotaur kept by King Minos in a labyrinth at Knossos. The idea was later taken over by the Church, as representing the difficult path of a believer, and the Cretan labyrinth pattern is to be found on the floors of many continental churches. From this it was a small step to turf mazes, and of these a number of early examples survive in Britain: at St Catherine's Hill, near Winchester, Hampshire; at Wing, Leicestershire; at Troy Farm, Somerton, Oxfordshire; and at Braemore, Hampshire. These may have had a religious significance, but an alternative theory is that they were for races, or derive from a game on horseback called The City of Troy, enjoyed by the Romans. One such turf maze survives at Trojeborg (Troy Town) in Scandinavia. See also GARDENS.

Mead. One of the oldest alcoholic liquors – certainly known in Britain in the Bronze Age; made by dissolving honey in water and boiling with spices; when it cools yeast is added, causing a fermentation. A Celtic chief's bodyguard drank his mead and, in return, fought in his battles,

known as 'paying for mead'. In later times it was drunk at church festivals in the richer monastic houses, being more readily available than
imported wines. Mead-drinking declined when wine from Gascony
became cheap and plentiful in the reign of Henry II (1133–89).

Meals, times of eating. In medieval times breakfast was eaten at 6 or
7 a.m.; dinner, the main meal of the day, at 10 a.m.; and supper around
5 p.m. The tendency was for the main meal to be eaten progressively
later: in 1740 at Bulstrode Park (the now-demolished home of the
Dukes of Portland) in Buckinghamshire, dinner was at 2 p.m. People
in the country generally kept earlier hours: by 1776 the fashionable
hour in London for dinner was 4.30 to 5 p.m. Coming up to London
from Surrey in 1776 for a rare visit, Mrs Boscowen (1719–1805), the
widow of Admiral Boscowen, having dined in Surrey at 2 p.m., was
amazed to find that she could get another dinner at 5.

One reason for later London hours was that by the late eighteenth
century, as speeches became longer, Parliament was sitting later; the
Prince of Wales liked late hours, and encouraged the fashion.

In the nineteenth century, the yawning gap between breakfast and
dinner was filled by the new fashion for a midday luncheon or 'nun-
cheon' and afternoon tea. Lord William Russell wrote to Lady Holland
in 1841: 'We are 30 at table, great profusion, and admirable cuisine,
besides repasts at every hour of the day. From 10 to 12 breakfast, from
2 to 3 luncheon, from 5 to 6 tea, at 7 dinner, and after balls and theatres hot suppers, otherwise cold.' By the First World War breakfast was
eaten earlier and luncheon was served at 1 p.m., tea at 4 p.m. and dinner
at 8, a timetable which is loosely maintained today. See also DINING
ROOMS, SERVANTS' HALL and SERVICE OF MEALS.

Mechanical tiles. See MATHEMATICAL TILES.

Mechanics' Institutes. Organizations which in the nineteenth
century provided further education for the growing class of skilled
workers. Founded in 1823 by Dr George Birkbeck (1776–1841), in
whose honour the London Institute was renamed Birkbeck College; it
became a constituent college of London University in 1920. The idea
quickly found popularity and by mid century every city and town and
many rural areas had their own institutes.

Medicine. For centuries medical science was based on principles
developed in the school associated with the name of the Greek physician, Hippocrates (*c.* 460 BC). The general theory was based on a belief
that good health consisted of a perfect balance between four 'humours'
in the body – blood, phlegm, yellow bile (choler) and black bile
(melancholy); ill-health resulted from an excess or lack of one or other
of these humours. A cure might be achieved by blood-letting, thus
reducing the proportion of the ill-humour. The collection by Galen,

who lived in Rome in the second century AD, of all ancient medical knowledge made up the corpus of medieval medical principles. Only the toughest of patients survived the treatments prescribed, yet any physician who veered from this ancient path was branded as a charlatan. For example, Jonathan Arderne (1349–70) had great success in operating on horrific fistulas, and published a book on the subject: he lost very few patients, because he sterilized his instruments, yet his example was not followed because it flew in the face of contemporary medical principles.

The circulation of blood was discovered in 1628 by William Hervey, but it was some time before the importance of this was recognized. Progress was gradual: the truths of evolution, demonstrated by Charles Darwin (1809–82) inspired research into new fields of study; discoveries by Louis Pasteur (1822–95) and others led the way to the understanding of toxins in blood produced by bacteria. Surprisingly, rubber gloves were first used by the surgeon Lord Moynihan (1865–1936) as recently as the late nineteenth century. For centuries the sick were often better off *without* medical attention. Goldsmith's elegy on Mrs Blaize sums up popular opinion: 'The doctor found, when she was dead – Her last disorder mortal.' See also HOSPITALS and SALERNO, SCHOOL OF.

Mendicant friars. A movement of poverty inspired by St Francis of Assisi (1181–1226) that began in the thirteenth century. The friars belonged to one of four orders: Augustinian Hermits (Austin Friars), CARMELITES, DOMINICANS and FRANCISCANS. St Francis's ideal was a return to the basic principles and simplicity of primitive Christianity; his followers were to live by the labour of their hands, relying on begging only when they could not earn their livelihood. As their establishments were not endowed with lands, the movement was eventually found to be unworkable as originally conceived. Established mainly in the slums of towns and cities, friars were forced to beg for alms. In time they came to acquire property – a contradiction of the original inspiration, although the personal poverty of the friars remained a principle. See also AUGUSTINIANS, BENEDICTINES, CARTHUSIANS, CISTERCIANS, CLUNIACS, GILBERTINES and PREMONSTRATENSIANS.

Mercantilism. An eighteenth-century economic theory which measured the wealth of a nation by the amount of gold and silver it held, resulting in artificial restraints to prevent money going out of the country. Toward the end of the eighteenth century, when the policy was dominant, heavy duties were put on imports, and taxation was used to prevent exports. The earlier Navigation Acts of 1651–96 had excluded the Dutch from British trade, and colonial trade was rigidly controlled for the benefit of British interests. The colonies were looked upon as an exclusive market for British manufactured goods, in exchange for raw materials. The EAST INDIA COMPANY benefited enormously from these advantages; later, North America became an important new market for the products of the Industrial Revolution. Mercantilism only worked in practice when colonies provided an expanding market. See also Adam SMITH.

Merchant Adventurers Company. A trading company, developed from ancient trading GUILDS, founded in the Netherlands in 1296 by the Duke of Brabant and active in England from the reign of Edward III (1327–77), for the export of raw wool to the Netherlands; the term 'adventurer' denoted any merchant engaged in foreign trade. The Merchant Adventurers as an organization retained many similarities to a guild, being subject to the same disciplines and form of internal government. It was a legal personality, and held the monopoly of the export of wool. From the fifteenth century the export of unfinished woollen cloth became more profitable, and from 1407 London-based merchants had ousted their northern counterparts; from 1446 the headquarters of the activities of the Merchant Adventurers was in Antwerp. From the sixteenth century their story was one of slow decline, until the company was dissolved in 1808 when Hamburg (their headquarters since 1611; hence an alternative name, 'Hamburg Company') was taken by Napoleon.

Merrybegot. An illegitimate child. See also BLANKET, WRONG SIDE OF THE; BYBLOW and CHANCELING.

Methodism. An evangelical movement originally within the Church of England, founded at Oxford in 1729 by John and Charles Wesley. Methodists emphasized the love of God, and individual salvation. Growing antagonism denied the Methodists church pulpits, while their open-air evangelical meetings and their concentration on those neglected by the Church of England increased both their popularity and the hostility to them within the Anglican Church. Methodism finally broke away from the Church of England in 1795, from which time the sacraments were administered by Methodist preachers in their own chapels.

Methodism took a rather different course in Wales, based on CALVINISM, with PRESBYTERIAN organization. For decades the Welsh Church had been in decline, and when English Methodists extended their revival there, c. 1735, they found fertile ground. Welsh Methodists maintained their place within the established church until 1811, when they seceded; they quickly became a dominant religious force in Wales, particularly in rural areas. See also ANGLO-CATHOLICISM and EVANGELICALISM.

Methredate or **metredate.** A compound in the form of a powder, comprising many ingredients; regarded in the sixteenth and seventeenth centuries as a universal antidote or preservative against poison and infectious diseases.

Mews. A mew was originally a cage or place for keeping hawks, particularly while they were 'mewing' or moulting; the royal stables, built on the site at Charing Cross in London where the royal hawks had formerly been mewed, were still known as 'The Mews', and thus began the word's association with stabling. The first private mews to be built were those behind the houses in Grosvenor Square, in the 1720s. Parallel rows of houses were served by common back-streets, called mews, lined all along with stables having accommodation above them for stable-hands. Each mews was at the bottom of the gardens of the houses it served.

Michaelmas. The Feast of St Michael, 29 September; a quarter-day for payment of rents, a law term, and an academic term at Oxford and Cambridge universities.

Middle Temple. See INNS OF COURT.

Midsummer Day. Falls on June 24th; a quarter-day for payment of rents.

Militia. A body of armed men enrolled for local defence and for keeping law and order in emergencies, originating with the Anglo-Saxon *fyrd* or general levy of every free adult male for the defence of his shire. The Assize of Arms of 1181 and the Statute of Winchester of 1285 specified what arms each man should carry, according to his status, when called upon by the SHERIFFS and later the LORDS-LIEUTENANT to deal with civil disturbances. First referred to as 'militia' in 1642, when conscripts were recruited by means of the PRESS GANGS. One of the discords between Charles I (1625–49) and Parliament concerned the control of local militias, or TRAIN BANDS: Parliament won, under the terms of the Militia Ordinance of 1642. The Militia Act of 1661 restored control to the sovereign, and subsequent Acts in 1662 and 1663 reorganized these local forces. The demand for greater skill and training led to the Militia Act of 1757 which introduced proper training and made a three-year county service by ballot compulsory. An Act of 1852 reversed the compulsory element, reorganizing militia service on a volunteer basis. The Militia ceased to exist when the Territorial Army was established in 1907.

Mirror silvering. Until the mid nineteenth century mirrors were silvered with tin foil on to which mercury was applied with a hare's foot. Glass was laid on the mercury side of the tin foil and pressed down until the backing adhered. Silvered mirrors were known as Venetian mirrors until the mid seventeenth century, when the Murano monopoly was broken.

Misericord or **miserere.** A ledge under the hinged seat of a choir stall which, when the seat was turned up, served as a support for the standing priest or monk during interminable services. The underside of the ledge is often richly carved with amusing scenes of contemporary life. Most date from the fifteenth century.

Miss. An abbreviation of 'Mistress'. A form of address applied to unmarried women in polite society from the early eighteenth century, while elderly unmarried women were addressed as MRS out of courtesy. Earlier, all women, whether married or not, were addressed as MRS, which is also an abbreviation of 'Mistress'. Although modes of address changed in fashionable society, below stairs the HOUSEKEEPER continued to be addressed as Mrs in the old-fashioned way, whether married or not. See also MR.

Mockadoe. Perhaps from the Italian *mocaiardo*, mohair. A wool cloth with a velvety pile, used for clothing in the sixteenth and seventeenth centuries. The term may be the origin of the 'moquette' used for upholstry and carpeting.

Monk. A male member of a religious community living apart from the world under vows of poverty, chastity and obedience. The term has no clear technical meaning, but contains the notion of a secluded community and should be distinguished in use from the members of later religious orders such as CANONS REGULAR and MENDICANT FRIARS. In the course of time monks became divided into two classes: (1) the quire monk, who devoted his time to religious duties, leaving the manual work of the monastery to (2) the lay brothers. In medieval times quire monks were often of noble or gentry blood or of yeoman stock, because of the requirements of literacy, and many superiors were of distinguished family. Nuns were also often from the upper ranks of society; some nunneries only received noblewomen, such as the priory of Dominican nuns founded at Dartford in Kent in 1346, to which 'the best and noblest families of the county send their relatives both for education and for nuns'.

Monteith. A deep oval bowl of silver or porcelain with a scalloped rim. Filled with ice or iced water, it was used to cool wine glasses suspended in the scallops by the foot. Called after a Scotsman named Monteith who wore a cloak with a scalloped bottom, according to an entry (1683) in the diary of Anthony à Wood (1632–95) of Oxford. See also WINE–GLASS COOLERS.

Morris dancing. See DANCES.

Motor cars. In the beginning the motor car was, understandably, regarded as a horseless carriage; the engine, logically, was put in front where the horses should have been; design and bodywork were in the hands of coach-makers and carriage-builders; the old leaf-spring was used for suspension; and the driver was perched up high where the coachman would have been; early motor-cars did indeed resemble carriages – but no car has ever been as elegant as an open four-wheeled carriage.

By 1756 driving on the left over London Bridge had become customary, but the first regulation about driving on the left in Britain came into force during the French Revolution: London had become crowded, and London Bridge was often jammed with horse-drawn traffic. An Act of Parliament of 1835 enforced the 'Keep Left' rule throughout Britain and the colonies. Like the design of the motor-car, the reasons for the 'Keep Left' rule also derive from carriage-driving practice. Most coach drivers, being right-handed, sat on the right-hand side of the seat and tended to drive on the left of the road, which gave the coachman a better view of the road ahead; it followed that the driving wheel of a car would be positioned on the right, where the coachman had sat. On the Continent, however, coaches were customarily driven (on better roads) by a postilion riding on the left horse of a pair, controlling the unsaddled horse with his whip; in consequence, continental traffic tended to hold to the right-hand side of the road, to give the postilion a clear view. And, inevitably, on the continent the driving wheel of a car was placed on the left.

Development of the motor car was slow in Britain, as a result of various restrictive laws which hampered the operation of the early steam carriages. Toll road and bridge charges were prohibitive, and between 1878 and 1896 a 'man with a red flag' (or, at night, a red lantern) was required to precede any motor-driven vehicle; the maximum permitted speed was 4 mph. For most of the nineteenth century it was left to the Germans, the French and the Americans to perfect what, in Britain, was looked on as no more than a rich man's foible.

CARRIAGES seldom carried spare wheels, so inevitably early cars carried none; journeys were likely to be fraught with mischance when the possibility of mechanical failure was added to punctures (the pneumatic tyre was patented in 1845). However, motorists soon came to demand more efficiency than they had expected in a horse-drawn vehicle: windscreen wipers, spare wheel, a horn, acetylene lamps, safer brakes (coaches had none until the nineteenth century), speedometers and rear-view mirrors were early developments. Self-starters became standard in the 1920s, but heaters only in the 1960s.

There was no headlong rush into buying cars, and horse-drawn carriages were still common in the 1920s. The Harpur-Crewe family banned all cars from their park at Calke Abbey in Derbyshire until the 1920s. But some took to the novelty with enthusiasm, like the Duchess of Sutherland, who regularly drove herself in London in a huge Mercedes with her chauffeur sitting behind in case of breakdowns, and to swing the starting handle. In 1903 the 20th Earl of Shrewsbury, whose family name was Chetwynd-Talbot, founded the Clement Talbot motor company, later the Talbot Car Company. The Earl was also an early victim of a speed trap – when the limit (imposed in 1903) was 20 mph. In 1908 the *Daily Telegraph* reported that he had been fined 3 guineas for excessive driving near Garlock in Scotland: his speed was exactly 31 mph! Edward VII (1901–10) was an enthusiastic motorist and, as a style-setter, undoubtedly helped to make motoring acceptable in Britain.

Inevitably the coach house became the motor house, the coachman (grudgingly) became the chauffeur, and the horses were sold. In 1919 George Bernard Shaw summed up the most widely-held reaction to motors: 'Go anywhere in England where there are natural, wholesome, contented and really nice English people; and what do you find? That the stables are the real centre of the household.'

Mound or **mount.** A late medieval garden might have a mount or mound, a small man-made hill, the top of which was reached by a spiral path, often culminating in a GAZEBO. Its purpose was to permit a view outside the enclosed garden. Some mounds still survive: at Dunham Massey, Cheshire; in the botanical gardens of Oxford and Cambridge; at Little Moreton Hall, Cheshire; and (a recreated one) at The Dutch House, Kew Gardens, London. See also GARDENS.

Mr. An abbreviation of 'Master'; a form of address for a man of some status in polite society. See also MISS and MRS.

Mrs. An abbreviation of 'Mistress'; the usual form of address in polite society for all women, whether married or not, until the early eighteenth century; young unmarried women then gradually came to be addressed as MISS, while mature unmarried as well as married women continued to be addressed as Mrs. See also MR.

Mudie's Circulating Library. A subscription library founded by Charles Edward Mudie (1818–90), a publisher and bookseller who began to lend books from his Bloomsbury shop in 1842, then opened premises in Oxford Street, London in 1852. The moral scruples displayed by Mudie in selecting his stock brought accusations of censorship. See also LENDING LIBRARIES.

Mule chest. A low storage chest with one or two drawers below, to be found from *c.* 1650 through the eighteenth century. See also CHEST OF DRAWERS.

Mullion. A vertical upright or post dividing a window into two or more 'lights'. See also TRANSOM.

Mundella's Act, 1880. Made secondary education compulsory in England; so-called after A.J. Mundella (1825–97), the MP who sponsored the Bill which led to it.

Music. Has played a part in household life through the centuries. The medieval dinner was announced by a fanfare of trumpets from the gallery over the SCREENS PASSAGE, where minstrels played during the meal. In the romance *Sir Gawain and the Green Knight* (*c.* 1370), King Arthur, Guinevere, and their family are dining on the dais, 'And many a trusty man below at the long tables./ Then forth came the first course with cracking of trumpets/ On which many bright banners bravely were hanging;/ Noise of drums then anew, and noble pipes/ Warbling wild and keen, waken their music/ So that men's hearts rose high on hearing.' From the sixteenth century, it was expected that women in the upper ranks of society should be able to play the HARPSICHORD or VIRGINALS, and the staffs of larger households often included talented musicians.

In village inns and farmhouses there was usually someone who could play a woodwind instrument or the fiddle. A painted frieze of *c.* 1585 in the GREAT CHAMBER of Gilling Castle, North Yorkshire shows three men and three women seated at a long table playing stringed instruments with sheet music by their sides. The court MASQUES of the early seventeenth century featured music, and often ended with dancing. At this time, too, the GREAT HALLS, no longer used as originally intended, were the venue for musical occasions at all times of the year. During the Commonwealth (1649–60) non-religious music was discouraged as frivolous, and of course immediately enjoyed renewed popularity at the RESTORATION of Charles II in 1660. At Longford Castle, Wiltshire, a music gallery had been added to the Great Hall by 1678.

The Duke of Chandos had a sixteen-piece orchestra on his payroll at Cannons in 1722. Music rooms became a household feature after 1750; although they were not necessarily used exclusively for music, decorative elements such as plasterwork often reflected the musical theme. Private concerts were becoming fashionable. Robert ADAM designed an organ case for the music room at Kedleston Hall in Derbyshire, and Newby Hall in North Yorkshire has an Adam organ (*c.* 1771) in the entrance hall; the music room at Killerton House in Devonshire has a chamber organ of *c.* 1807. At Fenton House in London is an important collection of musical instruments, the earliest being a five-sided Italian spinet of 1540. See also HARPSICHORDS and PIANOFORTES.

Musical-box. A nineteenth-century invention, consisting of a tuned musical comb plucked by teeth set in a drum revolving by clockwork; usually housed in an oblong wooden case, often elaborately inlaid and an object of beauty in its own right. The earliest date from *c.* 1810; they immediately became popular. Subsequent improvements were the addition of woodwind, bells and drum by 1850, and the interchangeable cylinder of about the same date. By 1870 musical-boxes were so advanced as to produce acceptable chords, and by 1875 long-playing, three-hour cylinders had been developed: the only means of playing music without instruments before the invention of the gramophone; quite often people danced to them, as they did later to the gramophone.

Music rooms. See MUSIC.

Mystery Plays. In an age when few of the laity could read, varied forms of spoken drama played an important part in religious instruction. Church ritual itself was full of drama, and by means of sermons congregations became familiar with the stories of the saints; it was then but a short step to religious plays built upon the Miracles of Christ, the lives of the saints, and allegorical morality plays. Only four great cycles of 'mystery plays' survive; those of York, Chester, Wakefield and N-Town (because it is not known where it came from) can be dated to probably between the thirteenth and fifteenth centuries; they are full of references understandable to the audiences of their day which over the centuries have become increasingly obscure and now leave us somewhat mystified about aspects of the dialogue and plot.

Nabobs. The eighteenth- and nineteenth-century nickname given to those who had made fortunes in India and retired to England. The name comes from *Nawab*, a Mogul governor; a female Nabob was a Nabobess. A classic example of the home and estate of a successful nabob is Sezincote in Gloucestershire. It was built *c.* 1805 in an Indian style with domes and oriental detail for Sir Charles Cockerell, Bt by his architect brother Samuel Pepys Cockerell (1754–1827), assisted by the Indian topographical artist Thomas Daniell (1749–1840); Humphry REPTON was also consulted about the house and park. A connection may be traced between Sezincote, which the Prince Regent visited *c.* 1807, and the Brighton Pavilion (1815). Sir Charles, an employee of the EAST INDIA COMPANY, had made a colossal fortune in India.

Nanny. A familiar name current from the nineteenth century for a children's nurse; a figure remembered with nostalgia by many. From the late sixteenth century, small children of both sexes were looked after by a nurse in the NURSERY, where they spent most of their time. Hardwick Hall in Derbyshire had a nursery on the ground floor in 1601, a rather gloomy oak-panelled room then furnished with two BEDS, two tables, one chair and a CLOSE STOOL. In the sixteenth and early seventeenth centuries it became the custom among the wealthy to put their children, from the age of twelve, into other wealthy households to learn manners and social graces. Nannies were only concerned with boys until they were sent away to school, and until the arrival of a GOVERNESS to educate the girls. See also NURSERY.

National Trust, The. Founded in 1895 as 'The National Trust for Places of Historic Interest or Natural Beauty' by Octavia Hill, Sir

Robert Hunter and the Revd Hardwicke Rawnsley, Canon of Carlisle and honorary Secretary of the Trust. Concerned at first to preserve places of natural beauty, the conservation of large houses was far from their minds. They had little in the way of funds – after the first ten years, the total annual income amounted to just £837. The National Trust Act of 1907 made the Trust a statutory body, and also conferred upon it the unique power to declare its land and buildings inalienable. The National Trust Act of 1937 (when the Trust owned two houses) enabled it to set up the Country House Scheme, by which an owner could transfer a house and its contents to the Trust in the knowledge that it would be safe for all time. The first house acquired under the scheme was Blickling Hall, Norfolk in 1940, through the generosity of Lord Lothian, who was partly responsible for the Act. Today the Trust owns more than 300 major houses and gardens, and with half-a-million acres is the largest landowner in Britain after the Crown.

Navvy. A labourer, originally one employed in excavating a 'navigation' or CANAL, when he was known as a 'navigator'. In later use, a labourer employed on road works, railways and similar kinds of earthwork.

Navy, Royal. See ROYAL NAVY.

Navy List. Official list of all Royal Navy Command officers in service and of those on the Reserve.

Neo-classicism. An international style encompassing all the arts which emerged in the eighteenth century as a reaction to the excesses of late BAROQUE and ROCOCO and aimed at recapturing the simplicity and nobility of Greek and Roman art. Originating in PALLADIANISM it was given new motivation by archaeological discoveries being made in Greece and Italy. In the place of a composite style, architecture adopted a more primitive purity. Neo-classical buildings tend to be solid, linear and generally severe, although Robert ADAM, one of neo-classicism's greatest exponents, gave it a lighter and more elegant touch. By the end of the eighteenth century it was being overshadowed by the emergence of the GREEK REVIVAL, having become very popular throughout Britain.

Nesfield, William Eden (1835–88). Trained briefly in G.E. Street's office with Norman SHAW and then with his uncle by marriage, SALVIN. A brief period in Paris introduced him to the French GOTHIC REVIVAL, and he then shared an architectural practice (1863–76) with Shaw. His small Wren Revival lodge (1866) in Kew Gardens was the first example of the 'Queen Anne' style. Kinmell Park, Clwyd (1868–71), in a 'Revived Classical' style, is another pioneering 'Queen Anne' design. Nesfield also designed gardens, mainly for the houses built by Salvin.

Newman, John Henry, Cardinal (1801–90). An English theologian who converted from the Anglican Church to Roman Catholicism in

1845. He was a charismatic personality and his sermons and publications had a powerful effect; he was also a leading figure in the OXFORD MOVEMENT. In 1864 he published his autobiography, *Apologia pro vita sua.* He was created a cardinal in 1879.

Newspapers. The first English-language newspapers – small, single-sheet (two page) affairs, but not pamphlets, containing more or less current news rather than gossip and rumour, and published on a more or less regular basis – were translations from Dutch or German news-sheets or corantos, and entitled *Corante, or, Weekely Newes from Italy, Germany, Hungarie, Spaine and France,* six of which were published in the autumn of 1621 in London, at irregular weekly intervals. From 1662 similar publications proliferated until 1632, when they were suppressed until 1638.

With the abolition of the STAR CHAMBER in 1641 and the consequent freeing of the press, weekly papers appeared detailing domestic news – which in that decade of the CIVIL WAR meant the struggle between King and Parliament. Many included the word 'diurnal' in their titles, and at first most supported the Parliamentarian side. The first Royalist diurnal appeared at Oxford in January 1643 – *Mercurius Aulicus, a Diurnal communicating the intelligence and affaires of the Court to the rest of the Kingdome* – and continued until September 1645, when it was succeeded by *Mercurius Academicus*; similar publications on the Parliamentarian side were *Mercurius Civicus*, the first regularly illustrated London paper, and the PURITAN *Mercurius Britannicus*. The licensed press was completely suppressed from October 1649 (Charles I was beheaded 30 November 1649) to June 1650, but official journals – obviously containing only the news the Commonwealth leaders wished people to know – were issued. There was some revival of news dissemination between 1650 and 1655, but thereafter Cromwell kept a tight rein on the newssheets, permitting only the official *Mercurius Politicus* and *Publick Intelligencer*, which were published between October 1655 and April 1660.

Press censorship continued during the RESTORATION. The twice-weekly *Oxford Gazette* first appeared in November 1665 and in February 1666 became the *London Gazette*: it has appeared ever since, on Tuesdays and Fridays, as the Government's official newspaper. After the Revolution of 1688 control of the press and censorship were relaxed, and many new papers came into being, some lasting only weeks, sometimes days. The oldest of the provincial papers, the *Lincoln, Rutland and Stamford Mercury*, was founded in 1695. Censorship was finally abandoned in 1693.

The first daily newspaper was the *Daily Courant*, established in 1702. But the Newspaper Tax of 1712 (the first in a succession of duties on newspapers which were finally abolished in 1855), initially one penny for a full sheet, spelled the end of the penny newspapers; even Addison's *Spectator*, first published in 1711, collapsed, although it had a brief renaissance (80 issues) in 1714. *The Times* began life on 1 January 1785 as the *Daily Universal Register*, but changed its name to *The Times* on 1 January 1788. The *Morning Post*, first founded as an advertising sheet in 1772, developed into a national newspaper after 1795, and was absorbed by the *Daily Telegraph* (founded 1855) in 1937.

George Orwell (1903–50) commented: 'Early in life I had noticed that no event is ever correctly reported in a newspaper.' In grand houses, newspapers were often ironed below stairs before being placed on the breakfast table or tray.

Nobility. The English nobility of medieval times was essentially feudal and military, based on land holdings, its origins in the personal relationship between lord and vassal. Modern nobility only resembles the feudal version in that it may possess landed estates; it now consists of a body of peers, some of whom sit in the House of Lords; many peerages are of fairly recent creation, and there are also Life Peers, first created in 1958.

In theory nobility followed principles of selective breeding, the idea being that certain stocks should be given the opportunity and encouragement to develop and reproduce those qualities which are: (a) most desirable in the higher administrative spheres; (b) difficult to acquire without leisure and economic independence; (c) readily lost in a few generations of unfavourable environment. In Britain, emphasis is laid on lineal descent, allied to wealth. Henry V (1413–22) laid down that arms are 'tokens of nobility' – although not everyone entitled to bear arms is a member of the nobility: BARONETS and KNIGHTS are not. See also ARISTOCRACY and the PEERAGE.

Nonconformists. In modern usage, a member of a Protestant religious body separated from the Church of England (QUAKERS, PRESBYTERIANS, BAPTISTS, etc.); historically, Nonconformists adhered to the doctrine of the Church of England, but refused to conform to its discipline, organization and practice; sometimes called Dissenters. In the sixteenth and seventeenth centuries Nonconformists, like ROMAN CATHOLICS, suffered penalties under the law for their nonconformity; the Conventicle Act of 1593 and the Act of UNIFORMITY of 1662, which outlawed their meetings, are two such acts. The Toleration Act of 1689 allowed them freedom of worship, repealing most of the penalties previously imposed on them, although they were excluded from public office until 1828. See also METHODISTS and PURITANS.

'Nonsuch' chests. Sixteenth-century chests elaborately decorated in marquetry depicting fantastic architecture. Unconnected with Henry VIII's (1509–47) palace of Nonsuch in Surrey begun in 1538, unfinished at his death and demolished in 1687. Engraved prints of the palace published in 1582 and 1598 show buildings similar to those depicted on these chests.

Norman architecture. The architecture of England, mainly seen in castles, churches, cathedrals and abbeys, from the time of the Norman Conquest or just before until the introduction of GOTHIC at the end of the twelfth century. Known in Europe as Romanesque, it is distinguished by an overall feeling of strength and mass, by the use of the Roman round arch, and by cylindrical piers and flat buttresses. It introduced a new system of ribbed vaulting, of which Peterborough Cathedral shows a good example. Norman architecture was first used in England shortly before 1066, in Edward the Confessor's (1042–66) rebuilding of Westminster Abbey.

The mainly Norman bishops and abbots who followed in the wake of the Conquest began the greatest rebuilding programme of cathedrals and abbeys of all time in England; most of the medieval cathedrals were Norman in origin, as were many of the abbeys which never achieved cathedral status, such as Malmesbury, Tewkesbury and Romsey. Variations evolved between the Romanesque style of Normandy and the Norman of Britain: the gallery inserted under the arcade arch at Jedburgh originated in Burgundy, as do the huge round pillars of Gloucester and Tewkesbury, while the single west tower of Ely and the vast niches on the west fronts of Lincoln and Tewkesbury originated in northern Germany. Norman decoration is usually geometric, its hallmarks dog-tooth, zig-zag and crenellation.

Durham (1093) has the first rib-vaulting in Europe, and forecast the evolution of the pointed arch and the Gothic style.

Nursery. A room for children, usually on the top floor of a house; however, in the sixteenth century nurseries were sometimes found on the ground floor, as at Hardwick Hall in Derbyshire (1590–7). By the mid seventeenth century the attic floor was the place for the nursery, and Hardwick also mirrors this change: the state WITHDRAWING ROOM had its ceiling lowered for the insertion of a mezzanine nursery floor. The pattern for the next 300 years was now established; children were looked after by a NANNY, helped perhaps by nursery maids, taught by a TUTOR or GOVERNESS, and only brought down to see their parents once a day (when their parents were at home).

The windows of nurseries often have iron bars, to prevent children from falling out. At the end of the eighteenth and through the nineteenth century, day and night nurseries were provided for children in wealthy families. The day nursery was in effect a living room, used also for the meals brought up from the kitchen by a nursery-maid who served the children and the nurse. The night nursery was essentially for sleeping; the nanny or governess also slept there, to keep an eye on her charges.

Lady Maud Baillie, a daughter of the 9th Duke of Devonshire, describes her childhood memories of Hardwick in 1908: 'There was no gas or electricity, and the darkness of the rooms, lit only by a very small lamp, was terrifying. All seven children lived up there [the nursery on the top floor] with a nanny, under-nurse and nursery maid, also any visiting maids who might be staying at Hardwick with their ladies. The older children had tea [for breakfast] on the refectory table in the Great Hall, supervised by two governesses (we had already had 40 minutes' lessons by then). The school party were promoted to the dining room for luncheon. If there were many visitors, we were relegated to our own table in the bay window . . . The nursery party had all their meals upstairs in the Day Nursery, i.e., three nurses, the latest baby and any other child under five; after that age one was promoted to the dining room. The transportation of nursery meals was a major operation. The tray containing the food for meat meals was carried by the ODD MAN. All the other meals were carried by the nursery maid, who was probably only 14 or 15 . . . as there were 97 steps in all it can be appreciated that her life was a hard one . . . as I remember them they were generally smiling and frequently singing.'

The nurseries at Nunnington Hall, North Yorkshire and Landhydrock House, Cornwall have been preserved. At Dalemain in Cumbria the nursery has been restored, and there are museums of childhood at Arreton Manor on the Isle of Wight and Sudbury Hall in Derbyshire; there are toy museums at Belton House, Lincolnshire, Penshurst Place, Kent and Sudeley Castle, Gloucestershire.

Odd man. The odd-job man was available for various heavy tasks the other servants were unable (or unwilling) to perform, such as getting in logs, lighting the hall fire and taking meals to the nursery at the top of the house; see the quotation regarding life at Hardwick Hall, Derbyshire in 1908, under NURSERY.

Old Style calendar. See CALENDAR.

Open or **common fields.** The most usual arrangement for farming in early medieval England was the open field system. This was doubtless of ancient origin, from the days when the first agriculturalists co-operated in clearing woodland and heath to provide arable land, each taking a share in the newly-cleared land. Initially each settlement might have shared two, three or four fields, perhaps added to over time as more land was brought into cultivation; then eventually a farmer would have smallholdings, called *furlongs*, *selions* or *shots*, distributed over several fields. The shape of the furlongs conformed to the needs of a plough drawn by teams of four to eight oxen; as this was a cumbersome thing to manoeuvre the furlong was therefore long and narrow, reducing the number of turns of oxen to the minimum. Each farmer cultivated his own strips; the plough seems to have been held in common, but the oxen were individually owned. Eric Kerridge defines a common field as 'one in which various parts or parcels of land (or the use of them) belong to individual proprietors, who exercise sole proprietary rights when the land is in crop but leave them in abeyance when not. When the land is not in crop it is under the general management of all proprietors in common or by common agreement.' See also ENCLOSURE and RIDGE-AND-FURROW.

Orangeries. From the sixteenth century, attempts have been made to grow citrus fruit in England. William Cecil, Lord Burghley, ordered a lemon tree from Paris in 1562 – he already had an orange tree. At first, temporary structures were erected over the trees to protect them in winter (described by John Evelyn as 'a tabernacle of boards warmed by means of stoves'), and these structures were known as orangeries. The trees usually died. In the seventeenth century, more permanent orangeries were built. In 1611/12 Salomon de Caus laid out a garden at Somerset House in The Strand, London, for James I's queen, Anne of Denmark, which included 'a house for orange trees', and in the 1640s André Mollet's layout for Charles I's queen Henrietta Maria at Wimbledon included a large 'Orange House' with south-facing windows where 60 trees in tubs could be stored during the winter. One survives at Chatsworth dating from the 1690s, but not in its original position; it has also, at some stage, been fitted with a glass roof. It was some time before the importance of light was generally realized but once it had been grasped and the means for providing it were to hand, the building of 'orangeries' proliferated, and they can be seen all over the country, attached to or in the grounds of large country homes – today, often used as gift shops. The fashion for having orange trees in tubs passed by the middle of the eighteenth century, and the buildings called orangeries were then effectively used as winter gardens, CONSERVATORIES in the original sense of the word, or greenhouses.

Ordeal, trial by. A method of determining innocence or guilt in criminal cases by appeal to God. There were three methods of ordeal, supervised by the church: (1) for the VILLEIN or serf, ordeal by water; the accused was bound and thrown into cold water; if he sank he was innocent and if he floated he was guilty (this remained a test of witchcraft for some centuries); (2) for a freeman, ordeal by fire: he had to carry heated iron a distance of nine feet into a church during mass, and show no scars after three days under bandages; (3) for the clergy, eating the cursed morsel (a feather or other foreign body was placed in blessed bread) without choking: it was believed that a perjurer could not swallow such food. Queen Emma, mother of Edward the Confessor, survived ordeal by fire; a variation on this was to walk between two closely-placed fires and show no sign of harm after a recovery time.

Trial by ordeal was abolished in 1212 by Pope Innocent III (1198–1216) and the clergy forbidden to be associated with such trials; Justices in EYRE were advised on replacement procedures in 1219. This marked the beginning of the evolution of CRIMINAL LAW and the JURY system.

Orders, the five architectural. The Greeks evolved a series of logical mathematical proportions for the posts or columns they used in building, and three forms of decoration – as well as the technical names for them – for the various parts of the column and entablature (the beam supported by the column). The three types of column, or 'order', are the Doric, the Ionic and the Corinthian. The Romans, when they superseded the Greeks, adopted their architecture, with modifications, and when Vitruvius (first century AD) wrote his treatise on architecture, *De Architectura*, he included the early Roman Tuscan (or Etruscan) order as well as the later Composite. The parts of the column are the base (except for Greek Doric), the shaft, the capital (the decorated head) and the entablature.

The five orders are usually ranked according to their height. The stubbiest, Tuscan, has a column height of seven times the diameter at the lower part of the shaft, and little decoration; Greek Doric, the oldest order, has twenty-five flutings on the shaft and no base; the Roman version includes a base, a simpler capital and a taller column, seven-and-a-half to eight diameters instead of the Greek six. The most distinguishing feature of the Ionic, originating in Asia Minor in the sixth century BC, is the capital decorated with four projecting volutes (or scrolls); the column is sometimes decorated with twenty-four flutings and the height is nine times the base diameter. The Corinthian order has a very ornate capital of sprouting acanthus leaves and a height of ten diameters. The final order, evolved by the Romans, is the Composite, a mixture of Ionic and Corinthian and, like the Corinthian, ten diameters in height. When more than one order is used in a building, the 'grammar' or rules of architecture dictate that the orders must be used in their correct sequence. At the entrance of the Old Bodleian Library, Oxford, all five orders can be seen, one above the other in correct sequence – but four of the bases are incorrect.

Ormolu. From the French *dorure d'or moulu*, the literal meaning of which is 'gilding of ground gold'. Strictly speaking, ormolu work is bronze figures and decorative mounts gilded with an amalgam of gold and mercury; this forms a rather messy paste and when it is fired the mercury evaporates, giving off highly toxic fumes and leaving the gold adhered to the bronze. Josiah Wedgwood's 1770 spelling 'Or-Molu' continued in use as late as 1878. Today the term is used to refer to any gilded metalwork applied to furniture. See also GILDING.

Orphrey, Orfrey, or **Orphray.** An ornamental strip or border, particularly on ecclesiastical vestments; often richly embroidered. See also CASSOCK and CHASUBLE.

Ostler. A stableman or groom at an inn. From 'host(e)ler', itself from the old French '(h)ostlier', hôtelier.

Outdoor servants. Usually connected with the stables and the garden. Elizabethan and Jacobean household orders are very precise on this point in their instructions. Those of Viscount Montague (1595) state that his Gentleman of the Horse 'shall take charge of all my horses . . . with the furniture and all other thinges perteyninge to the stable'. But the Gentleman of the Horse was scarcely an outdoor servant; it was the Yeoman of the Horse who ordered hay and straw and saw that the grooms did 'nott frequente ale howses', or otherwise misbehave; he and the grooms lived in dormitories over the stables. These sixteenth-century household orders do not mention coachmen, because a coach was used only in London. At Audley End. Essex in the 1770s the 4th Lord Howard de Walden had a groom, a coachman and two postilions, the coachman at £21 a year being the most highly paid. At the same time Lord Clive, at his luxurious London house in Berkeley Square, had first and second coachmen (the former at £30), three postilions and a groom. In 1881, at Kimbolton Castle, Cambridgeshire the 4th Duke of Manchester had a coachman at £45 a year, an under-coachman, and only a stud groom, while at Thoresby Hall, Nottinghamshire the same year the 3rd Earl Manvers had a head coachman at £32 a year, an under-coachman, a postilion, two grooms and four 'stable helpers'.

Other outdoor staff are not mentioned in the early 'instructions', but at Audley End in the 1770s they included a gardener, a gamekeeper, a huntsman and a whipper-in, the two last presumably in connection with Lord Howard de Walden's mastership of the local hunt. Neither at Kimbolton Castle nor at Thoresby are other outdoor staff mentioned.

Anthony Heasel, in *The Servants Book of Knowledge* (1773), states that 'The person who acts as gardener to noblemen or gentlemen must take care to make himself well acquainted with the cultivation of fruits, flowers, vegetables and . . . everything growing in gardens either for pleasure or use.' This is a reflection of the eighteenth-century passion for display, a time when owners competed in embellishing and improving their estates. One of the curiosities of the time is that so many gardeners were Scottish; Tobias Smollett, in *The Expedition of Humphry Clinker* (1771), has Matt Bramble, a Welsh squire, being told that 'almost all the gardeners of South-England were natives of Scotland'. The head gardener of the eighteenth century would have charge of hotbeds, greenhouses and ORANGERIES, and have under him a number of gardeners, according to the size of the gardens. In 1779, for example, Erddig in Clwyd employed six gardeners, mainly in growing fruit and vegetables for the squire's household. The head gardener was paid 1s. 4d. a day, but less in winter; by 1841 a head gardener at Erddig was paid £35 a year. It is interesting to compare these figures with the annual pay of the head gardener at Audley End in 1771, which was £30, with £16 for the kitchen gardener. No under-gardeners are mentioned, but probably farm labourers were recruited as necessary. Many of the gardens of the nineteenth century involved enormous upkeep, employing twenty or more in the garden. See also GARDEN STAFF and GARDENS.

Ovolo moulding. A simple, wide, convex moulding, sometimes referred to as a quarter-round.

Oyster veneer. Thin slices of veneer taken from branches and roots, mainly walnut or laburnum, which when inlaid on furniture and polished makes a repetitive pattern of whorls resembling oyster shells. Their use originated in Holland, and was principally a fashion of the late seventeenth and early eighteenth centuries.

Oxford Movement. The Oxford Movement dates from an ASSIZE sermon on 'National Apostasy' given at Oxford on 14 July 1833 by John Keble (1792–1866), in which, while ostensibly attacking a Bill suppressing ten Irish bishoprics and condemning the latitudinarian (toleration of a broad spectrum of thought) tendencies of the Church of England, he asserted its claim to a heavenly origin and a divine prerogative. His intention – and that of his followers – was to revive the High Church traditions of the early seventeenth century, and to counter the subordination of Church to State. Keble's sermon inspired R.H. Froude (1803–36), NEWMAN and E.B. Pusey (1800–82), like him Fellows of Oriel College, Oxford (hence the Movement's name), to launch their series of *Tracts for the Times*, setting out their views (hence also 'Tractarians', and 'Puseyites', after E.B. Pusey's involvement).

The response at Cambridge was J.M. Neale's (1818–66) founding in 1839 of the Cambridge Camden Society (later, as now, The Ecclesiological Society), whose publication, *The Ecclesiologist*, suggested that Anglican clergy might 'improve' their churches by sweeping away the furnishings of the previous 300 years, and focusing the service again on chancel and altar. The suggestion was acted upon: box pews were dispensed with – they interfered with the view of the altar – the font was placed by the south door, chancels were raised in height from the nave by a step, and the altar, the focus of ritual, was raised from the chancel by two steps. It is to the influence of the Ecclesiologists and

Tractarians of the nineteenth century, diametrically opposed to the PURITAN iconoclasm of the CIVIL WAR, that we owe the interiors of the majority of our 8,000 pre-twentieth-century parish churches. See also BROAD CHURCH MOVEMENT.

Oxgang. See BOVATE.

Pagan survivals. The early church successfully absorbed and adapted the greater part of pre-Roman and Roman beliefs, of which folk memories linger in such survivals as the MAY DAY dance round the may pole, a direct descendant of pagan dancing around a tree; May Day itself comes directly from the Roman festival of *Floralia*, and the GREEN MAN, so often found carved on church bosses, was the pagan tree spirit, adopted by the church. Primitive astrological beliefs were closely allied to religion, and as deeply entrenched – the stars must be consulted, demons placated: Mars, Jupiter and other Roman gods were seen as demons, and featured in the constellations, which were also linked to health, dictated by the humours (see MEDICINE): blood was under the signs of Aries, Taurus, and Gemini; yellow bile under Cancer, Leo, and Virgo; black bile under Libra, Scorpio, and Sagittarius; phlegm under Capricorn, Aquarius, and Pisces. The days of the week and the months of the year are mainly Roman. December 25th, the date of the pagan religious ceremony celebrating the beginning – or birth – of the yearly course of the sun, was adopted by the church in the fourth century as Christ's day of birth, CHRISTMAS Day.

Paine, James (*c.* 1716–89). Architect; born and lived in London, but the majority of his buildings are country houses in the Midlands and North of England. Work on six public buildings and more than seventy houses is attributed to him. He was strongly influenced by Inigo JONES and William KENT; his solid and conservative work is characterized by practical planning based on antique prototypes, with dignified exteriors and good workmanship, and spanned the NEO-CLASSICAL years between Lord BURLINGTON and Robert ADAM. His interiors reflect the changing fashions of the period, from the ROCOCO of the Mansion House, Doncaster (1745–8) to the Grecian and Adam influences later in his life. At Nostell Priory, West Yorkshire (built *c.* 1737–*c.* 1750) he supervised the work under James Moyser (*c.* 1688–1751) and designed many of the details and interiors (the work was later completed by Adam). Among many other commissions, he was the architect of Brocket Hall, Hertfordshire (*c.* 1760–75) and designed the north-west wing at Kedleston Hall, Derbyshire (1759–60).

Painted cloth hangings. A cheap alternative to TAPESTRIES, in vogue in Britain for farmhouses and cottages in the sixteenth and seventeenth centuries. In the Chapel at Hardwick Hall, Derbyshire is a set of biblical scenes made in the 1590s, and at the Luton Museum in Bedfordshire, an early seventeenth-century set of biblical subjects. Owlpen Manor in Gloucestershire has another early seventeenth-century set, depicting Joseph and his brothers. Shakespeare's Falstaff recommended painted hangings to Mistress Quickly in *The Merry Wives of Windsor*.

Painted furniture. As little survives of the customarily painted medieval furniture, the term in general refers to the NEO-CLASSICAL fashion developed by Robert Adam from the late 1760s. Like his interiors, his table and chair legs were decorated with garlands of flowers and chains of Classical husks, the tops and backs of chairs with ovals and roundels containing scenes from Classical mythology. Almost any and every furniture surface might be treated in this way, from bed-heads to COMMODES and POLE-SCREENS. In 1788 the cabinet-maker George HEPPLEWHITE wrote: 'A new and very elegant fashion has arisen within these few years, of finishing them [chairs] with painted or japanned work which gives a rich and splendid appearance to the minutest parts of the ornaments.' For many years painted furniture was little regarded and, between the wars particularly, could be picked up fairly cheaply; today, it is unfortunately rather scarce and expensive. However, there was a brief revival of painted furniture by the Omega Workshop, founded by Roger Fry in 1913 and featuring such artists as Wyndham Lewis, Duncan Grant, Vanessa Bell, and others. Now, in the last years of the twentieth century, there is renewed interest in this and the associated arts of GILDING and marbling among a new generation of architects, artists and craftsmen.

Palladianism. The style derived from the Venetian architect Andrea Palladio (1508–80); his *Quattro libri dell'architettura*, published in 1570, became the bible for the Palladians. In 1613 Inigo JONES visited the Veneto in Italy, where Palladio had practised, and studied his buildings. When he returned home he brought back a copy of the *Quattro libri* (now in the Library of Worcester College, Oxford). His designs for the Queen's House, Greenwich (begun 1616) and the Banqueting House, Whitehall (begun 1619) were strongly influenced by Palladio, and introduced the Palladian style to England. Thereafter it languished until the beginning of the eighteenth century, when it was revived by Colen CAMPBELL and Lord BURLINGTON, a revival given particular impetus by the publication of Cambell's *Vitruvius Britannicus* (1715–25). Colen Campbell's Wanstead House (1714; now demolished), which became the model for large Palladian houses, was the Palladian answer to Blenheim and Castle Howard; he also Palladianized Houghton Hall, Norfolk, for Sir Robert Walpole. By the 1730s, Palladianism had become established as the accepted style for English country houses and public buildings. Chiswick House, Middlesex and Holkham in Norfolk are fine examples of the Palladian spirit in architecture.

Apart from Nero's Golden House in Rome, there had in Palladio's time been no excavations of ancient Roman villas; the only remains above ground were those of Roman public buildings. Palladio assumed that Roman domestic architecture was similar, and his villas therefore derive from Roman temple architecture, with its ORDERS and ENTABLATURES. Moreover, his villas were designed for the hot summers of the Veneto, and every breeze was directed through a PORTICO to a cool and shady central hall: in icy British winters, the same device gives no comfort whatsoever. The style was always alien to the British climate; its popularity, particularly with the eighteenth-century WHIG aristocracy, represented a conscious attempt to recreate the art, architecture and civilization of ancient Rome. See also NEO-CLASSICISM and RENAISSANCE.

Panes. A sixteenth- and seventeenth-century term for hangings consisting of broad strips of contrasting colours, or rectangular panels framed by another material. There are some good re-created examples of this fashion of the 1670s used as bed hangings and as wall coverings at Ham House, Greater London.

Pantry. The Pantry was a medieval household office under the Yeoman of the Pantry, who was responsible for supplying bread at meal times (dry goods); in the course of time he also came to be responsible for the wine. The pantry door was one of the three doors off the SCREENS PASSAGE. See also BUTTERY.

Pantes. The lower valances of a bed; from the French *pente*.

Pargetting. Exterior plastering, on a TIMBER-FRAMED building, on which are modelled decorative designs such as figures, animals, vines and foliage.

Paperweights, glass. Decorative glass paperweights originated in Italy and Bohemia as recently as the 1840s; the fashion quickly spread, particularly to France, where famous makers were at Baccarat, Clichy and St Cloud, and to Britain (Bacchus). Many are based on the *millefiori* ('thousand flowers') technique, dating back to Early Egyptian and Classical Roman mosaic glass; the 'flowers' are made from transverse slices of coloured glass canes embedded in a clear glass body.

Papier-mâché. A material made of pulped paper mixed with glue, chalk and sometimes sand, molded into shape (furniture, trays, screens, boxes, picture frames and the like) then baked and decorated. Invented in France in the seventeenth century, it came to Britain *c.* 1670 but was little used until the eighteenth century, when it was also used for decorative details applied to ceilings and walls, and for the fillets masking the edges of silk damask wall coverings. Some early (*c.* 1620) gilded SCONCES, probably French, can be seen at Hardwick Hall, Derbyshire; a later example (1747) is the ceiling of the church of St Michael at

Witley Court, Worcestershire, where what appears to be STUCCO work is in fact papier-mâché. Henry Clay, a Birmingham japanner, patented in 1772 a type of japanned papier-mâché which became very popular and led to his appointment as Japanner-in-Ordinary to the King and the Prince of Wales. His method used built-up sheets of paper, rather than paper pulp, which were then pressed in a wooden mould before being japanned; his japanning used the then fashionable 'eastern' colours of black, crimson and green. Japanned papier-mâché is often inlaid with mother-of-pearl.

The best papier-mâché furniture was made in the 1840s, mainly at Wolverhampton and Birmingham; it did not escape the general falling-off in design standards evident by the time of the Great Exhibition of 1851. See also 'COMPOSITION', GESSO, JAPANNING and LEATHER MÂCHÉ.

Parian ware. An unglazed type of hard-paste white procelain with the appearance of marble; cast in moulds to make dolls' heads, busts and figures. It was introduced by Copeland & Garret of Stoke-on-Trent in the 1840s and due to its popularity was quickly taken up by other makers, in particular Minton. The subjects cast were popular and national heroes, such as Lord Byron, members of the royal family, and Wellington. The name is from the Aegean island of Paros, where the Greeks and Romans mined marble.

Parish registers. The local church's register of baptisms, burials and marriages is kept by the parish incumbent. From 1538 registers on paper were mandatory; from 1597 the registers had to be kept on vellum, and old entries were to be copied into them. Such registers are still kept; some 812 of the earliest survive, but both those and often later ones have in general been deposited in County Record Offices.

Parquet. A French design for wood-block floors in which the blocks are laid with contrasting grain in 'herring-bone' pattern. The first recorded parquet floors in England were laid at old Somerset House after Charles I's widow, Henrietta Maria (1609–69), returned to England in 1660. The Dowager Queen had lived at Saint-Germain and the Louvre during her exile, and brought back with her notions of French decorative fashion. It is unlikely that anyone in England was capable of doing such work, so French joiners were employed at Somerset House. Another example, of c. 1670, can be seen in the LONG GALLERY of Drayton House in Northamptonshire. William III and Mary (1689–94) used parquet patterns in the State Apartments at Hampton Court in 1688, and thereafter the fashion quickly spread; parquet floors were laid at Boughton House in Northamptonshire, and Chatsworth in Derbyshire in the 1690s.

Parquetry. A similar technique to PARQUET flooring, in which furniture veneers, using the same wood applied with contrasting grain, or different woods in different colours, are used to form a pattern. The term is also used to describe a pattern of what appear to be cubes in light and dark veneers, and similar geometric patterns. See also MARQUETRY.

Parterre. A level space in a garden formally laid out and occupied by flower beds. See also KNOT GARDENS.

Paterae. Small bas-relief circular or oval ornaments, often decorated with ACANTHUS leaves or rose petals; applied to buildings and furniture as part of the Classical repertory of decorative motifs.

Patent. (1) as 'Letters Patent', open letters from the sovereign detailing the grant of some title, dignity, office, monopoly, franchise or other privilege; (2) a Government grant of the sole right to make, sell or use a process or invention.

Peasants' Revolt, 1381. Widespread uprisings against authority, the result mainly of distress among the poorer classes arising from agricultural depression, finally sparked into revolt by the authorization in November 1380 of a flat-rate POLL TAX of one shilling a head. The most serious outbreaks were in Kent and Essex. In Kent Wat Tyler (d. 1381) led the storming of Rochester Castle before marching on London (13 June) to rendezvous with the rebels from Essex. The Fleet and Newgate prisons were seized, the Tower surrendered to the rebels, and unpopular figures such as the CHANCELLOR and the Archbishop of Canterbury were beheaded. On 14 June Richard II (1377–99) met the rebels at Mile End and agreed to some of their demands, including freedom from villeinage, and the commutation of all servile dues to a rent of 4d. an acre. At a further meeting at Smithfield the following day Wat Tyler spoke insolently to the King; the Mayor of London, William Walworth, knocked Tyler down with his mace, and he was killed by one of the King's squires, John Standwick (or Standish). Richard coolly saved a now very threatening situation with the much-quoted cry 'Sirs! Will you shoot your King? . . . I will be your leader. Let him who loves me follow me!' and led the peasants away. Other parts of the country were brought under control by September; Richard reneged on his promises, but agreed to a general amnesty.

Pediment. A triangular or low-pitched gable over a PORTICO; a feature of Classical architecture, used also purely decoratively by the Romans to crown doors, windows and niches. A *segmental* pediment has a curved top; a *broken* pediment has an apex not joined by the sloping sides but left open; an *open* pediment has a gap in the base and is sometimes called *open-bed*. Where many decorative pediments appear in a row – as over windows – the Romans (and later designers in the Classical taste) often made them alternately triangular and segmental in shape. The term is also applied to the topmost decorative element in such furniture as cabinets, bookcases and long-case clocks designed in the Neo-classical style.

Pedlars. See HAWKERS AND PEDLARS.

Peerage, The. Members of the degrees of NOBILITY whose adult holders may sit in the House of Lords. They rank in descending order: duke (addressed formally as Your Grace, socially as Duke), first created in 1337; marquess (addressed formally as my Lord Marquess, informally as Lord X——), first created 1385; earl, first created before 1066; viscount, first created in 1440; baron, first created in 1387; the last three peers are addressed formally as my Lord, informally as Lord Y——. The title usually descends through the direct surviving male heir but in exceptional circumstances a woman might have been created a peeress in her own right, or the patent of creation might allow for the descent through the female line when there is no direct male heir.

Many peers possess more than one title, and as a courtesy the eldest son (and grandson, if one exists) of a duke, marquess or earl may be known by the second (and third, if available) ranking title borne by the peer. Younger sons of dukes and marquesses are styled 'Lord', plus their name and the family surname (for example, the younger son of a Duke of Rutland would be known as Lord John Manners); all the daughters are styled 'Lady', followed by their name and family surname (for example, Lady Diana Manners), and this also applies to all the daughters of earls; wives of younger sons of dukes and marquesses are styled 'Lady', followed by their husband's name and surname (if Anne Smith marries Lord John Manners, she becomes Lady John Manners – *not* Lady Anne Manners). The younger sons of earls and all sons and daughters of viscounts and barons are styled 'The Honourable' – but unlike the other coutesy titles described, 'The Hon.' is confined to formal written use only. No courtesy title carries the right to a seat in the House of Lords.

It was always felt that a peerage should be supported in a certain style, so patents of nobility were often – though not inevitably – accompanied by grants of lands and/or funds: when John Churchill became Duke of Marlborough in 1702, Queen Anne gave him funds to build Blenheim Palace; after the First World War, Earl Haig was given £100,000 with his peerage.

The sale of titles has always been held to debase their value; if he did not set the precedent, James I (1603–25) at least continued it with the creation and sale of the title of BARONET. The Cavendish of the day was only one among many: he paid £2,000 for a barony in 1605, and was created Earl of Devonshire in 1618 against a payment of £10,000 (in fact, he got his titles cheaply: Lords Dormer and Haughton paid £10,000 each in 1615 and 1616 for their baronies, and Haughton a further £5,000 for his earldom in 1624); the dukedom of Devonshire was awarded to the 4th Earl by William III (1689–1702) in 1694, but no money changed hands. In the 1920s Lloyd George (Prime Minister 1916–22) sold titles to raise funds for the Liberal party; the first Lord Vestey (1859–1940) is said to have paid £25,000 for his peerage, provoking an angry letter from George V (1910–36) to Lloyd George. More recently, Harold Wilson was felt to have bestowed some Life Peerages undeservedly in his 1974 Resignation Honours List, so debasing this honour.

Life peerages rather than hereditary peerages have been the rule since 1958, with the exception of William Whitelaw and George Thomas in 1983 – each received an hereditary peerage but as they have no male heirs these will not survive them. The title, which normally ranks as a barony, is awarded to both men and women, and dies with the bearer; children of life peers bear for life the same courtesy titles as the children of an hereditary peer. There are ancient precedents for life peerages: earldoms granted for life have included Huntingdon in 1377 and Yarmouth in 1740; dukedoms for life have included Hamilton in 1660 and Kendal in 1719. Both Yarmouth and Kendal were created for women. More traditionally, life peerages are granted to the Lord of Appeal in Ordinary, and to the 'Law Lords', lawyers who have judicial functions in the House of Lords as the final Court of Appeal. The Peerage Act (1963) provided for the disclaimer for life of certain hereditary peerages, and for the first time permitted hereditary peeresses to sit in the House of Lords. See also HONOURS and NOBILITY.

Pele towers. A current term for a defensive tower house. In fourteenth-century Scotland a pele was a defence ditch with an earth and timber rampart, and from this a new form of building evolved: the tower house, in which the usual rooms of the period were unconventionally arranged – the floor plan was upended, to become vertical instead of horizontal – for ease of defence. Some 150 tower houses survive in Cumberland and Northumberland; they consist of three storeys, with a vaulted basement for cattle or storage, an attached ground-floor hall, a chamber on the first floor, and a smaller chamber above. Most were built around the time of the accession of James I (1603–25) and abandoned after the final Act of Union with Scotland of 1707. Pele houses, often known as bastle houses, were scaled-down versions of tower houses, built by farmers during the same period.

Tower houses were not confined to the Scottish borders; Longthorpe in Cambridgeshire dates from c. 1250; one at Halloughton in Nottinghamshire was built c. 1400; and Prior Overton built a brick tower house at Repton, Derbyshire in 1437 as part of a priory of AUSTIN CANONS. Curiously, these English examples share the common factor of having been built for clerics; the reason (if any) is so far undiscovered.

Perfuming pans, perfume (or **pastille**) **burners.** Vessels, often highly decorative and made in silver or other metals, for burning sweet-smelling pastilles (aromatic infusions bound in gum arabic) to disguise offensive body or other odours; known since Elizabethan times. Hardwick Hall, Derbyshire had many fine perfuming pans in 1601. The practice of burning sweet-smelling pastilles continued even after washing became more general in the nineteenth century; in the 1830s and 40s the Staffordshire potteries turned out many small porcelain and pottery burners in the form of cottages and other buildings; the aromatic fumes escaped through chimneys and windows. A *cassolette* is a late eighteenth-century pastille burner of bronze or gilt metal, like a small brazier on a stand, and an *Athénienne* is a multi-purpose lidded urn on a three-legged stand which could be used as a perfume burner (late eighteenth century).

Perpendicular style. An arbitrary division of English GOTHIC architecture, covering the period *c.* 1335–50 to *c.* 1530. The bald assertion that 'This church is Perpendicular' may sound ridiculous to the uninitiated – clearly it is not horizontal – but it is nevertheless a graphic description of the ecclesiastical style in which vertical thrust was emphasized, and columns soared heavenwards to support stone fan-vaulted roofs on the slenderest of pillars, with ever-greater window space. The ultimate expression of the Perpendicular style is perhaps King's College Chapel, Cambridge, begun in 1446. The term was devised *c.* 1811 by Thomas Rickman (1776–1841). See also DECORATED, EARLY ENGLISH styles and GOTHIC ARCHITECTURE.

Perpetual curate. The incumbent of a parish of which the tithes are impropriated (transferred to lay ownership), with no endowed vicarage. Perpetual curates were authorized to describe themselves as vicars by an ACT of 1868. See also CURATE.

Petty Sessions. An extension of QUARTER SESSIONS, at which two or more JUSTICES OF THE PEACE met at regular intervals to hear minor offences to do with the POOR LAW, highways, licensing, etc. Since 1949 Petty Sessions courts have become merged in magistrates' courts.

Pewter. An alloy metal used in Britain for mugs, tankards, plates and bowls, and church vessels, from early medieval times. A Pewterers' Guild was formed in 1348 and wares were marked with the Guild mark, a hammer or rose, crowned or uncrowned; from 1503 individual maker's marks were compulsory. The alloy used was of varying constituents in varying proportions: tin, lead, bismuth, copper and zinc. The best medieval pewter was made from tin and 25 per cent copper, which was hard enough for plates. Mugs, tankards and bowls used an alloy of tin with 25 per cent lead. A set of pewter is called a 'garnish'; originally it would have been proudly displayed in the GREAT HALL on a BUFFET, but today is often hung on the kitchen walls of large country houses. See also GUILDS and PLATES.

Phaeton. A light, open, four-wheeled carriage usually drawn by a pair of horses. See also CARRIAGES.

Photography. Pioneering work in photography was done by Sir Humphrey Davy (1778–1829), who in 1802 carried out experiments for copying paintings on glass. In 1814 a Frenchman, Joseph Niepce (1765–1833), managed to obtain images on bituminous film, and produced the first successful photograph in 1822, using silver chloride. He became a partner with Louis Daguerre (1787–1851) in 1829, and in 1839 the Daguerrotype process was perfected, in which an image could be produced by exposing an iodized silver plate in a camera to mercury vapour. Independently, W.H. Fox Talbot (1800–77) produced the first successful photographic process on paper in 1834, when he made impressions of fern leaves and similar flat objects, on paper sensitized with sodium chlorate and silver nitrate. Fox Talbot's oldest negative is of an oriel window at Laycock Abbey in Wiltshire, taken in 1835. In 1839 he published his results, and in 1841 patented his Calotype process, which produced a negative on paper: a positive image was obtained by printing through this negative on to sensitized paper.

In 1848 Claude Niepce de Saint-Victor (1805–1870; nephew of Joseph Niepce) took Fox Talbot's paper negative a stage further by suggesting that the negative should be produced on a glass plate. In 1889 the first roll-film negatives, using celluloid in place of glass, were manufactured and marketed by George Eastman (1854–1932) under the Kodak brand name.

One result of the invention of photography was that for the first time well-known paintings could be examined without actually standing in front of them. The publication and circulation of photographs of pictures encouraged an educated interest in art. See also CAMERA OBSCURA.

Pianoforte. Invented in Padua *c.* 1709 by a HARPSICHORD-maker, Bartolomeo Cristofori (1665–1731), as a *gravicembalo col piano e forte*, a 'harpsichord with soft and loud': he had substituted hammers for the quills of the harpsichord, and louder or softer sounds were produced by applying greater or less force to the finger-keys. To produce a perfect instrument took about a hundred years of experimentation and improvement. Part of the difficulty arose from the higher tension of the strings (approximately 12 tons on a modern pianoforte), which seriously distorted the wooden frames originally used; it was only when strengthening iron rods and bars were used that this problem was solved. In his twenties Thomas Broadwood founded his famous piano manufactory in London (1751) and married the daughter of the Swiss harpsichord maker Tschudi, who had settled in London in the first half of the eighteenth century. A Tschudi–Broadwood piano of 1782 graces the State Music Room at Chatsworth in Derbyshire. At Killerton House in Devon is a small square piano (horizontally strung) made in 1778 by Johannes Pohlman, one of twelve German piano makers in London at that date; another was George Astor, a flute maker, born near Heidelburg *c.* 1763, who came to London *c.* 1778 and was making pianos in Cornhill, London, in 1779. Another immigrant harpsichord-maker, Jacob Kirckmann, also made pianos in London from the mid eighteenth century, as did a Scot, Robert Stodart, who founded William & Matthew Stodart – their 'grand piano-forte, with an octave swell' was a noteworthy improvement. See also MUSIC.

Piano nobile. A term, principally applicable to PALLADIAN buildings, meaning the principal storey of the house, containing the state reception rooms; usually the first floor, marked externally by the size of the windows, with a basement below and a low storey above.

Picture galleries. In the early sixteenth century PORTRAITS of past sovereigns were commissioned by Henry VIII, probably to form part of an historical gallery. By the time of Elizabeth I (1548–1603) both royal portraits and (mainly imaginary) portraits of ancestors were hung in (LONG) GALLERIES, and provided something both improving and inspiring to look at while taking exercise. By the late sixteenth century the approach to pictures was gradually changing from dynastic glorification to an appreciation of art for its own sake. In the second half of the seventeenth century, collections of paintings made on the GRAND TOUR were at first shown in their owners' CABINETS, the small private rooms we might today call studies; but for serious collectors a cabinet was not big enough, and by the end of the eighteenth century galleries specifically designed to display paintings were being built. The example of the Uffizi in Florence undoubtedly influenced many. Corsham Court, Wiltshire, has a Picture Gallery designed by Capability BROWN in the 1760s: Lord Berwick added a picture gallery in 1805 at Attingham Park, Shropshire, and the North Gallery was created at Petworth, West Sussex by Lord Egremont in the 1830s to display his collections of sculpture and paintings.

Goethe (1749–1832) saw that a collection of paintings conferred prestige on a connoisseur, and said of art collections: 'They outweigh any splendour which the richest man can gain for himself' – a point already made by the Medicis in the fifteenth century.

The first public picture gallery in Britain was Dulwich Picture Gallery, designed by Sir John SOANE, which opened in 1814 in the building it still occupies. See also PICTURE HANGING, below.

Picture hanging. In the time of Elizabeth I (1548–1603) portraits of sovereigns and ancestors were invariably hung in the (LONG) GALLERIES,

those of near family and intimate friends in the more private WITH-
DRAWING ROOM. The first advice on where to hang pictures was given
in 1624 by Sir Henry Wotton (1568–1639), who recommended '. . .
Cheerful Paintings in Feasting and Banqueting Rooms; Graver Stories
in [long] Galleries: Landscaips and Boscage, and such wilder works, in
open terraces or in Summer Houses'. A book by William Sanderson
published in 1658 gave further advice: the hall should be reserved for
shepherds, peasants, milk-maids and flocks of sheep, the staircase was to
have architectural scenes, either new or ruined. In the GREAT CHAMBER
there were to be landscapes (unusual for the time), and pictures of
hunting, fishing, fowling, histories and antiquities. The WITHDRAWING
ROOM, being a less public place, was recommended for portraits of
'Persons of Honour' and intimate friends. The 'banqueting rooms' were
suitable for 'merry paintings of Bacchus, centaurs, satyres, syrens and
the like', but Sanderson warned that obscene pictures should be
avoided. The bed chamber was reserved for portraits of 'wives and children', with the proviso that the picture of the owner's wife should not
be prominently hung, in case 'an Italian minded guest gaze too long' at
it. Sanderson made no recommendations as to which artists were desirable; at the time, the attribution of unsigned work was based on hope
rather than experience – art history was unknown.

A late seventeenth-century fashion was to have portraits in the eating
room; in the 1760s, Robert ADAM recommended that eating rooms
should have pictures of game, food, Bacchus again, plus Ceres and
related pictures of sowing and harvest times. Saltram House in Devon
has a good example of an unaltered Adam hang.

In the mid eighteenth century the fashion was to hang pictures in
balanced tiers, as can be seen at Corsham Court in Wiltshire (1760s),
and at Squerryes Court, Kent (a collection made between 1740 and
1800). Old Masters and portraits were now separated, the latter commonly hung over library shelves. By the 1770s, dressing rooms were
held to be suitable for Italian paintings.

The 4th Earl of Bristol and Bishop of Derry (1730–1803) began
building Ickworth, Suffolk, in 1795; he died before the house was finished, but intended – unusually – to have Italian paintings in one of the
two wings (connected to the main house by corridors) and German
and Dutch in the other: no other connoisseur of his time had thought
of segregating paintings in schools.n See also PICTURE GALLERIES, above.

Picturesque. An eighteenth-century term applied to the kind of landscape that appeared to echo paintings by Claude Lorraine (Claude
Gelée) (1600–82) or Nicolas Poussin (1594–1665). The term developed in the late eighteenth and early nineteenth centuries to describe
an aesthetic approach to and pleasure in rough nature, as exemplified

for example by curious rock formations, and particularly applied to rustic landscapes and ruined buildings. The Picturesque supplemented Edmund Burke's (1729–97) 'Beautiful and Sublime'. A great deal of energy went into defining the term, and its sillier manifestations were satirised by Jane Austen (1775–1817) in *Sense and Sensibility* (1811) and *Northanger Abbey* (1818).

Pier-glass. A tall rectangular mirror set against the pier, or section of wall, between two windows, and usually placed above a pier-table. Its purpose was to reflect light in the dark space between windows; at night, the light from a candelabrum placed on the table would be reflected back into the room. Because of the difficulty and cost of producing large pieces of flat glass in Britain until the late eighteenth century, pier-glasses are usually made up of two or more pieces of glass, the joints covered by modelled decoration. The French, however, had been making large sheets of glass at St Gobain in Picardy since the seventeenth century; French glass was costly to import but there are French pier glasses at Newby Hall in North Yorkshire, at Osterley, Greater London (fitted out by Robert ADAM), and at Moor Park, Hertfordshire. It was only from the 1790s that the Ravenhead Glass Works in Lancashire was able to compete with the French in producing large sheets of glass. See also MIRROR SILVERING, WINDOW GLASS and TRIAD.

Pietra dura. An Italian term meaning 'hard stone', referring to an inlaid mosaic of coloured marbles and semi-precious stones used for table-tops, most fashionable in the seventeenth and eighteenth centuries.

Pilaster. A section of a shallow rectangular column or pier projecting from the wall, usually conforming to one of the Classical ORDERS.

Pilgrim bottle. A spherical bottle with flattened sides and loops on either side of the neck through which a cord or chain could be passed. Bottles of this shape were known in Ancient Egypt, and used by the Romans and also in China, in the Ming dynasty (1368–1644). Originally in some form of pottery, in more recent times they have been made in silver, porcelain or glass, purely as decorative objects.

Pillowberes. A Tudor (and earlier) term for linen pillowcases.

Pinder or **Ponder.** A village official appointed by the manorial court, responsible for rounding up stray animals and detaining them in the village pin-fold or pound.

Plagues. These were bubonic (but sometimes pneumonic) and carried by the flea of the black rat. Bubonic plague was almost endemic in Britain until the 1780s and local outbreaks were frequent. The Black Death, in pneumonic and bubonic forms, is held to have originated in Central Asia and spread to Europe along the trade routes, reaching England in 1348. Further outbreaks occurred in 1361, 1369 and 1379.

The population, estimated variously between 2.5 and 4 million, was reduced by about one-third. Mortality was heaviest where black rats were most numerous, such as in corn-growing areas, and towns. The immediate economic consequence of the Black Death was a shortage of labour, a rise in wages and a reduction in prices.

Serious outbreaks of plague occurred in London in 1603, 1625 and 1647; the last major outbreak in Britain, the Great Plague, raged in London from April 1665, reached its peak in September, and had died out by the autumn of 1666. The Great Fire of London of 1666 has usually been credited for ending the epidemic, but as the disease is cyclical in nature, it probably subsided spontaneously. Total deaths in London are estimated at 100,000, and graphic descriptions of the Great Plague may be found in Pepys's *Diary*, and also, though it was written after the event, in Defoe's *Journal of the Plague Year* (1722).

During the eighteenth century, plague died out generally in western Europe and was practically restricted to India and China, although Russia, Turkey and the Danube basin suffered occasionally; by the end of the nineteenth century it had largely retreated to the Far East, although a few cases occurred in other regions – for example, North America – in the first decades of the twentieth century.

Plates. Today plates are taken for granted, but it was many centuries before they superseded the messy TRENCHERS. Yeoman families were eating off copper and PEWTER plates by the mid sixteenth century, and the wealthy off plates of silver and silver-gilt – the best of which would be ostentatiously displayed on a BUFFET or CUPBOARD, the Tudor equivalent of a SIDEBOARD. Pottery plates appeared in the late sixteenth century; the first examples came from Delft, but a pottery was soon established at Lambeth in London, copying the distinctive Delft designs. The earliest surviving English pottery plate, which can be seen in the Museum of London, dates from 1602 and is painted in tin-enamel in blue, green and yellow designs outlined in dark purple. Even when plates had become the general rule (and, as with FORKS, it took a long time), the same plate would be used throughout the meal: a trencher was not removed, so why a plate? The English are, of course, innately conservative: as late as 1752 Horace Walpole (1717–97) was astonished to see the Duke and Duchess of Hamilton eating their entire meal off the same plates.

Playing cards. Of uncertain origin but variously attributed to the Chinese, Egyptians, Arabs and Hindus, and first introduced into Europe in the late fourteenth century, as much for divination as for gaming. They were being used in Venice in the late fourteenth century.

Tarots, or picture cards, seem to have been indigenous to Italy; there were 22, spotted or chequered on the back, used by themselves for fortune-telling or simple games and, combined with 56 number cards, for a game called *tarocchi* which is still played in northern Italy. The number cards consisted of four suits of four court (sometimes called 'coat') cards plus ten cards numbered one to ten. The four suits were chalice, sword, money and baton, and the court cards were king, queen, knight and knave. From this deck of 56 cards developed the 52-card French (in the later fifteenth century), the 40-card Spanish and the 32-card German decks. The French abandoned the knight from each of the four suits, which were called 'pique' (spade), 'coeur' (heart), 'carreau' (diamond), and 'trèfle' (club), and this was the deck adopted in England.

Ploughland. The area of land that could be tilled in one year by one plough-team of eight oxen. The actual size varied according to the type of soil on which it lay: it would be smaller on a heavy clay soil than on a light sandy loam – an average 120 acres. See also BOVATE and CARUCATE.

Plough Monday. The first Monday after Twelfth Night, and traditionally the day on which the new season's ploughing began. In some villages the ploughmen paraded from door to door with their ploughs, their faces blackened, to cries of 'God speed the plough'.

Plunge-baths. An open-air bath – in the nature of a BATHING-pool rather than a tub – filled with unheated water. Plunge-baths were a health-fad of the early eighteenth century, ungrounded in medical evidence but recommended by doctors; they may however have gone some way to curing the inevitable hangovers from drinking too much PORT. The fashion probably derived from Italy and the GRAND TOUR; the Villa Garzoni in Tuscany has a bath dating from the 1640s built over a Roman bath. There was a plunge-bath for public use at Clerkenwell in 1697, and another at Widcombe near Bath in 1707, both long since disappeared. The earliest surviving private plunge-bath in Britain is possibly that at Rufford Abbey, Nottinghamshire, dating from 1729, while one at Rousham, Oxfordshire dates from the 1730s. The majority, however, are from the late eighteenth century: Corsham Court, Wiltshire has a Gothic bath house by Capability BROWN of the 1760s; Wynnstay, Denbighshire has one of *c.* 1780 built like a Classical temple; and at Wimpole Hall, Cambridgeshire there is a particularly luxurious plunge-bath of the 1790s, with a fireplace, by Sir John SOANE. After a game of cricket in 1936, twenty-two policemen crammed into Soane's masterpiece. In the 1780s Lord Clive of India had one installed in the basement of Claremont House in Surrey, for treatment of a nervous disorder, and at Newstead Abbey in Nottinghamshire, Lord Byron flooded a cellar (*c.* 1800) to make a plunge-bath. Cragside in Northumberland has a complete suite of bathing rooms built in 1870.

Pluralism. The simultaneous holding of more than one BENEFICE, discouraged by the Roman Catholic Church from the thirteenth century and by the Church of England from the DISSOLUTION. A canon (decree of the Church) of 1703 permitted pluralism to a cleric who was an MA (Master of Arts) in two parishes only, provided that he lived part of the year in each. Unfortunately such rules were often ignored, and by the early nineteenth century there was much opposition to the practice both within and without the Church. In his 'Barsetshire' novels of the mid nineteenth century, Anthony Trollope illustrates the injustices of pluralism by contrasting the pluralist and absentee parson living in Italy, the Revd Dr Vessey Stanhope, with the impoverished Revd Mr Quiverfull, vicar of Puddingdale, and his abundant family, struggling to live on £400 a year.

Police Forces. By the middle of the eighteenth century it was proving impossible to maintain law and order by the old method of unpaid CONSTABLES acting under the authority of magistrates. BOW STREET RUNNERS were set up in 1748 by Henry Fielding (1707–54); until 1757 they operated only in the Westminster area; the Middlesex Justices Act of 1792 established a small force of men to aid magistrates in that area. In 1829, Sir Robert Peel (1788–1850), as PRIME MINISTER, was responsible for the Metropolitan Police Act which set up a police force (hence the old nicknames Peelers and – more enduringly – Bobbies) for the London area (except for the square mile of the City of London, which had its own police force from 1839), under the control of the Home Secretary. Further legislation led to the setting up of 171 provincial police forces by 1847. In 1835 the Municipal Corporations Act required BOROUGHS to establish and maintain police forces under the control of watch committees. It was felt that a co-ordinated national system of policing would offend local feeling, but the need for such co-ordination came to be recognized and the County and Borough Police Act of 1856 gave the Home Office powers of inspection in all boroughs and counties, and offered financial aid towards the provision of efficient local police forces. Central grants towards pay and clothing allowances were awarded in 1874; the Local Government Act of 1888 joined county councils with the magistracy in the control of local forces; and in 1919 central grants covering half the annual expenditure of county and borough forces were established.

Although the Police Act of 1919 standardized police conditions and pay, the way in which local policing evolved has resulted in autonomous county police forces, independent and uncentralized. This system, while sometimes less efficient than it might be, for example in tracing and arresting today's highly mobile criminals, does at least counter any suggestion of a 'police-state' and its inherent danger to public liberty –

the argument used from the beginning against the idea of a police force maintained, even only partly, from Government funds.

Poll Tax. A tax of a uniform amount levied on each individual; a tax of so much per head (Middle English *polle*, a head), levied periodically from the Middle Ages onwards; always unpopular, and widely evaded. The Poll Tax of 1380 was a contributory cause of the PEASANTS' REVOLT of 1381.

Polo. A ball game played on horseback, and one of the most ancient of games. It is played four-a-side, and bears some resemblance to field-hockey-on-horseback, using long-handled mallets (polo sticks). Each match lasts for about an hour, divided into 'chukkas' of 7.5 minutes. It was certainly played in Persia in 500 BC, and is illustrated in many of the illuminated Persian manuscripts to be seen in the British Museum. The game found its way to China and Japan and from there to Tibet and India. The first recorded description of an international game (between Persia and Turkey) is in Firdusi's eleventh-century *Shahnama*.

The origin of the modern game in England dates from 1869, when officers of the 10th Hussars at Aldershot knocked a billiard ball over turf with hockey sticks, on horseback, having read an account of polo in India. The game quickly became popular, particularly with the army, and clubs were founded in London (Hurlingham, 1874; Ranelagh, 1896; Roehampton, 1902), Dublin and Rugby. The word 'polo' is derived from an Indus Valley dialect word *polo*, ball, from the Tibetan *pulu*, ball.

Pomander. A portable container for aromatic herbs, spices or perfumes, used to counteract objectionable smells. Generally spherical with pierced sides, the finest were made in precious metals. The first references to pomanders date from the early sixteenth century. They were looked on as articles of adornment, much like jewellery, and they are often to be seen in Tudor PORTRAITS, hanging round the neck or wrist or from a girdle. By the seventeenth century pomanders had become much smaller, sometimes less than an inch across and frequently set with precious stones. See also PERFUMING PANS and POUNCET BOX.

Poor Clares. Clarisses; female members of the order of Friars Minor (or Franciscans); known as Poor Clares after their foundress St Clara (*c.* 1219), and also as Minoresses. They are the 'Second Order of St Francis' (the friars being the 'First Order'), and follow a rule of great poverty, seclusion and austerity of life. Later, they split into Urbanists and Colletines. The Minories, near Aldgate in London, takes its name from a convent of Minoresses established there in 1293.

Poor Law. A particular system of giving alms to the destitute. The DISSOLUTION of the monasteries, hitherto the principal support of the poor, combined with various complex economic developments of the Tudor period to produce the perplexing phenomenon of 'dearth in the midst of plenty'. Attempts to deal with the problem were more political than compassionate in impulse, and met with varied lack of success. An Act of 1601 codified previous law on the subject and firmly established the parish as the normal unit of administration of poor relief, based on local taxation. Administration was the responsibility of the parish 'overseers of the poor', consisting of churchwardens and two to four householders annually nominated by the local Justices of the Peace. The responsibility of every parish for its own poor had the effect of preventing poor people from moving out of their parish in search of work, and of strangers being firmly 'moved along' to another parish. Much later, an Act of 1819 empowered a parish vestry to manage its poor through a committee of substantial householders – always conscious that any unusual relief would have to come out of their own pockets.

In 1834, on the recommendation of a Royal Commission, important Poor Law amendments established a central Board of Commissioners in London, to oversee local administration under locally-elected boards of commissioners; within three years dramatic savings of three million pounds annually were being made on the relief of the poor.

The vast body of legal provisions for alleviating poverty was consolidated by the Poor Law Act of 1929, which repealed some sixty earlier Acts and partly repealed thirty-one others. This made the county and BOROUGH councils, created in 1888, responsible for administering the Poor Law. Poor Law Relief was soon changed again and termed Public Assistance, administered under the Public Assistance Order of 1930.

Central government did not assume full responsibility for the poor until 1946, with the passing of the National Insurance Act and National Health Service Act. The National Insurance Act provided comprehensive cover for all, in sickness, old age, and unemployment, against the 'ravages of poverty and adversity'.

There were unexpected side-effects of many Poor Law Acts. For example, the repeal of the Laws of Settlement in 1865 deprived landowners of casual labour and encouraged them to build cottages for a permanent work force, something positive that had not been foreseen by the legislators. ENCLOSURE of common land had the effect of ejecting those who had settled on the commons, who then became a charge on the parish – an unforeseen negative result. See also BADGE-MEN, GILBERT'S ACT, SETTLEMENT, SPEENHAMLAND SYSTEM and WORKHOUSE.

Population. The population of England and (from 1300) Wales has been estimated as follows. Figures before the first CENSUS return of 1801 can be no more than a rough estimate:

1080	1,000,000	1700	5,300,000
1350	3,800,000	1750	6,500,000
1377	2,400,000	1801	8,900,000
1400	2,000,000	1851	17,927,609
1500	2,250,000	1901	32,527,843
1600	4,500,000	1951	43,758,000

Porringer. A straight-sided vessel with two handles and a cover, which may have been used to serve porridge, probably in its original meaning of *pottage* – stewed vegetables, herbs and meat. Now more usually a small straight-sided bowl with a single (or pair) of tab or flat horizontally set handles, and no cover, used by children. ('Here's milk for his porringer . . .': A.A. Milne)

Port. A fortified wine popular from the late seventeenth century. Many of the Portuguese wines were too light to travel well, and too harsh for the English palate, but English merchants in Portugal discovered that the fuller wines of the Douro valley, when fortified with brandy before all the grape sugar had fermented out, both travelled better and were more acceptable to the English palate. The two countries had long enjoyed amicable relations, cemented by Charles II's marriage to Catharine of Braganza in 1662. Worsening relations between Britain and France at the beginning of the eighteenth century led to the Methuen Treaty of 1703, which gave preferential treatment to Portuguese wines (a duty one-third less than on French wines) in exchange for free entry into Portugal of English woollens. The drinking of French wines became unpatriotic, as well as expensive.

Even fortified port lasted no longer than four years in cask, or two in the squat upright BOTTLES stoppered with linen. With the introduction in the 1770s of cylindrical bottles, stoppered with cork, which could be laid on their sides, keeping the corks moist and maintaining a better seal, port could be fortified with a greater proportion of brandy to produce a rich, mellow, heavy wine that could mature for ten to fifteen years in bottle.

The three- or four-bottle-a-day men of the eighteenth century are not apocryphal; port was drunk throughout meals which lasted for many hours, and special equipment was developed for it. Horseshoe-shaped 'drinking tables' with a swinging holder for the port decanter, made to be put before the fire with the drinkers sitting on the outside of the table, are sometimes to be seen in country houses. Port formed a crust in the bottle, so was customarily decanted into large, fine, cut-glass decanters; in the nineteenth century, a decanter running on a railway track laid on the table was developed, running clockwise of course, because the port decanter always circulates around the table in that direction. See also BOTTLES, CLARET, SACK and WINE.

Porte-cochère. A French term of which the literal meaning is a 'coach-doorway'. This was a PORTICO or archway, over the front entrance of a house, sufficiently wide to allow coach access, under which passengers could descend without getting wet in rainy weather.

Porter. A black beer brewed from malt partly charred or browned by drying at a high temperature, with a long fermentation, and heavily flavoured with hops. First brewed in London in the 1720s, it quickly became very popular throughout the country. It was exported to Ireland, where Arthur Guinness of Dublin established his own brew with such success that this was exported to London, to the detriment of the local brewers there. Guinness remains the most famous porter to this day. See also STOUT.

Portico. Derived from Classical architecture: an open colonnaded porch with a pediment, attached to a building as the centrepiece of a façade. According to the number of columns supporting the pediment it is called *Tetrastyle* (4), *Hexastyle* (6), *Octastyle* (8), *Decastyle* (10), or *Dodecastyle* (12). This architectural feature was used mainly by the PALLADIANS in the first half of the eighteenth century. As Palladio used Classical Roman monuments as his models, he included the attached porticos to be found on Roman temples in his own designs.

Inigo JONES, a genius in advance of his time, built the first English Classical portico at St Paul's, Covent Garden, London (1631–8), contrived as an entrance to an Etruscan temple. The earliest Classical portico to be attached to an English country house was in 1654 at The Vyne, in Hampshire, designed, according to Horace Walpole (1717–97), for Chaloner Chute (d. 1659), Speaker of the House of Commons, by John Webb (1611–72), for 24 years a close assistant of Inigo Jones. A portrait of John Chute (1701–76), painted in Rome in 1758 by Pompeo Batoni (1708–87), shows him with The Vyne and its portico in the background – this is unusual for Batoni, who more commonly set his subjects against a background of Classical Roman architecture. See also PORTE-COCHÈRE.

Portraits. Initially the Church was almost the only patron of art, and its restrictions and requirements are expressed by the Council of Nicaea, AD 325: '[the] composition of pictures should not be the invention of the artist but the rules and traditions of the Church'; and by Gregory the Great, pope and saint (590–604): 'Let the churches be filled with paintings that they who do not know their letters may be able to read on the walls what they cannot read in the manuscripts.' In dealing, not with the here but with the hereafter, there was no demand for portraits – until Giotto, in the thirteenth century, introduced into his (religious) frescos groups of spectators, for whom his friends posed.

The earliest known royal portrait in oils, of Henry V (1413–22), was painted *c.* 1518, probably for Henry VIII (1509–47), and during the sixteenth century portraiture, whether imaginary or from life, became increasingly popular. Painters' workshops produced series of portraits of the Kings of England, of which several part-sets survive; one, belonging to the National Portrait Gallery, hangs at Montacute House, Somerset; another is at Burghley House in Lincolnshire, and a third at Hardwick Hall, Derbyshire, where it has been since 1601. See also PICTURE-HANGING and PORTRAIT PAINTERS.

Portrait painters. *Hans Holbein 'the younger'* (1497/8–1543), the greatest portraitist of the northern RENAISSANCE, visited England between 1526 and 1528 and was introduced by Erasmus to Sir Thomas More (1478–1535), for whom he painted the first domestic family group (now lost, but known through copies), and a brilliant portrait of More as Lord Chancellor (1527; now in the Frick Gallery, New York). He returned briefly to Basle, but settled in England in 1532, where he painted many court and other figures; he was one of the great miniaturists, and his influence on painting was huge.

Royal and court patrons, having had their portraits painted by a master such as Holbein, would send to a workshop for a copy whenever they wished to give a portrait of themselves as a present. Two such 'master portraits' by Holbein may be seen in the National Portrait Gallery, London: one of St John Fisher (1469–1535), Bishop of Rochester, the other of Sir Henry Sidney (1529–86).

Hans Eworth (*c.* 1530–after 1573) was the official Court Painter to Mary I (1553–58); pictures attributed to him may be seen at Arbury Hall, Warwickshire and Sudeley Castle, Gloucestershire.

George Gower (d. 1596) was Serjeant-Painter to Queen Elizabeth I (1558–1603); the 'Armada' portrait of Elizabeth (*c.* 1588) at Woburn Abbey, Bedfordshire is attributed to him, as is a portrait at Longleat, Wiltshire, of the Countess of Leicester (*c.* 1585).

Daniel Mytens (*c.* 1590–1647) trained at The Hague but was in London by 1618, painted James I (1603–25), and later became 'picture drawer' to Charles I (1625–49). His work stands out by comparison with the Elizabethan painters, and he dominated court painting until the arrival of Van Dyck. His portraits may be seen at Arundel Castle, West Sussex; the Duke of Buckingham, James I's favourite, at Euston Hall, Suffolk; and Charles I as Prince of Wales at Parham Park, West Sussex.

Sir Anthony Van Dyck (1599–1641), the most important Flemish painter of the seventeenth century after Rubens, first visited London in 1620/1; in 1632 Charles I (1625–49) lured him to settle in England, (except for 1634 and 1635 when he was in Antwerp) with the position of Painter-in-Ordinary, a pension of £200 a year, and a knighthood. The elegance and refinement Van Dyck gave to his sitters and his skill in painting rich materials remained the model for portraitists until John Singer Sargent's (1856–1925) day. He is undoubtedly one of the greatest of portrait painters. A series of more than forty sketches in oils made for his *Iconographia* hangs at Boughton House, Northamptonshire, and his well-known family group of the Earl and Countess of Pembroke is at Wilton House, Wiltshire. There are twenty-six Van Dycks in the Royal Collection.

William Dobson (1610–46), who succeeded Van Dyck as Serjeant-Painter in the early years of the CIVIL WAR (1642–6), was one of the great English painters of the seventeenth century. Some sixty portraits by him are known, all of Royalists. He favoured half-lengths, with hands, and a lack of elegance (as compared with Van Dyck) was compensated for by deep Venetian-inspired colours and a more robust feeling.

Sir Peter Lely (1618–80), born at The Hague, came to England in the 1640s; although he is best known for his portraits of the RESTORATION Court, he also painted Charles I (1625–49) and Oliver Cromwell (1599–1658). His early portraits are Dutch in feeling, soon altered under Van Dyck's influence to a coarser style with brighter colours. He ran an efficient studio, usually painting only the heads and leaving the rest for his pupils and employees to finish. There is a series of *Windsor Beauties* in the Royal Collection at Hampton Court, and the series of thirteen English admirals who fought in the Second Dutch War (1672), in the National Maritime Museum at Greenwich, are thought to be superior to his many 'Court' portraits.

Sir Godfrey Kneller (1646–1723), a German-born portrait painter who studied in Amsterdam under Rembrandt's pupil Bol and afterwards in Italy, before settling in England *c.* 1676. By the mid 1680s he had succeeded Lely as the leading Court portrait painter; he was Principal Painter to William III (1689–1702) and Mary (1689–94) jointly with John Riley (1646–91) until Riley's death. William III knighted him in 1692, and he was the first painter to be made a baronet, by George I in 1715. There are hundreds of signed and dated portraits by Kneller, but the best-known are the forty-two portraits of the KIT-CAT CLUB in the National Portrait Gallery, London, and the *Hampton Court Beauties* in the Royal Collection at Hampton Court.

Sir Joshua Reynolds (1723–92). The son of a Devon clergyman, he trained in London (1740–3) under Thomas Hudson (1701–79), a competent but unimaginative portrait painter, then moved back to Devon. In 1750–2 he was in Italy studying BAROQUE painting, the principles of which he applied to his own work when he returned to London. He was a social and professional success; as first President of the ROYAL ACADEMY OF ARTS (1768) he probably did more to raise the status of painters than anyone else of his time; he was knighted in 1769, and appointed Painter to the King in 1784, a post he occupied until his death. His style echoed the Old Masters and bestowed a 'senatorial dignity' upon his sitters. Unlike Gainsborough he employed many assistants, and because of poor technical procedures his work is often in a bad state of preservation. The often ghostly pale faces of his sitters are a result of his use of carmine (a fugitive red), which has completely faded with time. Examples of his portraits may be seen in many country houses and art galleries throughout Britain.

Thomas Gainsborough (1727–88) was born in Suffolk and in 1740 moved to London, where he studied painting under the Frenchman Hubert Gravelot (1699–1773) who introduced him to the ROCOCO style of Antoine Watteau (1684–1721). Marrying in 1745, he moved to Sudbury in Suffolk, to Bath in 1759, and flourished both as a portrait painter and a painter of landscapes. Influenced by Van Dyck, he was able to make a more natural likeness than Reynolds and was always a fine handler of paint; moreover, and contrary to general eighteenth-century practice, he painted every part of his portraits himself. His technique of diluting his colours with turpentine to the consistency of water-colour paint has resulted in his pictures lasting better than those of his contemporaries. Gainsborough was a founder member of the ROYAL ACADEMY OF ARTS in 1768. He painted some 500 pictures, and his work may be seen in many country houses and in every major art gallery.

Allan Ramsay (1713–84), a Scottish-born painter whose distinctive portraits combine the grace of Gainsborough with the learning of Reynolds. After early training in Edinburgh he worked briefly in London before moving to Rome and Naples (1736–8) where he studied under Francesco Solimena (1657–1747); on his return he established himself in London, but often revisited Italy (1755–7, 1775–8 and 1782–4). Ramsay was a serious rival to Reynolds: Horace Walpole stated that while 'Mr Reynolds . . . is bold and has a kind of tempestuous colouring, yet with dignity and grace the latter [Ramsay] is all delicacy. Mr Reynolds seldom succeeds with women. Mr Ramsay is formed to paint them.' To Reynolds' irritation, Ramsay was appointed Painter-in-Ordinary to George III (1760–1820) in 1760, and produced the Coronation portraits of the king and queen which are in the Royal Collection. He gradually withdrew from painting after 1773 and devoted himself to archaeology and politics. Ramsay's best works are in the National Gallery of Scotland and the National Portrait Gallery in Edinburgh, but may also be seen in country houses, particularly in Scotland.

Sir Thomas Lawrence (1769–1830), born in Bristol and precocious enough to be apprenticed in Oxford as a portrait draughtsman at the age of ten. He never doubted his high ability as a portrait painter. From the time when he exhibited at the ROYAL ACADEMY in 1787 he was hugely successful, being elected ARA in 1791 and RA in 1794. He was appointed Painter to the King on the death of Reynolds in 1792, knighted in 1815, and succeeded to the Presidency of the Royal Academy in 1820. After the defeat of Napoleon in 1815 he was commissioned by the Prince Regent (1811–20) to paint a series of twenty-four full-length portraits of the victorious European leaders, for the Waterloo Chamber at Windsor. His output was small, and only some forty of his paintings survive.

Franz Xaver Winterhalter (1805–73), a German portrait painter and a favourite of Queen Victoria, who first commissioned him in 1841 when he was living in Paris. His female sitters are imbued with a glossy, romantic charm, and there is often a touch of Lawrence in his style. Many of his portraits are in the Royal Collection.

John Singer Sargent (1856–1925), an American born in Florence who studied there and in Paris before settling in London, where he became the most celebrated society painter of his time. His work is instantly recogizable by his slim elongated figures, brilliant flattery and rich brushwork in the tradition of Lawrence, presenting the memorable Edwardian age in a way no other painter could attain. His output was such that examples of his work are to be seen in many country houses; notable is the family group of the Duke of Marlborough and his American Duchess at Blenheim Palace.

Posh. The dictionary definition is 'stylish, smart, first-rate'. The word is widely believed to be an acronym for Port Out, Starboard Home, arising in the days when the Peninsular & Oriental Steam Navigation Co. ran a passenger service from Britain to India (from 1840 until after the Second World War). On the voyage east to India the cabins on the port side were shaded from the blistering tropical sun, and therefore more expensive, as were those on the starboard side on the voyage west and home. The posh were those who could afford the shaded cabins. But 'posh' was also late nineteenth-century slang for a dandy, perhaps derived from the Romany *posh*, half, used in criminal cant to mean 'money'.

Posnet. A small metal pot with three feet and a handle, used for boiling liquids in the fire, and heating *possets*.

Posset. A hot drink popular in Tudor times and earlier, consisting of rich milk curdled with ale or wine, often sugared and spiced, and drunk, or rather eaten, both as a delicacy and as a remedy for colds. See also POSNET.

Post. A word derived from the Latin for 'place', and applied to the series of men with horses stationed at intervals along the highway with the duty of carrying letters forward to the next post stage. Postmasters were usually innkeepers, and post horses could be hired by travellers at so much a mile, with a fee for the guide at each stage. Lady Catherine de Bourgh (in Jane Austen's *Pride and Prejudice*) travelled 'Post'; the advantage of putting fresh horses to the carriage at every stage or two was speed – a steady ten or twelve miles an hour. See also POST-CHAISE and POST OFFICE.

Post Captain. A commissioned officer in command of a vessel of more than twenty guns. The captain who 'takes post' is thus distinguished from captains by courtesy and acting captains of smaller vessels.

Post-chaise. A fast travelling carriage driven by postilions, which could be hired from post-stage to post-stage, or drawn by horses so hired. See also CARRIAGES, HORSE, and POST.

Post Office. The present postal system grew out of the need of government officials to transmit correspondence quickly. The cost of paying *nuncii* to carry letters was a big item of royal expenditure as early as the mid thirteenth century, when the method of transmission was by relays of men and horses maintained at royal expense under the supervision of a government servant. Such bodies as universities and guilds of merchants established their own private posts, and these were commonplace by the middle of the sixteenth century. In 1516 Henry VIII (1509–47) appointed Sir Brian Tuke his Master of Posts, charged with the task of maintaining not only contact between his peripatetic sovereign and London, but also a regular service along the main routes to London. Post-masters were appointed charged with the duty of passing mail to the next POST and with the provision of mounts for royal couriers, and private correspondents were permitted to use the service. In 1635 Charles I (1625–49) appointed Thomas Witherings post-master, with the task of establishing a post travelling night and day between London and Edinburgh, '. . . to go thither and come back in six days'. Oliver Cromwell was well aware of the desirability of government control of the posts and the consequent opportunities for intelligence-gathering and censorship, and it was his Act of 1657 which established a government monopoly, first provided for the office of Post-master General, centralized the operation of the system, and prescribed rates of postage both inland and foreign. During the Commonwealth (1649–60) the postal service was farmed out at an annual rent of £10,000; later the revenues were settled on the Duke of York and his heirs. Attempts were made to break the royal monopoly, notably by William Dockwra (d. 1716) with his establishment in 1683 of a London penny post, but no sooner did he begin to show a profit than the Duke of York asserted his monopoly, and in 1682 Dockwra was condemned to pay damages and his business was incorporated into the general system; he was eventually appointed comptroller. In the days of Withering and Dockwra and for the best part of the subsequent two centuries, the charge for letters outside London varied according to the distance; it was Sir Rowland Hill (1795–1879) who advocated the establishment of a universal penny post throughout Britain, instituted in 1840.

Pounce. A fine powder rubbed into parchment to slightly roughen it and make it receptive to ink; also, before the invention of blotting paper in the eighteenth century, used (as was fine sand) to dry the ink on letters, etc. Pounce pots or boxes often form part of the fittings of silver inkstands or standishes of the eighteenth century. (Pounce-work is a design of small dots or holes in silver or other metal: hence perhaps POUNCET (for 'pounced') BOX, below.)

Pouncet box. Like the POMANDER, this was a container with a perforated lid for holding a sweet-smelling substance, such as a sponge soaked in aromatic oil, used to counteract offensive odours. Fashionable from Tudor times to the mid eighteenth century, they were usually flat and circular, later often mounted on the top of a walking stick. See also PERFUMING PAN.

Pratt, Sir Roger (1620–84). Learned and widely travelled, a country GENTLEMAN and amateur architect, Pratt was the most gifted of the followers of Inigo JONES, and a pioneer of Classical architecture in England. He was one of the three Commissioners appointed by the King to supervise the rebuilding of the City of London after the Great Fire of 1666. His five houses were influential, based on the work of Jones and Palladio (1508–80): Coleshill, Berkshire (c. 1650–62, burnt down in 1952); Kingston Lacy, Dorset (1663–5, altered by Sir Charles Barry in 1845–9); Horseheath, Cambridgeshire (1663–5; demolished in 1777); Clarendon House, Piccadilly, London (1664–7, demolished 1683); and Ryston Hall, Norfolk, for himself (1669–72; altered 1786–8 by Sir John SOANE).

Premonstratensians (Norbertines; White Canons, from the colour of the habit). An order of CANONS REGULAR founded by St Norbert at Prémontré (Aisne), c. 1120, they followed the Augustinian rule (but with supplementary rules of great austerity), and came to England in 1143. At the time of the DISSOLUTION they had in England thirty-one abbeys, usually consisting of twelve canons and an abbot, and two nunneries. The most impressive ruins are at Dryburgh, Borders Region, and Easby, North Yorkshire. Titchfield Abbey in Hampshire is on the site of a Premonstratensian foundation of 1232, and Welbeck Abbey, Nottinghamshire, on one of 1153–4. The canons returned to England in 1872 and have established three foundations. See also AUGUSTINIANS,

BENEDICTINES, CARTHUSIANS, CISTERCIANS, CLUNIACS, DOMINICANS, FRANCISCANS, GILBERTINES and MENDICANT FRIARS.

Pre-Raphaelite Brotherhood. Formed in 1848 by Holman Hunt (1827–1910), Dante Gabriel Rossetti (1828–82), John Millais (1829–96; Bt. 1884), George Stephens (1828–1909) and James Collinson (1825–73) (all painters), together with Rossetti's brother William (1829–1919; a writer and art critic), and Thomas Woolner (1825–92; a sculptor); dedicated to re-creating art as they believed it to have been practised before the time of Raphael (1483–1520). The aims, as noted by William Rosetti, were (1) to express genuine ideas; (2) to study nature attentively (evident from their use of time-consuming natural detail); (3) to exclude self-parading and learning by rote (a hit at current art teaching methods which consisted of copying the Old Masters); and (4) to produce good paintings and sculpture. Hunt was the first to use the initials PRB after his signature, in 1849, and the practice was adopted by the other members. The PRB briefly established its own journal, *The Germ*, which ran for only four issues. By 1854 each of the leaders of the movement had begun to follow his own path, but the PRB had enormous influence on such figures as William Morris (1834–96) and his friend, the painter (Sir) Edward Burne-Jones (1833–98), leading in turn to the creation of the ARTS AND CRAFTS MOVEMENT.

Presbyterianism. The Established Church of Scotland: a system of Protestant Church government by elders (or presbyters), rather than by bishops, as in Episcopalianism. Presbyterians were the original PURITANS. John Knox (*c*. 1513–72), an early zealot for the Lutheran reformation in Scotland, was appointed one of six chaplains to Edward VI (1547–53) but fled to Geneva on the accession of the Catholic Mary Tudor (1553–58); he returned to Scotland in 1558 and was instrumental in establishing Protestantism there (the Confession of Faith signed by members of the Scottish Parliament, 1560). See also ANGLO-CATHOLICISM, EVANGELICALISM and METHODISM.

Preservation (of food). Many things we eat today are the result of very ancient methods of food preservation; the biscuit, for example, derives from the method of preserving bread by baking it two or three times; bacon derives from a method of preserving pork; and soused herring is pickled fish.

Before the invention of refrigeration in the nineteenth century, the preservation of food for periods of dearth (such as winter) was a problem. The earliest process was that of drying in a hot sun – 'Bombay Duck', for example a small dried and salted fish, or the dried beef or 'jerky' of the North American Indians; a logical extension of this was curing in the smoke of a fire, of which ham, bacon and kippers are examples. Salting and pickling in brine followed, and remained for centuries the most widespread method of preserving meat. They are not much used today as they destroy all original flavour – compensated for by the extensive use of herbs in their cooking. Pickling in vinegar (pickled onions, for example) was a comparatively late development which had to wait for the discovery of a yeast-promoted fermentation to produce the vinegar; the Celts on the French Atlantic coast had vinegar in the first century BC.

Sugar, introduced to Europe by the Arabs in the eighth century AD, became recognized as an excellent preservative of fruit, hence today's use of 'preserve' to mean jams and marmalade. No new developments occurred until the sixteenth century, when it was discovered that a limited preservation which did not affect flavour might be achieved by sealing food with a layer of fat (potted meats and pâtés). Bottling of vegetables and fruit, first tried in the 1690s with no great success, was not properly developed until the late eighteenth century. Canning, perfected in the early nineteenth century (probably by a M. Appert of Paris in 1810), was used chiefly for army and navy rations. Tinned mutton was imported from Australia in the late 1860s. The eventual refinement and extension of refrigeration beyond the ICE HOUSE stage, in the late nineteenth century, solved nearly all problems of food preservation.

In a large medieval household, the messy process of brining and salting of meat was done by the butcher; pickling troughs may be seen at Haddon Hall in Derbyshire, but were acquired for the house in the early twentieth century. Pickled and dried fish was bought at big fishing ports like Hull, Bristol and London, and transported overland. Dried fruit ('raisins of the sun', dates and figs) was bought at large ports. In a sizeable household it was the HOUSEKEEPER's job to oversee the preserves made by the STILL ROOM maid, and she was also responsible for bottling fruit from the orchard. See also SALT.

Prie-Dieu. From the French, literally 'pray-God'; originally a small desk with a low platform on which to kneel in prayer and a shelf on which to put devotional books, in use from medieval times. The term was later applied to a chair with a high back incorporating an upholstered arm-cum-book rest, with a low seat for kneeling on. These were very popular in the middle of the nineteenth century, under the influence of the High Church movement, and are often beautifully embroidered, but they are much too low to be *sat* on with any comfort.

Priest-holes. Mention of a priest-hole in a house usually induces a *frisson* of anticipatory imagination, involving secret doors, traps in the floor, and hidden passages. Alas, imagination generally outstrips reality; the few genuine priest-holes date from the hundred years or so when Roman Catholicism was forbidden, from the reign of Elizabeth I

(1558–1603) to the relaxation of the penal laws in the late seventeenth century. Spurious priest-holes are very often no more than voids left in walls and between floors by builders during alterations. However, Harvington Hall, near Kidderminster in Worcestershire, once owned by the Catholic Packington family, has no fewer than seven genuine priest-holes dating from *c*. 1630. Carlton Towers in Humberside, although rebuilt in the 1870s, preserves in the new nurseries a trap-door from an earlier house of 1615 built by the Catholic Stapletons.

The many legendary stories of underground passages arise from the practice of organizing an escape route, called a 'safe passage', or quick way above ground, for an escaping priest. See also UNDERGROUND PASSAGES.

Prime Minister. The head of the government, leader of the political party with the largest number of seats in the House of Commons, chairman of the CABINET, and First Lord of the Treasury. After the Hanoverian Succession in 1714 the king attended cabinet meetings irregularly, so leaving the way open for a cabinet member to take the leadership: Sir Robert Walpole, 1st Earl of Orford (1676–1745), as First Lord of the Treasury in 1741–2, presided over cabinet meetings in the absences of the monarch, and may be reckoned the first Prime Minister. The nineteenth and twentieth centuries saw increasing power devolving on the Prime Minister at the expense of the sovereign. Today, although the office of First Lord of the Treasury continues with the Prime Minister, its functions are carried out by the Chancellor of the EXCHEQUER.

Primogeniture. A term used to signify the preference in inheritance which is given by law, custom or usage to the eldest son and his issue, or in exceptional cases to the line of the eldest daughter.

The origins of primogeniture are thought to be connected with the feudal duty of KNIGHT-SERVICE, but it was never universal throughout Britain, thanks to the survival after the Conquest of earlier customs: the Saxons, for instance, often divided property between children, and in Kent the system of inheritance known as GAVELKIND, which was generally superseded by primogeniture but not finally abolished until the Law of Property Act, 1922 and the Administration of Estates Act, 1925 (gavelkind had the effect of creating many small, uneconomical agricultural holdings).

Primogeniture worked against the interest of younger male children, who would have to make their own way in the world. Some made fortunes by means of the law, others emigrated to the colonies; in the nineteenth century it came to be accepted that the second son went into the army or the navy, and the third into the Church, but even so there seemed to be a plethora of unlanded but well connected bachelors who could not marry because they were unable to support a wife. An essential element in Victorian country-house accommodation was the Bachelor Wing, where these unfortunate guests without prospects were lodged. See also BOROUGH-ENGLISH.

Print rooms. A charming mid eighteenth-century fashion for decorating rooms with cut-out prints pasted to the walls and often surrounded by cut-out decorative paper frames. In 1746 Lady Cardigan paid for pasting up 'Indian pictures' in her dining room. These would have been pieces of Chinese wallpaper showing views, many things Chinese being referred to at this date as 'Indian'. They were not strictly prints, but it is the earliest evidence of the beginning of a vogue. One such room survives at Erddig, Clwyd, made in the 1770s. In 1750 that indefatigable correspondent, Mrs Delany, kept indoors by bad weather, was 'cutting out frames for prints'. Some eighteenth-century print rooms are still extant; at Uppark in West Sussex, a dressing-room survived the fire of 1989; at Blickling Hall, Norfolk the National Trust has 'restored and re-created' the print room; Thomas CHIPPENDALE designed that at Mersham-le-Hatch, Kent; Rokeby Park, County Durham has one with a remarkable selection of borders set on a coral background; Ston Easton Park, Somerset has one on a pale blue background. Later print rooms survive: one at Calke Abbey, Derbyshire has, uniquely, Gilray prints from *c.* 1805; another of *c.* 1815 is at The Vyne, Hampshire. At Stratfield Saye, Hampshire, in the 1820s the Duke of Wellington created eight such rooms, each including a print of himself.

Privy Council. A body of royal advisers which, originating in Norman England as the council of barons and great officers of state, became the chief governing organ under the Tudors and early Stuarts. Meeting regularly wherever the monarch resided, the Council resolved matters of government. One consequence of this practice was that members of the Court circle who might entertain their sovereign built houses large enough to accommodate the Court and the Privy Council. After the Commonwealth (1649–60), the RESTORATION, and the Glorious Revolution of 1688, power was gradually transferred to the CABINET, a committee formed of members of the Privy Council, and today the Cabinet is the policy-making committee of government. The Privy Council now has only formal duties, its membership consisting of those who have held high government, ecclesiastical or judicial office; however, the Lord President of the Council is a Cabinet member. In 1833 a Judicial Committee of the Privy Council was appointed to hear appeals from civil law courts. It advises the monarch what judgment should be given, and is not bound by previous decisions.

Prize money. A prize of war (normally a vessel and its cargo) is property captured at sea by a belligerent; the prize would be taken to port, sold and the proceeds divided under the rules and jurisdiction of the Court of Admiralty. Ordinary seamen in the capturing crew were entitled to share a quarter of the proceeds and lieutenants an eighth, while the captain kept the rest.

Probate. The official proving (or recognition), by a competent court, that a given will is the Last Testament of a deceased person and his, or her, lawful act, together with the grant of authority to the executor(s) to see that its terms are carried out. Until the middle of the nineteenth century, most probate was dealt with by an ecclesiastical court. A testator having all his property within the area of one archdeaconry would normally be granted probate by the Archdeacon's Court; in cases where property was in more than one archdeaconry, but in the same diocese, probate was granted from one of the Bishop's courts (the Commissionary Court or the Consistory Court); and where property was held in more than one diocese, by the Prerogative Court of the archbishop of the province (York or Canterbury). An Act of 1858 transferred jurisdiction over the probate of wills to the Court of Probate (which in its turn, by the Judicature Act of 1873, was transferred to the Probate, Divorce and Admiralty Division of the High Court).

After 1529 no fee was charged for probate where the deceased's estate was less than £5 (a proportionate charge was made for larger estates), though in practice small estates might be left unproved. From 1717 to 1791 the wills of Catholics had to be enrolled in Quarter Sessions or in one of the central courts, and until 1733 the record of Probate was written in Latin.

Prospect towers. See BELVEDERES.

Public schools. Called in the United States 'private schools', a more accurate description because they are largely only available to those able to pay the fees. However, they originated with the endowed grammar schools of the late medieval period, and in that sense were then public. By the mid fourteenth century some three or four hundred grammar schools had been established in England by monasteries, cathedrals, hospitals, guilds and chantries. Clever boys of humble origin learnt Latin and rose through the schools to become clerks and priests of the Church. William of Wyckham founded a grammer school at Winchester in 1382 for the education of secular clergy, which, like Eton (founded by Henry VI in 1440), became a model for later foundations. A certain proportion of the scholars were to be 'sons of noble and powerful persons', and this has been called 'the germ of the public school system', but the children of prosperous yeomen went, too: in 1477 William Paston was sent to Eton from his family's Norfolk manor house.

Shrewsbury was founded in 1552, Rugby in 1567; Harrow School was founded by John Lyon in 1571, a grammar school for boys where Greek was taught in the upper forms; Uppingham and Oakham, both Northamptonshire grammar schools, were also Elizabethan foundations.

By the beginning of the nineteenth century there were three kinds of secondary school: (1) the fashionable public schools, such as Eton, Winchester and Harrow, still few in number, where fees were charged but some local boys attended free; (2) private academies for Dissenting members of the middle classes; and finally (3) the old endowed grammar schools. The grammar schools were of little importance to the Victorians, the academies petered out with increasing religious toleration, and educationists saw in public schools the ideal breeding ground for the leaders required by increasing British growth and colonization. Dr Thomas Arnold (1795–1842), the great educational reformer of the 1830s at Rugby, laid emphasis on religion, chapel services and the monitorial system whereby senior boys were given positions of power to maintain discipline over the younger boys. Arnold was largely successful in suppressing the vices of bullying, drinking, and profligacy of the old 'bear-garden' type of public school, and his principles were quickly adopted by other head masters. 'Organized games' were not a part of the curriculum emphasized by Arnold, but grew up spontaneously. The burgeoningly prosperous middle classes found the reformed public schools a sure pathway into the 'governing classes', and the success of the Victorian public school was assured.

Pugin, Augustus Welby (1812–52). Architect and designer of genius, and a key propagandist of the GOTHIC REVIVAL. An astonishingly swift draughtsman, he designed not only buildings but, above all, their contents: altars, screens, furniture, metalwork. It was this versatility that led to his work with Sir Charles BARRY on the Houses of Parliament from 1836. His fame was established with the publication in 1836 of his book *Contrasts*, a passionate plea for the honesty and integrity of medieval Catholic architecture over the vulgarity of the architecture of his own day. This made him unpopular among Protestant Classicists, and his conversion to Catholicism also cut him off from many commissions. Three of his best buildings in the GOTHIC style are Nottingham (RC) Cathedral (1841–4), Scarisbrick Hall, Lancashire (1837–45), and Alton Towers, Staffordshire (1837–52). St James's (RC), Reading (1837–40) is one of his rare designs in the Romanesque style. In addition to Nottingham, Pugin built two other Roman Catholic cathedrals: St Chad's, Birmingham (1839–41) and St Mary's, Newcastle upon Tyne (1841–44), again in the Gothic style. His publications between 1827 and 1851 (some fifteen books) were immensely influential in promoting his favourite Gothic; he was also a skilful etcher.

Pulhamite. A composite material, manufactured from the 1830s by the Pulhams, a father-and-son team, and consisting of Portland cement mixed with clinker to give a hard rock-like appearance; used for making rock gardens. The Pulhams' first large contract was in 1838, for Hoddesdon Hall in Hertfordshire; between 1847 and 1884, they constructed several massive rockeries at Highnam Court in Gloucestershire. Battersea Park in London, a more generally known site, has Pulhamite rockeries dating from 1866 to 1870; Sandringham in Norfolk has some installed in the 1870s; and Bearwood in Berkshire has an artificial ravine constructed 1879–83. See also ROCK GARDENS.

Punch. An alcoholic drink consisting of spirits, fruit juice, sugar, spices and hot water, the recipe for which originated in India. It became fashionable in Britain in the late seventeenth century and maintained its popularity through the eighteenth century, when a stronger version known as toddy was drunk. Punch clubs were established, and the serving of punch became something of a ritual. The correct equipment was required: a deep punch-bowl of silver or porcelain, long-handled punch-ladles for serving (with handles made from a material such as wood or whalebone that does not conduct heat), strainers, sugar-bowls, sugar-dredgers, nutmeg-graters, and punch-glasses (stemless and cup-shaped, with a handle).

Punch and Judy. The name 'Punch' is a shortened form of the name of a stock character in sixteenth-century Italian *commedia dell'arte*, Pulcinella, an immensely popular character adopted, like several others, by seventeenth-century puppet showmen. Both Samuel Pepys (1633–1703) and John Evelyn (1620–1706) refer to an Italian puppet show at Covent Garden in the 1660s, so it is likely that travelling Italian puppet shows, like so much else Continental, followed in the wake of the RESTORATION of 1660.

The Punch and Judy puppet play is performed in a portable cloth booth, tall and narrow, with a stage opening in the upper part. Glove puppets are manipulated by a single operator concealed in the lower part of the booth. Charles II (1660–85) was fond of Mr Punch and his supporting cast. Punch has a hooked nose, hunched back and squeaky voice (contrived with a swozzle), and carries a stick with which he beats opponents and often his wife Judy. 'Punch and Judy fought for a pie. Punch gave Judy a knock in the eye' was part of the busker's song. Punch is the anarchic hero who overcomes all adversity and outwits all enemies. See also GNOMES, GARDEN.

Punch, or *The London Charivari*. An illustrated weekly periodical, at first strongly Radical in tone. The first issue was published 17 July 1841, under the joint editorship of Mark Lemon (1809–70) and Joseph Coyne (1803–68); Lemon continued as editor until his death. Thackeray, Hood, Leech and Tenniel were early contributors, and George Du Maurier (1834–96) drew for the magazine from 1860 before joining the staff in 1864. The well-known cover featuring Punch and his dog Toby was designed by Richard 'Dickie' Doyle (1824–83) and used from 1844 to 1956 when it was replaced by a different full-colour design which until 1969 retained Punch and Toby. The cartoonist Kenneth Bird ('Fougasse') was the editor from 1949 to 1952; other well-known cartoonists who have been featured include Ronald Searle, Norman Thelwell, and Gerald Scarfe. Recent contributors have included Melvin Bragg, Alan Brien and Hunter Davies. *Punch* ceased publication in 1992 and was relaunched in 1996 by Liberty Publishing Ltd.

Purgatory. From the Latin *purgare*, to cleanse; in Roman Catholic theology, the place where the souls of those departed who have died in a state of grace but without having fully expiated their sins at the moment of death are detained until cleansed of all stain. The doctrine, derived from early Christian tradition, was defined by the Council of Florence (1438–45) which held that souls in Purgatory were helped by the prayers of the faithful on earth. The Protestant belief in justification by faith, rather than by works, led logically to the rejection of the idea of Purgatory (e.g., by Martin Luther, 1483–1546); but the doctrine was reaffirmed by the Council of Trent (1545–63) and is still held by the Roman Catholic Church, though in a modified form. See also CHANTRIES.

Puritans. Puritanism was a development of CALVINISM; the term 'Puritan' was in use as early as 1564, by themselves, to distinguish a party within the Anglican Church who wished to 'purify' it of popish abuses. The movement itself originated in Protestant disappointment at the lack of real reform by Henry VIII (1509–47), once he had achieved his independence of Rome, and flourished anew under Elizabeth I (1559–1603) despite her opposition. The Millenary Petition of 1603, in which 750 clergymen requested James I (1603–25) to reform church liturgy in accordance with the principles of Puritanism set out therein, was rejected by him at the Hampton Court Conference (1604). The Puritan cause met with most success in Parliament between 1640 and 1660 but, discredited, was swept away at the RESTORATION in 1660.

Some ideals lingered, and their adherents became NONCONFORMISTS; those who actually broke with the Church of England became QUAKERS, Independents, BAPTISTS and Brownists.

Purle. A coiled metal thread or cord made of silvered base metal (or 'Venice Gold') wire, used in Tudor needlework. As it was too thick to be drawn through the material, it had to be 'couched down', that is, held in place with small stitches.

Quakers. The Society of Friends. Founded by George Fox (1624–91), a Leicestershire shoemaker, who began preaching in 1647 and soon had a large following in northern England. The Friends' practice of interrupting services, and their abjuration of creeds, formal services and oath-taking, brought them into conflict with other NONCONFORMIST sects as well as with the government of the day. Under the Commonwealth they were tolerated but, like other nonconformists, suffered after the RESTORATION under a series of acts known as the CLARENDON CODE, in particular the Quakers' Act of 1662 which inflicted severe penalties on their unlicensed meetings for worship. The Toleration Act of 1689 permitted Friends to make a declaration instead of an oath and ended their prosecution for non-attendance at Church of England services, but the various civil disabilities under which they and other Dissenters remained were only gradually removed over the following two centuries. Friends were early campaigners for the abolition of SLAVERY, and in the early nineteenth century successfully led agitation for prison reform, particularly under the leadership of Elizabeth Fry (1780–1845). During both World Wars, many Friends were imprisoned as conscientious objectors.

The name Quakers was originally used contemporaneously and derived from the physical manifestations of religious emotion common during the intense religious excitement which characterized the mid seventeenth century. In proportion to the small numbers of members of the Society of Friends, the number of men and women of Quaker profession or origin who occupy or have occupied positions of influence is striking. Fox emphasized the importance of repentance and of personal striving after the truth, but there is no evidence that his first intention was to establish a religious body separate from the Church of England.

Quarter-days. The days which begin each quarter of the year: Lady Day (March 25th), Midsummer (June 24th), Michaelmas (September 29th) and Christmas (December 25th). The days on which rented tenancies customarily begin or end, on which rents fall due, and on which periods of employment begin and end.

Quarter Sessions. From 1368 JUSTICES OF THE PEACE were empowered to hear criminal charges, and from 1388 they were directed to 'keep their sessions in every quarter of the year'. The Criminal Justice Act of 1925 provided that they should be held within the three weeks before or after the four QUARTER DAYS. Quarter Sessions were abolished in 1971. See also PETTY SESSIONS.

Queen Anne's Bounty. A perpetual fund confirmed by statute in 1703, and established in 1704, for 'augmenting the livings of poorer clergy'. The income, a gift from Queen Anne (1702–1714), was derived from FIRST-FRUITS AND TENTHS, which since the REFORMATION had been vested in the Crown. Under the provision of two Acts of 1707 and 1708, some 3,900 poor livings of an annual value of less than £50 were discharged from the liability to pay first-fruits and tenths. Loans for repairs of old and building of new parsonages were paid from 1777. In the early nineteenth century the fund was increased by government grants. In 1925 the Bounty was made responsible for tithes, and in 1948 it was finally merged with other elements of church funds, under the control of the Church Commissioners.

Queen Charlotte's Ball. First held *c.* 1923 by the Dowager Lady Howard de Walden, to raise funds for Queen Charlotte's Hospital. The ball was for DEBUTANTES who were to be presented at Court, and also for girls who were ineligible for presentation at Court because their parents were divorced. The choice of the hospital was deliberate, as Queen Charlotte (wife of George III, 1760–1820) was believed to be the first queen to receive debutantes. Lady Howard de Walden had a very large cake drawn into the ballroom, before which the debutantes curtsied. The ball was given until 1976, even though presentation at Court ceased in 1958, and was revived, as the opening 'event' of the autumn or 'little' SEASON, in 1989. See also COURT, PRESENTATION AT.

Quincunx Garden. A pattern like the design for 'five' on a dice, used mainly in planting trees, less often in laying out a garden, introduced to Britain in the early seventeenth century. There was a quincunx garden at St John's College, Oxford in 1733. The pattern is derived from ancient Egyptian net work, and Xenophon's description of the plantations in King Cyrus's garden at Sardis. No original quincunx gardens survive today, but an idea of how they may have been used may be seen at Westbury Court, Gloucestershire. See also GARDENS.

Quoins. Dressed stonework at the corners of a building, usually laid so that the faces are alternately large and small. The same effect is achieved in a brick building with groups of brickwork.

Railways. The first regular passenger service in Britain, from Manchester to Liverpool, opened on 15 September 1830. Within ten years main-line tracks were being laid to link all parts of the country. Transport had been revolutionized, but the revolution was not always welcome. The Duke of Wellington (1769–1852) felt that modern transport was all right for some, but that it 'encouraged the lower classes to move about'. Some landowners fiercely resisted the invasion of their property by railway surveyors, and running battles were fought. The 5th Duke of Grafton (d. 1863) energetically opposed the laying of the London-to-Birmingham line in Northamptonshire, on the grounds that trains would disrupt his HUNTING – he was Master of the Hunt. In Scotland railways were viewed favourably; successive Dukes of

Buccleuch, for example, saw their advantages, and invested in them to open up the Highlands.

Money was made – and lost – and some large country houses were built with railway money. Thomas Brassey, the most successful of the railway contractors, made a fortune and built Normanhurst in Sussex (now demolished); George Glyn (later Lord Wolverton) financed railways with great success and built a large, gloomy house at Iwerne Minster, Dorset; Thomas Hudson made a huge fortune, and then lost it, but not before he had remodelled Canford Manor, Dorset; and Sir Morton Peto made a railway fortune which crashed in 1866 – after he had built Somerleyton Hall in Suffolk.

The famous headmaster of Rugby School, Dr Arnold, was surprisingly positive about the railways: 'I rejoice to see it and think that feudality is gone for ever. It is a blessing that any one evil is really extinct.' Rugby was near a main line.

One unpredictable result of easy rail travel was the institution of the country-house 'weekend' – though this expression was considered vulgar: 'Saturday to Monday' was the accepted phrase. Houses within two hours or so of London by rail came to life after the London SEASON; in the country, balls were held on a Saturday evening, at which smart London society mixed with local families. Country-house games became popular – CHARADES, TENNIS, CROQUET, above all whist – to avoid or alleviate boredom during these three days in the country.

Rams' heads or **skulls** (*Aegricanes*). An ornament much used in Greek and Roman times, deriving from the custom of hanging the heads of animal sacrifices on temple walls; revived in the RENAISSANCE and much used on furniture in Britain in the late eighteenth century.

Recusants. A name (from the Latin *recutare*, to refuse) given in the sixteenth and seventeenth century to those who persistently refused to attend Church of England services and so became liable to prosecution under the Acts of UNIFORMITY of 1552 and 1559; the fine of a shilling for each non-attendance was increased to £20 a month in 1581. A further act of 1587 provided for the seizure of two-thirds of the offender's property. Although the measures were initially aimed chiefly at Roman CATHOLICS, Jewish and dissenting Protestant recusants were also punished.

Reeve. The manorial farm manager who supervised the VILLEINS' work on the DEMESNE.

Refectory table. From the late Latin *refectorium*, the room in religious houses where meals were taken. A modern term for a long narrow wooden table on two supports, little different in form from the medieval trestle table it was replacing by the fifteenth century. Also known as joined or long tables, these were often used as the high table in the GREAT

HALL, and often very narrow because the lord, his family and important guests sat on one side only and were served across the board.

Reform Acts. Universal suffrage is now taken for granted but until the first Reform Act of 1832 only a few 40 shillings-a-year freeholders had the right to vote. By the Act of 1832 the FRANCHISE was extended to £10 copyholders and to £10 householders in BOROUGHS, and most ROTTEN BOROUGHS were disfranchised. The effect of this extension of the franchise and redistribution of seats was to increase the electorate by 50 per cent. The Reform Acts were strongly resisted by land-owners who rightly feared loss of power. The 4th Duke of Newcastle (1785–1851), who was strongly against the Bill, had his Nottingham Castle burnt down by rioters in 1831.

Scottish and Irish Reform Acts of the same year increased representation from 45 to 53 Scottish seats, and from 100 to 105 Irish seats.

A lowering of the property qualification in the Act of 1867 extended the franchise to two million people; the Act of 1884 gave illiterate agricultural labourers the vote, and brought the total to five million. An Act of 1885 redistributed seats to correct anomalies in the sizes of constituencies.

The Representation of the People Act, 1918 (sometimes called the Fourth Reform Act) conceded full adult male suffrage and, as a result of the SUFFRAGETTE MOVEMENT, extended the vote to women over the age of 30 who were, or whose husbands were, local government electors; this added some two million more male and six million female voters. Universal adult suffrage was not finally achieved until 1928; in 1969 the voting age was lowered to 18 years.

Reformation, The. The religious revolution of the sixteenth century, which divided western Christendom into Catholic and Protestant camps, and its attendant political consequences. As early as the twelfth century powerful heretical sects had arisen, such as the Waldensians of France and Germany, and the Lollards of early fifteenth-century England, but these were mercilessly driven underground. A contributory factor in the ultimate success of the religious revolution was the rise in Europe of centralized, absolute monarchies which resented both the power and the wealth of the papacy.

The Reformation began in Germany with Martin Luther's (1485–1546) *protest* in 1517 against the sale of indulgences; the term 'Protestant' was in general use by 1529. The Lutheran version of Protestantism was essentially north European, adopted by Sweden in 1527 and by Denmark in 1536; the northern and western German states became Protestant in 1555, following the Peace of Augsburg.

The English Reformation was more political in its origins than religious, and sprang from the refusal of Pope Clement VII (1524–34) –

dominated as he was by the Emperor Charles V (1500–58) – to annul the marriage of Henry VIII (1509–47) to Charles's aunt, Catherine of Aragon (1485–1536). In 1529 Parliament passed a series of Acts which destroyed papal authority in England; by the Act of Supremacy (1534) Henry became 'supreme head' of the English church; but despite her repudiation of papal supremacy, England remained liturgically Catholic. However, an influx of religious refugees from the continent spread the teachings of Huldreich Zwingli (1484–1531) and John Calvin (1509–64), and by the time of Henry's death Protestants were in the majority in Parliament.

In Scotland the Reformation was, initially at least, more clearly a religious movement; it gained ground in the 1540s and was strengthened by a visit from the Calvinist John Knox (*c.* 1513–72) in 1555–6. In 1557 the Protestant Lords of the Congregation signed a covenant to advance the Protestant cause, the next year petitioned for a reform of the church, and in 1558 summoned Knox to return from Geneva. Subsidized by French money and soldiers, the Regent, Mary of Guise, outlawed the Reformed Preachers, a move so unpopular that it led to the destruction of church and monastic property by mob violence. The Regent's death the following year (1560) enabled the Estates to abolish papal jurisdiction, adopt the Calvinist 'Confession of Faith', and thus complete the Reformation in Scotland. See also BOOK OF COMMON PRAYER.

Regency style. The general term for the English late Neo-classical style (*c.* 1790–1830), a style characterized by its restrained simplicity and its imitation of ancient Classical architecture, especially Greek. It took its name from George IV (1820–30) – who was Regent for his father George III between 1811 and 1820 – and very much reflected his tastes at the time. One of the principal promoters of the style in Britain was Thomas HOPE, a collector and antiquarian whose designs (in his *Household Furniture and Interior Decoration*, 1807) were widely copied.

Regiment. A term used – but without much consistency either over the centuries or, across the different corps, as to the size of unit – to denote a body of soldiers united, in the British Army, by a common cap badge and uniform. In the Infantry of the Line a regiment may be made up of one or more battalions (the fighting unit, of about 800 men, divided into companies and commanded by a Lieutenant-Colonel). Typically, in the nineteenth century, the first battalion served abroad while the second was stationed at home as a depot to recruit the first with trained soldiers. In the Cavalry the regiment is the fighting unit, of equivalent size to a battalion and divided into squadrons. Confusingly, the units of the ROYAL REGIMENT OF ARTILLERY are also called regiments, as are most of the Lieutenant-Colonels' commands in the supporting arms.

Renaissance Style, The. From the French word for 're-birth', 'Renaissance' in general usage refers to the great release of creative energy that came with the rediscovery of Classical civilization and learning in Italy from about the fourteenth century and spread through the whole of Europe, finally replacing the GOTHIC.

Architecturally, the Renaissance was an Italian movement of the fourteeth and fifteenth century based on a recognition of the artistic values of Classical antiquity. Although the Renaissance proper was over in Italy by 1520, its influence was to reach England later; in Scotland, however, through that country's long alliance with France, it was evident much earlier. Stirling Castle, Central Region (built 1460–88), was perhaps the first true Renaissance building in Britain; Falkland Palace, in Fife (1537–41), was still far ahead of anything being built at that time in England, although in 1511 the Italian Torrigiano (1472–1528) was employed in the design and construction of the tomb of Henry VII (d. 1509) in Westminster Abbey. Cardinal Wolsey employed a group of Italian artists, to whom the screen and stalls at King's College, Cambridge (1533–5) may be attributed, and there are other isolated examples of Renaissance influence. Nonsuch Palace in Surrey, which Henry VIII (1509–47) was building at his death, incorporated many Renaissance features; some panels believed to be from Nonsuch are at Loseley House, Surrey (see GROTESQUES). At this period few in England were able to see for themselves at first hand what was taking place in Europe; more information was found in the pattern books published mainly in the Low Countries and northern Europe, but this was the Renaissance seen through an increasingly obscured filter, its principles only partly understood. At Longleat House in Wiltshire Sir Francis Thynne employed a Frenchman, Allen Maynard, from 1563 until Thynne's death in 1580.

Inigo JONES, one of the first English architects to make a visit to Italy and the Veneto (1613–14), to study Palladio's buildings, was responsible for the first truly Renaissance buildings in England: the Queen's House at Greenwich (begun 1616 but not completed until 1635); the Prince's Lodging at Newmarket (1619–22; now destroyed); and the Banqueting House, London (1619–22). But the time for a general acceptance of Classical building in England had not yet come, and few were inspired to copy these.

Renaissance elements of decoration and proportion may be seen at Raynham Hall in Norfolk where the east façade, for example, has a centre bay of four Ionic columns supporting an entablature. Raynham was begun in 1622 by the remarkable Sir Roger Townshend, who took his mason, William Edge, abroad to gain first-hand knowledge of current trends in architecture; they may also have studied Inigo Jones's work in London and Newmarket. Lees Court in Kent, begun in 1640 to designs by an unknown architect, has giant Classical pilasters reaching through two floors from ground-level to the roof, with Ionic capitals.

Sir Roger PRATT, a follower and acquaintance of Inigo Jones, was responsible for designing Coleshill House, Berkshire (1650–5; burnt down 1952), which was an almost pure expression of Palladian Renaissance architecture using restrained Classical detail round the windows and a segmental pediment over the main entrance. Pratt went on to build Kingston Lacy in Dorset (1663–5); Horseheath Hall, Cambridgeshire (1663–5; demolished 1792); Clarendon House, London (1664–7; demolished 1683); and Ryston Hall, Norfolk (1669–72) for himself. All were in a style similar to that he had used at Coleshill. Inigo Jones having died in 1652, Pratt, as one of only a handful of educated men in England after the RESTORATION with a serious interest in and knowledge of architecture (the others included Hugh May (1621–84) and Christopher WREN), was influential in disseminating the Palladian Renaissance style. The south front of Thorpe Hall, Northamptonshire (1654–6), by Peter Mills (1598–1670), has been compared to designs by Inigo Jones, while Combe Abbey, Warwickshire (1682–8), certainly by William Winde (?–1722), and Belton House, Lincolnshire (1685–8), possibly by him, follow the pattern of Pratt's Clarendon House.

The Restoration of the Monarchy in 1660 opened the door to French influence and the BAROQUE style, used to such great effect by the genius of Sir Christopher Wren.

Repton, Humphry (1752–1818). If 'Capability' BROWN is the first famous country-house landscape gardener who comes to mind, Repton is probably the second. The son of a Collector of Excise, he was intended for a mercantile career, spent some time in Holland, and on his friend William Windham of Felbrigg's appointment as Chief Secretary to the Lord Lieutenant of Ireland, accompanied him there in 1783, as his private secretary. On his return he settled in Essex, lost most of his money in a business speculation, and – so it is said – decided in the small hours one night that he had all the qualifications to become a landscape designer; he wrote to his friends the next morning to announce his new profession, and met with instant success. Lancelot Brown, MP, son of 'Capability' Brown (who had died in 1783), seems to have considered Repton as his father's successor, since he gave him access to his father's papers. Like Brown, Repton was untrained, and interested in architecture – but he had his own ideas. The garden historian Miles Hadfield makes a distinction between Brown's landscape 'pictures' lying *around* the house, and Repton's perception of the house (sometimes improved by John Nash (1752–1835)) as an integral part of a Claudian landscape; both men used the 'belting and clumping' of trees in creating distant views.

Always conscious of the value of publicity, Repton produced for prospective clients his famous 'Red Books', in which coloured illustrations showed the landscape before and after 'improvement', by means of overlays. Repton once calculated that he had produced over a million and a half explanatory sketches during his lifetime, of which about 3,000 were in private hands. Although fewer than one in ten of those for whom he produced designs actually engaged him to carry out his proposals, it is likely that a great many others used his ideas in 'improving' their grounds themselves; and indeed, Repton recalled being shown landscapes and gardens which it was claimed he was responsible for, but with which he had never been involved.

The British 'landscape' as we know it probably owes as much to Repton as to Brown; examples of Repton's many landscapes may be seen at Sheringham Hall, Norfolk; Attingham Park, Shropshire; Ashridge Park, Hertfordshire; Woburn, Bedfordshire; and Cobham Hall in Kent. He had the doubtful distinction of being recommended by Miss Bertram in Jane Austen's *Mansfield Park* (published in 1814). Mr Rushton of Sotherton Court, engaged to Miss Bertram of Mansfield Park, felt his estate to be in need of improvement: 'I must try to do something with it, but I do not know what. I hope I shall have some good friend to help me.' 'Your best friend upon such an occasion,' said Miss Bertram, calmly, 'would be Mr Repton, I imagine.' Miss Austen's own preference for 'the Picturesque' is voiced by Fanny, who deplores the proposed felling of an ancient avenue of limes and other suggested 'improvements'.

Reredos. An ornamental background to an altar. Sometimes the reredos is a painting or a hanging, but more often it takes the form of a carved stone or wooden screen at the back of the altar. A very large and beautiful stone reredos of 1475 may be seen at Winchester Cathedral.

Restoration, The. The Restoration of the Monarchy on the accession of Charles II in 1660, following the CIVIL WAR, the Commonwealth, and Oliver Cromwell's Protectorate.

Retainer. In medieval usage from the fourteenth century, a retainer was one whose services were retained, to be called upon when needed. On the strength of a written contract and payment of a small annual retainer (exactly the modern usage), a man so retained agreed to attend upon, and fight for, whoever retained him. Originally providing something in the nature of a private army, in the fifteenth century retainers might be called on to supplement the usual household whenever a show of power and wealth was required. This is clearly rather different from the 'old retainer', the long-established country-house servant.

Ridge-and-furrow. The visible evidence on the ground of the medieval strip-farming or OPEN FIELD system, often surviving in pasture which has not been ploughed since ENCLOSURE, particularly in parts of Gloucestershire, where the depth between the ridge and the furrow is often more than three feet.

In a medieval village the great open fields designated for ploughing were divided up into long, narrow strips a 'furrow-long' (furlong) or about 40 poles in length and four poles in breadth, constituting roughly an acre of land. There were sometimes half-acre strips, the same length but only two poles' width; standardization of the size of a strip was not fixed by statute until the reign of Edward I. These long strips were divided from each other by 'baulks' of earth, and lie in the shape of an elongated, gently curving, reversed S; the heavy plough team of four or more oxen – not easily manoeuvred – took this line so that the team should be partly turned when it reached the end of a furrow. The 'headland', the strip along the top at right angles to the furrows, was the last to be ploughed. See also BOVATE.

Riot Act. Riot has long been held to be the gravest breach of the peace in English law, short of treason, and is an indictable offence in COMMON LAW. A riot has been legally defined as a tumultuous disturbance of the peace by at least three persons, it being immaterial whether the purpose is lawful or unlawful. The Riot Act of 1715, in the wake of Jacobite disturbances following the accession of the Hanoverian George I, created certain statutory offences of riot and defined some terms: if twelve or more people gather unlawfully to the disturbance of the public peace, it is the duty of a magistrate, sheriff, mayor or other authority to read a proclamation ('the Riot Act') calling on them to disperse; if, after an hour, the rioters have not dispersed, they may be dispersed by force; to continue longer is a felony punishable by death (a sentence since abolished).

Rock gardens. The remains of rock gardens sometimes to be found in forgotten corners of country-house GARDENS bear witness to the Romantic Movement of the late eighteenth century and its veneration of mountains and wild terrain, as extolled by the Romantic poets of the Lake District. The first such garden was perhaps that made by William Beckford (1759–1844) at Fonthill Abbey, Wiltshire in 1795: it was an alpine garden in a quarry, and like the Abbey has long since vanished.

By 1838 Lady Broughton's famous model, at Hoole House in Chester, of the mountains surrounding the valley of Chamonix was complete. It was huge (the outer perimeter was more than 150 yards), but it was a disaster: roots and frosts split the rocks and rain washed away the soil. Rocks of vast size were also used by Joseph Paxton and the 6th Duke of Devonshire in making the Wellington Rock and the Strid at Chatsworth, Derbyshire in the 1830s, and a bizarre rock garden inhabited by GNOMES was made by Sir Thomas Isham at Lamport Hall, Northamptonshire in 1848.

PULHAMITE was often used in the construction of rockeries, but their planting was not always such as would be approved by today's purists. They might be extensively planted with ferns, for which there was something of a mania in the 1850s. Rock gardens never went completely out of fashion, and the publication by William Robinson (1838–1935) of *Alpine Flowers for English Gardens* (1870) gave a fresh impetus. Later still, at Friar Park, Berkshire Sir Frank Crisp used 7,000 tons of rock in a *chef d'ouevre* in which a white-painted Matterhorn towers above alpine valleys: the herd of carved chamois, thankfully, is no more. See also FERNERIES and ROMANTICISM.

Rococo. A development of the BAROQUE style, originating in France in the early decades of the eighteenth century, taking its name from the *rocailles* or artificial grottoes and fantastic rock-work of Versailles, and dominated by curving motifs based on natural forms; 'C' and 'S' scrolls, shells and ribbons, and asymmetry are hallmarks of the style, and oriental motifs are common. Often associated with LOUIS XV (1715–74), rococo was never as popular in Britain, where it reached its peak in the 1740s and 1750s. As a decoration, it could be applied to old rooms to achieve a modish appearance at comparatively little expense. A late and extreme example is the interior of Claydon House, Buckinghamshire, created for the Verney family in the 1760s by Luke Lightfoot, using carved wood rather than the usual plaster, and featuring CHINOISERIE. The name of Thomas CHIPPENDALE is closely associated with furniture in the rococo and chinoiserie styles; and the Chelsea porcelain works, copying France, turned out rococo figures and decorated china. The influence was less marked in painting, but Hogarth (1697–1764) and Gainsborough (1727–1788) were mildly affected by the style. In France, Honoré Fragonard (1732–1806) and François Boucher (1703–70) were the principal Rococo painters. See also BOISERIES.

Roman Catholic. A member or adherent of the Church of Rome. The concept that a nation should follow the religion of its ruler led, once England had become a Protestant country, to a deep suspicion of Roman Catholics. Priests smuggled into England were arrested and tortured, and the 4th Duke of Norfolk (1536–72) was imprisoned for many years, essentially because he was a Roman Catholic. Elizabeth I (1557–1603) was finally persuaded to order the execution of Mary,

Queen of Scots (1542–87) when her ostensible involvement in the Babington Plot to put her on the throne proved her to be a danger, as a rallying point for Roman Catholics. Catholics who refused to attend Church of England services were labelled RECUSANTS and fined; this was the era of the secret PRIEST HOLE. In fact, the majority of Roman Catholics were loyal supporters of the monarchy, their religion notwithstanding. The easy-going Charles II (1660–85) favoured toleration, but the hysteria arising from a fictitious 'Popish' plot to murder Charles and his brother James led to the TEST ACT of 1678 which barred Catholics from holding political office. The blundering attempts of James II (1685–88) to promote Roman Catholicism resulted in his overthrow, the 'Glorious Revolution' of 1688, and the invitation to the Dutch William III (1689–1702) to take the throne in right of his wife Mary (d. 1694), James II's daughter. Thereafter, although the machinations of Roman Catholics were no longer particularly feared, the apparatus of the law remained in place. Growing political pressure resulted in a series of CATHOLIC EMANCIPATION acts between 1780 and 1839.

Romanticism. The 'Romantic Movement' of the late eighteenth/early nineteenth century was a reaction against the severe NEO-CLASSICISM of the eighteenth-century Enlightenment, linked with contemporary revolutionary and nationalist movements; by extension, romanticism also covered 'romantic' ideals and behaviour, especially when deliberately adopted. Freedom from articially-imposed form and a sense of rapport between humanity and Nature were hallmarks of Romanticism. Both neo-classicist and romantic might admire a temple: but the neo-classicist preferred his temple new and whole, while to the romantic an ancient, ruined temple was suggestive of the passage of time, and of human frailty.

The informal, Romantic garden was pioneered by the architect Batty Langley (1696–1751) in his *New Principles of Gardening . . . Wilderness . . . Labyrinths, Etc.* (1728). William KENT (1685–1748) designed a GOTHIC garden building in the Romantic style in 1735 for Queen Caroline (1683–1737). Writers such as Alexander Pope (1688–1744), stimulated by 'the amiable Simplicity of unadorned Nature' in contrast to the formal gardens of Versailles (and especially of its imitators) and drawn to tame wildernesses and 'venerable' ruins, influenced architects to provide striking, sometimes bizarre, effects. It was soon realized that Gothic shapes were even more effective than ruined temples. Sir Francis Dashwood made a 'Romantic' garden at West Wycombe Park, Buckinghamshire as early as 1738; he continued to improve it until his death in 1781, so that the earlier creation is overlaid by later work. In painting, Nicolas Poussin's (1594–1665) and Claude Lorraine's (1600–82) imaginary landscapes littered with ruins were considered romantic in the eighteenth century. The landscapes of the latter inspired Henry Hoare II (1705–85) who, in an excess of romanticism, created Claudian vistas, ruins and temples in his memorable garden at Stourhead, Wiltshire, in 1741 – an example of Nature being made to imitate Art. See also PICTURESQUE.

Rotten Boroughs. Those which, so 'decayed' as to no longer have a real constituency, were completely under the control of a patron or the Crown. As the English philosopher John Locke (1632–1704) said, 'We see the bare name of a town, of which there remains not so much as the ruins, where scarce so much housing as a sheep cote or more inhabitants than a shepherd is to be found, send as many representatives to the Grand Assembly of Lawmakers [Parliament] as a whole county numerous in people and powerful in riches.' He doubtless had in mind such famous rotten boroughs as Old Sarum with 7 voters and Dunwich with 14, which each returned two MPs – although Old Sarum had become depopulated in the thirteenth century when Salisbury grew up around the new cathedral, and even in 1714 Dunwich was half under the sea. Wealthy and populous cities like Birmingham and Manchester, which had come into existence since 1600, returned no representatives to Parliament, while the counties, like Old Sarum and Dunwich, also returned two members each – and there were 17,000 voters in Yorkshire. But it was particularly BOROUGH representation which William Pitt the Elder (1708–78) described as 'the rotten part of the Constitution'.

Royal Academy of Arts. The Academy was founded on January 2nd 1768, under the patronage of George III (1760–1820) and the Presidency of Sir Joshua Reynolds (1723–92), 'for the purpose of cultivating and improving the arts of painting, sculpture and architecture'. There were, and are, forty Academicians, artists by profession, who each present an approved sample of work on admission – the diploma work – to form the basis of a permanent collection. But the first act of the Academy was to establish schools of instruction, for which professors of painting, architecture, perspective, geometry and anatomy were provided. In addition to the forty academicians there are thirty (increased in 1876 from twenty) Associate members.

The schools of the Royal Academy were opened in Pall Mall, and the first exhibition was held there on 26 April 1768; in 1781 the Academy transferred to the old Somerset Palace; in 1837 it moved to the National Gallery; and to Burlington House in Piccadilly in 1867.

The Summer Exhibition, of work by living artists, held annually at the Royal Academy from the first Monday in May to the first Monday in August, has long been one of the essential social events of the London summer SEASON, caricatured as such by Rowlandson (1756–1827).

There is also an annual Winter Exhibition, of works by Old Masters and deceased British artists. The initials RA after an artist's name indicate that he is a Royal Academician, ARA that he is an Associate, and PRA that he is President of the Academy.

Royal Air Force. The youngest of the three services, the RAF was formed, under the Air Force (Constitution) Act, on 1 April 1918 as a merger between the Royal Naval Air Service and the army's Royal Flying Corps.

Royal Company of Archers. The Sovereign's bodyguard in Scotland, supposedly founded in 1509 as the personal bodyguard of James IV of Scotland, but constituted in its present form in 1676 by an act of the Privy Council of Scotland. Several of the leading insurgents in the JACOBITE rebellion of 1745 were members, but the company did not suffer from this in any way.

When George IV (1820–30) visited Scotland in 1822 it was thought appropriate, especially in light of the tradition of an archer bodyguard, that the Company should act as his bodyguard during his stay, performing the duties usually assigned to the GENTLEMEN-AT-ARMS; the King authorized the addition to their former name that of 'The King's Body Guard for Scotland' and presented the Captain-General with a gold stick, thus constituting the Company part of the Royal Household. Membership of the Company totals about 400 and is considered an honour; on ceremonial occasions the Company parades in green jackets, carrying yew bows, and arrows. See also YEOMEN OF THE GUARD.

Royal Marines. The early history of the Marines ('sea soldiers') is one of false starts. The first marines were 1,200 men of the Duke of York and Albany's Maritime Regiment of Foot; raised in 1664, they were disbanded by William III (1689–1702) after the Glorious Revolution of 1688. However, he recreated them in 1690 for the war with France, when the 1st and 2nd Marine Regiments were formed, and then disbanded when peace was signed. Six regiments of Marines were raised in 1702 for the War of the Spanish Succession, of which three were incorporated into line regiments and three disbanded in 1713. Ten regiments were raised for the War of the Austrian Succession (1739–40), to be disbanded in their turn at the end of 1748 and their officers put on half-pay. It was only in 1755, in the run-up to the Seven Years' War, that a corps of Marines, formed of 50 companies each 100 strong, was permanently established as a fighting force, for the first time under the complete financial and administrative control of the Admiralty. The Marines expanded during the Napoleonic Wars and were awarded their 'Royal' title in 1802; they wore the red infantry uniform. In 1804 three companies of the Royal Marine Artillery were formed, known as the 'Blue Marines' from their blue uniform. In 1923 the

Royal Marine Artillery and the Royal Marine Light Infantry were amalgamated to become the Royal Marines. The marines are subject to army discipline when ashore and naval when afloat.

Royal Marriages Act, 1772. An Act, still in force today, stipulating conditions for marriages of the descendants of George II. It was brought in after two brothers of George III (1760–1820), the dukes of Cumberland and Gloucester, married commoners without the king's approval. By its terms, no member of the royal family under 25 can marry without the sovereign's consent; over 25, a marriage disapproved of by the sovereign may be solemnized if 12 months' notice in writing is given to the PRIVY COUNCIL, unless both Houses of Parliament disapprove.

Royal Navy. After the Conquest, the Cinque Ports (Dover, Hastings, Hythe, Romney and Sandwich) provided men and ships for a short period each year for naval defence, in lieu of the customary feudal levy; however, the main part of the navy was formed of the king's own ships under his direct command. Edward I (1272–1307) seems to have had it in mind to make the Cinque Ports ships the basis of a navy for use in his wars in France (from 1293). In March 1297 William Leyburn was described as 'admiral of the sea of the King of England' – probably the first recorded use of the word 'admiral' in England. It may be that Edward had brought it back from the CRUSADES: it is from the Moorish *Amir-el-ma*, meaning 'commander of the water'. Already by this date the Cinque Ports harbours were silting up, and when Edward III needed transport to take his troops to France in 1338, he had to conscript large numbers of merchant and fishing vessels.

The High Court of Admiralty was the Court of the deputy or Lieutenant of the Admiralty. In the *Black Book of the Admiralty* the High Court of Admiralty is said to date from the reign of Edward I, but it is generally considered to have been established as a Civil Court by Edward III (1327–77) in 1360, although the powers of admirals in matters of discipline, fines etc. undoubtedly pre-date this. In its earliest days there were separate admirals of the north, south and west, having each their own deputies and courts, but these were merged into one high court early in the fifteenth century.

Between the latter part of the thirteenth century and the early years of the sixteenth, the necessity for a navy which could give England command of the Channel and transport her knights, men-at-arms and archers to France varied according to the relationship between England, her French possessions and France at any given time. Because the navy was seen as providing transport for men (and correspondence), the sailors who navigated the ships were of secondary importance. By Henry VIII's time this attitude had changed, mainly due to the confidence in ships inspired by successful voyages of discovery, such as those of the Cabots at the end of the fifteenth century, and the need to have a majority on board capable of navigating the vessels. Consequently the military complement on naval vessels declined and the number of seamen increased. This, allied to the ability to build large ships, led to the creation of the first truly Royal Navy. James I (1603–25) further expanded the concept of a Royal Navy, and the post of Lord High Admiral was given to a commission, rather than being vested in one individual. There was further expansion under Charles I (1625–49), and the first 'Ship Money' (an ancient device, in fact, stemming from those levies on the Cinque Ports) was imposed to provide funds for this increase. During the Commonwealth (1649–60) the forty ships of the navy were taken over by the Parliamentarians, and rivalry and war with the Dutch led to its expansion to three times this size by 1660. Under Charles II (1660–85) proper naval training was instituted and the service was opened to volunteer seamen rather than being manned by the press gangs' recruits. Under the Duke of York (later James II (1685–1688)), Lord High Admiral until 1673, the fleet grew to 170 ships, manned by 42,000 men. Samuel Pepys (1633–1703), Secretary to the Navy, recorded a great deal of the period in his diaries. After the Glorious Revolution of 1688 control of the navy passed into the hands of Parliament. Thereafter there were few changes until the nineteenth century. The first steam warship was launched in 1814 and, due to the greater penetrative power of missiles, armour-plating was used after 1854. The first iron-clad vessel, HMS *Warrior*, was launched in 1860; later in the decade, the first turret guns, capable of firing in all directions, were fitted, leading to changes in naval strategy: manoeuvring to fire broadsides was no longer necessary. From 1880 a programme of naval expansion was instituted based on the size of the navies of other European nations. In 1906 HMS *Dreadnought* was launched; with ten 12-inch guns, she was better armed and faster than any other warship hitherto, thus provoking other navies to follow in 'the Dreadnought Race', a contributory cause of the First World War. From this came the super-Dreadnoughts carrying ten 16-inch guns, at a cost of eight million pounds; which evolved into the even more costly battleships. The purpose of the navy was essentially that of guarding the trade routes of the Empire. After the Second World War, and the demise of the Empire, the size of the navy was reduced and its principal role became one of deterrence by means of nuclear-rocket-firing submarines.

Royal Regiment of Artillery. In 1716 the Board of Ordnance created the Royal Regiment of Artillery, and in 1812 it became an independent Corps. The Board was abolished in 1855, when the Regiment came under the direct control of the War Office. Unlike other corps, this Regiment does not carry its colours as a flag or standard: 'Our guns are our colours'.

Royal Visits. For centuries it was the custom for the sovereign and his entourage to move about from place to place, and the burdensomely expensive visits of Elizabeth I (1558–1603) to her subjects are well documented. Sir Nicholas Bacon (1509–79) added a new wing to his house at Gorhambury (Hertfordshire) for one of her visits, and her godson Sir Christopher Hatton (1540–91) ruined himself building additions to his house at Holdenby (Northamptonshire) in anticipation of a visit which never took place.

Apart from providing the necessary accommodation, how was the host to behave? How was he to receive and amuse the monarch? In 1729 George II's Queen Caroline and all the royal family visited the Duke of Newcastle at Claremont House, Surrey. The major event was a dinner, after which they drank '. . . a bumper rack of punch to the Queen's health . . . her Majesty sent word that she was going to walk in the garden . . . We walked till candle-light, being entertained by very fine French horns . . .'. On returning to the great hall '. . . Mr Schutz played there at quadrille, in the next room the Prince had the fiddlers and danced . . . country dances . . . The Queen came from her cards to see that sight . . .' The visit, though in no way remarkable, seems to have been a success.

Detailed advice survives, sent to the Howards at Audley End, Essex, when a visit to them by George III (1760–1820) and Queen Charlotte in 1786 was being planned. The STATE APARTMENTS having been extravagantly refurbished for the event, instructions were given as to how the Howards were to receive their royal guests. 'Your Lordship and Lady Howard are to receive their Majesties at the door yourself either in full dressed Coat (with your sword) or your uniform, Lady Howard in a sack, without a Hat. Your Lds will have a glove on to hand the Queen into the Drawing Room – the carpet to be laid for their Majesties to step out of the coach on.

'Your Ldp & Lady Howard know that during the whole time of their Majesties stay with you, you are their Lord and Lady of the bedchamber and supersede any Lord or Lady they may carry with them.

'Your Lds & Lady Howard are supposed to wait on the K & Queen at Table, therefore no servants can be in the Room when they go to Dinner etc – but their Majesties will probably order you to call them in – no servant in Livery can ever wait at any time, or even on any occasion appear before them and the King's Pages never wait.

'Your Lords and Ladys will carve for their Majesties or the dish they chuse will be sent off the Table & carved by a servant, as it may happen.

They are very indifferent as to what they eat. The dinner is to be served in the usual style of great entertainments – Two courses & a dessert are sufficient.' The visit was never made.

Queen Victoria stayed with the Duke of Buckingham at Stowe, Buckinghamshire in 1845, and '. . . would have been far better pleased had her bedroom and dressing room been more simply furnished.' Entertaining the sovereign was never easy. See also DESSERT, 'SACK' GOWNS and SERVANTS.

Ruff. A fashion of the mid sixteenth to early seventeenth century, the ruff began in Spain as a ruffled or frilled collar to a shirt or chemise, worn by both sexes, and attached to the garment. As the fashion spread it became exaggerated – the ruffles became ruffs, separate from the garment, made of long strips of linen, lawn or cambric, pleated and set into a neckband, usually completely encircling the neck, and tied in front with fine tassled cords called band-strings. Ruffs became ever larger after the introduction of starch about 1565, requiring frequent and expert laundering and 'goffering', to set the pleats (from the French *gaufre*, a waffle or honeycomb). When dry they were kept from harm in a band-box. By the 1580s the ruff might extend nine inches either side of the neck and face, consist of 18 yards of material, and require a support behind, of wire, or of pasteboard covered with white, pleated cotton. The edge of the ruff might be wired, and lace edging, or an entire ruff of lace, was fashionable in England. In the late sixteenth/early seventeenth centuries women often wore an open ruff extending either side of a low neckline and supported behind to frame the face. A smaller ruff circled the throat inside the main ruff. From the 1640s, when the PURITANS condemned all vanity, including starch, ruffs then collapsed about the shoulders as the 'rabat', the falling ruff or falling band, the forerunner of the CRAVAT.

Sack. A dry white wine from southern Spain and the Canaries, hardly known before Henry VII's (1509–47) reign. The Elizabethans required it to be sweetened with sugar: 'If sacke and sugar be a fault, God helpe the wicked!' (Shakespeare, Henry IV Pt 1). By Samuel Pepys's time the Spanish trade was centred on Jerez, exporting to Bristol, where Pepys enjoyed the variety of 'Sherry-sack' known as 'Bristoll milke'. A sweeter variety was imported from the Canary Islands. See also CLARET, HOCK, PORT and WINE.

'Sack' or sacque gowns. Originally a rather shapeless morning gown or over-gown, somewhat tent-like, worn over another or for relaxation. In March of 1669 Samuel Pepys observes that 'my wife this day put on first her French gown, called a *sac*'. These gowns were pleated to the neck at the back, low and wide and laced across in front. Sir Godfrey Kneller (1646–1723) often portrayed his female sitters in 'sacks', believing them to be a timeless fashion – and indeed, having become high fashion in the 1720s–30s, they lingered on in various guises until about 1780. Note the reference under ROYAL VISITS to the 'sack' Lady Howard was instructed to wear to receive George III and Queen Charlotte at Audley End in 1786; Court Dress has often languished behind the current mode, but it may be that by this time a 'sack' was no more than a sort of silk train attached at the shoulders, worn on such august occasions.

Salerno, School of. Hippocratic and Galenic medical traditions survived at the remarkable school of MEDICINE which flourished at Salerno, south-east of Naples in Italy, a centre of international repute by AD 1000. At its most distinguished in the mid twelfth century, its decline dates from 1224 when the Emperor Frederick II (1212–50) founded a university at Naples. The most famous medical treatise of the Salerno School, *Regimen Sanitatis Salerni*, addressed to an apocryphal 'King of England', reached England *c.* 1250. Its rules for healthy living through diet and an appreciation of the 'four humours' were influential throughout Europe.

Saloon. Or *salon*; borrowed from the French with other fashions following the RESTORATION. The Saloon was the principal reception room, usually immediately off the entrance hall at the back of the house, and the centre-piece of a suite of reception rooms. It served the same purpose as the old GREAT CHAMBER, and like it was used as a room of assembly as well as a grand eating room. When it was needed for the latter use, its occupants would withdraw into the next room, the 'withdrawing' room. There was probably, off the saloon, a suite of apartments including the principal bedchamber, sometimes called the STATE APARTMENTS. Houses belonging to members of the Court circle might also include an additional, very grand saloon on the first floor, like the one at Burley-on-the-Hill, Rutland, built by the Earl of Nottingham and Winchilsea in 1698, access to which is by an impressive staircase decorated by Gerard Lanscroon (d. 1737); such a room was used for the entertainment of royalty and visitors of higher rank than the host. But as the eighteenth century progressed fashion shifted again; a DINING-ROOM specifically fitted for use on formal or state occasions came to take over the dining function of the saloon, which was subsequently relegated to a lesser position on the reception-room circuit.

Salt. In the Roman army an allowance of salt was made to officers and men: in Imperial times this *salarium* was converted into an allowance of money for the purchase of salt – hence salary. Salt was a commodity always of importance to our ancestors, from its use in preserving meat and fish through the winter. The brine springs of Worcester and Cheshire have yielded salt at least since Roman times, as have the rock-salt mines of Droitwich, and salt was also produced on the coast by evaporating sea-water in heated pans. By the fifteenth century the demand for salt exceeded its production in Britain, and 'Bay Salt' was imported from France. This was produced, by natural evaporation, first in the Bay of Bourgneuf, eventually along the whole Atlantic coast of France, still under the name 'Bay Salt'. The sharp, sweet taste of coarse-grained 'Bay Salt' was preferred for PRESERVING, the fine white salt from mineral springs and mines for the table. Both came to the house in either bricks or sacks.

Salt, to sit above or **below the.** An indicator of social rank. The ancient importance of salt was emphasized in medieval times by its provision at the eating-table in a rich and elaborate container – the salt, or salt-cellar – often in silver or silver gilt. The salt would be placed on the high table to the right of the host, whose most important guests also sat to his right; those to his left and below, in the body of the hall, were 'below the salt'. Later, when the high table was abandoned, the salt was placed in the middle of the table with the host and his more honoured guests at the upper end (above the salt) and less distinguished guests 'below the salt' at the lower end. Other diners had to help themselves to salt from 'little' salts placed at the ends of the high table and on the tables in the body of the hall.

Some dazzling late medieval salts survive, especially in Oxford colleges: the silver-gilt New College Monkey Salt, made c. 1500, is a chimpanzee sitting on a cushion while on its head is a crystal disc supporting the salt bowl; the Corpus Christi silver-gilt salt given by Bishop Fox in 1517 displays the badge of its donor, animals, scenes of the Virgin Enthroned, and an angel holding a scroll. Perhaps the most elaborate is one in the Royal Collection (since 1550); its silver-gilt hexagonal base is set with shell cameos of Roman emperors, supporting a crystal column that once contained a table clock.

Salvin, Anthony (1799–1881). A prolific and long-lived architect known for his country houses in the Tudor and Jacobean ('Jacobethan') styles. A pupil of Nash, he had designed three country houses by his early thirties: Mamhead, Devon (1828–38) in the Tudor style; Moreby Hall, Yorkshire (1828–32), also Tudor; and above all Harlaxton Manor, Lincolnshire (1831–8), in an Elizabethan BAROQUE style. By the end of his life he had built, rebuilt, altered or extended some 76 houses; he also worked on the restoration of castles, for example, the Tower of London, Windsor Castle and Norwich Castle.

Sanctuary. From Anglo-Saxon times all churches provided refuge for safeguard of their life to felons. Under COMMON LAW, the felon in sanctuary must go before the CORONER within forty days, confess the felony, and take an oath of Abjuration of the Realm, by which he undertook to leave the country. In 1486 second offenders, and those guilty of treason, were barred from seeking sanctuary. Most rights of sanctuary were abolished at the REFORMATION under Henry VIII (1509–47), but he established seven cities as 'peculiar' (by grant of Royal Charter) sanctuaries – Derby, Lancaster, Manchester, Northampton, Norwich, Wells and York – to give sanctuary to debtors. Right of Sanctuary was abolished for criminal offences in 1623, and for civil wrongdoers by Acts of 1697 and 1723.

Saye, say. A fine-textured cloth resembling serge; made in the sixteenth century partly of silk, later all of wool.

Scagliola. An imitation marble or PIETRA DURA made from marble chips, colouring and cement or plaster, especially popular in the seventeenth and eighteenth centuries. The earliest English example, made in the 1670s, may be an overmantel in the Queen's Closet, Ham House, Greater London.

Scarlet cloth. The most expensive form of Tudor woollen cloth, often encountered in inventories; a speciality of the mills in the Stroud Valley in Gloucestershire.

Sconces. Wall-mounted candle-holders, usually with two or more branches, commonly made in brass and sometimes with sheet silver or a mirror behind to reflect the light. In the last half of the seventeenth century silver sconces were fashionable.

Scott, Sir George Gilbert (1811–78). The foremost practitioner and spokesman for the mid Victorian GOTHIC REVIVAL. Scott became a casualty in the Battle of the Styles (Gothic *v.* Classical) when Lord Palmerston rejected his Gothic design for the new Home Office and Foreign Office in Whitehall (1868–73) and obliged him to revert to a more Classical, Italianate style. Scott was the leading architect for Victorian churches, and was often criticized for his over-enthusiastic church restorations. Scott's St Mary's Episcopal Church, Edinburgh, a late work consecrated in 1879, is his most successful recreation of thirteenth-century Gothic. Scott is perhaps best known for his façade at St Pancras Station (1866–76), and for the High Victorian extravaganza of the Albert Memorial (1863–75), both in London.

Scullery. From the Anglo-French *squillery*, in turn from the Old French *escuelier*, a maker or seller of dishes; that part of the service area of a household where dishes, pots and pans were washed and cleaned in medieval times by a scullion, later by a scullery maid. The *Shorter Oxford English Dictionary* makes no connection between 'scullion' ('of unkn. origin') and 'scullery' – but see the quote from Lady Stapleton under SERVANT PROBLEM.

Sculpture galleries. A well-known portrait of Thomas Howard, 14th Earl of Arundel (1585–1646), painted *c.* 1618 by Daniel Mytens (*c.*

1590–1642) shows the earl sitting before his sculpture gallery filled with Roman statuary at Arundel House, London; there was more in the garden. This is the earliest illustration of such a gallery; the collection and display of sculpture really only became a fashion in country houses in the eighteenth century, arising from the GRAND TOUR.

Sculptures dominate a room more than paintings, and require to be viewed from all angles, a problem recognized by the 3rd Earl of Burlington (1695–1753) and addressed in the VILLA at Chiswick which he designed c. 1724, as an adjunct to his existing house, to display the busts and figures he had collected on his recent Grand Tour. Other collectors followed suit, and galleries which survive today may be seen at Holkham, Norfolk (built 1734); Newby, North Yorkshire (1768); Petworth, Sussex (1780s); Woburn, Bedfordshire (1786); and Chatsworth, Derbyshire (1825). Not all galleries followed the pattern of the LONG GALLERY; indeed, the Palladian taste was often for something based on the Tribuna in the Uffizi in Florence, or the Pantheon – for example, Adam's Rotunda at Newby, North Yorkshire (1768), and the room known as The Pantheon at Ince Blundell Hall, Lancashire (1802).

The plaster fig leaf, lending modesty to antique nudes, is not the Victorian invention we might suppose, but first appeared around the mid eighteenth century. Statues of nudes in the garden were one thing; but having them in the house was another, especially when women began to take an interest in antique art.

Season, The London. In eighteenth-century London 'The Season' was the period from early summer onwards, when mothers brought their daughters to London and opened their Town houses, engaging in a round of balls and social events as a means of launching them in society and finding them eligible husbands. It came into particular prominence at the end of the nineteenth century when the Prince of Wales enlivened society. Today, the private and semi-public parties and balls of the Season revolve around public events, usually under royal patronage, many of them sporting. The Season begins with The Summer Exhibition at the ROYAL ACADEMY, and the Chelsea Flower Show at the end of May, followed by the Derby in early June; Wimbledon in mid June; the Eton versus Harrow cricket match at Lord's at the end of June; Henley at the beginning of July; Goodwood at the end of July; and ends with sailing during Cowes Week at the beginning of August. Thereafter, everyone disperses to the moors for the opening of the GROUSE-shooting season on 12 August. See also 'COMING OUT'; COURT, PRESENTATION AT; DEBUTANTES and QUEEN CHARLOTTE'S BALL.

Seaweed marquetry. A furniture veneer, fashionable in Britain in the late seventeenth and early eighteenth centuries, in which light wood (usually holly or box) was set against dark (walnut) in symmetrical scrolls or arabesques. Parquetry is similar, but features a geometrical pattern. Floral marquetry used a variety of woods to create scrolls, vines, flowers, etc. See also BOULLE.

Sedan chair. An enclosed chair with a hinged door to the front, windows to the sides and a hinged roof so that an occupant could stand up, carried on horizontal poles by two chairmen. The name may come from the French city of Sedan, where such conveyances are said to have been first used. They were introduced to London from Naples in 1634 but did not become widely fashionable until the eighteenth century, at a time of muddy city streets when a sedan chair had the merit of keeping the occupant dry and clean. The chairmen were usually Irish, and fights between them were notorious. Sedan chairs are sometimes exhibited in the halls of historic country houses, which seems inappropriate for a town conveyance. There is a nice example in the Pump Room in Bath.

Sedilia. Seats for the clergy, in the south wall of the chancel. They generally run in threes, for priest, deacon and subdeacon, and are made of often highly decorated stonework.

Sensibility. A fashionable literary cult of the mid eighteenth century, in which the virtuous characters were possessed of a sympathetic heart and tender feelings, together with a strict code of morality and honour. Samuel Richardson's (1689–1761) *Pamela* (1740; generally considered to be the first modern English novel) and *Clarissa* (1747 and 1748, in five volumes: the longest novel in the English language), both widely read, may be said to have initiated the 'novel of Sensibility'. The heroine of each displays great sensibility and retains her virtue in the face of severe trials and temptations. Jane Austen's *Sense and Sensibility* (published in 1811, but written in 1797, by which time the cult was passing) satirises the excesses of an outmoded notion.

Serfdom. The legal status of a feudal peasant. He was bound to the manor on which he worked and was not free to leave. He was compelled to provide labour on his lord's DEMESNE in return for a rent-free small-holding. Serfdom features throughout the Domesday Book but had died out by the fourteenth century.

Servant problem. Not an affliction many people suffer from today, but until the Second World War the finding and keeping of reliable SERVANTS could be a very pressing problem. In 1730 Lady Stapleton wrote to an acquaintance from Grey's Court, Oxfordshire: 'I have a favour to beg of you to get me a good cook maid for I am at a loss for one, my cook being to go from me. I wo'd not have a young servant. She must boil and roast well, wash the dishes (for I keep no scullion) clean the kitchens and larder [see SCULLERY]. Salt all the meat but the bacon (which the diary maid do's) wash the kitchen linen and help scour the pewter, and take care she be of quiet temper if possible.

'PS. I give but £8 a year wages.'

The Countess of Kildare, of Carton in Ireland, needing a HOUSE-KEEPER, wrote to her husband from London in 1761: 'This morning I had a long conversation with Mrs Clarke, our new housekeeper. She seems a sensible, notable, genteel sort of woman; not fine, but just the manner to create a little respect from under-servants, and enters perfectly into our schemes. We are to give her £25 the first year and £30 if we approve of her afterwards.' A year later the good Mrs Clarke was grumbling about the difficulty of getting the maids up in the mornings.

Kenneth Rose's Life of Lord Curzon (1859–1925) reports a revealing comment. After serving Lord Curzon for many years a BUTLER gave in his notice, and was asked to recommend a successor. 'There are', he replied, 'only two people who could take my place. One is Jesus Christ. I am the other.' See also SERVANTS and SERVANTS' HALL.

Servants. The conception that service is degrading is an attitude surviving from the nineteenth century. In medieval times, to be in the service of a lord was an honour which also ensured one's protection as part of his household. Under the STEWARD's management gentlemen servants such as the Usher of the Hall, the Usher of the Chamber, or the Clerk of the Kitchen were 'officers' over the yeoman servants, and all were considered part of the lord's family. Women were of minor importance in the hierarchy, as ladies' maids, nursery maids, or in the LAUNDRY. The more powerful the head of the household, the more servants he had: in 1420 the Earl of Warwick had 125, the Duke of Norfolk 144 in 1526. In his *A Description of England* (1577), William Harrison fulminated against 'Swarms of idle serving men' – he had a healthy PURITAN bias against idleness, and tended to find it everywhere, but he may have had a point. Overstaffing as an expression of power – but containing also an element of *noblesse oblige* – continued through Tudor times, until the early seventeenth century when James I (1603–25) put many of his household servants on board wages, or sacked them. It was only a matter of time before his courtiers followed his example.

Through all these centuries servants, whether gentlemen or yeomen, were in service because it was to their advantage. By the RESTORATION, the conception of the gentleman servant was in decline, although Pepys's *Diary* indicates that servants still lived more as members of the family than was to become the case in succeeding centuries. There was, however, a general reduction in the number of servants employed, due to rising wages.

The real break in tradition, however, came with the Industrial Revolution. Alternate booms and slumps caused extreme poverty in cities, driving people into service at very low wages and with employers who had no tradition of looking after servants, thus leading to exploitation. So began an aversion to service in a household. Women were taken on to do some jobs which had formerly been a male preserve, because they were paid less. Female servants were organized under the HOUSEKEEPER, the men under the steward or BUTLER. A nineteenth-century tax on male servants further increased the number of females in service.

By the mid nineteenth century the household of a wealthy earl or duke might number around fifty, correspondingly fewer lower down the social scale. Although the First World War generally saw a considerable reduction in households, some wealthy families continued to maintain a full staff. Harold Nicolson, visiting Cliveden in 1936, wrote to his wife Vita Sackville-West: 'Oh my sweet, how glad I am that we are not so rich. I simply do not want a house like this where nothing is really yours, but belongs to servants and gardeners, there is a ghastly unreality about it all.' The Second World War virtually saw the end of large households. See also RETAINERS, SERVANT PROBLEM, SERVANTS' HALL, SHOVEL BOARDS and VAILS.

Servants' Hall. With the demise of the GREAT HALL in the early seventeenth century, the Servants' Hall 'below stairs' came into existence, its hierarchy reflecting social customs long since discarded above-stairs. The customs of the old Great Hall were mirrored, and who sat where at first remained unchanged: as gentleman SERVANTS, the STEWARD and the Clerk of the Kitchen ate at a high table, the rest at long tables, and the scullery maids ate in the kitchen. After the RESTORATION, when the conception of the gentleman servant no longer existed, wages had risen, staffs were smaller and more women were employed under the HOUSEKEEPER, the Servants' Hall became more as we picture it today. By 1700 a peer could live quite comfortably with forty servants – half the number of a hundred years earlier. The BUTLER gradually became all-powerful, and he and the housekeeper ruled the Servants' Hall, imposing rigid discipline. The old custom of taking the DESSERT course in another room, away from the eating-room, was maintained as the housekeeper and butler withdrew, usually to the housekeeper's sitting-room. In many Servants' Halls there were 'Rules and Orders' painted on a board, with stated fines for offenders. Meals were taken in the Servants' Hall before meals were served above stairs.

By the turn of this century the custom of the higher servants withdrawing for dessert was still followed, but by this time they also often ate meals other than dinner separately from the lower servants. Restored Servants' Halls may be seen at Raby Castle, County Durham, and at Erddig, Clwyd.

Service of meals. Little or nothing is known about the Norman service of meals. However, the late medieval custom among the wealthy of covering tables with every sort of food and leaving guests to help themselves was imported from the dukedom of Burgundy where profligacy, waste and display were used as expressions of wealth and power.

This way of serving meals became known as *service à la française* and lasted, with modifications, until well into the nineteenth century. A variety of dishes was set on the table and guests helped themselves from those nearest them. The mixture of dishes might seem chaotic, with beef, fish and sweet jellies all set out at the same time, but there was an order in the method. The first course would be that which the guests found when they sat down to dinner, as today soup would be first, served by the mistress of the house, and other dishes would be served to lady guests by the gentlemen guests sitting next to them. During this course there would be 'removes', which is defined by Dr Johnson in his *Dictionary* (1773) as 'a dish to be changed while the rest of the course remains'. Soup could be one remove, followed by boiled or roast meats. Removes would be carved or served by the master and mistress alternately, the guests either accepting or rejecting what was offered, as they pleased. The second course was less elaborate, with no removes being served, and was followed by the DESSERT course.

A new way of serving grand dinners was observed by the great chef Carême at the Court of Czar Alexander II in 1818, and this *service à la russe* eventually replaced the *service à la française* which had been the norm. Dishes were now served in succession. Soup was followed by *entrées*, perhaps cutlets or tongue or sole, then the main dish was brought in and presented to the host and guests, to be admired in all its glory before being carved at the sideboard or portioned out in the kitchen. Extravagance now lay not in the amount of food spread before the guests at one time, but in the number and quality of a succession of dishes – and in the number of servants required for the last-minute preparation and the individual serving of diners.

It is difficult to be precise about the date of introduction of the *service à la russe* in England. In 1857 Charles Pierce, *maître d'hôtel* at the Russian Embassy in London, noted in *The Household Manager* that '*Service à la Russe* derived from the Czar's mode of dining . . . [and was] introduced into France and England at the peace of 1814, out of compliment to the Emperor of Russia.' A grand dinner was indeed given by the City of London for the Prince Regent, the King of Prussia and the Czar of Russia on 18 June 1814, but City records do not clearly indicate how it was served. In his book *Host and Guest* (1864) A.L. Kirwan stated that '. . . since 1815 no sensible Englishman would think of going to Russia to learn how to serve a dinner . . .'; even so, it was a long time before the custom became universal. Mrs Beeton (*The Book of Household Management*, 1861) was of the opinion that 'Dinners *à la Russe* are scarcely suitable for small establishments: a large number of servants being required to carve and to help the guests . . .' – so it seems likely that even by the mid century, *service à la russe* was still confined to the higher echelons of fashion and society.

Sestern, cistern. A large vessel for holding liquids; most often, a wine cooler.

Settled Land Act, 1882. The first ACT to overturn the strict principle of ENTAIL, which had hitherto prevented the beneficiary of an entail from disposing, to the 'damage' of subsequent heirs, of any part of the entailed (or settled) land. At the time it was estimated that two-thirds of the estates of England were held under entail. The Act gave the beneficiary the power to sell to life tenants, so releasing capital to pay for repairs and other estate costs.

Settlement. The legal right to poor relief arising from a right to settlement in a parish. By the Poor Law Act of 1601 a settled inhabitant was one who had lived in a parish for a month. Those not qualifying were escorted by the constable, or a series of constables, back to their official parish of settlement. This was only done after examination of the case by two JUSTICES OF THE PEACE. Unless the person being examined could provide an indemnity, or guarantee, against becoming a charge on the parish, they were removed.

Illegimate children had a right to settlement where they were born, which led Overseers of the Poor to behave harshly in moving poor pregnant women quickly out of their parish before the birth could take place. Otherwise, a child's place of settlement was that of its father, and a wife took the same place of settlement as her husband. By the Settlement Act of 1662 the period of residence was raised to forty days for anyone occupying a property worth less than £10 per year.

The principle of 'Settlement' remained a legal force until 1876. Much of the injustice was removed in 1795 when Overseers were forbidden to move anyone on *before* they became a charge on the parish. See also BADGE-MEN, GILBERT'S ACT, POOR LAW, SPEENHAMLAND SYSTEM and WORKHOUSE.

Sewage. The disposal of human waste was always a matter of concern in country houses, but often also taken for granted, with the consequence that after centuries of neglect whatever system was employed became inadequate. For example, in 1844, no fewer than fifty-three overflowing cesspits were found under Windsor Castle; although they were cleared out, Queen Victoria convinced herself (wrongly) that Prince Albert's death from typhoid fever in 1861 was due to the drains.

Monasteries were the first to tackle the problem satisfactorily. Rere-dorters (communal GARDEROBES) situated off the monks' dormitories commonly discharged into a running river or stream, down-stream from the kitchens, or into culverts, as at Audley End, the site of a Bene-dictine Monastery. Where running water was not available, a cesspit would be utilized, as at St Alban's Abbey (excavated in 1924), where the cesspit consisted of a 25-foot deep pit, 18 ft 8 in. long by 5 ft 3 in. wide beneath the cloister floor. At Tintern Abbey on the Severn the tide was harnessed to clear the garderobes, to such effect that at the highest tides the monks must have been flushed from their seats.

Until the late sixteenth century, country house owners were content with such old medieval garderobes as continued in use, but gradually these came to be replaced by the more convenient CLOSE-STOOL, which was used well into the nineteenth century. Many bedchambers of this period have a small closet attached, for a close-stool, of which luxuri-ous examples may be seen at Knole in Kent, Ham House in Surrey, and at Hampton Court Palace. The close-stools were emptied by a personal servant (using the back stairs) into an outside privy or pit.

As early as 1596 Sir John Harrington invented a flushing WC, but Queen Elizabeth I preferred her close-stool, and without royal patron-age Harrington's invention languished. In 1660 Chatsworth in Derby-shire was unusual in having at least ten WCs – but as Derbyshire is full of rushing streams, piped water posed no problems. By the mid nine-teenth century WCs were becoming more popular, but the regular piped water supply on which they depended was something many country houses lacked until the twentieth century. The wide use of WCs exacerbated the problem of overflowing cesspits; the need for a sewerage system to remove the waste was first felt in cities. In 1189 London was served by open sewers, as it continued to be for another five or six centuries. London Bridge was said to be 'for wise men to go over and fools to go under'. From the mid eighteenth century the paving of city streets was introduced, drains were covered over, and iron pipes for sewage were introduced from 1746. The river Fleet, an open sewer from early times, was only culverted in 1841. In 1748 the Duke of Bedford installed a sewerage system at Woburn Abbey, with four water-closets – but only one was in the house. Often in the eight-eenth and nineteenth centuries CHAMBER POTS were kept handy for use in the dining room, behind a screen discreetly placed across the corner of the room. In 1860 the Revd Henry Moule invented the earth-closet, a seat placed over a bucket or pit, with behind it a hopper filled with dry earth or ashes which, when a handle was pulled, allowed a measure of earth to fall into the bucket or pit. For cottages without water, and for the closely-terraced houses of mining and mill villages, the earth closet was a decided improvement on the outdoor privy. See also WATER.

Shaw, Richard Norman (1831–1912). Trained under William BURN, in whose office he began a lifelong association with William Eden NESFIELD, and shortly afterwards took Philip WEBB's place as Chief Assistant in G.E. Street's office. Shaw, in private practice with Nesfield, evolved a new sophisticated range of domestic styles employing vernacular motifs which became the basis of much of the late Victorian Domestic Revival. Cragside, Northumberland (1869–84) is an early masterpiece in a mixture of styles, but at Bedford Park in London, the earliest garden suburb (1878), Shaw compromised between 'Queen Anne' and 'Old English'. New Scotland Yard, London (1887–90 and 1906) is in the then fashionable BAROQUE Revival style.

Shell rooms and **houses.** A fashion inspired by the shell-decorated grottoes seen in Italy on the GRAND TOUR. The Shell Room at Woburn Abbey, Bedfordshire dates from the mid seventeenth century. The Shell House was a later development, and one of the best in Britain is at Goodwood House, Sussex, the interior decorated with shellwork designs: in the 1740s it took the 2nd Duchess of Richmond and her daughters seven years to make. A la Ronde in Devon is an extraordinary rustic cottage, built in the 1790s literally 'in the round', in which shells are used extensively in the decoration; even in the round gallery above the hall, the walls are completely covered with shell and feather designs. Eastleigh House, also in Devon, has a polygonal shell-encrusted Shell House designed in 1810 by Sir Jeffry Wyattville (1766–1810).

Sheraton, Thomas (c. 1750–1806). Furniture designer. Sheraton is first heard of in London c. 1790, but is not recorded as having his own workshop, and no piece of furniture made by him has been identified. He was best known in his own day through his influential publications, *The Cabinet-Maker and Upholsterer's Drawing Book*, published in parts, 1791–4, and *The Cabinet Dictionary*, published in 1803, and his enduring fame is based on these. Many of his designs were influenced by the straight lines of the French LOUIS XVI STYLE. His influence on furniture design was considerable and continued after his death into the REGENCY period, since his style adroitly met the ever-growing public demand for comfort, and for specialized pieces such as dining tables, sofa tables, breakfast tables, and leather-topped writing desks; it was characterized by grace, simplicity, and an extensive use of satinwood. Examples of furniture made to his designs are at Harewood House and Nostell Priory, both in West Yorkshire.

Shooting. In the early days of shooting game, either with long-bow, cross-bow or, from the fifteenth century, the gun, the sportsman crept up on sitting birds. Even the gun was at first a very imperfect weapon: early models often blew apart, injuring the sportsman; there was a time-lag between pulling the trigger and the discharge of the shot; the barrels were long and the gun unwieldy. All things considered, shooting was a true sport and a fine test of skill, and game stood a very good chance of survival.

By the seventeenth and eighteenth centuries the best guns were made in Italy, France or Germany; John Evelyn (1620–1706) noted his purchase of a sporting gun in northern Italy in 1646. The custom of shooting flying birds originated in France (where, even now, anything that flies is liable to be shot). Three inventions made this possible: the patent breech, allowing fast loading; the manufacture of regular-sized shot by means of dropping lead from a great height in shot-towers; and the percussion cap that replaced the flint-lock in 1808. These improvements gradually made guns so much more efficient that wild game had less chance against them: the balance was corrected artificially by the introduction of shooting by licence (1784), and by means of GAME LAWS to protect game from slaughter during the breeding season (end of January to autumn).

The main game bird in the eighteenth century was the partridge, not the pheasant, as today. The grey partridge is native to England, while the red-legged bird (generally called the French Partridge: nothing to do with France, but named after the French soldiers' uniform) was introduced by the 2nd Marquess of Hertford (1743–1822) in the 1770s; it rapidly became naturalized, preferring heavier or more infertile soils than the native grey. The red-legged partridge has proved particularly well suited to the driven shoots which became possible as guns improved; it is claimed that Holkham in Norfolk was the first estate to drive flying birds over standing guns.

Inaccessible GROUSE moors had to await the coming of the railways before organized shoots became possible, and hence are a comparatively recent development. Unlike pheasant and partridge, grouse do not readily breed in captivity, but require encouragement; grouse-rearing is very subject to the vagaries of the weather. Controlled burning of heather to improve stocks was first carried out on the Scottish estates of the 5th Duke of Portland (1809–79) in 1859. From this time the annual shooting calendar became established; grouse from 12 August to 11 December, partridge from 31 August to 2 February, pheasant from 30 September to 2 February.

The nineteenth century also saw the introduction of highly-organized 'battues', in which landowners competed to score the highest day's bag, following the introduction of the French-designed break-and-load shotgun at the Great Exhibition of 1851. The more rapid firing possible with this gun led to the high-flying pheasant taking the place of the patridge as *the* game-bird on most estates.

The record for the highest single bag by one gun in one day is held by the 6th Lord Walsingham (1843–1926), of 1,070 grouse on 30 September 1888. The highest tallies for single guns, as recorded by Purdey's the gun-makers, who hold their game books, go to the 1st and 2nd Marquesses of Ripon; the 1st Marquess (1827–1909) downed 142,343 pheasant, 97,759 partridge and 56,460 grouse between 1867 and 1900, while the score of his son the 2nd Marquess (1852–1923) stands at 241,232 pheasant and 124,193 partridge, from 1867 to his death, in a tally running 23 years longer than his father's; the annual average is similar. The 2nd Marquess died as he no doubt would have wished, after shooting his fifty-second bird on the morning of 22 September 1923.

A point too often overlooked is that we have the planting of cover for game birds in the eighteenth and nineteenth centuries to thank for some of the finest country views in Europe. See also SHOOTING-BRAKE.

Shooting-brake. A nineteenth-century vehicle used to take guests to the shooting butts. Originally horse-drawn with rows of seats; there were subsequently motorized versions. See also CARRIAGES.

Shovel-board. At least three historic houses have boards for playing shovel-board, shuffle-board, or shovel-penny (now shove-ha'penny). In the GREAT HALL at Littlecote, Berkshire is a vast table dating from *c.* 1600, which had been converted to a shovel-board by the mid seventeenth century. Too big to move, the table has remained in the room in which it was built, used as both a dining table and a games board. Stanway House in Gloucestershire also has a shovel-board in the Great Hall, made about 1620. The shovel-board in the Audit Room at Boughton House, Northamptonshire was made in 1702 at a cost of £3 17s. 6d.

Shutters. Before glass became readily available (oiled cloth or thin sheets of horn were other and earlier alternatives), windows were covered by interior shutters, which served to reduce draughts slightly. A set of shutters in the medieval hall at Stokesay Castle, Shropshire, gives an impression of their effectiveness. Shutters were not generally a feature of Tudor houses, which is surprising in view of the amount of draught filtering through in spite of the small diamond-shaped glass quarries. By the latter half of the seventeenth century they were fitted to many new houses; when closed with a cross-bar they provided a certain security, and also insulation – an early form of double glazing. Cottages have traditionally had shutters fixed to the outsides of their windows, for these very reasons. Window CURTAINS were not at all commonplace until well into the eighteenth century, so shutters were highly visible decorative features. The festoon curtains fashionable in the 1720s were often left drawn up to reveal richly decorated shutter-panels, clearly intended to be seen, but by the 1770s paired curtains which concealed the shutters had come into vogue, so undecorated shutters in plain panelling were fitted. The popular unrest and rioting of the first three decades of the nineteenth century bought shutters back into use once more as a security measure, but by the end of the nineteenth century, when the majority of the population of the British Isles lived in small houses with better glazing, and large-scale rioting belonged to the past, shutters went out of fashion again.

Sideboards. Developed from the side-tables which from the fifteenth century supplemented the court CUPBOARD or BUFFET, with their displays of plate or pewter. Sideboards were often originally very plain tables, richly cloth-draped, but by the early Georgian period had become important pieces of furniture, massive in marble-topped mahogany – but, as they lacked so much as a single drawer, of strictly limited utility. By the middle of the eighteenth century side-tables or sideboard tables had become lighter in design under the influence of CHIPPENDALE, and were usually flanked by a freestanding pedestal either side, the same height as the table, and topped with a covered urn. These pairs of urns and pedestals were fitted out in various ingenious ways, as KNIFE (or cutlery) BOXES, plate warmers, cellarets, or to contain water in which the butler might wash glasses between toasts. Robert ADAM designed a fine suite to decorate the apse at one end of the dining room at Kedleston Hall, Derbyshire (in the 1760s); the fitments include a PERFUME-BURNER. Other sideboard-table and pedestal arrangements can be seen at Harewood House, West Yorkshire (attributed to CHIPPENDALE, 1769–71); and at Culzean Castle, Strathclyde Region, c. 1780.

By 1788 Thomas SHERATON was illustrating a new design of sideboard in which the sideboard-table and flanking pedestals were joined into one impressive piece of furniture. Sheraton made many inventive designs for the fitting-out of these all-in-one sideboards; smaller versions were intended for rooms too small for the full pedestal arrangement, and it is these, which have continued to be made in infinite variety, which we would most readily recognize as a sideboard today.

Slavery. The ownership of one person by another. In 1772 Lord Mansfield's judgment in the case of a runaway Negro, James Somerset (one of over 15,000 estimated to be then in Britain), held that as soon as a slave set his foot on the soil of Great Britain he became free.

England had been involved in the slave trade since the days of Sir John Hawkins (1532–95), and fortunes were made in the interrelated traffic in slaves, sugar and tobacco, centred on Liverpool but also carried on from London, Bristol and Lancaster: the wealth of the Codingtons of Dodington House, Gloucestershire, the Lascelles of Harewood House, West Yorkshire, and the Beckfords of Fonthill, Wiltshire was based on sugar and slaves. In his early Parliamentary life, even William Gladstone (1809–98) spoke in defence of the fortune made by his father from this source.

The QUAKERS were among the first to oppose slavery, speaking out against it as early as 1671, and in 1783 they formed an association 'for the relief and liberation of the negro slaves in the West Indies, and for the discouragement of the slave trade on the coast of Africa', the first such society established in Britain. Under the aegis of William Wilber-force (1759–1833) a committee was formed in 1787 for the abolition of the slave trade which soon attracted numerous people remarkable in their day, such as Josiah Wedgwood (1730–95). After various attempts an Act was passed in 1807 to put an end to the British slave trade to supply foreign markets, and forbidding the importation of slaves into British Colonies. In the face of habitual violation of the provisions of this Act, another of 1811 declared the traffic in slaves to be a felony punishable by transportation, and this effectively ended the trade in the British dominions.

The abolition of slavery itself took longer to achieve. An anti-slavery society was established in 1823 but their attempts to legislate for a gradual abolition came to nothing, and in 1833 Earl Grey's ministry carried the complete abolition, establishing a seven-year apprenticeship system as a transition measure; the slaves were in fact granted their freedom in 1838, before this period was up.

It is extraordinarily difficult to discover much about the domestic employment of slaves who lived in Great Britain, evidence of which has been very much swept under the carpet. In eighteenth-century portraits showing fine ladies accompanied by a black male in household livery, the inference must generally (though not invariably) be, if they were painted before 1772, that the man is a household slave. Sir Joshua Reynolds (1723–92), c. 1769, 'had had a black footman for several years', and an unfinished portrait by him of a 'Young Black' (1761; now in Houston, Texas, USA) may well portray a London slave. Reynolds' painting of Lady Elizabeth Keppel (also 1761, formerly at Woburn) shows a female black with straight hair holding a garland behind Lady Elizabeth, and his portrait of the Marquess of Granby (in the Royal Collection) shows a black male holding the Marquess's horse. In the servants' hall at Erddig in Clwyd hangs an early eighteenth-century portrait of a black coachboy. Dr Johnson (1709–84) employed as a servant a freed slave, Francis Barber, who when his master was away played host to other freed black servants. On his tour of Scotland in 1773 Johnson met another freed slave, employed by Lord Monboddo (1714–99). Ignatious Sancho (1729–80), the black butler to the Duke of Montague (1712–90), later became a Mayfair grocer.

Smallpox or **Variola**. A highly contagious and infectious viral disease characterized by a fever followed by an eruption of pustules or 'pocks' which then dry up, leaving more or less scarred skin tissue. Low standards of nutrition and general uncleanliness predispose to infection; every case can be traced to an earlier contact. Smallpox was introduced to Europe from the East by returning Crusaders and reached the Americas by way of Spanish expeditions. An attack normally confers immunity against infection; inoculation with the smallpox virus itself, generally producing a milder case of the disease, was the method of protection until Edward Jenner (1749–1823) developed VACCINATION with cowpox in the 1790s. It was his observation of the fine, unblemished complexions of dairy-maids that led Jenner to his discoveries: he deduced that those girls must have experienced mild cases of cowpox, which gave them resistance to the smallpox virus.

Smith, Adam (1723–90). A Scottish economist born at Kirkcaldy, Fifeshire, Scotland; professor of moral philosophy at Glasgow University, 1752–63. In *Inquiry into the Nature and Causes of the Wealth of Nations* (1776) he propounded the theory that the labour of a nation was the source of its wealth – a theory in direct opposition to MERCANTILISM, which maintained that money is the only form of wealth. He also supported the case for Free Trade, and deplored the costly wars and imperial rivalries of mercantilism. His theories formed the basis of the classical British school of political economy, and he may be said to have established economics as a subject of study.

Smith, Francis and **William, of Warwick** (1672–1738; 1661–1724). Master-builders/architects, sons of a bricklayer of The Wergs, nr Tettenhall, Staffordshire; William became a bricklayer and Francis a stonemason. William remained at The Wergs but Francis married and settled in Warwick, where he restored St Mary's Church after the fire of 1694. They often worked in partnership, mainly in the Midlands, and were involved in work on more than forty houses, while sixteen others are attributed to them; they also worked on ten churches. Francis, known as 'Smith of Warwick', was the dominant partner and designer and one of the most successful master-builders in English history. A typical Smith house is of three storeys with the centre bays slightly projecting or receding, uniform fenestration, and little external ornamentation – in fact, the typical late seventeenth- or early eighteenth-century house. Smith interiors might be surprising: at Mawley Hall, Shropshire (1730) there is amazing ROCOCO plasterwork; and the plasterwork from Sutton Scarsdale, Derbyshire (1724), itself now a roofless ruin, is in the Philadelphia Museum of Art, USA.

Smoking jackets, smoking rooms. With the Victorian passion for specialization it was only a matter of time before a special room was set aside, and special clothing devised, for smoking. One of the main reasons for this was the way the smell of tobacco clung to clothes and curtains. Earlier, men smoked in the garden, on the terrace, in the service wing, or in the stables. In 1839, Lord Melbourne (1779–1848) railed against it as a dirty German habit: 'I always make a great row about it; if I smell any tobacco I swear for perhaps half an hour.' The Prince Consort (1819–61) introduced smoking at Court, and included a smoking-room at Osborne House, Isle of Wight (1845); the door bore only the initial 'A' above it, not the entwined 'V & A' to be seen over other doors; cigars were for men! Mentmore in Bedfordshire, built 1850–1 for the 1st Lord Rothschild (1840–1915), had a very small smoking room isolated off the conservatory; perhaps the Rothschild ladies also used it, for in 1858 they were observing that, while to see a lady smoking regularly was not acceptable, '. . . at times a chance cigar is very pleasant.' Other smoking rooms were in towers, as at Breadsall Priory, Derbyshire (1861) and Tyntesfield, Somerset (1866); Cardiff Castle (1868–71) had two, for summer and winter. A more common practice was to place the smoking room next to the BILLIARD room. By the 1890s the well-equipped male smoker would have his frogged and quilted smoking jacket and, if he were really fashionable, a matching fez. These jackets were more loosely cut and comfortable than the highly-tailored coats worn formally, and the quilting was not only luxurious but necessary, since the rooms in which smoking was permitted were often unheated. The fez perhaps reflected an association of ideas with Turkish smoking-rooms, where hookahs were used; there is a smoking-room in the Moorish style at Rhinefield, Hampshire (built 1888–90). See also TOBACCO.

Smythson, Robert (1534/5–1614). The first architect to be so described ('Architector', on his memorial in Wollaton Church, Nottingham) and, although trained as a stonemason (like most at that time who designed buildings), the foremost architect of his age. He came from a family of Westmorland tenant farmers who had settled at Crosby Ravensworth; his father may also have been a stonemason. Smythson is first heard of on his arrival in 1568 at Longleat, Wiltshire (where Sir John Thynne was building from 1547 until his death in 1580) with his lodge of four masons and a letter from Humphrey Lovell, the Queen's Master Mason, saying that he was 'Laytt with Master Vice-Chamberlaine'. Smythson and his men worked at Longleat with a French mason, Alan Maynard, until 1575, and during that time he also made some alterations to Old Wardour Castle for Thynne's neighbour Sir Matthew Arundell. Smythson then vanishes from our view until 1580, when Sir Francis Willoughby, Arundell's brother-in-law, commissioned Wollaton Hall, Nottinghamshire (completed in

1588); Smythson's memorial states that he built 'the most worthy house of Wollaton and divers others of great account'. Thereafter Smythson's work can only be attributed stylistically, and from his drawings in the RIBA. It would seem to include Worksop Manor, Nottinghamshire (*c.* 1575, burnt out 1761); Hardwick Hall, Derbyshire (1590–7); Barlborough Hall, Derbyshire (1583); and Worksop Manor Lodge, Nottinghamshire (*c.* 1594–5) – all in the Earl of Shrewsbury's circle. Other houses attributed to him are: Doddington Hall, Lincolnshire (begun *c.* 1595); The Hall, Bradford-on-Avon, Wiltshire (*c.* 1597); Burton Agnes, Humberside (1601–10); Chastleton House, Oxfordshire (*c.* 1602); Fountains Hall, North Yorkshire (*c.* 1611); and the plan of Bolsover Castle, Derbyshire, begun in 1612 for Charles Cavendish, son-in-law of the 6th Earl of Shrewsbury, and completed by Robert's son John. Smythson's style is distinguished by soaring height, façades with square turrets which act as buttresses to support walls pierced by large windows, and compactness and ingenuity in planning.

Snob. A person who apes gentility from a disposition to be ashamed of socially inferior connections and a vulgar admiration for wealth and social position. The origin of the term in this sense, which came into use in the mid nineteenth century, is not known. In the eighteenth century 'snob' was slang for a cobbler or shoemaker; it was used at Cambridge to denote a 'townsman' (as opposed to a 'gownsman'); and Thomas de Quincey (1785–1859) observed that 'those who work for lower wages during a strike are called snobs'.

William Thackeray (1811–63) republished in 1848 as *The Book of Snobs* a collection of papers first written for the magazine PUNCH in 1846–7 under the title 'The Snobs of England by One of Themselves', which satirized the various types of snobbery encountered in society: 'Country Snobs', 'Clerical Snobs', 'Military Snobs', etc.

Snooker. See BILLIARDS.

Snuff-boxes. Snuff, powdered tobacco inhaled through the nostrils, was known in Europe from the time of the discovery of the Americas, but only became fashionable in Britain after the RESTORATION – a habit picked up in the French and Dutch courts. At first snuff-takers grated rolls of TOBACCO on a grater, and did not need a snuff-box; coarser sorts of snuff were later known as 'rappee' from the French *râper*, to grate. In time tobacco came to be available ready-ground and the snuff-box came into its own, the earliest examples dating from *c.* 1700. The fashion for snuff-taking ran throughout the eighteenth century. Many snuff-taking rituals evolved – taking snuff from a lady's wrist was considered elegant, dashing, and (doubtless) erotic. Enthusiasts blended their own special mixtures to suit mood and season, and collected boxes to complement them: Lord Petersham was said to have a box for every day of the year. It is hardly surprising that many snuff-boxes survive, made in an almost limitless variety of materials. The mull, a silver-mounted ram's head, is a large snuff box, to sit on a table.

Soane, Sir John (1753–1837). Studied architecture under George Dance and Henry Holland and later, like so many of his contemporaries, pursued his studies in Italy and Greece. His individual interpretation of Classical architecture and his eccentric style are instantly recognizable. His exteriors exhibit a restrained linear decoration and the occasional dramatic skyline introducing urns and sarcophagi, as at Dulwich Picture Gallery, South London (1811–14). Soane's interiors are equally dramatic in their use of CLERESTORY lighting and intersecting arcs and domes. He is perhaps most widely known for his own house, 13 Lincoln's Inn Fields (now Sir John Soane's Museum), with its highly eccentric interior which glories in the use of mirrors, arches, recesses, and an ingeniously contrived PICTURE GALLERY displaying, among other treasures, the eight engravings of Hogarth's *The Rake's Progress* (c. 1735).

Solar, sollar, soller. The name given to the upper floor of the two-chambered, two-storied house which became common in England after the Norman Conquest. May be connected with the Latin *solarium*, a gallery or terrace exposed to the sun; or, as some authorities think, connected with the French for floor-joist, *solive*, and originally applied to the timber floor which divided the upper chamber from the lower (a house with a stone-vaulted ground floor was described as having a 'stone solar' above it; consider the French for 'mezzanine', a low storey between two others: *entresol*). The use of 'solar' to mean either the GREAT CHAMBER or a bower-like room in which maidens languished is a solecism of the early nineteenth-century Romantics – the heroines of Sir Walter Scott's *Waverley Novels* or the earlier-set *Ivanhoe*, for example, were often to be found in wrongly-designated solars.

Solicitor. A term originally applied to those who 'solicited' or took care of suits, bills and petitions in the EQUITY courts and before Parliament and the PRIVY COUNCIL, or who conducted private negotiations not involving, or arising out of, litigation. At the date of the Solicitors' Act of 1843, the 'junior profession' of the law consisted of solicitors, ATTORNEYS and proctors (see ADMIRALTY, COURT OF); by the Judicature Act of 1873 it was enacted that all such persons should thenceforth be known as 'solicitors of the Supreme Court'. In the Solicitors' Act of 1877 provision was made for qualifying examinations and the issue of certificates by the Incorporated Law Society. The term 'solicitor' is unknown in the USA, where 'attorney' is used instead.

Solicitor-General. A law officer of the Crown who acts as the deputy for the Attorney-General or, in Scotland, for the Lord-Advocate.

Souls, The. An élite group of late Victorians and Edwardians who prided themselves on their taste and aesthetic sensibility. Its members included such intellectuals and politicians as Arthur Balfour, George Curzon, Lord Elcho, Wilfrid Blunt, George Wyndham, Henry Cust, and above all women such as Margot Asquith and her sisters. Ettie Grenfell and Lady Elcho, daughter-in-law of the Earl of Weymss, were great hostesses in whose houses The Souls met – houses such as Stanway in Gloucestershire, Taplow Court in Buckinghamshire, and Mells Park in Somerset. The best-known house associated with The Souls is perhaps Clouds in Wiltshire, built by Philip WEBB in 1885 for Madeleine and the Hon. Percy Wyndham and furnished with William Morris carpets and fabrics.

South Sea Company. A joint stock company formed in 1711 and granted the monopoly of British trade with Spanish America, mainly in slaves. It was initially highly successful, and in 1720, by agreement with Parliament and in competition with the Bank of England, it took over half the national debt in return for certain privileges and an extension of its monopoly to the South Seas – a highly speculative move. Share prices in the Company rocketed, followed inevitably by a crash (the 'South Sea Bubble' bursting), a considerable financial disaster which ruined all those who had held onto their shares; three ministers were charged with corruption. The resulting scandal reached as far as George I (1714–27), two of whose mistresses were involved. Sir Robert Walpole (1676–1745), LORD CHANCELLOR and effectively PRIME MINISTER, who had not been involved in the scandal, restored credit by transferring £9 million of South Sea Stock to the EAST INDIA COMPANY and £9 million to the Bank of England. The South Sea Company continued in existence as a financial trading house until 1856, but abandoned their concessions in South America in 1750.

Sovereign. A gold coin worth twenty silver shillings (the 'pound sterling'), introduced by Henry VII (1457–1509). The pound as a unit of account remained based upon a silver standard until the eighteenth century, during the course of which gold gradually took over from silver as a monetary regulator; it became the standard monetary unit in 1817. The sovereign disappeared from currency soon after the outbreak of the First World War in 1914, and the last gold sovereign was struck in 1917. See also GUINEA.

Spanish blankets. Woollen blankets from Catalonia, imported to Britain in the sixteenth and seventeenth centuries.

Sparver. A bed canopy suspended from the ceiling. See also BEDS.

Spectacles. Said to have been invented in Florence by a monk in the thirteenth century, but not widely needed until the invention of printing in the late fifteenth century. It is not known precisely when they were first introduced into Britain, but in 1629 Charles I (1625–49) granted a charter to the Spectacle Makers' Guild. Bifocals were devised by Benjamin Franklin about 1760.

Speenhamland System. A method of poor relief devised by Berkshire justices (Speenhamland is near Newbury) in 1795, and subsequently adopted in much of England and Wales, at a time when wages were low and prices high. Under it farm workers' wages were supplemented out of parish rates according to the price of wheat and size of family. This systematized the 'outdoor relief' provided for under GILBERT'S ACT of 1782 and endorsed by a further act of 1796 abandoning the WORKHOUSE test. The system had the effect of encouraging farmers to pay inadequate wages, throwing the burden on rate-payers rather than employers, and demoralizing the recipients. See also BADGE MEN, POOR LAW and SETTLEMENT.

Spices. Pepper with everything was the rule in Roman cooking, and other spices such as cinnamon, sugar (then considered a spice), mustard, ginger, saffron, and coriander were popular. With the withdrawal of the Romans from Britain in the fifth century AD and the virtual closure of the Mediterranean to Christian trade in the centuries of Moorish domination, imported spices became all but unavailable, until the CRUSADES reopened the Levant trade. Most spices followed the expensive silk route from the Far East, and so the use of the rarest was restricted to the wealthy. The price of spices fluctuated according to supply, but cinnamon, pepper and ginger were usually the cheapest, mace and cloves more expensive, and saffron most costly of all.

Returning crusaders certainly brought with them a taste for spicy dishes, but it is hard to judge how heavily spiced medieval and later food was, because few contemporary recipes give quantities; however, the combination of spices and the foods in which they were used often seem very adventurous. Undoubtedly they disguised the taste of tainted fish and meat – and once palates had become accustomed to strong flavours, unspiced foods tasted dull. Until the end of the fifteenth century Venice controlled the European end of the silk route, setting her own (high) prices. The Portuguese broke the monopoly, rounding the Cape of Good Hope in 1488, but though Portuguese spice ships were in Falmouth by 1504, their prices were little different from the Venetians'. By mid-century the Dutch were also bringing spices from the Far East. The EAST INDIA COMPANY was set up in 1600 to fill the trade vacuum left by the decline of Portuguese power, and with so much competition the cost of spices fell and they became more widely available.

Kitchen fireplaces of the seventeenth century often have a small spice cupboard set in the wall near the chimney; round wooden boxes with radiating compartments inside served the same purpose and were closed with lock and key.

Spinet. See HARPSICHORD.

Spit. A slender steel or iron bar on which meat was fixed before being roasted in front of an open fire. At first the spit was turned by hand, or sometimes by a small dog on a caged wheel (turnspit boy, or dog) – as in the kitchens at St Fagan's Castle, South Glamorgan. Eighteenth-century technology introduced a fan in the flue which by means of convected heat drove an arrangement of cogs, chains and wheels, turning the spit on the hearth; the eighteenth-century CLOCK-JACK was a clockwork spit. See also KITCHENS.

Spittoon. An open or conical metal or ceramic container for spitting into, varying in size from those small enough to hold in the hand to larger models to stand on the floor.

Squire. Originally, a young man of good birth attendant upon a knight (see ESQUIRE); subsequently, the form of address often used for a country GENTLEMAN, especially for the chief landed proprietor of a district. It is no more a title than 'MR', although there is still a Leicestershire land-owner who is known to prefer the use of 'Squire' as a prefix to his SURNAME.

Stables. So important was the HORSE to civilized Europe that many houses provided them with luxurious accommodation. At Seaton Delaval in Northumberland, designed by Sir John VANBRUGH between 1718 and 1728 for Admiral George Delaval (1660–1723), the stable block was considered an appropriate place for a banquet to celebrate its completion. Hovingham Hall, North Yorkshire (1750s) is uniquely dedicated to horses: the entrance, under a high tunnel-vaulted archway, tall enough to ride through on horseback, is by way of the riding school and magnificent stables, from which a visitor is allowed to mount stairs to the house above. The stable block at Peover Hall, Cheshire (1654) has ornamental plaster ceilings; at Avery Hill, Greenwich (1880s), the stables were centrally heated.

In London as in other towns horses remained essential until the advent of the MOTOR CAR; those belonging to richer families were stabled in MEWS, the first of which were built when Grosvenor Square was laid out in the 1720s.

Stag-hunting. Anciently, 'hunting at force' – the chase, on horseback with a pack of hounds, of deer. As William I (1066–87) demonstrated in appropriating large forested tracts of England as royal hunting demesnes, stag-hunting was extremely popular among the Normans. Heavy dogs such as the stag-hound and buck-hound were bred for the chase; the Queen's Privy Buckhounds (belonging to Elizabeth I, 1558–1603) were kept by Lord Leicester at Kenilworth. Population growth, better farming methods and ENCLOSURES had forced deer into the remoter parts of Britain by the eighteenth century. Stag-hunting continued even during the Second World War, with Government encouragement, to supplement the meat ration and control the deer population, and does so today despite increasing opposition from animal rights activists. See also FOX-HUNTING.

Standard. A large trunk or chest.

Standing. After a serious fall while hunting in 1536 Henry VIII took to shooting at driven deer from a platform called a 'standing'. Standings were quite large timber-framed constructions, often of two storeys with an attic, and offered accommodation for the king and his courtiers, and often the court ladies. Two were built at The More, one of Henry's smaller houses in Hertfordshire, in 1538 and 1542. A private house at Chingford in Essex, now known as 'Queen Elizabeth's Hunting Lodge', was another originally built for her father. An early seventeenth-century 'hunting-stand' is at Ledstone Hall in South Yorkshire, but the Stand at Swarkestone, Leicestershire – an early seventeenth century stone construction – may be a bowling alley house rather than a hunting stand.

Stanhope. A light open, two- or four-wheeled carriage for one, named after The Revd The Hon. Fitzroy Stanhope (1787–1864), for whom it was first made. See also CARRIAGES.

Star Chamber, Court of. The Star Chamber, a room in the old Palace of Westminster – accounts of 1398 refer to the 'sterred chambre' – came to give its name to the judicial functions exercised by meetings there of the King in his Council, reinforced from time to time by judges and others. In public hearings, without a jury, the Court of Star Chamber dealt particularly with violations of the Royal Prerogative, and with offences for which the law had made no provision. But litigants might petition for their cases to be heard before it, and often did so, as its processes were swifter than those available at COMMON LAW. The Court of Star Chamber is popularly associated with Henry VII (1485–1509), but he did no more than strengthen its existing powers to offset and deal with irregularities in the administration of justice caused by the influence of over-mighty local magnates which had arisen during the chaotic years of the WARS OF THE ROSES. Hearings of the court were public, but there was no jury; torture was sometimes used to obtain confessions and mutilation was sometimes decreed as a punishment, but in general the court's punishments took the form of imprisonment and/or fine: the sentence of death was never pronounced. Star Chamber continued as an active court, and a powerful weapon in the hands of the Crown, until its abolition in 1641 by an Act of the Long Parliament, in Puritan and Parliamentary opposition to its misuse by Charles I (1625–49).

State apartments. A series of rooms set aside for the reception of important visitors, developing from the suites of rooms used by the master of the house in the medieval period. In courtiers' houses of Tudor times the sequence comprised a GREAT CHAMBER (often containing a CHAIR OF STATE), WITHDRAWING CHAMBER, and State Bedchamber, with closets and smaller bedchambers off. The Great Chamber, the first room of reception, was also used for dining in, its occupants moving to the Withdrawing Room while it was set up for dinner. While these rooms might be used on a variety of grand occasions, the State Bedchamber was customarily reserved for use by the sovereign, or by visitors of higher rank than the host. This sequence of rooms was a modified version of that to be found in the royal palaces, where the Great Chamber was preceded by a guardroom and followed by a Presence Chamber, which we would recognize as a throne room. Hardwick Hall, Derbyshire, has almost unaltered state apartments of the 1590s.

At the RESTORATION of the monarchy in 1660 continental Court practice became a strong influence, and the arrangement of royal state apartments became more complicated. WREN's estimates for finishing the King's Side at Hampton Court in 1699 cover the following sequence: Guard Chamber, Presence Chamber, Privy Chamber, Withdrawing Room, Ante-Room, Great Bedchamber and Gallery. Stuart courtiers, however, felt no need to provide equally lavish accommodation (as may be seen in the untouched apartments at Boughton House, Northamptonshire, built in the 1690s for the 1st Duke of Montague (1638–1709) and comprising Great Chamber, Withdrawing Chamber and bedchamber with a closet off it), as government officers now remained in London instead of travelling about with the sovereign.

The change in the relationship between sovereign and Parliament following the abandonment of the principle of the DIVINE RIGHT OF KINGS at the Glorious Revolution of 1688 led the grandees of the period to express their new-found and growing power by the building of vast houses. Although state apartments became much less important, until the 1760s state bedrooms on the French pattern, with ante-rooms and closets, continued to be provided on the main reception floor. Almost the last to be built were at Kedleston Hall, Derbyshire, begun in 1758 for the 1st Lord Scarsdale (1726–1804). Existing state apartments were maintained somewhat haphazardly. By the late eighteenth century the State Bedchamber at Wilton in Wiltshire had no bed in it; when a visit from George III (1760–1820) and Queen Charlotte was announced, a bed was borrowed and brought over in a cart from neighbouring Fonthill Abbey. In the event, their Majesties brought their own bed with them, which was set up alongside the Fonthill state bed. See also BEDS.

Statute. Defined by Sir Edward Coke (1552–1634) as 'an Act of Parliament made by the King, the Lords and the Commons' – though nowadays the consent of the House of Lords is not essential. A statute is a written declaration reforming old or establishing new rights, procedures and laws. Early statutes concerning charters, codes or laws, ASSIZES and instructions to justices derived their authority from the king's will agreed in council; as the power and influence of Parliament grew, its agreement came to be required too. The presentation of new proposals to Parliament in the form of Bills arose during the fifteenth century, their three readings in Tudor times.

The courts regarded statute law as new law, as against the old, unwritten COMMON LAW. No ACT OF PARLIAMENT can become inoperative by disuetude, only by repeal or supersession by a later Act. The Statute Law Revision Committee of 1863 looked into the accumulated mass of Acts, repealing those considered to be obsolete, such as the statutes forbidding the consumption of meat, eggs and milk during Lent, and published a collection of those currently applicable, *Statutes Revised*; the Statute Law Revision Act of 1927 also repealed a large number of obsolete Acts. See also STATUTE LAW.

Statute Law. Law promulgated by the sovereign body. Compare COMMON LAW and EQUITY.

Steeplechasing. A form of racing which arose in Ireland as early as 1752, allegedly when a homeward-bound party after a dull day's HUNTING decided to race to the steeple of the village church, visible two miles distant. The first to touch the church with his whip was the winner. Not introduced to England before about 1800, when younger members of fox-hunts took it up. The first English steeplechase (point-to-point) is said to have taken place at Nacton in Suffolk in 1803, and the first Grand National, the most important steeplechase event, was run over a two-mile course at Aintree near Liverpool in 1839. Steeplechases are run over a selection of artificial fences, water-jumps and other obstacles. See also HORSE RACING and the HORSE.

Steward. The head of a grand medieval household, a GENTLEMAN, perhaps even a KNIGHT, in charge perhaps of upwards of a hundred household SERVANTS, almost all male, and many themselves gentlemen – who would in turn have their own servants. As the need to display wealth and power by means of a large retinue and household died away, so did the need for a steward. By the eighteenth century only the very grandest households (or those aspiring to be so) had stewards, their place at the head of a smaller staff, which included more women, having been taken by the head BUTLER. The Royal House of Stuart came to prominence as hereditary stewards of an earlier line of Scottish kings.

Stew ponds. Ponds to contain live fish, constructed in medieval times, near monasteries and manors. The word is derived from the Latin *studiare* meaning 'to take care of'. In an age of poor communications when fish was an important alternative on the many meatless fast days, it was useful to have a place where fish could be kept until needed. By the sixteenth century they were more often known as fish ponds. In the 1590s, Bess of Hardwick (Hall, Derbyshire) had a series of fish ponds (still in existence) and employed a fisherman to manage them.

Still-room. Of medieval origins; a room in which was kept the still and other apparatus for the distillation and preparation of scented waters and cordials, used to counteract the smell of rarely-washed bodies and clothes and in the basic doctoring practised at home by most country housewives of high or low degree; sweet cordials were very popular with the Tudors. The home preparation of such items languished in the eighteenth and early nineteenth centuries, but in the 1840s, when afternoon tea came to be widely taken, to fill the void between luncheon at one and dinner at seven, the still-room came into its own again. By then it was the province of a still-room maid, where, under the supervision of the HOUSEKEEPER, she kept teas and made jams and jellies and small sandwiches. The ideal place for the Victorian still-room was below stairs, but with near access to the drawing room, and conveniently placed for the housekeeper's supervision.

Stout. A strong dark BEER brewed with roasted malt or barley. See also PORTER.

Strapwork. A Mannerist decoration originating in the Netherlands *c.* 1540 and brought to England with Flemish religious refugees, popular in the later Elizabethan period. Interlaced bands of cut stone, carved wood or moulded plaster, in appearance similar to a pattern made of leather straps or ribbons, were used to decorate overmantels, balustrades, ceilings, screens and funerary monuments, and were also stamped, cast or engraved on silver, and painted on ceramics. Strapwork evolved in the mid sixteenth century from Italian GROTESQUE decoration, itself probably of Islamic origin. The style was copied from book plates published in the Netherlands which used curling straps as a decorative feature. See also MANNERISM.

Stucco. A cement or plaster rendering used to cover walls or moulded into decorative architectural features such as cornices. Stucco was extensively used by Palladio (1508–80) in his buildings in the Veneto in Italy; many of them were painted on the outside with classical figures and scenes. The exterior use of stucco poses no problems in the dry atmosphere of Italy, but the English Palladians of the first half of the eighteenth century, slavishly following their mentor, discovered that it flaked off in the damp British climate. See also PALLADIANISM and PARGETTING.

Sublime, The. An eighteenth-century notion associated with the wonders and vastness of nature, religious awe, and the mystery of natural forces, which particularly intrigued writers, marking a movement away from the imitation of Classical authors (Neo-classicism) and towards the emotionalism of the Romantic movement in literature. Edmund Burke's *Philosophical Enquiry into the Origin of our Ideas of the Sublime and Beautiful* (1757) was widely read, and his attempts to explain the effect of emotions, particularly of terror, were popular and influential, leading to such manifestations as the macabre paintings of Henry Fuseli (1741–1825) and the 'GOTHIC' novels of Anne Radcliffe (1764–1823). See also PICTURESQUE and ROMANTICISM.

Suffragette. A term denoting a militant supporter of women's parliamentary suffrage, first used around 1906. Mary Woolstonecraft (1759–97) first put forward the notion of women's suffrage in *A Vindication of the Rights of Woman* (1792); the early Socialist William Thompson (*c.* 1785–1833) advocated votes for women in his *An Appeal of One Half of the Human Race* (1825), and although a clause to this effect was included in the first Reform Bill (1832), it was thrown out. Another unsuccessful parliamentary attempt was made in the late 1860s. The first women's suffrage society was formed in Manchester by Lydia Becker (1827–1890) in 1865 under Elizabeth Wolstenholme, later succeeded as Secretary by Lydia Becker. Many others followed, and all were affiliated in 1893 to the National Union of Women's Suffrage Societies under its first president, Mrs Henry Fawcett. Neither the Liberal nor the Conservative parties supported the demanded legislation. In 1903 Mrs Pankhurst founded the Women's Social and Political Union and began a more aggressive political programme in an unsuccessful attempt to influence the Liberal Government. In frustration, and to draw public attention to their demands, suffragettes embarked on a law-breaking programme, even arson. Imprisoned suffragettes went on hunger strikes, and authority responded with forced feeding.

The First World War interrupted the campaign but gave women the opportunity to emphasize their worth by taking over men's work, and in 1918 the Representation of the People Act gave the vote to married women, women householders, and women university graduates over the age of 30. Final victory was not won until 1928, when women were, like men, given the vote at 21. See also REFORM ACTS and the FRANCHISE.

Sugar-loaf. The form in which cane sugar arrived in the kitchen; cone-shaped, white, and crusty on the outside, it was broken into lumps by means of sugar nips. Near the centre the sugar was brown, with molasses in the centre. The shape was acquired after the cane was boiled, and the sugar stacked up to dry. The name 'Sugar Loaf' is often given to cone-shaped hills, such as the Sugar Loaf outside Abergavenny in Wales.

Suits (men's). The suit, comprising jacket, waistcoat and trousers in matching material, came into use in the 1870s, its origins in the vest, knee-length coat and breeches of the seventeenth century and the *habit à la française* (coat, waistcoat and breeches) of the eighteenth century. Trousers (often spelt 'trowsers' up to the 1870s), anciently worn, came into fashion again with the French Revolution, when long pantaloons replaced the knee-breeches (or *culottes*) and hose of the aristocracy. They were not widely worn in England until *c.* 1825 and, borrowed from working-men's garb, are a contradiction of the theory that style descends through the social scale. Turn-ups date from the 1890s, as a protection from country mud. In cities the frock coat and morning coat, worn with trousers with no turn-ups, were universal for all GENTLEMEN. The tail-less jacket coat replaced the ubiquitous long-tailed coat, but these 'lounge suits', as they came to be called, were worn only in the country, and very informally. Evening lounge suits or 'dress lounge' suits – dinner jacket and trousers – were introduced in the 1880s for informal evening wear, but until after the First World War would never be worn at any function where ladies were present.

Surgeon. Originally, a setter of bones and dresser of external wounds; surgeons were considered to be of lower status than physicians. Because they originally qualified by licence or diploma, rather than by taking a medical degree, they were addressed as 'Mr', not 'Dr', a convention which is maintained to this day.

Surnames. In use by the Norman nobility by *c.* 1100, but not widespread until the thirteenth century. The derivation of surnames generally falls into one of the following categories: (1) Patronymic (father's name); 'son of' varied among the Norman, Scots, Irish and Welsh: the old Normans used *Fitz*, as in Fitz-Herbert; Fitz might also signify illegitimacy, as in Fitzroy, Fitz-Clarence. The Scottish Highlanders used Mac and its variations Mc, M^c, as in Macdonald, son of Donald. The Irish favoured O', for grandson, as in O'Donnell, O'Neal. The Welsh used Ap, as in Ap Richard (son of Richard), Ap Rhys, Ap Owain; eventually the prefix came to be elided, giving Pritchard, Pryce, Bowen. Germanic or Scandinavian patronymics end in -son: Jackson (Jack's son), Robinson (Robin's son). (2) The occupation or calling of an ancestor: Smith, Miller, Tailor. (3) Derived from a place-name; often early English, Celtic, Norse, German or, after 1066, French: Johnston (the *ton* or holding of John), Marsh. (4) Nicknames indicative of physical features or characteristics, such as Brown, Short, Campbell ('crooked-lip'), Goodfellow, and sometimes animal names, of which Lamb is an example. (5) Clan or tribal names (see CLANS).

When surnames began to be widely used and written down, mistakes were made which obscured the meanings of many old English stems; first names were misinterpreted or regarded as meaningless; and spelling was not standardized until as late as the eighteenth century.

By the nineteenth century the social use of surnames had also become standardized; men used surnames one to another unless they were related, while close women friends invariably used Christian names among themselves. Conversely, and to distinguish SERVANTS from guests, male servants were called by their Christian names, female by their surnames; the first footman was often known as 'James', whatever his own Christian name might be.

Swaddling. The custom of tightly binding newly-born children in bandages to prevent movement of limbs, common in England from at least the Middle Ages.

The baby remained in swaddling clothes for up to four to six months, the arms being freed at about four months. It was thought to prevent the baby's soft bones from bending and malforming. In *Some Thoughts Concerning Education* (1673), the philosopher John Locke (1632–1704) included, with other practical advice on the upbringing of the sons of gentlemen, the recommendation that swaddling should be abandoned in favour of lighter clothing, and during the eighteenth century upper-class babies at least were unbound after about six weeks. During the latter part of the eighteenth century medical opinion turned against swaddling, and by 1785 *The Lady's Magazine* was doubting whether any of its readers knew how it was done. Swaddling is mentioned in the Bible and is clearly an ancient practice. Modern investigation shows that it slows down a child's heartbeat, induces sleep and reduces crying: a swaddled baby was little trouble, could be passed around like a parcel, put down or even hung on a peg, while a rural, working mother could easily carry it on her back.

Tallboy. A piece of furniture made in two parts, consisting of one chest of drawers on top of another ('chest-upon-chest' is a name also applied to this type of piece). Of Dutch origins and introduced at the end of the seventeenth century, they continued to be made until the late nineteenth century.

Tally. A notched wooden stick used for accounting. This use combines the two primitive notions of notching or scoring a piece of wood for counting, and a broken stick shared between the two parties to an agreement. Its use in England predated the earliest EXCHEQUER organization, and it continued to be the recognized form of receipt for payments into the Royal Treasury until 1826. In all this time the tally changed little in appearance apart from a continually increasing length (originally about 9 inches), due solely to the increase in the numbers of thousands (notches of the thickness of a mans hand) it was required to show: the Bank of England has one 8 feet 6 inches long.

Tallies are often mentioned in Pepys's *Diary* – 'Thence to the Exchequer and there got my tallies for 1750O*l* . . .' – but are memorable today chiefly because the destruction in 1834 of centuries'-worth of tallies in the furnaces of the House of Lords, and the consequent over-heating of the flues, is generally held to have been responsible for the burning down of the old Houses of Parliament.

Tapestries. Tapestries became a major art-form and an important element of interior decoration in the fourteenth and fifteenth centuries, when the tapestry works at Arras, Bruges, Brussels and Tournai exported sets of hangings throughout Europe. The early designs were based on cartoons (drawings on stout paper, used as a blueprint) by known designers, showing biblical scenes, history, hunting and romance. As tapestry-weaving is laborious and consequently expensive, their use was always an expression of wealth. A cheaper, coarser version known as *Tapisseries de Bergame* and made in Rouen and Elbeuf was not pictorial but had large repetitive patterns; these may be referred to as 'Dornix' (Doornick, the Flemish for Tournai) in seventeenth-century inventories. By Tudor times many English and Scottish houses were filled with tapestries, most of which have long since perished. PAINTED CLOTH hangings were an even cheaper substitute for tapestries.

The earliest surviving English tapestry was made for the Earl of Leicester before 1588 by Richard Hicks at the tapestry works of William Sheldon, Barchester, Warwickshire, and now hangs in the Victoria & Albert Museum; there is another Sheldon tapestry in St Denys's church, Sleaford, Lincolnshire. The Mortlake Tapestry works opened in 1620, and for a short time Flemish weavers there, brought over by James I (1603–1625), produced some of the finest tapestries in Europe. Between 1620 and 1636 Mortlake was under the direction of Sir Frances Crane, and examples from this period have the initials *F.C.* or *Car. Re. Reg. Mortl.*; it continued under a succession of owners until 1771. From the 1670s the original Mortlake designs were 'farmed out' to several other workshops. In the eighteenth century, English tapestries were also made at Fulham, Lambeth and Soho, but had gone out of fashion by the end of the century. In the second half of the nineteenth century two important workshops were opened in England, one at Windsor set up by weavers from Aubusson, and another at Merton Abbey founded in 1881 by William Morris.Over the centuries tapestries have tended to fade from exposure to daylight, which can also variously alter the colours of the vegetable dyes used before the mid nineteenth century; a look at their backs, however – hung always in the dark and so protected from fading – will give an idea of their original bright colouring.

Taxation. Taxation in forms we ourselves would recognize began in the seventeenth century, and its remorseless incidence has continued since then. Although Magna Carta was in part about land tax, the LAND TAX introduced in 1643 replaced old Parliamentary subsidies and dues of WARDSHIP, and was followed by an excise tax on consumption of a wide range of articles, narrowed after 1660 to beer, cider, spirits, tea, coffee and chocolate, but expanded again between 1688 and 1713 to include also malt, hops, candles, soap, leather and paper. These early taxes were crude in their operation; clearly the land tax fell on land-owners – but the main burden of consumption taxes fell on the poorer part of the population. A finer tuning of taxation was the aim of Adam SMITH, of whose principles the most important was that the subjects of a state should contribute towards its support as nearly as possible in pro-portion to their means.

Income tax was first levied in 1799 by William Pitt the Younger (1759–1806), as PRIME MINISTER, at a rate of two shillings in the pound, to pay for the war with revolutionary France; the tax continued until 1816, except for the years of peace 1802–3. It was re-imposed by Sir Robert Peel (1788–1850) in 1842, and has now persisted for more than 150 years. See also AIDS, DEATH DUTY and WINDOW TAX.

Taxidermy. No nineteenth-century country house was complete without a collection of stuffed birds, beasts and fish realistically dis-played in glass cases – an embarrassment to later heirs because of the space they occupied, and therefore many were simply thrown away. However, a very large collection of stuffed animals remains at Calke Abbey in Derbyshire, where the Harpur-Crewes simply stored things they did not want in rooms they did not use, thus preserving them for posterity. Most taxidermy dates from the nineteenth century; some examples survive from the eighteenth century, but most have perished as a result of imperfect preservation techniques.

The nineteenth-century fad arose from the Victorian interest in science, coupled with improvements in taxidermy. The skins were the problem: not their preservation, which was easy enough, using the same materials used in preserving food – alum, saltpetre, sodium chlo-ride – or simply tanning. The drawback was that the preserved skins subsequently became infested with insects, which ate them away. Arsenic, which came into use early in the nineteenth century, not only preserved the skins but, being poisonous, prevented infestations. Once mounted, specimens were coated (or, in the case of birds, feathers were dusted) with arsenic, as a preventive measure.

Teddy bears. The first teddy bear was made in Germany by Margaret Steiff in 1902 after she saw a cartoon in *The Washington Post* of President Theodore ('Teddy') Roosevelt refusing to shoot a bear cub. Margaret Steiff was born in 1849, stricken with polio at the age of three, and left with the use of only one hand. She began making pincushions on a sewing machine in 1879, but soon diversified into making animals, including a stuffed bear on four wheels. In 1902 it was only a short step to making the much loved teddy bears. The Steiff bears are regarded by enthusiasts as the *best* of bears: by 1908 the factory had exported more than a million. Others followed where Steiff had led the way, but the factory is still producing all manner of soft toys today. There is a fine collection of teddy bears in the Museum of Childhood at Sudbury Hall, Derbyshire.

Teinds. Scottish TITHES, which were managed differently from those in England. Most parishes in Scotland (some 1,100 in all) had been established by the end of the thirteenth century – the majority in the more settled areas of the south and east. Each parish was endowed with sufficient land to support a rector or parson, but as early as the twelfth century King David I (*c.* 1084–1153) had encouraged, in addition, the payment of teinds to ensure an adequate endowment for the parishes, a step later reinforced by an ecclesiastical council in 1177.

In the course of time some eighty-five per cent of Scottish parishes were taken over by religious foundations, and more than half had their incomes and teinds appropriated. Where the income was not completely appropriated vicars were put in to serve the parish on a very small stipend.

Temperance Movement. By the beginning of the nineteenth century it was recognized that drunkenness had become a major evil, a cause of crime and of the ruin of families. Distilled spirits (such as gin, whisky and brandy) were held chiefly to blame – a reversal of the viewpoint which saw them as the 'water of life' (see AQUA VITAE) on their first discovery. William Hogarth (1697–1764) had caricatured the ruinous aspects of the availability of cheap gin in *Gin Lane*, and in 1847 and 1848 George Cruikshank published *The Bottle* and *The Drunkard's Children*, which were reproduced in their tens of thousands.

The Temperance Movement came into being in 1826 and those who gave up alcohol ('signed the pledge') were given blue ribbons to wear in their buttonholes. A largely successful and well-organized attack on drunkenness was made by the 'Blue Ribbon Army'. The Temperance Party became a force in Liberal politics in the 1870s, but their fanatically extreme proposals, which included suppression of the drink trade, for long worked against their success. Balfour's Licensing Act of 1904 regulated the number of outlets for the sale of alcohol, and successive increases in duty went far to solving the problem, pricing distilled spirits beyond the reach of many.

Although the Temperance Movement was particularly strong among the NONCONFORMISTS, all religious groups supported its principles: in 1909 there were 639,000 members of the Church of England Temperance Society.

Templars. The Knights Templar, The Poor Knights of Christ and of the Temple of Solomon; a military order of KNIGHTHOOD founded in 1118 by a French knight, Hugues de Payns, to give protection and hospitality to the pilgrims who flocked to the Holy Land following the first CRUSADE. They won the support of the influential Bernard of Clairvaux, and adopted a modified form of CISTERCIAN rule, sanctioned by the Council of Troyes in 1128; their badge was a red cross on a white background. Recruits were readily found among the European nobility, and the order (under the Grand Master of the Temple at Jerusalem) was organized like the HOSPITALLERS, into national *langues*, or tongues.

The English headquarters was the Temple, now the site of two INNS OF COURT, just off Fleet Street to the south, in London, where the Temple Church was dedicated in 1185. King Stephen (1135–54) and his wife Matilda granted them lands at Cowley in Oxfordshire and Cressing in Sussex, where their first English preceptories were established. By the thirteenth century the Order had fifty houses in England, of which two were hospitals. Additionally, the English Master was summoned to the king's councils, and the Order frequently lent the king money.

The wealth and influence of the Order combined with its privileges and immunities provoked jealousy and unpopularity leading to accusations of immorality and heresy. Philip IV of France (1285–1314) plotted their downfall; the Pope was manoeuvred into issuing a Bull for their arrest (1308), Philip seized much of their French property, the Order was suppressed in 1312, and in 1314 the Grand Master was burned at the stake. The property of the Templars in England passed to the Crown, and in 1324 was granted by Edward II (1307–27) to the Knights Hospitallers.

Tennis. (1) *Real or Royal Tennis*. One of the oldest ball games. Its origins are disputed, but it was so popular in France and Spain, from at least the twelfth century, that two Spanish kings, Philip the Handsome and Henry I, and two French, Louis X and Charles VIII, are recorded as having died as a direct result of playing tennis. In England it was known to Chaucer, who refers to 'players racket to and fro', but forbidden by royal command between 1305 and 1388; Shakespeare famously mentioned the playing of tennis at the Court of Henry V (1413–22), and it was certainly played in the reign of Edward IV (1461–83): at St Peter's,

Elford (near Litchfield in Staffordshire) is a tomb-effigy, *c.* 1460, of a child, John Stanley, killed by a tennis ball. Henry VII was a player and enthusiast; a 'tennis-play' was made for him at Kenilworth in 1492–3, and he had courts at Richmond, Woodstock, Windsor and Westminster; records show that Henry VIII employed a Keeper of 'tennis-plays' in 1528. Two versions of the game were played in the late fifteenth century, the more ancient on a '*jeu quarré*' court (of which the only surviving example, much restored, is at Falkland Palace in Scotland, made in 1539 for James V and still in use today), about 60 feet by 23 feet. Another version was played on a larger court of about 100 feet by 38 feet, examples of which are to be found at Hampton Court (the oldest such court in the world, and still used) and at Holyroodhouse in Edinburgh. The older form of the game had passed from wide popularity by the end of the seventeenth century, but the larger-court game was played until the nineteenth century, and has its enthusiasts to this day. The court is very different from that used in lawn tennis: a sloping roof runs round the two ends and along one of the side walls, and a net that sags is strung across the middle.

(2) *Lawn Tennis.* A comparatively late derivation from Real or Royal Tennis. The *Sporting Magazine* of 1793 mentions 'Field Tennis', but unfortunately no details are known of how this was played. The earliest tennis club, the Leamington Club, when the game was called Polota or Lawn Rackets, was founded by Major Harry Gem in 1872. Major Walter Clopton Wingfield patented a 'new and improved portable court for playing the ancient game of tennis' – an hour-glass shaped court which he called 'Sphairistike' and his detractors shorted to 'Sticky'. About the same time the All England Croquet Club at Wimbledon added 'Lawn Tennis' to its name and laid down several grass courts, and the first championship was held there in 1877, with 22 competitors, most of them real tennis or rackets players. See also BADMINTON.

Terracotta. An Italian word meaning 'baked earth', applied to unglazed moulded and fired clay, much used for the making of detailed decoration for buildings, and also for modelled figures. Terracotta differs from brick in that finer, sieved clay is used, fired at a temperature beyond 1375 °C, far higher than that used for brick-making. The first use of terracotta in Britain was probably by Italians working *c.* 1514 for Cardinal Wolsey (*c.* 1475–1530) at Hampton Court Palace, where he placed Italian medallions of Roman emperors on his gatehouse. On his acquisition of the Palace in 1529, Henry VIII (1509–47) continued to use the Italians and their terracotta detailing, and thereafter terracotta came to be more widely popular, obviously following this inspiration. Some examples, all dating from around this period, include the tombs of two Lords Marney (d. 1523 and 1525) at Layer Marney in Essex; a group of terracotta window mullions at Shrubland Old Hall, Suffolk (*c.* 1525), and in the nearby churches at Henley, Barham, and Barking, using the same moulds, pointing to a local workshop; and some terracotta window mullions at Kneesall Old Hall, Nottinghamshire, built *c.* 1523 as a HUNTING LODGE for Lord Hussey (1466–1537), probably using unwanted items from Hampton Court; there are other examples, but after this brief outbreak, terracotta was scarcely employed again until the nineteenth century, when it was used extensively by architects for decorative details, and often for facing entire buildings.

Tester. A canopy, particularly those over BEDS.

Theatricals. A painting by Hogarth of 1732 shows the children of John Conduit, Master of the Royal Mint, and their friends, dressed to play parts in Dryden's *The Indian Emperor* – an exceptionally extravagant amateur production, which was performed before royalty. Amateur theatricals were probably introduced to England after the RESTORATION of 1660, and have held their appeal down the centuries. The 6th Duke of Devonshire built a private theatre at Chatsworth in Derbyshire in 1833, now the only survivor of others built but since demolished: at Blenheim in Oxfordshire; Wynnstay in Denbighshire; and Wargrave in Berkshire.

The 5th Marquis of Anglesey had the distinction of being the only peer to have bankrupted himself by over-indulgence in amateur theatricals, FANCY-DRESS and jewellery: he built a theatre in the chapel of his house, Plas Newyd, Anglesey, and financed his own company of players, with whom he unfailingly performed his Butterfly Dance whatever the production. In debt to the tune of £250,000 in 1904, he died in Monte Carlo the following year, aged only 30. See also ACTRESSES.

Tiger. A liveried servant who rode out with his master; the equivalent attendant for a lady was known as a page.

Tilbury. A light, open, two-wheeled carriage popular in the first half of the nineteenth century; invented by a Mr Tilbury. See also CARRIAGES.

Tilting. The last breath of CHIVALRY, and one of the principal Court entertainments between 1470 and 1536: mounted knights, fully armoured and carrying lances, charged one another, two at a time, either side of a timber barrier, 'the lists'. Points were scored for dismounting an opponent, breaking his lance, or making contact with his armour. Henry VIII was a keen participant in his youth, but his enthusiasm was tempered when in 1524, having omitted to drop his vizor, he received a helmet-full of splinters; he finally gave up tilting altogether in 1536, when he was knocked unconscious for two hours. Tilting was revived as part of the chivalric pageantry which so often marked the reign of Elizabeth I (1558–1603), but died out again under James I (1603–25). Other uses were found for tilt-yards. See also TOURNAMENTS.

Timber-framing. A method of house construction in which the walls are built of a timber framework carrying the load, the spaces between the timbers filled in with BRICKWORK (nogging) or WATTLE AND DAUB. Sometimes the timber is plastered over, or covered with horizontal boards (weatherboarding).

Tipping. See VAILS.

Tithes. The literal meaning is one-tenth, applied to a man's property or produce. Until the ninth century one-tenth of all living things were expected to be voluntarily donated to the Church for the support of religious activities. From the reign of Edgar (959–75), the payment of tithes became compulsory, and from the tenth century tithes became the support of the parish priest, their collection greatly resented by many parishioners. After the Norman Conquest, lords of the manor were given free use of tithes and a large proportion was donated to supporting or establishing monasteries. As tithes came progressively into the possession of monasteries, bishops and cathedrals, the rectors who had direct rights to all tithes in their parish – see CLERGY – were replaced by vicars, who were usually given only the small tithes, the rectorial, or great, tithes being retained by the possessor.

The practice of exacting tithes survived the DISSOLUTION and was viewed with increasing intolerance, particularly by NONCONFORMISTS and Roman CATHOLICS who were, of course, outside the Church of England. Commutation of the tithes for an annual stipend was instituted before 1600, but no provision was made to revise them in times of inflation, when the clergy were the losers. Dissatisfaction was further increased by parish ENCLOSURE. Tithe Commutation Acts between 1836 and 1860 attempted to replace tithes with a single 'tithe rent charge' determined by a Tithe Redemption Commission; however, problems continued to arise and discontent provoked further Tithe Acts in 1936 and 1951, whereby tithes were commuted to a lump sum, payable in instalments up to the year 2000. The Tithe Redemption Commission was dissolved in 1960 and its responsibilities transferred to the Inland Revenue. See also TEINDS.

Tobacco. Christopher Columbus found the natives of Central America smoking tobacco for ceremonial and medicinal purposes. It is thought to have been introduced to England from North America (where the American Indians also smoked it) as early at 1565, but the story of Walter Raleigh introducing it to the Court of Queen Elizabeth I (1558–1603) in 1585 is so well known as to pass for fact; at this time smoking was confined to Indian pipes and the Central American cigar.

From the beginning tobacco incurred a duty of 2d. a pound. By the end of Elizabeth's reign smoking was fairly widespread and James I (1603–25), who regarded the habit as disgusting, raised the duty to 6s. 10d. a pound, which proved an effective discouragement. Nevertheless, tobacco was reputed to act as a disinfectant, particularly against PLAGUE, and was employed as a remedy for various maladies (nicotine is indeed a pesticide, as GREENHOUSE owners may know). The use of snuff displaced smoking in the eighteenth century; by 1773 Dr Johnson (1709–83) was reporting that 'Smoking was gone out', but its popularity increased with a reduction in taxation. The Peninsular War reintroduced Europeans to the forgotten cigar or cigarillo, first brought to Spain in the sixteenth century, and returning officers brought them into fashion in England. The Crimean War (1854–6) gave the popularity of tobacco another boost when troops were introduced to the cheaper cigarette. This led to the first hand–rolled cigarette factory in Britain being opened at Walworth by Robert Gloag, ex–paymaster to the Turkish troops. By 1883 W.D. & H.O. Wills, using mass-production machinery, were making 150 million Woodbines a year, selling at a penny for five. The First World War finally brought the cigarette social acceptance, even for women, who had hitherto smoked clandestinely. The Second World War had a similar dramatic effect on annual cigarette sales, which increased by 25,000 million in the United Kingdom in 1945.

Skilfully pitched advertising on the part of tobacco manufacturers gave smoking a glamorous image, but its connection with cancer was first published in Germany in 1939 – to be ignored until the publication of similar findings in the USA (1950) and Britain (1951). Smoking reached its peak in 1956, when 57 per cent of United Kingdom males were smokers. See also SMOKING JACKETS, SMOKING ROOMS and SNUFF BOXES.

Tokay (Tokaj, Tokai). A rich sweet, dessert wine, long famous, which takes its name from a town in Hungary at the foot of vineyards said to have been introduced by Italian colonists in the thirteenth century.

Toleration Act, 1689. Legislation permitting Protestant Dissenters, other than UNITARIANS, to worship in their own licensed meeting places.

Tolpuddle Martyrs. These were six farm labourers of Tolpuddle in Dorset, who in 1834 under the leadership of George Loveless formed a branch of the Friendly Union of Agricultural Workers, to resist payment of lower wages. This was no longer an offence (see COMBINATION ACTS) but the Government, alarmed by waves of rick-burning and machine-breaking since 1831, had determined to support local magistrates who dealt harshly with trades unionists. The six were prosecuted under the terms of the Unlawful Oaths Act of 1797 for 'administering illegal oaths' for 'seditious' purposes and, out of all proportion to their offence, were sentenced to be transported to Tasmania for seven years. The trial cannot be said to have been fair, as the jury was composed of local farmers with a vested interest in resisting Union power, but the Home Secretary, Lord Melbourne (1779–1848), refused to receive a petition containing half a million signatures, and upheld the sentence. Widespread protests and a further TRADES UNION petition eventually secured a pardon for the six, in 1836; five subsequently emigrated to Canada, and only one returned to England.

Tontines. A financial scheme introduced in France in 1653 by a Neapolitan, Lorenzo Tonti; first used as a means of raising money by the British government in 1693. Each subscriber to a government tontine invested the same amount of capital in the scheme, which then paid each an equal annuity; as the subscribers died, the annuities paid to the survivors increased, until the last survivor enjoyed all the income. On his death, the capital sum reverted to the Government. Other government tontines were in 1773, 1775, 1777 and 1789.

Topiary. Defined as the art of growing and clipping trees and shrubs in ornamental or fantastic shapes, fashionable in Britain particularly from the sixteenth century until the beginning of the eighteenth. At Packwood House in Warwickshire is a nineteenth-century creation, perhaps based on an early yew garden of *c.* 1650, representing the Sermon on the Mount, with the Multitude. The Dutch were masters of this art and the accession of William III (1689–94) and Mary in 1689 brought topiary increased popularity. They employed the well-known gardeners London and Wise to design gardens to complement their alterations at Hampton Court, and the great semi-circular yew garden remains of the topiary work dating from this period. London and Wise also designed a topiary garden at Melbourne Hall, Derbyshire, *c.* 1700. At Levens Hall in Cumbria is a topiary garden of 1690–4 laid out for Colonel James Graham by a Frenchman, Guillaume Beaumont, who had been gardener to James II (1685–88) at Hampton Court. An interest in topiary revived in the nineteenth and early twentieth centuries, and examples survive at Elvaston Castle, Derbyshire; Hidcote Manor, Gloucestershire; and Nymans, Sussex. See also GARDENS.

Tories. Originally, applied to Irish Roman Catholic bandits who lived by plundering and killing English settlers; later applied (by those later called WHIGS) to those who supported the hereditary right of the Roman Catholic James, Duke of York (1633–1701) to succeed to the throne, despite his faith. As a political grouping the Tories emerged in the 1680s; they enjoyed some favour under Queen Anne (1702–14), but following the Hanoverian succession of 1714, they became associated with the JACOBITES, and in consequence were out of power until the reign of George III (1760–1820). Under William Pitt the Younger (1759–1806) a new and more vigorous Tory party emerged which held power from 1783 to 1830, when their opposition to Parliamentary reform brought defeat. In the next decade began the transformation of Toryism into the Conservatism of Bejamin Disraeli (1804–81), since when the names 'Tory' and 'Conservative' have been synonymous.

Tournament or **Tourney.** Originally a tournament was a series of jousting matches between mounted knights in full armour who charged at each other in the lists with lances, each attempting to unhorse his opponent. The tournament provided the medieval mounted knight – the armoured tank of the time – with practice and training for battle. With advances in warfare and the invention of gunpowder the mounted, armoured knight became outmoded – but tournaments were revived as a form of entertainment in the reigns of Henry VIII (1509–47) and Elizabeth I (1558–1603), when knights competed at jousts for the favours of the Queen, as part of the renaissance of CHIVALRY, which lasted until the 1620s.

Under the inspiration of the GOTHIC REVIVAL, a joust was held by Viscount Gage at Firle Place, Sussex in 1827, but more famous was the Eglinton Tournament, held at Eglinton Castle, Ayrshire in 1839. The young and dashing 13th Earl of Eglinton, encouraged by his friends, produced a three-day pageant far bigger, more impressive and costly than he had originally intended. The event was ruined by a torrential downpour, and history only remembers the rained-out fiasco and the knights holding umbrellas. It was the last of the medieval-revival tournaments. See also TILTING.

Tractarians. See OXFORD MOVEMENT.

Trades Unions. From the beginning of the INDUSTRIAL REVOLUTION in the eighteenth century, skilled craftsmen from time to time organized themselves into trade societies in order to bargain for better wages and working hours, rather in the style of the earlier GUILDS. Frequent riots over wages and working conditions in the Midlands during the latter part of the century resulted in the COMBINATION ACTS of 1799 and 1800, which forbade two or more to 'combine' in order to seek better wages, etc., thus effectively making Trades Unions illegal. The Acts were repealed in 1824, but replaced in 1825 with measures which, while admitting the legal right of unions to exist, imposed many restrictions on their actions. Government paranoia about organized insurrection was fuelled by Robert Owen's (1771–1858) attempt (1833) to combine trade societies and unions into a Grand National Consolidated Trades' Union. Owen's GNCTU collapsed in 1834, its fall hastened in part by the Government's over-reaction in the case of the TOLPUDDLE MARTYRS.

Improvement of trade in the 1840s and 1850s permitted higher wages, fears of riots receded, and the Union movement began to develop on a national scale. The Miners' Association of Great Britain and Ireland was formed in 1841, The Amalgamated Society of Engineers in 1851, and The Amalgamated Society of Carpenters and Joiners in 1862 – models of national union organization, but of doubtful legal status. In 1868 the Trades Union Congress (TUC) was formed, with the object of exerting pressure on Parliament for labour law reform. The Trade Union Act of 1871 granted legal status to Unions, and legal protection of Union property and funds.

A depression in the 1880s saw Union expansion into unskilled trades such as agriculture, railways and docks given further encouragement by a successful dock strike in 1889. These unskilled unionists tended to be more militant and socialist than their skilled 'brothers', and their political activities led in 1893 to the creation of the Independent Labour Party, under James Keir Hardie (1856–1915).

The Taff Vale Judgment of 1901, when the Taff Vale Railway Company successfully sued the Amalgamated Society of Railway Servants for damages (loss of profits) caused by its agents' actions during a strike, threatened the Unions' right to strike, but was reversed by the Trade Disputes Act of 1906 which gave trade unions immunity from suits for damages and upheld the legality of peaceful picketing. The Osborne Judgment of 1909 successfully restrained the Amalgamated Society of Railway Servants from levying funds to be spent in support of a political party – as the levy was mostly used to provide financial support for Labour MPs, at a time when MPs received no salary, this was a blow to the Labour Party. However, the Trade Union Act of 1913 effectively reversed the Osborne Judgment: the political levy was deemed legal, but provision was made for those who objected to paying it to opt out.

The period 1910–14 saw acute industrial unrest, many strikes, and an increase in the power of the unions; by 1914 there were 4.1 million union members. However, the declaration of an industrial truce on the outbreak of the First World War demonstrated the possibility of co-operation between unions and employers.

The GENERAL STRIKE of 1926 proved a serious set-back to both employees and employers. One outcome was the Trade Disputes Act of 1927 which, making sympathy strikes and intimidation illegal, was designed to ensure that another general strike would be impossible; this Act was repealed in 1946.

After the Second World War the unions followed a restrictive policy of specialist working, so that jobs were not interchangeable on the shop floor. In the 1970s and 1980s, the Miners' Union under Arthur Scargill followed an aggressive policy of strikes and violence, provoking heavy police interference and losing the miners public sympathy. Under Prime Minister Margaret Thatcher in the 1980s the Government revised the Trade Union legislation, removing anomalies and bad working practices along with many hard-won privileges.

Train Bands. A term particularly applied to the London MILITIA during the period of the CIVIL WAR. The use of locally-raised forces under commissions from the Crown for the purpose of putting down civil disturbances dates back at least to the thirteenth century. As the men were unpaid, and any assembly and exercise time came out of their working time, they were understandably never very keen, and seldom adequately trained or disciplined; their strong local character made them unwilling to serve outside their own county.

Transom. A horizontal bar of wood or stone across a window opening. See also MULLION.

Tray. Because of the many SERVANTS available to carry things, trays made a comparatively late appearance, in the seventeenth century, as 'voiders' or 'voyders', used for clearing scraps from the dining table; this later evolved into the butler's tray. Trays were of plain, inlaid or lacquered wood, tin or silver. During the eighteenth century lacquered PAPIER MÂCHÉ was also used, and oval inlaid mahogany trays with handles, in the SHERATON style, were popular.

Treason. Generally, the crime of attacking the safety of a sovereign state or of its head; the violation of allegiance owed to the sovereign. The first Statute of Treasons of 1531, still in force today, declared the following offences to be high treason: (1) imagining or compassing the death of the king, his queen, or his heir; (2) violating the king's companion, the king's eldest unmarried daughter, or the wife of his heir; (3) levying war against the king within his realm, or adhering to his enemies within his realm, or giving them aid and comfort in the realm or elsewhere; (4) murdering certain royal officials and judges engaged on the king's business; (5) forging his coins or his seal.

Other offences have been temporarily added, but subsequently removed; for example, in 1536 it was treason to refuse to take the Oath of Supremacy; in 1571, to make a declaration that the queen was a heretic. In 1597 rioting against ENCLOSURE was included, and in 1688 'rioting' was stretched to include apprentices who pulled down brothels.

The original punishment for high treason was hanging, drawing and quartering; after 1795, simple beheading; and since 1870, hanging. The Treason Felony Act of 1848 included three offences punishable by life imprisonment only: (1) attempts to depose the sovereign; (2) attempts to deprive him/her of his/her dominions; (3) attempts to levy war against him/her. Since the abolition of CAPITAL PUNISHMENT for muder in 1965 and arson in 1972, high treason is one of only two crimes for which the death penalty may be imposed; the other is piracy with violence.

Tree house. What is probably the world's oldest tree house survives at Pitchford Hall, Shropshire, in a 600-year-old lime tree. Built in 1692 and half-timbered, from its windows in 1832 the future Queen Victoria, then aged 13, watched a fox-hunt.

Treen. Early wooden household utensils usually made of sycamore, such as TRENCHERS and bowls, which preceded the use of pewter. The word was never used contemporaneously but is derived from the Old English word *trëowen*, tree.

Trenchers. From early medieval times to the fifteenth century, plates for eating from were all but unknown; instead, two or four slices of stale bread were used, with a further slice over the centre join. The word comes from the French *trancher*, to slice, cut or carve. A hungry diner could eat his trencher, but more commonly it was scraped into a bucket with all other leavings and given as DOLE to the poor at the gate. Because of the nature of the foundation from which the diner ate – it is impossible to cut anything up on soggy bread – food had to be cut into manageable pieces before being served; conversely, food could not be too mushy. These limitations inevitably restricted recipes. During the fifteenth century the bread trencher came to be replaced by square wooden plaques – a great improvement, but still called trenchers. See also FORKS, PLATES and TREEN.

Triad, triolet. This describes a suite, consisting of table, looking-glass and pair of candlestands, designed to fill the pier or wall space between two windows; popular from the 1670s to the early eighteenth century (see also PIER GLASS). The arrangement (which can be seen at Ham House, Greater London) was practical – the looking-glass reflected the face lit by window-light during the day, and reflected candle-light back into the room at night – and could be used anywhere, the table serving as a dressing-table in the bed-chamber or as a writing-desk elsewhere. However, unless very carefully positioned the candles tended to set curtains alight, and the arrangement was gradually altered to the familiar pier glass and table or console, with a candelabrum placed on the table at night, an arrangement widely used by Robert ADAM in his interiors from the 1760s.

'Turkie' or 'Turkey' work. English knotted woollen pile carpet pieces (not imported Turkey carpets), often used from the sixteenth century for covering chairs and stools, as bed or table coverings, or, later, as carpets. 'Turkey' work was less expensive than imported velvets and carpets, but still not cheap. It might be used as foot carpet in wealthy households, and as table carpet in lesser establishments. An industry centred on Norwich. See also AXMINSTER CARPETS and FLOORS AND FLOOR COVERINGS.

Turnpike roads. After the departure of the Romans the road system in Britain was more or less neglected; every parish through which a road passed was responsible for its maintenance, by means of six days a year of unpaid labour given by the local people, one of whom was chosen as surveyor; the work was supposed to be completed by midsummer. Needless to say, in the majority of parishes this amounted at best to the filling-in of potholes. With the increase in commerce and improvements in the design of wheeled CARRIAGES, including springing, from the beginning of the seventeenth century, the demand grew for better roads. The first Turnpike Act (1663) passed the burden of the costs of road building and maintenance to trusts supported by local interests and authorized to raise capital and levy tolls. Each turnpike required its own ACT OF PARLIAMENT; the Act of 1663 applied to main roads in Hertfordshire, Cambridgeshire and Huntingdonshire, and an Act of 1695 to the London to Colchester road.

The turnpike was the gate or barrier across the turnpike road, at which the traveller paid his toll or charge. Between 1760 and 1770, 452 separate Turnpike Acts were passed, and in 1773 a General Turnpike Act became law. By 1800 there were 1,600 turnpike roads covering many parts of the kingdom: it was possible to travel from Leicester to London by horse-drawn carriage in two days. The coming of the railways in the 1840s killed the turnpike system, and by 1890 only two remote turnpike roads survived. Today, turnpike cottages are the only visible evidence of these roads. Built close to the sides of country roads with bay windows giving views up and down the turnpike, they were provided for the men who kept the gate and collected the tolls. See also the HORSE.

Tweenie. See BETWEEN-MAIDS.

Typhus. A highly infectious and often fatal disease, most commonly caused by a microbe in the excreta of lice, fleas, mites and ticks. It usually enters the body through abrasions, often on the feet, and is endemic in overcrowded and filthy conditions. The symptoms are a high fever with eruption of purple spots.

Umbrellas. It is unsurprising to find that the Chinese had umbrellas in the eleventh century BC; they were carried by slaves to shade people of rank from the sun in Ancient Egypt, Assyria, Babylon, Persia and Greece. In the Orient and the Middle East they have long been used, made of leather, for protection against rain too. The modern umbrella came to Britain via France from Italy, where the Venetian Doge was, from the twelfth century, carried in state beneath a ceremonial umbrella, and where Italian clergy used umbrellas from the late sixteenth century. In Britain umbrellas of oiled silk were used by women in the reign of Queen Anne (1702–14), but their use by men was for long considered effeminate. James Hanway (1712–86) is said to have been the first man to use an umbrella in London, disconcerting SEDAN chairmen and porters. However, a footman, John Macdonald (1741–96), claimed in his autobiography *Travells of Various Parts of Europe, Asia and Africa* (1790) to have been the first, in the 1770s: 'If it rained I wore my fine silk umbrella: then the people would call after me "What, Frenchman, why do you not get a coach?"' He further tells us that 'At this time there was no umbrellas worn in London, except in noblemen's and gentlemen's houses; where there was a large one hung in the hall, to hold over a lady or gentleman if it rained.' Umbrellas with steel ribs, instead of cumbersome cane, were first made *c*. 1840. When used as a protection against the sun the umbrella is usually called a parasol.

Underdog. This one is curious; the underdog was the sawyer in the bottom of the sawpit, on whom the sawdust fell; the better position was that of the upper-dog (top dog, top-sawyer) on the top end of the two-handled saw. At Erddig in Clwyd a sawpit has survived with its equipment; set up as if it has just been used, it gives a very good impression of what the underdog must have endured.

Underground passages. There are various thrilling accounts of escapes through underground passages by papists or priests, or Royalists during the Commonwealth, but most are pure fiction. Underground passages and rooms there certainly are, but they usually served a utilitarian or eccentric purpose. At Calke Abbey in Derbyshire, a murky passage running from the kitchen garden to the park beneath the Pleasure Ground Plantation was constructed in 1816–18 because Sir Henry Harpur-Crewe (1763–1819) did not want to meet gardeners and outdoor servants when he was enjoying his garden. Welbeck Abbey in Nottinghamshire has an amazing underground complex built from 1860 by the reclusive 5th Duke of Portland (1809–79), who had a morbid fear of being seen. It includes a tunnel one-and-a-quarter miles long leading to Worksop station, a library and a picture gallery, a BALLROOM (at the time, the largest room in Europe without supporting pillars), and passages with tramlines so that food could be sent to the Duke in trucks from the KITCHEN. Harleyford Manor in Buckinghamshire has a separate service wing connected to the main house by an underground passage, as has Belton House in Lincolnshire. At Stoke Rochford Hall, Lincolnshire, begun in 1839, there is a short passage, again with tramlines, linking the kitchen to a food lift to the dining-room. Most eccentric of all is the BILLIARD room at Witley Park in Surrey, constructed in the 1890s at the bottom of a lake. See also PRIEST-HOLES.

Undertakers. Early uses of this word very often have little to do with funerals. In the sixteenth and seventeenth centuries, undertakers were tenants of Crown lands in Ireland; in the early Stuart Parliaments they were the 'fixers' who tried – usually without great success – to ensure that MPs who would support the Court party were elected. In the eighteenth century the word was used of Irish magnates who agreed to use their patronage to support the government in return for places and pensions. It was only in the early nineteenth century that the term became at all widely used for those who organize funerals.

Uniformity, Acts of. Legislation to establish the doctrinal and legal foundations of the Anglican church, as follows: (1) 1549: required that Archbishop Cranmer's gently Protestant BOOK OF COMMON PRAYER should be used for Anglican worship. (2) 1552: enforced a more Protestant Book of Common Prayer with more stringent penalties, particularly for the non-attendance of RECUSANTS. (3) 1559: both earlier Acts having been repealed under Mary I (1553–54), this Act, promoted not by the Church but by Parliament, restored a revised form of the 1552 Prayer Book. (4) 1662: although the Presbyterians who had helped restore Charles II (1660–85) looked for some reward, the first Parliament of the RESTORATION was violently anti-Puritan, and provided that all ministers not episcopally ordained or refusing to conform to the usages of the Church of England should be ejected. Some 2,000 NON-CONFORMIST clergy were forced to resign, marking the beginning of the Nonconformist breakaway from the Church of England. (5) 1666: applied the Act of 1662 to Ireland. See also the ELIZABETHAN SETTLE-MENT.

Unitarianism. A system of religious observance supporting the doctrine of the single personality of God, as opposed to the Trinitarian conception of a three-fold Being – Father, Son and Holy Ghost. The most notable figure among early Unitarians was Michael Servetus (c. 1511–53), burnt at the stake at the instigation of John Calvin for his heretical opinions.

The TOLERATION ACT of 1662 specifically excluded Unitarians from its provisions for Dissenting ministers to preach under licence, yet many chapels established at this time came to adopt Unitarian opinions, which hold that supreme authority is found in religious history and experience, interpreted by man's reason and conscience. Many congregations today (members of the General Assembly of Unitarian and Free Christian Churches) adopt the statement 'for the love of faith, and in the spirit of Jesus Christ, we unite for the worship of God and the service of man'.

Universities. Universities grew up in towns where there were already communities devoted to higher learning, apparently as more or less spontaneous combinations of teachers and scholars – on the analogy of the trades guilds – for mutual benefit and protection. Schools in the precinct of a former nunnery and of Osney Abbey are thought to have provided the nucleus for Oxford, where an eminent theologian from the University of Paris was delivering lectures on the Bible in 1133. An impetus was probably provided by the expulsion of foreign students from France in 1168. In 1209 a body of Oxford students migrated to Cambridge, where the new Priory of St Giles at Barnwell was already an important educational centre.

The thirteenth century saw the establishment of halls, places of licensed residence for students, followed by the foundation of colleges. The first were at Oxford – University College (1249), Balliol (1263) and Merton (1264); Peterhouse was the first Cambridge college (1284), followed in 1324–6 by Michaelhouse and King's Hall (later – 1547 – amalgamated into Trinity College), and another handful between 1347 and 1359 – Pembroke Hall, Gonville Hall, Trinity Hall, Corpus Christi, Clare Hall. Merton was the first college established for secular clergy, previous foundations having been designed solely for the benefit of one or other of the religious orders, and its statutes (drawn up by Walter de Merton) were such a rare combination of breadth of conception and discriminating attention to detail that they were taken as the model for later colleges, at Cambridge as well as at Oxford.

The course of studies at both universities was the *trivium* (Latin grammar, rhetoric and logic), leading to the degree of Bachelor of Arts, followed by the *quadrivium* (arithmetic, geometry, music and astronomy), leading to the degree of Master of Arts. Students entered at the age of sixteen and undertook a seven-year course; further residence was necessary for a doctorate. The subjects taught changed little until the nineteenth century, although under Sir Isaac Newton's professorship (1673–1702) Cambridge became a centre for mathematical science. A university degree, while it doubtless indicated a trained mind, was of slight practical use to any but clerics, which may in part explain the popularity of the GRAND TOUR, with its opportunities for the study of languages, art and architecture, and for generally broadening the mind.

In 1571 *An Acte for Thincorporation of Bothe Thunyversities* incorporated both Oxford and Cambridge, the corporation consisting of a Chancellor, masters and scholars, and confirmed to them all privileges held under charter or by prescription (ancient or continued custom). Between 1603 and 1948, each university returned two members to Parliament.

St Andrews, the first Scottish University, was founded in 1411, Glasgow in 1453, and Aberdeen in 1494; they were followed by Edinburgh in 1587; and Trinity College Dublin in 1591. Oxford and Cambridge remained the only English universities until the foundation of King's College, London in 1829, Durham in 1832 and Manchester in 1851.

Uranian. A term denoting homosexuality.

Vaccination. Inoculation with vaccine (literally, a virus of cowpox) to give immunity against specific diseases (originally SMALLPOX). Lady Mary Wortley Montagu (1689–1762) attempted to introduce vaccination, having learned of the practice in Constantinople where her husband was ambassador, 1716–18, and having herself been vaccinated. At that time the preparation for vaccination required the patient to consume a low diet for a month before the treatment, a course not without danger because the mild dose could cause a full-blown attack in an already half-starved patient. It was not until 1796 that real progress was made, when Edward Jenner (1749–1823), a Gloucestershire country doctor, observed that milkmaids infected with cowpox did not catch SMALLPOX. He met considerable opposition from the medical profession, but persevered, and free vaccination, introduced in 1840, was made compulsory for babies in 1853. Smallpox was quickly eradicated from Britain; compulsory vaccination ended in 1946.

Vails. Described by Dr Brewer in his *Dictionary of Phrase and Fable* (1897) as 'Blackmail in the shape of fees to servants'; a system of tipping that reached its apogee in the early eighteenth century. Visitors were expected to tip the SERVANTS on leaving any household in which they had been a guest, and the higher the rank of the host, the more generous were the vails expected. Some servants adopted a fixed scale.

The poet Pope (1688–1744) protested to the 2nd Duke of Montagu (1688–1749) that as it cost him £5 in vails whenever he dined at Montagu House in Bloomsbury, he couldn't afford to accept another invitation. In future, the good-natured Duke's invitations were accompanied by £5. In 1761 the *London Chronicle* reported a case in which an Admiral's valet had cut to pieces the hat of a visitor who left no vail.

Except in a few very grand houses, the custom of leaving tips on this scale had died out by the end of the eighteenth century. However, even today it is considered correct to leave a tip in one's bedroom for the housemaid if one stays in a house where staff are kept.

Valet. The modern meaning is a man's personal servant, but in medieval times he was a boy living in a household other than that of his parents in order to learn behaviour and manners.

Vanbrugh, Sir John (1664–1726). Dramatist, soldier and architect, one of the chief exponents of the BAROQUE style in England. Jonathan

Swift (1667–1745) wrote: 'Van's genius, without thought or lecture,/ is hugely turn'd to architecture.' In 1699 he made designs for Castle Howard (1700–26), North Yorkshire, based on Palladio's plans, for the Earl of Carlisle, but having had no practical training in building himself he relied on the expertise of Nicholas HAWKSMOOR, who assisted him at Castle Howard from 1700. Thereafter Vanbrugh worked on 22 houses, and a further 13 are attributed to him; on many of the houses he worked again with Hawksmoor, and it is not always easy to determine the part played by each man. Blenheim Palace, Oxfordshire (1705–16), built for the 1st Duke of Marlborough, is his best known work. Unfortunately he fell out with the Duchess, and the building was completed by Hawksmoor. Vanbrugh's buildings have been called 'heroic architecture'; they are certainly theatrical and dramatic, with detail drawn from Italian and French sources. Vanbrugh was one of the Commissioners under the Act for Building Fifty New Churches (in the suburbs of London: 1711). His buildings tend to have the appearance of great monumentality – hence the adjuration in Abel Evans's epitaph to him: 'Lie heavy on him, Earth! for he/Laid many heavy loads on thee.'

Vehicle Tax. First introduced in 1747, the tax had risen by the 1850s to £2 2s. for a four-wheeled vehicle. Anything having fewer than four wheels and weighing less than 4 cwt was taxed at 15 shillings. Any two-wheeled vehicle costing less than £12 was taxed only a few shillings – provided that the words 'tax cart' were clearly painted on it. The rates remained unchanged into the Second World War, when the tax on horse-drawn vehicles was dropped.

Vicar. See CLERGY.

Victoria. A low, light, four-wheeled, horse-drawn carriage with two forward-facing seats, a collapsible top, and a raised driving seat. Named after Queen Victoria, who owned one which may still be seen in the Royal MEWS. See also CARRIAGES.

Villa. In Classical Rome, a summer residence or elegant farmstead on a country estate; in Renaissance architecture, a country house; and in nineteenth-century Britain, a detached house for 'opulent persons' on the outskirts of a town or city. The first house in England to be built in the villa style created by Palladio was Mereworth Castle, Kent (1722–5), designed by Colen CAMPBELL for the 7th Earl of Westmorland (1682–1762); a close second is Chiswick House (1723–9), designed by the 3rd Earl of BURLINGTON for himself. Both are based on Palladio's La Rotonda at Vicenza.

Villein. A feudal serf holding manorial land in return for agricultural service. A villein was free of everyone except his feudal lord; this meant that he was bound to his holding, which also carried rights to a share in the common lands and grazing rights in the common pasture. His service was of two kinds: week work, regular agricultural work done weekly, and BOONWORK, extra work done at important times in the agricultural year. There were some restrictions on a villein's freedom: he could not marry without his lord's permission, nor could he bring a suit in the king's court. The villein status had all but died away by *c.* 1500, by which time the descendants of villeins had become entirely free, and held their land of the lord of the manor by right of COPYHOLD. See also HERIOT and MANOR.

Virginals. See HARPSICHORD.

Visiting card. A white, stiff card (usually 3 ins × 1½ ins for a man and 3¼ ins × 2¼ ins for a woman) printed or engraved with a person's name and address – the London address in the bottom left-hand corner, and/or the country address in the bottom right.

The protocol of 'calling' and 'leaving cards' throughout the nineteenth century and well into the twentieth was organized to be as convenient as possible to both parties. Ladies usually set aside one afternoon of the week, between 4 and 5.30 p.m., when they would be 'at home', receiving callers. On other afternoons, a caller might ask for the lady of the household; if she was 'not at home' – either literally absent, or not receiving callers that day – cards would be left. A married woman calling on another married woman and finding her 'not at home' would leave three cards – one of her own and two of her husband's; if calling on a widow or a spinster, one of her own and one of her husband's. A gentleman never left his wife's card. The top right-hand corner of the cards was turned down, to indicate that they had been left in person rather than sent by a servant. Cards were left (as distinct from a call being paid) as a formality, without the expectation of seeing anyone, after various social events; at times of illness or death; or when leaving to live elsewhere, when 'P.P.C.' (*pour prendre congé* – to take leave) was written in the bottom right-hand corner. Unmarried daughters rarely had cards of their own until the 1920s; they were included on their mother's card, or would write their names on it.

Older or married women or women of rank either asked younger, unmarried or less elevated ladies to call, or announced their intention of calling; newcomers to a district waited to be called upon by those already in residence; a bride waited to be called upon after returning from the honeymoon. It was incorrect for a first call to last more than 15 or 20 minutes, and if the lady called upon wished to pursue the acquaintance she returned the call within a fortnight; if she did not wish to pursue it, she merely left cards, without asking to see the other lady.

This formal calling and leaving of cards lingered on in some branches of the services until the 1960s, but is now scarcely encountered except in the Diplomatic Corps.

Wages. Because of changes in the purchasing power of money, particularly in the last 50 years, no absolute comparison of wages can be made. However, it is interesting to look at the wages of a more or less unchanging occupation, such as the agricultural labourer. In the mid thirteenth century he was paid two pence a day without board, or £2 10 shillings a year: in 1254 Henry III (1216–72) paid an anchoress a penny-ha'penny a day for living comfortably at Dover Castle. The Black Death of the mid fourteenth century caused a shortage of labour and pushed up wages: the farm labourer received fourpence a day, perhaps sixpence at harvest-time. Throughout the fifteenth and sixteenth centuries the labourer's wages remained steady at two shillings (24 pence) a week, but by 1650 had risen to six shillings, and by 1770 to seven. The Napoleonic Wars led to inflation: by 1800 the weekly wage was ten shillings, twelve by 1810. Thereafter weekly wages fell to nine shillings in 1824, but rose again to twelve by 1840, thirteen in 1870. In 1900 the labourer was paid eighteen shillings weekly, £1 12s. in 1924, £8 10s. in 1955, and nearly £10 in 1960.

Waggonette. An open, four-wheeled, horse-drawn pleasure vehicle with seats along each side facing inwards. See also CARRIAGES.

Wall Game. A ball game played at Eton College. The key match takes place between Collegers (Scholars) and Oppidans (non-scholars) on the nearest Saturday to St Andrew's Day (30 November) each year, under rules impenetrably complex. It is played, with a soft oval ball, between two teams of ten men each, against a 120-yard-long wall on a pitch 6 yards wide. At each end is a 'Calx' marked by a vertical white line on the wall. The object of the game is to put the ball in the opposing team's 'Calx'. The game begins when the 'bully' or scrum forms up in the middle of the Wall under the 'ladder', which is no longer actually there. When a team gets the ball into its opponents' 'Calx' area, special rules come into play and another 'bully' is formed. In this 'bully', team members attempt to 'furk' the ball backwards to another team member, but the ball must not be heeled out of the 'bully'. To score, a team has to raise the ball off the ground and hold it against the wall to the shout of 'Got it'. This merits the award of a 'shy', worth one point. Shys are rarely scored and most games are a nil-nil draw. The last time a 'shy' was scored was when the late Prime Minister, Harold MacMillan, was one of the College players – in 1909.

Wallpaper. The first wallpapers were imitations of textile hangings; the earliest so far discovered in Britain (in 1911, at Christ's College Cambridge) is a printed paper based on a needlework design of pomegranates, made *c.* 1509. Both John Evelyn (1620–1706) and Samuel Pepys (1633–1703) refer to wallpapers in their Diaries: Evelyn mentions 'India' hangings, which were probably Chinese hand-painted papers, while Pepys describes his wife's closet wallpaper as 'counterfeit damask', meaning a flocked paper. Their contemporary, John Houghton (d. 1705), gives us (1699) a graphic description: '. . . a great deal of Paper is nowadays printed and pasted upon walls to serve instead of Hangings'; he says it was supplied in rolls, some having printed wood-cut patterns, and explains that it was known as 'Paper Tapistry'. At Brympton D'Evercy in Somerset there was a paper with a late seventeenth-century printed design based on the well-known Florentine flame-stitch embroidery. The 'counterfeit damask' mentioned by Pepys was made in imitation of Genoese cut-velvet hangings, and such papers may have been produced in London by Jerome Lanyer as early as the 1640s; however, it was only in the 1730s that improvements in manufacturing made 'Paper Tapistries' fashionable – Clandon Park in Surrey has an example dating from 1735.

In 1755 Mrs Delany mentions in her correspondence 'mohair caffoy' paper; CAFFOY was usually a wool-velvet material, but in this case it appears to have been mixed with mohair.

Chinese (at first known loosely as 'India') papers were hand-painted; at first they were carried back from the Far East as part of a captain's 'private trade', to be sold at the tea centres at Mincing and Birchin Lanes in London – possibly as early as c. 1700 in Britain, although they were available in France in the mid seventeenth century. These were sold in sets of about twenty-five rolls, each 12 feet long by 4 feet wide, at from three to five GUINEAS each and painted with an unrepeating pattern of flowers, trees and shrubs. Often, in lower-ceilinged rooms, the top of the paper was cut off, leaving amputated trees at the cornice. Stuck-on, cut-out birds were a fashion of the mid eighteenth century. Dalemain in Cumbria boasts a good English imitation (1750s) of Chinese wallpaper. By 1800 the fashion was fading, and Sir Walter Scott's green Chinese wallpaper of 1828 was from one of the last shipments.

In the middle nineteenth century the fashion was for flat one-dimensional (mostly bad) designs; those of PUGIN were good, however, and one made for the House of Commons in the 1840s is still in production today. The Great Exhibition of 1851, with its endless displays of machine-made horrors, including wallpapers, inspired William Morris's reaction (see ARTS AND CRAFTS MOVEMENT): in 1864 his first wallpaper, 'Daisy', based on an embroidery design, was printed. Although it looks simple, it nevertheless required no fewer than twelve blocks to print it. 'Daisy' was followed by various natural designs, all having an amazing depth, such as 'Acanthus' (1875) and 'Chrysanthemum' (1876). In a lecture given in 1879 Morris commented: '. . . in all patterns which are meant to fill the eye and satisfy the mind there should be a certain mystery'; in achieving this he was outstandingly successful and his wallpaper designs are still sold today.

Walls, decorative treatment of. In medieval times, among the wealthy, walls were usually lime-plastered (the fashion for bare stone is relatively modern) and hung with TAPESTRIES; in farmhouses, plastered walls were finished with a lime wash, either off-white or coloured with natural earth pigments. Sometimes they were painted with scenes or figures. A very early example of a mural series was at Clarendon, Wiltshire, where Henry III (1216–72) had the walls of the Antioch chamber painted with subjects relating to the Crusades. By the sixteenth century panelling or wainscoting was common among the wealthy, often used in combination with tapestries and hangings of silks and other rich fabrics; the less wealthy used PAINTED CLOTHS in place of tapestries. The earliest existing WALLPAPER is printed with a design in imitation of needlework. Wall-paintings continued: Henry VIII (1509–47) commissioned several large murals, for Whitehall, Windsor, Hampton Court, Richmond and Greenwich, and also had GROTESQUE designs painted on many walls. However, the principal wall coverings remained tapestries, and panelling, either inlaid, decorated with stencils, or carved in linenfold design. In the background of *The Family of Henry VIII* (in the Royal Collection, by an unknown artist) may be seen panelling carved in GROTESQUES, painted and gilded. In the seventeenth century wallpaper was becoming a more common wall covering, but tapestries and rich fabrics remained popular among the wealthy. Examples of mural painting dating from the 1620s survive at Bolsover Castle, Derbyshire.

During the seventeenth century the so-called 'common colours' – browns, greys and fawns – were cheapest, and in consequence interiors were conspicuous for their drabness. Blue, made from azurite, had always been expensive, but about 1700 a cheaper substitute, blue verditer ('vert de terre', a bluish-green or light blue made by adding chalk or whiting to nitrate of copper), became available. Throughout the seventeenth and eighteenth centuries expensive fabrics were popular among those who could afford them, either covering the walls or set in STUCCO panels. Wood-graining became popular: in 1625 the stairs at Ham House, Greater London, were painted in imitation of walnut. By the end of the seventeenth century, BAROQUE history paintings of classical events were being used in important rooms, in combination with marbled and grained panelling; an early example of this treatment, dating from the 1670s, may be seen in the Queen's Bedchamber, again at Ham House, and the balcony room at Dyrham Park, Avon was grained in the 1690s. Marbling died out between 1730 and 1750; and where doorcases had been grained in 1730, by 1750 they were painted white. Wainscoting lost its popularity under PALLADIAN influence and stucco took over; where wainscoting was retained, it was painted stone colour, pale grey, or white in reaction from the dark colours of the Baroque period. Examples may be seen in the saloon of Beningborough Hall in North Yorkshire, and the Marble Hall at Petworth, West Sussex. From *c.* 1730 the use of wallpaper between wainscot and cornice became common, and throughout the eighteenth century GILDING was widely used in the finest interiors. Another Palladian fashion was the custom of using panels shaded to display the architectural features, a fashion which lasted until the 1760s when ADAM used a flat background with the plaster decorations picked out in white or natural colours.

In the eighteenth century three types of paint were used: distemper, a water-soluble finish made from whiting and size; oil paint, usually based on white lead mixed with linseed oil; and varnish, made of resins dissolved in linseed oil, turpentine or alcohol, to give a transparent finish or to JAPAN an opaque finish. Pea-green was a favourite wall colour from the mid eighteenth century, while crimson, usually in silk damask, was favoured as a background to display paintings. In the 1780s the publication of illustrations showing the collection of antiquities made by Sir William Hamilton (1730–1803) introduced dark earth-colours. Farmhouse interiors were finished in a whitewash often tinted with blue-bag or red ochre.

The light late eighteenth-century wall colours continued well into the nineteenth century, to be followed, inevitably, by dark, drab colours again. By the 1840s wallpaper was ubiquitous, in flat, lifeless patterns, and interior woodwork was painted brown or dark-stained. From the 1860s, however, the influence of the PRE-RAPHAELITES and the ARTS AND CRAFTS MOVEMENT began to be felt, through the brilliant designs of William Morris; these, used with white-painted woodwork, marked the brighter interiors popular until the close of the century.

Among the wealthy the twentieth century continued the taste for historical revivals which had been fashionable since the 1880s, perhaps because Morris's bright interiors, for all his neo-Medieval aesthetic, did not always sit happily in genuinely old houses, while Adam revival, Elizabethan and Jacobean styles were much more compatible. Although some daring, avant-garde spirits opted for Japanese rooms with bamboo wallpapers, the majority of Edwardians were content with dull pastel hues. Liberty of London commissioned designs for wallpapers in the Arts and Crafts style, while Elsie de Wolfe's *The House of Good Taste* (published in New York in 1913) recommended bright distempers. The years following the First World War saw another Adam revival, complete with plaster panels picked out in un-Adam colours, while others reverted to the 'Cottage Style', with plain-coloured walls. From the 1920s tastes veered between a bleak modern style, with plain white walls, and a taste for the antique, with corresponding wallpapers or textile hangings; 'Stockbroker's Tudor', of course, demanded plain-coloured walls or tapestry hangings. The 1930s saw an 'all-white' phase, a treatment which could scarcely offend, and which lasted until the Second World War.

Wardship, Court of Wards. Although it came to be regarded as one of the most iniquitous impositions of the Crown on landed proprietors, the feudal origins of wardship were logical enough. If the heir to land held by feudal right of KNIGHT-SERVICE was under the age of 21 and thus ineligible for knight-service, the estate was taken into wardship by the Crown until he came of age (in the case of a girl, until she was old enough to marry – 14). As knight-service came to be commuted to a money-payment of rent, the Crown took to selling wardships to the highest bidder. If the estate was taken over by a relative, there might be little exploitation, but often it went to a complete stranger, who did not hesitate to make what he could out of the estate during the years it was in wardship.

Henry VIII (1509–47) saw the ancient laws of wardship as a source of revenue, and in 1540 created the Court of Wards (which became the Court of Wards and Liveries in 1542) as a means of control; the old feudal rights thus revived were very strictly enforced.

Early marriage was one method employed by Tudor landowners seeking to avoid the possibility of wardship. Bess of Hardwick (later Countess of Shrewsbury) was married to Robert Barley over his father's deathbed in 1542, she being 15 at the time and he 13. For a married heir, there would be no question of wardship, but as Robert only lived a year the plan failed and the Barley lands were eventually taken into wardship. On the death of Bess's own father in 1528 she, with her mother, brother and three sisters, lost the Hardwick estate to wardship until the heir, James Hardwick, became 21 in 1547. Wardship was abolished by the Long Parliament in 1645.

Warming-pan. An early form of bed heating, consisting of a round pan with a hinged cover, made of copper or brass, with a wooden handle thirty to forty inches in length. Before bed-time the pan was filled with hot embers and passed under the bedclothes to heat and air all parts of the bed. If the pan was not kept moving the heat scorched the sheets, so some expertise was needed. The earliest known example was made in 1616, and several others survive made before 1630.

Wars of the Roses (1455–85). Dynastic wars between the Houses of York and Lancaster for the crown of England, named after the supposed emblems of white (York) and red (Lancaster) roses. Both factions claimed the throne by descent from Edward III (1327–77): the Lancastrians by direct male line from John of Gaunt, Edward's fourth son; the Yorkists by the female line from Lionel, Edward's third son. The causes of these wars, their course, and the ultimate triumph of the House of Tudor are the subject of Shakespeare's *Henry VI, Parts First, Second and Third,* and *Richard III.*

The long decline of respect for Henry VI (1422–61 and 1470–1), due to his incompetence and bouts of insanity, allied to the loss of Maine by Henry's marriage to Margaret of Anjou, and Normandy after an unsuccessful war with France which resulted in the impeachment, exile and murder of the Duke of Suffolk, permitted the personal power of the barons to increase, bringing disorder and local feuding in the counties. Open warfare between Yorkists and Lancastrians broke out at the first battle of St Albans in 1455, where the 2nd Duke of Somerset (1404–55) was killed, the royal army defeated, and Henry injured and captured. The Duke of York proclaimed himself Protector (1455–6), although Henry had not relapsed into madness, and Yorkists filled the high offices of state.

In 1460, Henry recognized York as his heir, disinheriting his own son Edward, Prince of Wales. York, attempting to put down Lancastrian support in Yorkshire, was killed at the Battle of Wakefield at the end of 1460. Queen Margaret, advancing on London, defeated the Earl of Warwick (the Kingmaker; 1428–71) at the second Battle of St Albans in 1461 and rescued Henry. But against this royalist victory must be set the destruction of a western Lancastrian army at Mortimer's Cross in early 1461 by Edward, Earl of March, York's son. March, now Duke of York, and Warwick joined their armies, secured London, and the young Duke of York was crowned king as Edward IV (1461–83, except 1470–1); there followed a series of crushing defeats for the Lancastrians, at the battles of Towton, Hedgeley Moor, and Hexham.

Edward secretly married Elizabeth Woodville in 1464, arousing the opposition of his brother George, Duke of Clarence (1449–78), and upsetting the plans of the Earl of Warwick for a marriage with the royal house of France. Clarence and Warwick briefly allied themselves with Queen Margaret, restoring Henry to the throne in 1470. Edward fled to the Low Countries, returning in 1471 to defeat the Lancastrians at Barnet, where Warwick fell, and at Tewkesbury, where the Prince of Wales was killed. Henry VI was murdered on 21 May 1471, and the Duke of Clarence met his end seven years later. On the death of Edward IV in 1483 his son Edward V (the elder of 'the Princes in the Tower') was briefly king for eleven weeks under the protectorship of Edward IV's brother Richard, Duke of Gloucester; he then disappeared from public view and Richard of Gloucester ascended the throne as Richard

III (1483–5). Richard's forces were heavily defeated and he himself killed at the Battle of Bosworth in 1485 by a group of disaffected Yorkists under Henry Tudor, a Lancastrian, who became Henry VII (1485–1509); Henry went on to defeat a revolt under Lambert Simnel at East Stoke in 1487.

Although the Wars of the Roses extended over thirty years, they took the form of a series of outbreaks between warring factions, rather than continuous warfare; Edward IV's reign was a period of comparative peace. However, only with Henry VII's capture of the impostor and pretender Perkin Warbeck (1474?–99) in 1497 did Yorkist attempts to retake the throne end.

Wash-coloured. This was probably pale blue. 'Wash', in its original meaning of stale urine, was used as a mordant or fixative for indigo.

Watch and Ward. The feudal policing duty of a community, dating from the thirteenth century, to set a watch at night and arrest (ward) strangers who could not give a good account of themselves. Subsequently 'The Watch'. See also CONSTABLE, HUE AND CRY and POLICE FORCES.

Watchet. Of a light blue colour (sometimes greenish); of unknown origin.

Water supply. We take the supply of piped water so much for granted that it is easy to forget that it is a comparatively recent arrival. Our earliest ancestors were careful to build their houses near water supplies. A well was essential to a medieval castle, and was often dug to a great depth. Water supply might be run by conduit from a well or spring, but such expensive works were usually undertaken only for monastic houses and royal buildings: the first recorded royal conduit (1234) supplied Westminster Palace from the Hyde Park area, and the conduit system in place at Eltham Palace in 1509 was probably installed by Henry VII. In the sixteenth century conduits became more common: Hatfield, Otford and Enfield all had them; at Ashridge, water was raised not by the usual means of hand pumps, but by a pump worked by dogs. The remains of a very long conduit dating from the 1620s have been found at Bolsover Castle in Derbyshire.

In 1600 Hardwick Hall in Derbyshire had a 'Well House' which enclosed a horse-pump for raising water from a well to a CISTERN, while in 1620 at Theobalds in Hertfordshire this was done by a double-barrelled pump. However, these were rarities, and hand-worked pumps were the generality in the seventeenth and eighteenth centuries: mid eighteenth-century household regulations at Hatchlands, Surrey stipulate that every servant shall 'assist to pump water for the use of the house'.

A water-wheel powering a pump at Euston Hall, Suffolk, dating from 1671, was used until 1921; and there is a water-wheel-powered pump concealed in VANBRUGH's bridge at Blenheim Palace, Oxford-shire. A very ingenious 'multiplying wheel bucket engine' powered by water was installed at Chicheley Hall, Buckinghamshire, c. 1729, and a horse-powered pumping system survives at Houghton Hall in Norfolk. There is a horse-pump in an outbuilding at Gosfield Hall in Essex, while Greys Court, Oxfordshire still has a donkey-wheel. From the mid eighteenth century, steam was occasionally used. In all these houses the water was pumped up from a well.

By far the most ingenious pump was the hydraulic ram, introduced to Britain c. 1830 and widely used from the mid nineteenth century. Needing no fuel, rams run endlessly on the power contained in a stream of water running down a pipe. A pair of valves, alternately opening and shutting, uses the force generated by that disagreeable 'thump' that is heard in a pipe when the water is shut off suddenly, to pump a part of the water up to a cistern situated at a greater height than the source of the stream. Thus part of the water flowing down the pipe pumps the other part up to the cistern above. The greater the height of the cistern above the source of the stream, the smaller the proportion of the flow that can be pumped up to it. Hydraulic rams were also often used to provide GARDEN water effects; though they may silt up over the years, the quality of their original construction was such that they can usually be brought back into operation. The ram installed at Stowe in Buck-inghamshire in 1843 for the Duke of Buckingham has lately been cleaned and restored to full working order by the firm who originally provided it.

Once water had been raised to a cistern, it then had to be distrib-uted to where it was needed. The water supply at Chatsworth in Derbyshire came from the moors above the house, and by the end of the seventeenth century running water was piped by gravity to all three floors; it was, however, some time before pipes came into general use in houses without similar natural advantages – hand power was cheap. Lady Diana Cooper remembered Belvoir Castle, Leicestershire in c. 1900: 'The water men are difficult to believe in today. They seemed to me to belong to another clay. They were the biggest people I had ever seen . . . On their shoulders they carried a wooden yoke from which hung two gigantic cans of water. They moved on a perpetual round. Above ground there was not a drop of hot water and not one bath, so their job was to keep all jugs, cans and kettles full in the bedrooms, and morning and evening to bring hot water for hip-baths. We were always a little frightened of the water-men.'

Wattle-and-daub. A method of wall construction used betweeen upright posts in a TIMBER-FRAMED building, consisting of thin oak (or other timber) laths (wattles) sprung between the posts; sometimes branches were used. The resulting screen was plastered with mud (daub) and smoothed over. The mud mix depended on the secrets of the specialist; often horse or cow dung was an ingredient, with animal hair and straw to bind the mixture.

Webb, Philip Speakman (1831–1915). A great architect of the late Victorian Domestic Revival. He trained with William Morris in G.E. Street's office in Oxford, and they became lifelong friends. In 1859 Webb designed Red House, Bexleyheath, Kent for Morris, a prototype of the English Domestic Revival, which provided houses for discriminating middle-income, middle-class clients: a new class of patron. Webb's houses were based on vernacular architectural styles. His last commission was Standen, near East Grinstead, Sussex (1891–4) in which local materials and the local vernacular style have been blended with infinite care and simplicity.

Weddings. The wedding celebration as we know it is quite a modern custom. In the earliest medieval times a church ceremony was considered unnecessary, and divorce by consent followed by remarriage was widely practised. In remote areas the 'handfast' – the holding of hands – was considered sufficient for a binding union. It was only in the thirteenth century that the Church began to assert the principle of marriage as a spiritual sacrament rather than an economic contract.

The wedding, when the couple pledged themselves to each other, often took place in the church porch. Later a public celebration – the 'nuptials', the 'gift', or the 'bridal' – when friends and relatives assembled to feast and to hear the financial details of the contract, might or might not take place. In the late seventeenth century a visitor to England remarked: '. . . one of the reasons that they have for marrying secretly, as they generally do in England, is that thereby they avoid a great deal of expense and trouble.' He goes on to explain that such a marriage usually only involved the bride and groom, their parents, two bridesmen and two bridesmaids. On the other hand, hundreds might attend a marriage between people of rank and fortune. Among long-enduring marriage customs were the bringing of gifts, and a mock resistance on the part of the bride. The most notorious custom was the 'bedding of the bride', when the bride and groom were escorted to the marriage chamber, and often sewn into their wedding sheets together, to the accompaniment of much ribaldry.

A party was not an inevitable accompaniment to a wedding: in 1770, when Jacob Houblon married Mary Archer at Welford House in Berkshire, ten people stayed in the house for three weeks, but there is no record of a celebratory party. When the Lord Newark, the heir to Earl Manvers, married the daughter of Sir Michael Robert Shaw-Stuart on 28 September 1880, the Earl spent only £268 at Thoresby Hall, Nottinghamshire. It is not recorded what was spent by the bride's father in Scotland. See also GRETNA GREEN; MARRIAGE, AGE AT; MARRIAGE ACT and MARRIED WOMEN'S PROPERTY ACTS.

Well-dressing. A curious spring custom peculiar to the county of Derbyshire and dating from at least 1350: it is suggested that survivors of the Black Death gave thanks by decorating their well-heads. However, it is likely that the custom is Roman in origin, a propitiation of the water gods in hopes of a sufficient supply in dry seasons. Beginning at Tissington on Ascension Day, Derbyshire wells are 'dressed' with thousands of petals stuck on clay-covered boards to make a picture. Other Derbyshire villages have their own dates for well-dressings – Wirksworth at Whitsun, Bonsall and Barlow in August. Youlgreave has no well – but piped water was laid on in 1829, and a central fountain and four standpipes are 'dressed' between 19 and 24 June.

Western Rebellion, The (June–August 1549). Provoked by the introduction of the new BOOK OF COMMON PRAYER (first used on Whit Sunday 1549) – part of the REFORMATION legislation of Edward VI (1547–53) – rebellions began independently in Devon and Cornwall. The rebels, who were almost exclusively peasants, took Plymouth and laid siege to Exeter before being subdued by government forces under Lord Russell at Clyst Heath (August 5th) and Sampford Courtney (August 17th).

Wet-nursing. In early modern Europe, breast-feeding of babies usually lasted for a year to eighteen months and could be a severe burden on the mother. By 1763 'the present fashion . . . is to let children suck only three or four months', although others strongly advised that breast-feeding should last six to twelve months, with nine the ideal.

It had long been the custom for upper-class mothers to put their babies out to wet-nurses – that is, to mothers who were already feeding a child or had just lost one. In 1682 the novelist and dramatist Aphra Behn (1640–89) noted that by this means 'both you and your wife are freed from tossing and tumbling with it in the night'. Breast-feeding became unfashionable, many mothers fearing that it would spoil the shape of their 'pretty breasts, firm nipples, round and smooth'. In 1748 a good wet-nurse cost £25 per year.

By the end of the eighteenth century medical opinion, always in favour of breast-feeding by the natural mother, was winning the argument. In 1789 Lady Craven reported 'that you will find in every station of life mothers of families who would shrink in horror at the thought of putting a child out from them to nurse'. The reduced likelihood of a mother conceiving during the months she was breast-feeding, although not infallible as a contraceptive measure, was also attractive. By the nineteenth century breast-feeding was firmly back in favour, to be replaced by bottle-feeding in the twentieth century. The debate continues.

Whigs. A political grouping originating in the late seventeenth century, which became the Liberal Party in the second half of the nineteenth century. The term was originally used of Scottish cattle and horse thieves and was later transferred, pejoratively, to Scottish Presbyterians. (*Whig* is a Scottish word meaning 'drive', and the 'Whiggamore raid' was made by a body of insurgents from the west of Scotland against Edinburgh in 1648.) With its connotations of Presbyterianism and rebellion, it came to be applied by the TORIES to the Exclusionists who claimed the power of excluding the heir, James, Duke of York (1633–1701), from the succession on account of his Catholicism. Following the Bloodless Revolution of 1688, largely instigated by the Whigs, they held power during the reign of William and Mary, gradually losing it to the Tories under Anne. After 1714, and as a result of the Tories' unpopular association with Jacobitism, they were able to form a ruling oligarchy until the reign of George III. They were not organized on party lines in the modern meaning, but held together by family ties and patronage rather than policy. In 1783 their long run of power gave way to the new Toryism exemplified by William Pitt the Younger. After the French Revolution, many Whigs joined the Tories. At this time Lord Byron (1788–1824) remarked, in *Don Juan*: 'Nought's permanent among the human race,/ Except the Whigs *not* getting into place.' In 1830 the Whigs returned to power, supporting the abolition of slavery in the colonies, the emancipation of the Catholic Church, and Parliamentary reform. In the Tory split of 1846 over the CORN LAWS, the Whigs were strengthened by defectors from the PRIME MINISTER Sir Robert Peel's policies. Under Gladstone the Whigs evolved into the Liberal Party (*c.* 1867).

Wife-sale. Although DIVORCE was difficult to impossible for any but the very wealthy until 1857, wife-sale was a cheap alternative practised by those on the bottom rungs of the social ladder. Readers of Thomas Hardy's *The Mayor of Casterbridge*, set in the early nineteenth century, will know that Michael Henchard, a hay-trusser, got drunk and sold his wife to a sailor for £5. The description of a real sale of 1727 tells how the husband put a halter round his wife's neck and led her to the market-place as if she had been a cow. Such sales frequently took place at Smithfield, but the sale was usually arranged beforehand, with the full agreement of the wife, for a price ranging from a few pence to a few pounds. In 1769 a Sheffield steel-burner sold his wife to a fellmonger for sixpence, and then paid half a guinea more to have her taken out of town. Although widely accepted, the practice (medieval in origin) never had a legal basis, and indeed attempts were made to stop it in the early eighteenth century. Wife-sales were most frequent in the eighteenth century, but the last recorded case was in 1887, and the LORD CHANCELLOR's ruling against it in 1891 effectively abolished the practice. See also GRETNA GREEN; MARRIAGE, AGE AT; MARRIAGE ACT; MARRIED WOMEN'S PROPERTY ACTS and WEDDINGS.

Wigs. Short for 'periwigs'. An ancient fashion, wigs were worn to augment natural hair, alter the coiffure for fashion's sake, and to designate professional status or rank. During the Gallic wars Roman women were partial to blonde wigs made from the hair of captured slaves.

Wigs of human hair or silk thread were worn by fashionable Italians of both sexes in the late fifteenth and sixteenth centuries, and their use spread to the rest of Europe. Queen Elizabeth (1557–1603) had a choice of eighty wigs to wear when her own red hair grew thin. Her cousin Mary, Queen of Scots, with naturally black hair, had 'perewykes', mostly red, for every day of the year. She went to her execution with 'her borrowed hair [wig] a bourne', and it was pulled off by the executioner, exposing her own hair, turned white in her forties. In 1593 Thomas Nash damned seekers after youth who wore periwigs, and Shakespeare mentions them in *Hamlet* (Act III, Scene ii).

In France in 1620 the Abbé de la Rivière wore a long golden wig at the court of Louis XIII, which led the king, who was going bald, to adopt the periwig.

Wigs were worn in Britain, mainly by men, and particularly from the time when long hair began to be the fashion in the 1620s, but only came into general use with the Restoration in 1660, when the long-haired periwig was fashionable. Samuel Pepys (1633–1703), attending church wearing his new periwig for the first time in 1664, noted: 'I found that my coming in a periwig did not prove so strange as I was afraid it would . . .'

Wig-wearers shaved off their hair for comfort and cleanliness, necessitating the wearing of a cap or nightcap when the wig was taken off indoors. Until 1675 wigs approximated a natural head of hair: a mass of irregular grey, blond, brown or black curls falling over the shoulders; subsequently the full-bottomed wig developed, with more and closer curls, from the 1680s often with a centre parting: this is the style of wig worn today by judges on ceremonial occasions. From about 1690 until the wheat famine and powder tax of 1795, hair was powdered for ceremonial occasions, but grey or white wigs did not become fashionable until the early eighteenth century. From 1710 wigs were worn by almost all men.

Wigs were uncomfortable to wear and the best, made of human hair, were very expensive; they were also quite impractical for any active pursuit – smaller wigs, tied with a ribbon at the nape, were worn for travelling and sport. Soldiers evolved their own 'campaign' wig, in which hair was arranged in three locks, one at the back of the head and one on each side, turned up and tied. Scholars and clergymen wore bob wigs, frizzed rather than curled. The 'Ramillies' wig (named after Marlborough's victory over the French in 1706, but not fashionable until the 1750s) carried simplification still further: the hair was drawn back and tied with two black ribbons in a pigtail. Because the full, heavy wig was so uncomfortable, smaller 'Dress' wigs, always grey and with the hair tied in a queue at the back (similar to those worn today by judges in court) were worn for formal events from the 1770s. These were called bag wigs because the tail of the hair, in wear, was encased in a black silk bag.

Women wore wigs, or for preference grew their hair long, for only a short period during which they were much influenced by the French court. In the 1690s the fashion was for very high hair arrangements, ironically called a 'tower', supported on a wire frame 'two or three stories high' according to the *Lady's Dictionary* for 1694. By 1699 this fashion had passed in France and lingered on in London for only a few years; it was revived again at the court of Marie Antoinette (1759–93).

A knowledge of the dates at which fashions in wigs changed can be helpful in dating portraits.

Wimple. A fashionable female head-dress from about 1150. So slowly did medieval fashions change that the wimple was still worn, though not by the fashionable, in the fifteenth century, and lingers on today in the habits of some nuns. The wimple was a piece of fine linen or silk, usually white, fastened to the hair and chin, neck and throat. The lower edge might be tucked into the neckline of the gown, or the ends drawn up and pinned to the top of the head beneath the veil, framing the face. Wimples are clearly shown on fourteenth-century brasses; that of Lady Margaret de Camoys (d. 1310) at St George's church, Trotton in Sussex, shows a particularly fashionable wimple.

Window glass. Often when light catches the windows of an old house one can clearly see curves (known as 'reams') in the glass, somewhat resembling the base of a large wine-glass: this is crown glass. Glass was manufactured in London from the fifteenth century, but became a localized industry all over the country because of the difficulties of transporting it. Crown glass was made by blowing a large bubble of glass, cutting the top open and spinning out the molten glass into a large flat disc three feet across. The disc, of varying thickness, could not be used in a window as it was, and was therefore cut up into small diamond-shaped pieces which were sorted into similar thicknesses, then set in lead to make up the required size of window. The centre of the disc, with a knob where it had been attached to the glass-blowing rod, was discarded, but sometimes reserved for use in cottage windows. By the early seventeenth century, small diamond-shaped panes had given way to slightly larger rectangles.

An alternative process produced 'broad' glass, in which the bubble of glass was worked into a cylinder shape on the marver (a polished slab of marble or iron). The cylinder was then slit down its length and laid on a flat bed of sand as a collapsed sheet about a foot wide and five feet long. Broad glass continued to be made in Britain until the late eighteenth century. See also WINDOWS and WINDOW TAX.

Windows. Most domestic windows in the medieval period had only shutters to keep out draughts, although they were occasionally glazed with oiled parchment or cloth, or thin sheets of horn. In the late fifteenth century the use of glass, though still restricted because of its cost, was more widespread and the casement window, often of metal and glazed with small diamond-shaped leaded panes, provided a great deal more comfort. Inward-opening, to avoid being buffeted by winds, such windows required space inside the room, and by 1620 they were being replaced by outward-opening wooden-framed windows with stronger glazing bars. This was gradually superseded in France in the 1640s by a primitive sliding sash window which, at first held in place by pegs or springs, did not acquire pullies and counter-balancing weights until the 1660s. The first sash windows in Britain are said to have been fitted at Chatsworth in the 1670s. Once the sash window was established it remained in fashion until the 1850s. In the 1840s techniques of manufacturing sheet and plate glass were developed, the removal of excise duty from glass in 1845 halved the cost, and in 1851 the WINDOW TAX was repealed: with such incentives it is not surprising that many fine old windows were (to their detriment, in our eyes) 'modernized' by the insertion of plate glass sash windows, which spoiled the proportions of classical façades. See also SHUTTERS and WINDOW GLASS.

Window Tax. A tax of two shillings annually on inhabited houses paying Church or Poor rates, first imposed in England in 1696 to replace the HEARTH TAX; an additional tax was payable according to the number of windows – on 10 to 19 windows the tax was four shillings. Scotland was exempt from the tax by the terms of the 1707 Act of Union. The tax was increased at various times, and in 1782 William Pitt the Younger (1759–1806) introduced a graduated tax starting at one shilling per window up to ten windows, and rising on every window thereafter; houses with fewer than seven windows were exempted in 1792, as were those with fewer than eight in 1825 – but in 1797, when Britain was at war with France, the tax was trebled.

Although there are cases of windows having been bricked up to avoid the tax, this was not so common as is supposed; 'blind' windows were often introduced on Georgian houses to balance a symmetrical façade. In 1851 the tax was replaced by a tax on inhabited houses. See also WINDOW GLASS and TAXATION.

Wine. Grape wine arrived in south-east England several decades before the Roman invasion. Wine making was known to the Greeks in Mycenean times and viticulture was taken to Marseilles in the seventh century BC by Greek colonists. From Marseilles the wine was traded with the Celts in the north of France, who drank wine undiluted. 'And since they partake of this drink without moderation, by reason of their craving for it, they fall into a stupor or a state of madness', wrote Diodorus Siculus (*Bibliothica Historica*, V, 25). In England tombs of Belgic princes often have three wine amphora and Roman drinking cups to serve them in the next world, and the ruler of Hampshire's Atrebates, Verica, issued a coin bearing a vine leaf shortly before AD 43.

By the fifth century viticulture had generally died out in Britain, although monastic vineyards continued to produce wine of sorts for the celebration of mass. The Normans revived viticulture in Britain, planting vineyards as far north as York, but by the time of Henry II (1154–89) imports of Moselle, Rhineland and Gascony wines had destroyed the home industry.

Wine-glass coolers. Round, small, flattish glass tumblers with straight sides and what look like pouring lips on opposite sides of the top, standing on glass saucers; these tumblers, when filled with iced water, were supposedly used for cooling empty wine glasses, particularly champagne glasses. The lips held the stems of inverted wine glasses and prevented them from rolling about. When several different wines were served at dinner, the coolers were used to wash out the glasses. The fashion for them lasted for about a hundred years, from the mid eighteenth century. See also MONTEITH.

Witch-ball. A ball of coloured reflecting glass, believed to repel witches; from the belief that they cannot bear to see their own reflection.

Witchcraft. A belief in the possession of supernatural powers by people in league with the devil or with evil spirits persisted, even among eminent scholars, well into the seventeenth century. Laws against witchcraft date from the Norman Conquest, and dealing with witches soon became the responsibility of both Church and secular courts. Except in the case of love philtres, all these laws called for the prosecution to prove that injury had been done or intended to persons or property, or that gain was intended. The seventeenth century saw the height of witchcraft trials; they were more numerous in Scotland where, in contrast to England, the law permitted torture to extract confession. Although belief in witchcraft was declining by the end of the seventeenth century, and with it prosecutions, the last recorded conviction in England was as late as 1712, that of Jane Wenham; in Scotland, a woman was burned alive for witchcraft in Sutherland in 1722. A common and much less drastic English punishment was the pillory. Although there had by that date been no convictions for nearly a quarter of a century, an Act of 1736 fixed the maximum punishment for witchcraft at a year's imprisonment.

An accusation of witchcraft was often a convenient way of ridding a small community of unpopular neighbours. A monument to the 6th Earl of Rutland (d. 1632) in Bottesford church, Leicestershire relates how his two sons by his second wife, whom he married in 1608, both died mysteriously in infancy, 'by wicked practice and sorcerye': the evil spells of three local women who were in dispute with the Rutlands. One woman died during the subsequent trial, while the other two 'confessed' and were hanged at Lincoln in 1618.

Witch marks to deter witches are sometimes seen over the entrance to fifteenth- and sixteenth-century buildings, while two or three shoes hidden beneath floorboards were thought to prevent sorcery.

Withdrawing. From the mid eighteenth century it became the custom for the ladies to retire from the eating room at the end of dinner, leaving the men to their PORT; the ladies went to the 'withdrawing' – later shortened to drawing – room, to gossip and make tea or coffee. François de la Rochefoucauld, visiting Houghton Hall in 1784, found that after the ladies left the dining room, the men got down to serious drinking (it must be remembered that dinner was then served at 5 p.m.): 'After two or three hours, a servant comes in to announce that tea is ready and to conduct *Messieurs le buveurs* into the drawing room to join the ladies, who are usually busy making tea or coffee. After the tea, one usually plays whist, and at midnight there is cold meat for anyone who is hungry. During the game, punch is on the table for those who want it.'

At Woburn in Bedfordshire, Frances, Lady Shelley, carefully noted in her diary in 1812: 'As soon as we left the dining room the Duchess went to her nursing employment (after a little edifying conversation on the subject) and we dispersed . . . through an enfilade of six rooms. The gentlemen soon joined us and in the first Shelley got a companion for billiards. In the next Lady Asgill established herself in an attitude, lying on the sofa with Sir Thomas Graham at her feet. In the next Lady Jane and Miss Russell at her harp and the pianoforte (both out of tune) playing the Creation. Alas, it was chaos still. In the gallery a few pairs were dispersed on the sofas . . . scarcely was I seated when the Duchess entered; and collecting her romping force of girls and young men, they all seized cushions and pelted the whist players . . . The romp was at last ended by Lady Jane being nearly blinded by an apple that hit her in the eye.'

By Victorian times dinner was served at around 8 p.m. and the men did not linger long before joining the ladies. Unless there were guests to be entertained, evenings could be so yawningly dull that they generally ended early – which also saved on candles.

Withdrawing room. In the fifteenth century, a withdrawing room might be any smaller room off a chamber, but by the mid sixteenth century, it had come to signify the room next to the GREAT CHAMBER into which one withdrew when the great chamber was being set up for a meal, or after it had been eaten, or to a room off one's bedchamber where one could sit, eat or receive guests in some privacy.

Wog. A derogatory term applied to natives of the Middle East; sometimes said to be an acronym of 'Wily Oriental Gentleman', but more likely to derive from the Golliwog dolls popularized by Florence Upton's illustrations for *Adventures of Two Dutch Dolls and a Golliwogg*, published in 1895 and followed by eleven more books which sold in vast numbers at the time, but would now be considered more than a little politically incorrect.

Workhouse. A means of provision for 'the able-bodied poor'. The POOR LAW Act of 1601 included a direction that every parish should provide 'a convenient stock of flax, hemp, wool, thread, iron and other ware . . . to set the poor on work', but parish authorities were more concerned with providing 'houses of correction' for vagabonds. In 1696 the Corporation of Bristol promoted an ACT OF PARLIAMENT specifically for the provision of workhouses in which the inmates were to be made to work in return for a pitiful board and lodging, an example quickly followed by other towns and parishes. To regulate their establishment, a general Workhouse Act was passed in 1723, which also denied relief to those refusing to enter. This Act was later amended by GILBERT'S ACT of 1782, and the SPEENHAMLAND SYSTEM of 1795–6 was a further adjustment. The workhouse became the central feature of the Poor Law Relief Act of 1834. See also BADGE-MEN and SETTLEMENT.

Workmen's Compensation Act. Introduced in Parliament by Joseph Chamberlain in 1897, this act for the first time imposed on the employer a liability to pay compensation, under certain conditions, in the case of an employee's injury or death. Previously, an injured man or his family could rely only on membership of a FRIENDLY SOCIETY, charity or whatever paternalistic feelings his employer might have. The case of Priestly v. Fowler (1837) was the first in which an employee sued an employer for injuries suffered at work. The case went against the worker, who had been injured by an overturned butcher's cart, the court ruling that an employer could not be held responsible when the negligence of one employee resulted in injury to another; this ruling was eventually overturned, in 1948.

Wren, Sir Christopher (1632–1723). Probably the most famous of English architects. The son of Dr Christopher Wren, Dean of Windsor, and nephew of the Bishop of Ely, his Church connections meant that he was well placed to take advantage of the RESTORATION of 1660. Known first as a brilliant scientist and mathematician, in 1661 he became Savilian Professor of Astronomy at Oxford. Two years later he was consulted by the commission for repairing St Paul's. His first commission was almost certainly for Pembroke College Chapel, Cambridge (1663–5), through his uncle the Bishop of Ely, followed by the Sheldonian Theatre, Oxford (1664–9). He made his only trip abroad, to Paris, in 1665. Wren had actually prepared a scheme for the restoration of St Paul's when the Great Fire of London (1666) destroyed it past repair. Its rebuilding is his masterpiece, its dome one of the most majestic anywhere in the world. Wren was appointed one of three Commissioners to advise on the rebuilding of the City, and in 1669 he was appointed to the post of Surveyor-General of the King's Works. Thereafter, his busy life was devoted to the rebuilding of fifty City churches, their plans based on his principle of 'a preaching box' in which the pulpit was the focus of the interior. He was also involved in some fifteen other churches, and in a wide range of secular commissions which include The Royal Hospital, Chelsea; Greenwich Observatory; a doorway at Longleat, Wiltshire (1683); Tring Manor, Hertfordshire (*c.* 1700, demolished in the nineteenth century); Arbury Hall, Warwickshire (a doorway, 1674); Thoresby Hall, Nottinghamshire (destroyed by fire in 1745); Easton Neston, Northamptonshire (*c.* 1685–95, with HAWKSMOOR); Bridgewater Square, London (*c.* 1688; demolished); Winslow Hall, Buckinghamshire (1699–1702); Marlborough House, London (1709–11).

Writ. A legal document issued by the Crown, ordering one or more persons to perform or not perform some act; also, a document issued by the Crown, summoning lords spiritual or temporal to attend Parliament, or containing directions for the holding of an election of a member of Parliament. Although writs were known in Anglo-Saxon times, the Normans developed their use, chiefly when issued by the COURT OF CHANCERY, to compel appearance in court; this is what is known as an original writ. In 1832 this procedure was replaced by a Writ of Summons. Today the serving of a writ of summons is the first step in a criminal or civil legal procedure.

Writers to the Signet. An ancient society of Scottish law agents who conduct cases before the Court of Sessions, with the exclusive privilege of the preparation of Crown writs, charters, etc; with others, such as the Procurators Fiscal, Writers to the Signet are the Scottish equivalent of English SOLICITORS. Originally, they were clerks in the office of the Secretary of State involved with the preparation of documents requiring the signet or seal.

Xystus. In Greek architecture, a covered portico, used by athletes for exercising; in Roman architecture, a long, open or covered walk bordered by trees or colonnades, in which to walk and talk.

Yeoman. Originally, a forty-shilling freeholder (holder of land worth £2 per year), and so qualified to vote and serve on juries; by Tudor times the term had come to mean a farmer working his own land, or a substantial tenant farmer. Also, an attendant in a royal or noble household, usually ranking somewhere between a SQUIRE and a page; also an official title (e.g., Yeoman of the Cellar).

Yeomen of the Guard. A sovereign's bodyguard established by Henry VII (1485–1509) at his coronation in 1485; originally 'Yeomen of the Guard of the body of our Lord the King'. Yeomen of the Guard were chosen for their skill in archery; Welsh archers were particularly proficient, and the Yeomen still wear their distinctive scarlet uniform symbolizing the dragon of Cadwaladr ap Cadwallon. Since 1669 they have numbered a hundred, under a Captain of the Guard; their function of attending the sovereign on the battlefield ceased only with the battle of Dettingen in 1743, the last occasion on which a British sovereign commanded an army in the field.

Today the colourful guardsmen, known as Beefeaters (allegedly from a comment of Cosimo, Grand Duke of Tuscany, in 1669: 'They are great eaters of beef, of which a very large ration is given them daily at court, and they might be called "Beefeaters"') perform purely ceremonial duties; every member of the Guard except the captain must be a former regular soldier, and they are selected for distinguished conduct. The Warders of the Tower form a separate corps, under the Constable of the Tower. See also GENTLEMEN-AT-ARMS and ROYAL COMPANY OF ARCHERS.

Zoophorus. Vitruvius' term for a frieze of animals and men carved in relief.

SELECT BIBLIOGRAPHY

Primary sources

Furnival, Frederick J. (ed.), *The Babees Book* (Early English Text Society, 1868)

Llanover, Lady (ed.), *Autobiography and Correspondence of Mrs Delany* (London, 1861)

Morris, Christopher (ed.), *Journeys of Celia Fiennes* (Macdonald, 1982)

Scarfe, Norman (ed.), *A Frenchman's Year in Suffolk in 1784* (Boydell Press, 1988)

——*Innocent Espionage, the Rochefoucauld Brothers' Tour of England in 1785* (Boydell Press, 1995)

Secondary sources

Bland, Olivia, *The Royal Way of Death* (Constable & Co, 1986).

Colvin, Howard, *A Biographical Dictionary of British Architects 1600–1840* (John Murray 1978; rev. edn Yale University Press, 1995)

Davenport, Millia, *The Book of Costume* (Crown (NY), 1966)

Durant, David N., *Living in the Past: An Insider's Social History of Historic Houses* (Aurum Press, 1988)

Entwistle, E.A., *The Book of Wallpaper: a History and Appreciation* (Redwood Press, 1970)

Fowler, John & Cornforth, John, *English Decoration in the 18th Century* (Barrie & Jenkins, 1974)

Gere, Charlotte, *Nineteenth-Century Decoration: the art of the Interior* (Weidenfeld & Nicholson, 1989)

Girouard, Mark, *Robert Smythson and the Architecture of the Elizabethan Era* (Country Life, 1966)

——*Life In the English Country House* (Yale University Press, 1978)

——*The Victorian Country House* (Yale University Press, 1979)

Litton, Julian, *The English Way of Death: the Common Funeral since 1450* (Robert Hale, 1991)

Macfarlane, Alan, *Marriage and Love in England, 1300–1840* (Basil Blackwell, 1986)

Mingay, G.E., *English Landed Society in the Eighteenth Century* (Routledge & Kegan Paul, 1963)

Smith, Charles Saumarez, *Eighteenth Century Decoration* (Weidenfeld & Nicholson, 1993)

Stone, Lawrence, *The Crisis of Aristocracy, 1558–1641* (Oxford University Press, 1965)

——*Family and Fortune: Studies in Aristocratic Finance in the Sixteenth and Seventeenth Centuries* (Oxford University Press, 1973)

——*The Family, Sex and Marriage in England, 1500–1800* (Weidenfeld & Nicolson, 1977)

——*Broken Lives: Separation and Divorce in England, 1650–1857* (Oxford University Press, 1993)

Summerson, John, *Architecture in Britain 1530–1830* (Penguin Books Ltd, 1970)

Thompson, F.M.L., *English Landed Society in the Nineteenth Century* (Routledge & Kegan Paul, 1963)

Thornton, Peter, *Seventeenth Century Interior Decoration in England, France & Holland* (Yale University Press, 1978)

——*Authentic Decor: the Domestic Interior 1620–1920* (Weidenfeld & Nicolson, 1984)

Wright, Lawrence, *Clean and Decent: the History of the Bathroom and the WC* (Routledge & Kegan Paul, 1996)